FRANCE
under
DE GAULLE

FRANCE
under
DE GAULLE

Edited by Robert A. Diamond

FACTS ON FILE, INC.   NEW YORK

FRANCE
UNDER
DE GAULLE

Library of Congress Catalog Card No. 70-122212
ISBN 0-87196-179-2

9 8 7 6 5 4 3 2 1

CONTENTS

PART II

THE FOREIGN POLICY YEARS (1963-1967)

PART III

CRISIS AND CONCLUSION (1968-1969)

PREFACE

This book is neither a history nor an analysis. It argues no thesis and reaches no conclusions. It is, however, a factual journalistic account of the 11-year period—from May 1958 to April 1969—when Charles de Gaulle governed France, initially as the last premier of the Fourth Republic and then from January 1959 on as first president of the Fifth Republic.

The book is divided into three major parts which later historians may well regard as the most logical chronological breakdown of the 11 years—from 1958 to 1962, when de Gaulle's primary concern was to end the Algerian war; from 1963 to 1967, when de Gaulle centered his attention on foreign policy; and finally, 1968-9, when the domestic upheaval of May 1968 forced de Gaulle to focus on France's problems at home.

It is understood, of course, that this three-part division is a simplification, that the periods overlap and that important domestic events occurred during times more remembered for foreign policy.

While the book can be read from cover to cover, it will probably be put to its best use as a volume to consult for quick easy reference to a variety of questions on the period:

● What were the main steps in extricating France from Algeria?

● Did de Gaulle's trip to the Soviet Union precede or follow the announcement of his decision to withdraw France from NATO's military command?

● What was de Gaulle's reaction to the U-2 incident and the collapse of the 1960 East-West summit conference?

● Did France modify its position on international monetary questions after the May 1968 domestic crisis?

The main source materials for this book have been FACTS ON FILE, volumes 1958-69; research in the American and West European press, primarily *Le Monde* of Paris; and the official translations of de Gaulle's speeches and press conferences provided by the Press and Information Division of the French Embassy.

PREFACE

This book's primary ambition is not an analysis. It aspires to thesis and reaches its conclusions. It is, however, a factual journalistic account of the [...] crisis—from May 1958 to April 1969—when Charles de Gaulle governed France. Initially as the last premier of the Fourth Republic, and then from January 1959 on as the first president of the Fifth Republic.

The book is divided into three major parts, which like the whole, may, with regard to the most logical chronological break-down of the 11 years—ran in 1958 to 1961 when de Gaulle's primary concern was to cap the Algerian war; from 1962 to 1965 when de Gaulle concentrated his attention on foreign policy; and finally, 1966-7, when the dramatic upheaval of May 1968 began definitely to take on proportions of a cataclysm.

It is understood, of course, that this breakdown division is a simplification, that these points overlap, and that many crucial moments events occurred during time periods remembered for or of politics.

While the book can be read from cover to cover, it will probably be put to its best use as a volume to consult for quick, easy reference to a variety of questions on the period:

• What were the main steps in achieving France from Algeria?
• Did de Gaulle's trip to the Soviet Union precede or follow the announcement of his decision to withdraw France from NATO's military command?
• When was de Gaulle's reaction to the LBJ incident and the call to save the LBJ Franc-West-gafront conference?
• Did France modify its position on international monetary questions following May's domestic crisis?

The main source materials for this book have been France in 1958-69, research from the numerous and frequent press books on France primarily De Gaulle on France, and the verbatim translations of the official speeches and press conferences provided by the Press and Information Division of the French Embassy.

CHARLES DE GAULLE

INTRODUCTION

Charles de Gaulle's return to power in 1958 and the creation of the Fifth French Republic were both precipitated by the four year old Algerian rebellion which had caused growing unrest and repeated political crises in France.

Algeria, a French territory since 1848, was since 1947 governed as an integral part of metropolitan (i.e., European) France with representation in the French National Assembly. More than eight million native Moslems and over one million Europeans lived in Algeria.

The Moslem rebellion against French rule had begun the night of Oct. 31, 1954 when Moslem guerrilla bands staged attacks on French military posts, farms, and travelers in northeastern Algeria. Moslem guerrilla forces, armed and trained from bases in neighboring Morocco and Tunisia, centered their operations in inaccessible mountain regions and began full-scale war against the French. By 1958, the guerrillas had grown in number to 50,000 full-time fighters and an unknown number of part-time auxiliaries. France by then had 375,000 troops stationed in Algeria and the cost of military operations was running at over $800 million a year. Casualties had mounted to 70,000 Moslem rebels and 6,000 French troops killed by the end of April 1958.

The Algerian rebellion created growing tension and discontent in metropolitan France. Inflationary pressures caused by the war increased the cost of living 10% in the last six months of 1957. Violence mounted — caused by French rightists demanding decisive military suppression of the Moslem rebellion and by terrorists among the 400,000 Algerians living in France. The National Assembly of the Fourth Republic voted the government special police powers July 18 to combat the rebel terrorism in metropolitan France and renewed these powers November 12. By the end of February 1958, over 600 deaths in metropolitan France were attributed to Algerian terrorists during the preceding seven months.

Inability to end the Algerian rebellion threatened the stability of the Fourth Republic and led to its downfall. Four French cabinets which held office following the beginning of the Algerian rebellion fell from power on the Algerian question or on closely related issues:

(1) Radical Socialist Pierre Mendes-France's government fell Feb. 5, 1955 when the National Assembly refused to give him a vote of confidence on his North African policy.

(2) Socialist Premier Guy Mollet resigned May 21, 1957 when the Assembly defeated a tax-increase bill to raise revenue to cover the cost of the Algerian war and check the foreign trade deficit.

(3) Radical Socialist Premier Maurice Bourges-Maunoury's cabinet fell Sept. 30, 1957 when the Assembly rejected a new basic statute for Algeria.

(4) Radical Socialist Premier Felix Gaillard resigned April 16, 1958 after the Assembly refused to accept a U.S.-British mediation effort to settle the dispute between France and Tunisia, following the French air force bombardment February 8 of Sakiet, a Tunisian village on the Algerian border. (Sakiet, the French charged, was being used by Algerian rebels as a base.)

French President Rene Coty May 8, 1958 named Pierre Pflimlin premier-designate after ex-premiers Georges Bidault and Rene Pleven had failed in attempts to form cabinets (April 20-22 and April 28-May 8 respectively).

The National Assembly met May 12 to debate the investiture of a cabinet headed by Pflimlin.

Charles Andre Marie Joseph de Gaulle was born Nov. 22, 1890. He graduated as a second lieutenant from St. Cyr Military Academy in 1912. During World War I, he was promoted to captain, twice wounded, and captured by the Germans and released at the end of the war. Between the two wars, de Gaulle wrote a number of articles and books on mechanized and tank warfare. At the beginning of World War II he was a colonel in command of an armored division. Following a success in turning back a German tank offensive at Laon, he was promoted to the rank of brigadier general. After the fall of France de Gaulle, then in London, made an historic radio appeal to France June 18, 1940 to continue the fight, thereby launching the Free French Movement.

De Gaulle triumphantly returned to Paris Aug. 25, 1944. The Constituent Assembly elected in November 1945 named him head of the government. He resigned Jan. 20, 1946 after he was unable to obtain from various political parties the unit he felt necessary for postwar reconstruction of France.

On Oct. 13, 1946 a draft constitution setting up the Fourth Republic was adopted — against de Gaulle's advice — by a small margin in a referendum. De Gaulle then organized the Rally of the French People (RPF) which gained almost 40% of the vote in municipal elections held in October 1947, but failed to gain a majority of seats in the National Assembly in the elections of 1951. On May 8, 1953 de Gaulle announced in Paris that the RPF would no longer put up candidates for elections or act in the Assembly as a party since the RPF had lost heavily in municipal elections held April 26. He withdrew from public life at that time to retirement at his home in Colombey-les-Deux-Eglises (100 miles east of Paris) where he wrote his memoirs of World War II but maintained his contacts with important political leaders. He was at Colombey May 12, 1958 as the National Assembly debated confirmation of the Pflimlin cabinet.

PART I

THE ALGERIAN WAR YEARS

(1958 – 1962)

CHAPTER I

DE GAULLE RETURNS TO POWER

May 13, 1958 — June 1, 1958

Algiers French Rebel, Call for Gaullist Rule. Rightist French civilians and army officers rebelled May 13, 1958 against Premier-designate Pierre Pflimlin's newly formed government. Headed by Brigadier General Jacques Massu, commander of the 10th Parachute Division, they proclaimed the formation of an Algiers Committee of Public Safety and warned that they would oppose Pflimlin's reported willingness to open negotiations with Algeria's Moslem rebels. The Committee, leading a mob of students and war veterans, occupied the headquarters of the French Ministry for Algeria and other government buildings in Algiers. The Committee was composed of three other parachute officers and seven civilians, among them Leon Delbecque, a liaison man between Gaullist supporters in Paris and Algiers. Massu, in a speech to the Algiers crowd May 13, addressed a public appeal to General de Gaulle "to take the leadership of a government of public safety" in Paris; de Gaulle alone, declared Massu, was capable of forming a regime that would "insure the everlastingness of French Algeria, an integral part of France." Massu's call for the return to power of de Gaulle was backed in Paris by demonstrations led by rightist deputies.

Assembly Votes Pflimlin Premier. Pflimlin, a centrist Catholic Popular Republican (MRP), was approved May 14 as France's 25th postwar premier by a National Assembly vote of 274-109 (136 abstentions). In an effort to regain control of events in Algiers, Pflimlin immediately ordered Lieutenant-General Raoul Salan, French army commander for Algeria, to assume military and administrative control in Algeria. Salan accepted Pflimlin's orders May 14 in a statement saying that the army would transmit commands to the Algiers Committee. Salan, in a midday speech May 15 to an Algiers rally, called for continuation of French rule in Algeria, and concluded his speech with the cry: "Long live France, Long live French Algeria. Long live de Gaulle." Six hours later, de Gaulle, in his first public reaction to the Algiers Committee's call for his return to power, declared in a statement issued in Paris: "I hold myself ready to take over the powers of the Republic." He warned that the "degradation of the state inevitably brings...the estrangement of the peoples of our territories," trouble in the Army and "the loss of our independence." General Massu May 16 sent a telegram to French President Rene Coty calling upon Coty to "accept the arbitration" of de Gaulle "so that a government of public safety may be formed [in Paris], headed by de Gaulle."

Pflimlin Voted Powers to Counteract Algiers Coup. A declaration of a state of emergency empowering the government of Premier Pflimlin to combat the Algiers revolt, as well as unrest in France among supporters and opponents of General de Gaulle, was voted by 461-114 in the French National Assembly May 16. Pflimlin decreed dissolution of four rightist youth groups and political organizations and cast doubt on the loyalty of General Salan and the French army in Algeria to the Paris government. He said that Salan had dismissed and replaced civil officials in Algeria without the "agreement of the government." He charged that "certain" army leaders had "embarked on a course that could lead to the splitting up of the nation."

De Gaulle, appearing before journalists in Paris May 19, 1958 issued a second statement confirming his readiness to serve "at the head of the government of the French Republic." Referring to the May 13 army-civilian rebellion in Algeria, he said that the French population in Algeria "has seen that the present system established in Paris cannot solve its problems." He understood "very well the attitude of the military command in Algeria"; the army, he asserted, had been "deeply affected by the [Algerian] drama" and by "the disability of the public authorities" and had acted "to prevent disorder from breaking out." He announced that his Algerian policy would attempt "arbitration" of the Moslem and rightist rebellions.

General Salan told an Algiers rally May 20 that de Gaulle's comments on the Algerian revolt and the army's role in it had given rise "to an immense hope of greatness and national unity." At the same rally, Jacques Soustelle, a right-wing deputy in the French National Assembly and supporter of de Gaulle, who had eluded surveillance by Paris police and had arrived in Algiers via Switzerland May 17, called for complete integration of the French and Moslem populations of Algeria on a basis of full equality. Soustelle, known to favor military suppression of Algeria's Moslem rebellion, said he had put himself "at the disposition of French Algeria." (Soustelle, former Governor General in Algeria from Jan. 26, 1955 to Feb. 6, 1956, had been Secretary General of the Gaullist Rally of the French People (RPF) movement.)

All-Algeria Committee of Public Safety Formed. A 71-member Committee of Public Safety for Algeria and the Sahara, formed to direct the local Public Safety groups set up throughout Algeria, was proclaimed in Algiers May 23, 1958 and recognized immediately by General Salan. Meeting in Algiers May 23 in a plenary session presided over by Salan, the Committee appealed to "French citizens of the metropolitan country, of the French Union and of the entire world" to establish local "Committees of Public Safety" to obtain "a government of public safety headed by General de Gaulle...."

Corsican Revolt Supports Algiers Coup. Rightists and pro-Gaullists formed a Committee of Public Safety on Corsica May 24 and, aided by French army parachutists, seized control of government buildings and communications in Ajaccio, the capital.

The Ajaccio Committee of Public Safety pledged its loyalty to the Algerian Committee and General de Gaulle. An Algerian delegation headed by Leon Delbecque, Gaullist political leader active in the formation of the Algiers Committee, arrived on Corsica May 26 to coordinate policies of the rebel groups. Parachutist Colonel Robert Thomazo was named military and civil commander for Corsica May 26 by General Salan.

Paris Acts to Quell Corsican Revolt. The Pflimlin cabinet declared May 24 that a state of insurrection existed on Corsica. The National Assembly moved May 27 to censure leaders of the Corsican rebellion. The Assembly voted suspension of parliamentary immunity for deputies guilty of criminal actions. A preliminary indictment charged Pascal Arrighi, a Corsican deputy and member of the Ajaccio Committee of Public Safety, with plotting against internal security. Pflimlin May 27 conceded, however, that he had not sent security reinforcements to Corsica for fear of undermining the government's ability to suppress disorders in France proper.

French Fleet Joins Rebellion. French naval forces under Admiral Philippe-Marie Auboyneau, French and NATO naval commander for the Mediterranean, put into Algerian ports May 26 as a demonstration of support for the Algerian insurrection. Auboyneau, Free French naval commander during World War II and reportedly an early member of the Algiers conspiracy, had declared open support for the Algerian and Gaullist revolt May 25.

De Gaulle Renews Bid. General de Gaulle, who had conferred secretly with Pflimlin near Paris the night of May 26-27, 1958 declared in a statement issued May 27 that he had "started yesterday the regular process necessary for the establishment of a republican government capable of assuring the unity and the independence of the country." He said he depended "on that process [of forming a cabinet] being carried through." He denounced "any action, from whatever side…that threatens public order" and said he expected all French armed forces in Algeria "to remain exemplary under the orders of their chiefs, General Raoul Salan, Admiral Philippe-Marie Auboyneau and General Edmond Jouhaud."

Left Declares Opposition. De Gaulle's assertion that he had begun forming a cabinet, made while the Pflimlin government still was in office, brought hardened opposition by leftist groups. Socialist deputies caucused May 27 and voted, 112-3, that they would "not in any case rally to the candidacy of General de Gaulle." The Socialist resolution, adopted despite opposition of Socialist leader Vice Premier Guy Mollet, charged that de Gaulle had been called to power by "seditionists" and that his candidacy was "a challenge to republican legality."

The Communist-led General Confederation of Labor (CGT), acting before de Gaulle made his cabinet statement, had called on French workers to strike May 27 as "a powerful demonstration…, of anti-Fascist action and of republican defense." The CGT strike was followed May 27 by Christian and Socialist unions' appeals for members to demonstrate May 28.

An estimated 125,000 leftists, led by Radical ex-Premiers Pierre Mendes-France and Edouard Daladier, Communist Party Secretary Jacques Duclos, Socialist Information Minister Albert Gazier, ex-Foreign Minister Christian Pineau and Francois Mitterand, leader of the Social Union of the Resistance (UDSR), paraded in Paris May 28 to protest efforts to restore de Gaulle to power. The demonstration had been called by the National Committee of Action and Republican Defense, an anti-Gaullist coordinating body set up May 23 by Socialists and Popular Republicans and joined by Radicals, the Democratic and the UDSR and smaller leftist groups.

Pflimlin Defends Contact with de Gaulle. Premier Pflimlin defended his secret talks with de Gaulle May 27 as part of his task to explore all possibilities "to spare our country the trial of civil war." He told the Assembly that he had met with de Gaulle to urge him to use his "moral authority" to curb rightist and military leaders "who were engaged in or were contemplating insurrection against republican order." Pflimlin asserted that he had not known of de Gaulle's claim to be forming a government until publication of the general's May 27 statement.

Pflimlin had opened contact with de Gaulle May 22 while still attempting to rally Assembly support for his own cabinet and constitutional reform program. He had accepted offers by Independent (conservative) ex-Premier Antoine Pinay to act as liaison with de Gaulle. Pinay, who met with de Gaulle May 22 and Pflimlin May 23, reportedly initiated efforts to bring about direct talks between Pflimlin and de Gaulle. A leader in the efforts to rally Gaullist support in the Assembly, Pinay was said to fear that de Gaulle would be swept to power by an armed coup if not made premier by legal means.

Pflimlin Resigns. Faced with growing military and civilian insurrection against rule by the French government and National Assembly in Paris, Premier Pflimlin submitted his resignation to President Coty early May 28, 1958 despite Assembly approval May 28, by 408-165, of a resolution declaring its intent to institute constitutional reforms aimed at strengthening executive powers of the cabinet and premier.

In a statement issued following the vote and a visit to President Coty, Pflimlin said that he had offered his resignation but had been asked to remain in office to avoid "a power vacuum" between regimes. He said he had based his decision to resign on the failure of "an important group," presumably Independents, to support the constitutional reform resolution.

It was generally thought that Pflimlin resigned to pave the way for a legal return to power by de Gaulle and forestall a possible coup d'etat by rebellious pro-Gaullist military and civilian leaders.

De Gaulle Accepts Coty's Call to Assume Power. De Gaulle agreed to attempt to form a new French government May 29, 1958 after President Coty had warned the National Assembly earlier that day that he would resign and abandon France to civil war unless de Gaulle was approved as premier. In an extraordinary message (read to the National Assembly by Assembly Speaker Andre Le Troquer), Coty warned that Frenchmen were "preparing for a fratricidal struggle" that could only end in "civil war." He said that he was asking de Gaulle "to examine ... what, within the bounds of republican legality, is immediately necessary to a government of national salvation ... for a profound reform of our institutions."

De Gaulle, in a statement issued May 29 after talks with Coty, indicated that he would assume the premiership on these conditions: "The government, once invested by the National Assembly, would receive for a fixed time the full powers necessary to act in the present ... grave situation." A "mandate would be given to the government" under constitutional procedure "to prepare and to submit to the country through a referendum the changes that must be made in it." These constitutional changes would concern "the separation and the balance of powers as well as the relations of the French Republic with the peoples that are associated with it."

Opposition to de Gaulle Weakens. Resistance to de Gaulle's return to power, led by the Socialist Party, dissident Radicals and lesser leftist groups with the support of Communist deputies, lessened May 29-30, 1958 following the Coty-de Gaulle statements and the publication May 29 of an exchange of letters between de Gaulle and Socialist ex-President Vincent Auriol.

In a letter written to de Gaulle May 25, Auriol called on the general to "break all solidarity" with Algerian rightist leaders. Auriol urged de Gaulle to submit all constitutional reforms to national referendum.

De Gaulle's reply, written May 29, asserted that the Algerian insurrection had been "carried out in my name without my being in any way involved." De Gaulle declared that he "could not consent to receive power from any source but the people, or at least its representatives." He said that he sought only "to form by legal means a government" which would "remake unity, reestablish discipline (particularly within the armed forces)... and promote adoption of a renovated constitution by the country."

Auriol and Socialist ex-Premier Guy Mollet met with de Gaulle May 30 in Colombey-les-Deux-Eglises and returned to Paris to attempt to rally a Socialist caucus to support the general. The joint meeting of Socialist deputies and senators voted by 77-74 to oppose de Gaulle but to leave the deputies free to vote as individuals on de Gaulle's confirmation as premier.

Independent ex-Premier Antoine Pinay and Pierre-Henri Teitgen, leader of the Catholic Popular Republicans, had met with President Coty May 28 and assured him of their parties' backing for de Gaulle's confirmation.

Communist-led riots broke out in working-class districts of Paris June 1, and 190 anti-Gaullists were reported arrested by police. Fears, however, that the CGT would attempt a nationwide general strike to oppose de Gaulle proved unfounded. The CGT, in an appeal similar to messages issued by the Christian and Socialist union federations, called May 30 for workers to remain vigilant but contained no orders for direct action.

Assembly Elects de Gaulle Premier. De Gaulle June 1, 1958 went before the National Assembly to seek confirmation as premier. In a brief speech he warned that the "degradation of the state is rapidly becoming worse," endangering France's domestic and international situation. He asked for "full powers to be able to act with all the effectiveness, speed and responsibility demanded by the circumstances ... for a period of six months, hoping that at the end of this time — order having been restored in the State, hope regained in Algeria, unity restored in the nation—it will be possible for the public powers to resume their normal course." He declared that he would demand "a mandate ... to formulate and then propose to the country, through a referendum, the indispensable changes" required by the constitution."...the Government will specify the three principles which must be the basis of the republican regime in France and to which it pledges that its bill will conform: universal suffrage is the source of all power; the executive and the legislative branches must be separate and apart so that the Government and the Parliament can, each for its own part and on its own responsibility, assume its full powers; the Government must be responsible to the Parliament."

In the debate following the speech, prominent Assembly members, including Radical Pierre Mendes-France, UDSR leader Francois Mitterand, Progressist Pierre Coty, and Communist Jacques Duclos, expressed opposition to confirming de Gaulle under threat of a rightist coup d'etat, but they made no effort to block a favorable vote. The Assembly then voted by 329-224, 52 more than the required absolute majority of those voting, to make de Gaulle premier, returning him to power as the 26th and last premier of the postwar Fourth Republic.

CHAPTER II

FROM THE FOURTH TO THE FIFTH REPUBLIC

June 1, 1958 — October 10, 1958

Cabinet Installed, Emergency Powers Voted. De Gaulle's 15-member cabinet, announced to the Assembly June 1, 1958 contained three former premiers (Mollet, Pinay, Pflimlin) and representatives of seven Assembly political parties. The cabinet contained no members known to have been involved in the Algiers rightist insurrection or the conspiracy presumed to have preceded it. The cabinet (with party affiliation in parenthesis):

> *Premier and National Defense Minister*— General Charles de Gaulle; *State Ministers*— Guy Mollet (Socialist), Pierre Pflimlin (Popular Republican), Louis Jacquinot (Independent), Felix Houphouet-Boigny (African Democratic Rally); *Foreign Affairs*— Maurice Couve de Murville (no party); *Interior*— Emile Pelletier (no party); *Justice*— Michel Debre (Gaullist); *Education*— Jean Berthoin (Radical); *Information*— Andre Malraux (Gaullist); *Labor*— Paul Bacon (Popular Republican); *Overseas France*— Bernard Cornut-Gentille (no party); *Armed Forces*— Pierre Guillaumat (no party); *Finance*— Antoine Pinay (Independent); *Industry and Commerce*— Edouard Ramonet (Radical); *Algeria*— Max Lejeune (Socialist); *State Secretaries*— Malraux, Lejeune, Cornut-Gentille, Bacon, Guillaumat, Ramonet.

De Gaulle's reliance on moderate Assembly leaders was viewed as an additional pledge of continuation of the republican system. Algiers rightists were reported disgruntled at the cabinet's composition and its exclusion of Gaullist leaders Jacques Soustelle and Leon Delbecque. De Gaulle's demand for full powers to rule France by decree for a six-month period was granted by the National Assembly June 2 by a vote of 322-232. The law empowered the de Gaulle government to take any action it viewed as necessary in the fields of taxation, economy, production, military reorganization and Algerian and North African affairs.

Constitutional Reform Powers Granted. The Assembly voted by 350-163 June 3 to grant de Gaulle powers to revise the French constitution and present the reforms to a national referendum without submitting them to the Assembly. The measure pledged de Gaulle to base reforms on republican principles. The Assembly abandoned efforts to debate amendments to the bill after de Gaulle threatened to resign, warning that his government "could not assume its responsibilities beyond this night" if they were adopted.

15

De Gaulle Goes to Algeria; Seeks Control of Rightist Coup, End to Moslem Rebellion. De Gaulle visited Algeria June 4-6, 1958 in an attempt to bring rebellious right-wing civilians and military leaders under control of the French government and to seek a political formula linking Algeria's more than eight million Moslems and over one million Europeans under French rule.

Arriving in Algiers June 4, he declared to a huge crowd of Europeans at a welcoming rally; "I have understood you." ("Je vous ai compris.") He hailed Algeria's Europeans for opening "in Algeria...the road of renewal and brotherhood." The French army, he said, had "accomplished here a magnificent work of understanding and pacification." He announced at the rally that "all Frenchmen, including the 10 million in Algeria," would, within three months, take part in elections to choose through "a single [electoral] college their representatives to the public powers." De Gaulle urged participation in the proposed voting even by Moslem rebels. "To those," he said, "I, de Gaulle, open the door to reconciliation." Offering the Moslem population equality, he proclaimed that "from today forward France considers that there...are only Frenchmen of the same sort, with the same rights and the same duties."

De Gaulle repeated his offer to Algerian Moslems June 5 in visits to Constantine and Bone. Refusing to take up chants for "French Algeria" and "total integration [with France]," de Gaulle told a Bone rally that "all barriers, all privileges must fall."

Rebels Reject French Bid. De Gaulle's appeal for reconciliation was rejected June 5 by the Algerian National Liberation Front's (FLN) ruling Committee of Coordination and Execution in Cairo. An FLN communique said de Gaulle's proposals for Algeria were a "perpetuation of the colonialist policy of France" and were "closing the door to all possibilities of negotiable settlement based on the independence of Algeria." In an interview in Cairo FLN leader Ferhat Abbas stated that Algeria's Moslems were "not French and never will be French."

De Gaulle Curbs Junta. Statements issued by de Gaulle June 6, 1958 before he left Algeria ordered the All-Algeria Committee of Public Safety to withdraw from political action. Meeting with members of the All-Algeria Committee June 6 in Oran, de Gaulle told them that the "authority here is in the hands of General Salan. It must not be contested."

In a letter to Salan, made public the same day, de Gaulle designated Salan his "delegate general" in Algeria and made clear that Salan was to communicate "directly with me, to whom you are subordinate and who assumes...control of Algerian affairs." De Gaulle said the Committee of Public Safety was to work under Salan's control.

The All-Algeria Committee demanded in a June 10 message to de Gaulle that de Gaulle suppress the French political party system and form a "real government of public safety" in France. It urged postponement of de Gaulle's plans, announced June 7 by Information Minister Andre Malraux, to hold municipal elections in Algeria within a month. It expressed the committee's pleasure at "having been able to obtain the promise of total integration without reserve of Algeria with metropolitan France," a position avoided by de Gaulle during his Algerian visit.

Replying to the Committee in a message to Salan, de Gaulle June 11 denounced the Committee's demands as "peremptory" and rebuked Salan for his evident approval of them. De Gaulle told Salan that the "regular authority, and first of all yourself, could not take a position on anything this committee... might express or demand."

New Regime Proposed. Addressing the French people in his first radio-TV broadcast since returning to power, de Gaulle declared June 13 that the French Fourth Republic's system of government had come to an end. He asserted that "for 12 years, the party regime, floating over a deeply divided people, in the midst of a terribly dangerous universe, showed itself incapable of assuring the conduct of affairs" or of solving the "enormous problems" facing France. He proposed constitutional revision to ensure "the Republic powers strong enough, stable enough, effective enough to answer for her destiny." He appealed to Frenchmen for their support in pacifying Algeria so that it would "always be body and soul with France," and in organizing "federal... links of metropolitan France with... Africa and Madagascar."

Algiers Leaders Retreat. European civilians and army officers in Algeria tempered their public opposition to de Gaulle's policies June 13-14 and pledged their loyalty and cooperation for the plans outlined in de Gaulle's broadcast appeal. In a message transmitted to General Salan June 13, members of the Algiers Committee of Public Safety pledged their "fullest confidence" and "respectful cooperation" to de Gaulle. General Salan was formally installed in the Algiers Government General building June 16 as de Gaulle's delegated administrator for Algeria. Salan June 15 named Air Force Major General Edmond Jouhaud as his deputy commander for Algeria charged with operational control of French air, land and sea forces. Jouhaud was a member of the All-Algeria Committee of Public Safety.

De Gaulle Revisits Algeria, Courts Moslems. De Gaulle returned to Algeria July 1, 1958 for a tour of Moslem centers and rural areas to seek Moslem backing for his program of Algerian equality. Arriving near Constantine, he visited Batna, Setif and Telergma, near Oran, urging French-Moslem unity and backing for Algeria's racial "reconciliation" movement. He told 2,000 Moslems gathered in a French-held enclave in the Traras Mountains near Morocco July 2 that "all men who live here must be equal ... and I give you my word that they will be." De Gaulle, accompanied by State Minister Guy Mollet, was accorded what newsmen termed a markedly cool reception by the European community on his arrival in Algiers July 2. (The de Gaulle cabinet had met June 28 to approve decrees limiting and defining the powers of General Raoul Salan's military administration in Algeria and to name Algerian Secretary General Rene Brouillet as central coordinator for the execution of de Gaulle's Algerian policies.)

De Gaulle ended his second visit to Algeria July 3 with an Algiers radio speech outlining a "vast plan" to give Algeria a "rightful share" in French progress. Avoiding any indorsement of rightist demands for total Algerian integration within France, he pledged: (1) participation of Europeans and Moslems, (2) a 15 billion-franc ($36 million) increase in the 62 billion-franc Algerian development budget for 1958; (3) specific programs for "new industries," agricultural modernization, and (4) doubling of

Algerian housing and expansion of the education system to provide schooling for all children within 10 years.

Soustelle Enters Cabinet. De Gaulle announced July 7 the appointment of Jacques Soustelle as Information Minister, replacing Andre Malraux, who remained in the cabinet with responsibility for youth, cultural and scientific affairs.

Soustelle announced July 11 that Brigadier General Massu had been promoted to major general and General Salan had been awarded the *Medaille Militaire*, France's highest military award. Massu and Salan were cheered by an estimated 500,000 Parisians July 14 when they accompanied General de Gaulle in the traditional Bastille Day military parade.

Algeria Offered Federal Tie. Premier de Gaulle, in a Bastille Day broadcast to French overseas territories July 13, 1958, asserted that Algeria would be offered a "choice place" in a new federal system linking France with its overseas dependencies. "We are moving," he declared, "toward a vast and free community. In 1958 we must build new institutions, establish the links of our union in the federal manner and organize a grand political, economic and cultural entity that will answer to the conditions of modern life."

Constitutional Reform Proposed. A draft constitution designed to create a new French federation composed of metropolitan France and its overseas territories under a Fifth Republic was prepared by the de Gaulle cabinet and made public July 29. The draft outlined a strong presidential system of government to replace the system of parliamentary supremacy of the Fourth Republic. It was attacked July 30 by moderates and leftists as a threat to French democratic institutions. Approval of the draft was considered assured in a referendum scheduled to be held September 28 in France and its overseas territories.

De Gaulle Tours Colonies, Urges Federation with France. Premier de Gaulle left Paris Aug. 20, 1958 on a tour of France's African territories to seek their acceptance of the proposed new French constitution. De Gaulle had warned the territories August 8 that their rejection of the draft would be tantamount to secession from the French Union. (The French Union had been established in 1946. It included all French colonies and Algeria, but Algeria was governed as an integral part of France, not as a colony.)

De Gaulle told a rally in Tananarive, Madagascar August 22 that African territories could choose between "separating their destiny completely from that of France" and participating in a "federal community" with "complete liberty" under French leadership. In Abidjan, Ivory Coast August 24, de Gaulle said it was "natural and legitimate" that African peoples should advance politically and assume "the entire responsibility for their external affairs and decide their own government." Madagascan Premier Philibert Tsiranana August 21 and Ivory Coast leader Felix Houphouet-Boigny August 24 both pledged support for the new constitution.

In response to demands by Guinea nationalist leader Sekou Toure for independence, de Gaulle August 25 declared in Conakry that Guinea was free to choose independence by voting against the constitution in the September 28 referendum.

At the conclusion of his African tour, de Gaulle declared August 29 in Algiers that approval of the new constitution in the referendum would insure "the necessary evolution of Algeria ... in a French framework." (Overseas Minister Bernard Cornut-Gentille, accompanying de Gaulle on his African tour, had told newsmen in Guinea August 25 that Algeria, unlike France's overseas territories, would not be given the right to secede because it legally was part of metropolitan [i.e., European] France.)

Exile Algerian Government Formed. A "Republic of Algeria" government-in-exile headed by Ferhat Abbas, an FLN leader, was established in Cairo Sept. 19, 1958. It was recognized immediately by the United Arab Republic, Iraq, Libya, Yemen, Tunisia and Morocco. The French government denounced it as an organization for "assassination and terror." Ferhat Abbas declared September 26 in Cairo the rebel government's desire to "bring to the Algerian problem a peaceful and negotiated solution" but on the basis of Algerian independence.

De Gaulle Speech on Draft Constitution. Premier de Gaulle September 4 defended the draft constitution at a rally in the Place de la Republique, a working-class center in Paris. Speaking after police had routed Communists who tried to disrupt the proceedings, de Gaulle called for adoption of the new constitution in the September 28 referendum. He outlined the main provisions of the document: (1) election of the president for a seven-year term by an electoral college consisting of members of Parliament, of general councils and assemblies of overseas territories and municipal council representatives; (2) power for the president to appoint the premier, dissolve the National Assembly and take extensive executive power during a "great national emergency"; (3) a premier and cabinet responsible to but not members of Parliament; (4) association in a "community of common interest" of France and overseas territories ratifying the constitution; (5) popular election of National Assembly deputies but abolition of the parliamentary confidence vote by which cabinets previously were overthrown; (6) substitution of an arrangement whereby a cabinet could be deposed by Assembly passage of a censure motion first signed by 1/10 of the deputies, with the proviso that a deputy could not sign another motion during the same session of Parliament if one that he signed had been defeated.

Besides the Communists, ex-Premier Pierre Mendes-France (a Radical Socialist) came out September 5 as chief opponent of the de Gaulle constitution which, he said, would imperil democracy in France. The proposed constitution was supported by ex-Premier Felix Gaillard (also a Radical Socialist) and was indorsed by a Radical Socialist congress in Paris September 14. The Socialist Party, in a Paris convention September 14, also indorsed the de Gaulle constitution and reelected ex-Premier Guy Mollet, state minister in the de Gaulle cabinet, as party secretary-general.

Constitution Approved in Referendum. The Fifth Republic constitution was approved in a referendum Sept. 28, 1958 by a 4-1 margin in France and overwhelmingly in Algeria and all other parts of the French Union except French Guinea, West Africa.

The new charter advocated by Premier de Gaulle won by 17,666,828 to 4,624,478 in France. In Algeria the constitution was approved by a 3,356,169 to 118,615 vote, with 79% of the registered voters, including Moslems, going to the polls despite a rebel decree boycotting the referendum. Voting was conducted Sept. 26-28 in rural Algeria. News reports said that most Moslems in French-controlled areas decided not to defy authorities by supporting a boycott and that French promises to improve the lot of Moslem women attracted many of them to the polls to vote for the first time.

Vote on the new Fifth Republic constitution in other areas of the French Union (the only rejection came in French West Africa-Guinea):

Possession	For	Against
Chad	182,028	1,734
Comoro Islands	63,899	1,755
Congo	296,359	1,361
Dahomey	399,422	9,289
Fr. Equatorial Africa-Gabon	137,650	11,376
Fr. Somaliland	8,661	2,851
Fr. Sudan	490,679	10,349
Fr. West Africa-Guinea	15,551	573,470
Ivory Coast	1,553,705	197
Madagascar	1,178,595	332,294
Mauritania	192,444	13,080
New Caledonia	26,085	500
Niger	214,840	59,856
Polynesian Islands	13,736	7,531
St. Pierre and Miquelon	2,325	46
Senegal	772,058	21,540
Ubangi-Shari	452,230	4,808
Upper Volta	768,639	6,822

Guinea Made Independent. The French government, acting on de Gaulle's pre-referendum declaration that a territory rejecting the constitution would be cut free of France, served notice on French Guinea September 29 of its separation from the French Union. The territory became an independent state with a government headed by Sekou Toure, leftist Guinea premier, who had led a successful campaign for Guinea's rejection of the constitution in favor of independence.

De Gaulle Discloses Algerian Plan. Returning to Algeria for his fourth visit since assuming power, Premier de Gaulle outlined Oct. 3, 1958 a five-year plan for creation of a prosperous, peaceful Algeria linked closely with France. Speaking in Constantine, a predominantly Moslem city in eastern Algeria, de Gaulle angered rightists when he again ignored European demands for Algerian integration with France and instead pledged the preservation of a distinct Algerian "personality." He promised: (1) equal Moslem-European participation in election of Algerian deputies, "at least 2/3" to be Moslems, to the new French Assembly; (2) distribution to Moslems of 625,000 acres of reclaimed land; (3) earmarking of 10% of civil service assignments in France and a higher proportion in Algeria to be filled by Moslems; (4) construction as public works of new housing for one million persons and hospitals, roads and ports in Algeria; (5) creation of 400,000 new jobs in Algeria through public works, a heavy French investment program and development of Saharan oil resources; (6) elevation of Algerian wages to French levels.

Army Officers Quit Algiers' Junta. Major General Jacques Massu and 11 other French army officers resigned their posts on the All-Algeria Committee of Public Safety October 14. Massu acted after de Gaulle ordered French army officers to withdraw from Algerian politics. The resignations marked the success of de Gaulle's efforts to deprive rightists in Algiers of army support and reassert government control over dissident military leaders in Algeria.

Fifth Republic Born. The French Fifth Republic formally came into existence October 5 with publication of the new constitution. Final referendum results reported by the French government October 4, showed that of 45,840,642 registered voters in France and French dependencies (Guinea excepted), 36,893,979 had cast 36,486,251 valid ballots — 31,066,502 for the constitution, 5,419,749 against it.

The de Gaulle cabinet announced October 10 that Algeria would be given 66 deputies in the new 585-member French Assembly to be elected in voting November 23 and 30. Metropolitan France would elect 465 deputies, the Saharan Department of Algeria 4, other overseas dependencies 39. The cabinet had announced October 7 the abandonment of departmental proportional representation in favor of small electoral districts empowered to elect one deputy by majority vote — a change in the election system that was to reduce the Communists' large Assembly bloc gained through the designed proportional representation system. Decrees issued by the cabinet October 21 fixed the size of the new French Senate and scheduled senatorial elections for March 1959.

CHAPTER III

ENDING THE ALGERIAN WAR

"CEASE-FIRE" TO "SELF-DETERMINATION" OFFERS
October 1958 — November 1959

De Gaulle Offers "Cease-Fire"; Rebels Reject Bid. Premier de Gaulle publicly offered Oct. 23, 1958 in Paris to meet with Algerian Moslem rebel-leaders and negotiate an "end of hostilities" in Algeria. Addressing his first press conference since becoming premier, he disclosed that rebel leaders already had been invited to France under a safe-conduct guarantee to discuss a cease-fire. Although he did not reject rebel demands for discussion of Algerian independence, he made clear that a settlement must "have as a basis the personality of Algeria and her close association with metropolitan France."

De Gaulle declared that the rebels had "fought courageously" but slowly were losing ground to superior French forces. He offered rebel troops a "brave men's peace" and promised that they would be treated honorably under truce flags. He reported that 77,000 rebels, 7,200 French troops, 10,000 Moslem civilians and 1,500 European civilians had been killed in Algerian fighting and that an additional 75 Frenchmen and 1,717 Moslems had died in terrorist attacks in France itself since the beginning of the war.

The Algerian Provisional Government rejected de Gaulle's negotiation offer October 25 as "a request for unconditional surrender." A rebel communique issued in Cairo made clear that negotiations would have to center on Algerian independence demands and could be held only on neutral territory.

Civilian Rule Restored in Algeria. De Gaulle Dec. 12, 1958 following his fifth visit to Algeria since returning to power, named Paul Delouvrier, European Coal and Steel Community financial director, as civilian delegate-general in Algeria replacing General Salan. Delouvrier's appointment ended the French Army's military regime in effect in Algeria since May 13.

Decrees issued by de Gaulle's cabinet gave Delouvrier full civil and military powers in Algeria as part of a general reorganization of Algerian administration. French Air Force General Maurice Challe was named to succeed Salan as French military commander for Algeria subordinate to Delouvrier. Major General Massu was made "superprefect" of Algiers and the Algiers district. Salan was named French Inspector General of National Defense.

23

De Gaulle Becomes President; Debre Cabinet Formed. De Gaulle was proclaimed first president of the Fifth French Republic for a seven-year term Jan. 8, 1959, succeeding Rene Coty, last president of the Fourth Republic. In his first official act January 8, President de Gaulle, who had relinquished the premiership to assume the presidency, appointed Michel Debre, a leading member of the Gaullist Union for the New Republic (UNR) as premier at the head of a 27-member cabinet. Debre's cabinet, including 16 members of the former de Gaulle cabinet, took office January 10.

Amnesty Decree. The Debre cabinet, at a meeting presided over by President de Gaulle Jan. 13, 1959, decreed broad measures of clemency and amnesty for captured Algerian rebel leaders, condemned rebel terrorists and persons detained on suspicion of rebel sympathies. The clemency decree was issued despite opposition expressed January 12 by the Algerian and Saharan group in the National Assembly.

The amnesty decree included these provisions: (1) Ahmed Ben Bella and four other Algerian rebel leaders, three of them named to the rebel Algerian Provisional Government after their capture in 1956, would be transferred from Paris' Sante Prison to more comfortable quarters; (2) the sentences of 140 to 200 rebels condemned to death were commuted to life imprisonment; (3) all rebel prison terms were shortened by 10%; (4) 7,000 interned rebel suspects would be released.

Truce Offer Renewed. President de Gaulle in messages January 15 to the opening sessions of the French National Assembly and Senate repeated his offer to assure Algerian rebel leaders safe conduct to Paris for negotiation of a cease-fire in the Algerian rebellion. He declared that "the pacification and transformation of Algeria" were "indispensable conditions" for an "(Algerian) political solution, which can only proceed from universal suffrage." He made clear that France would not negotiate a political settlement with the rebel Algerian Provisional Government.

Debre in Algeria. Premier Debre arrived in Algiers Feb. 8, 1959 and declared "in the name of the (French) Government" that "French sovereignty" would control "this side of the Mediterranean as it does the other." Debre's visit, his first to Algeria since assuming the premiership, was protested in Algiers February 7 by anti-Gaullist demonstrators favoring Algerian integration within France. Jeered as a "traitor" at Algiers war memorial ceremonies February 9, Debre denounced the "contemptible minds" who doubted President de Gaulle's pledge that "there will be no political negotiations" with the rebel government.

De Gaulle Affirms French Role. President de Gaulle, addressing a press conference in the Elysee Palace March 25, 1959, the first press conference ever held by a French president,* affirmed that France would continue to play a vital role in the "transformation that will enable Algeria to find itself." He cited the results of the September 1958 referendum in Algeria as evidence that "the vast majority of Algerian people trust me to secure for them peace, liberty and dignity and to act so that Algeria will thereby remain linked to France."

---

*De Gaulle held 17 formal Elysee Palace press conferences during his eleven year presidency. These conferences, held before upwards of a thousand people and in the presence of the complete cabinet, provided the occasion for de Gaulle to announce major decisions and policy orientations. At these conferences, he spoke from memory and only on subjects he had prepared in advance.

Algerian Elections Held Amid Violence. Moslem terrorists April 19 killed at least eight persons, wounded 80 and kidnaped 20 others, principally Moslem candidates, in attacks timed to coincide with the beginning of Algerian municipal elections. The rebels had ordered Algerians to boycott French-sponsored elections. Despite appeals by Major General Massu for Moslems to vote, only 40-50% of the electorate was reported to have cast ballots in major cities. Up to 95% voter participation was reported in rural areas, however, where the predominantly Moslem population voted under direct army supervision.

In Senatorial elections held May 31 to fill 32 seats for Algeria in the French Senate, 20 Moslems and 12 Europeans supporting de Gaulle's Algerian policy were elected by a body of 6,134 "grand electors," two-thirds of whom were Moslems.

Rightists Boycott May 13 Ceremonies. European residents of Algiers obeyed rightist orders May 13 and boycotted official ceremonies marking the 1958 Algiers coup. An estimated 40,000 Moslems were brought to the Algiers Forum to participate in the army-run ceremonies. Rightists had proclaimed the anniversary a "day of mourning" to protest President de Gaulle's alleged failure to carry out the aims of the 1958 uprising.

In a nationwide radio-TV address marking the first anniversary of the May 13, 1958 Algiers uprising, Premier Debre declared May 12 that France would maintain its position in Algeria permanently.

De Gaulle Hails Elections. De Gaulle told a cabinet meeting June 3, 1959 that recent Algerian elections had proved "the Moslem accession to political equality, to equality of rights and, definitely, the establishment of democracy in Algeria." In a reference to right-wing opposition to his Algerian program, de Gaulle warned that "whether one likes it or not, democracy exists in Algeria." He asserted that even the Algerian rebels had not been able to halt "free consultations" with Moslem moderates on Moslem participation in the elections.

Charges of Torture. Gaston Deferre (Socialist mayor of Marseilles) June 26 accused the French government of concealing the torture of Moslem prisoners. Charges that French police and troops had tortured suspected rebels to obtain information had been widespread following the publication and seizure in France of "*The Gangrene*," an account by four Moslems of their torture while held as rebel suspects. Premier Debre denounced the book June 25 as the work of Communists but told the Senate that he had warned French generals in Algeria they would be held "personally responsible" for maltreatment of Moslem prisoners.

Major French Offensive. Thirty thousand French troops began a major offensive July 22, 1959 against about 5,000 Algerian rebels operating in the mountainous Kabylia area east of Algiers. The French attack was directed personally by General Maurice Challe, French commander in Algeria. Challe announced September 21 that 4,400 rebels had been killed by French troops in the first two months of the offensive. He said the struggle would be "intensified" until "total pacification" of Algeria had been accomplished.

African Nations Back Rebel Government. Envoys from nine independent African states met Aug. 4-8, 1959 in Monrovia, Liberia to mobilize African support for the Algerian rebel government. Resolutions adopted

August 8 by the nine states (Liberia, Morocco, Tunisia, Ghana, Guinea, Ethiopia, Libya, Sudan and the UAR) called for (1) recognition of the Algerian Provisional Government by all countries; (2) withdrawal of French troops from Algeria; (3) peace negotiations between France and the rebels on the basis of French recognition of Algerian independence.

Algerian rebel Information Minister Mohammed Yazid told the conference August 7 that the rebels were prepared to "negotiate a political settlement" with France on neutral ground, but, he warned, if "France does not come to terms with our will for independence, it will mean war, war and war." He said an "Algerian Dienbienphu is possible not tomorrow or next month but in terms of years."

De Gaulle Hints at Self-Determination. De Gaulle visited Algeria August 27-30 and was reported to have persuaded French army leaders there to accept his developing plan for a "liberal" solution in Algeria: grant the territory self-determination but insist that it first be pacified. In a series of carefully-worded speeches during the tour, he hinted at a plan for self-determination without using the phrase. He said in Algiers August 28 that France must "pursue, complete and finish the pacification" of Algeria, "then the Algerians must freely decide their own destiny."

Self-Determination Offered. President de Gaulle, Sept. 16, 1959, offered the Algerian people freedom to choose their political future — including independence from France. In a radio-TV address to the French and Algerian peoples, de Gaulle made public his long-awaited program for ending the Algerian rebellion and assuring Algeria's Moslems the power to decide their country's future. De Gaulle rejected negotiations with the Algerian rebel government but invited rebel leaders to accept his previous offers of a cease-fire.

De Gaulle "proclaimed" all Algerians' rights to "self-determination." He called on "all Frenchmen to indorse their [Algerians'] choice" if the final decision required a French constitutional referendum. De Gaulle said that the "free choice which the Algerians themselves would make for their future" would be made from the following alternatives:

Secession— Algerians who chose separation from France would be free to "organize ... the territory in which they live, the resources which they have at their call, the government which they desire." Under secession, France would partition Algeria to arrange "regrouping and resettlement" of Europeans and Moslems who chose to "remain French" and would retain French-owned industry including oil interests in the Sahara.

Integration— If Algerians chose "out-and-out identification with France," they would "accede to all political, administrative and legal responsibilities" and "would benefit, from the point of view of salaries, social security, education ... by all measures provided for in Metropolitan France." "They would become part ... of the French people."

Internal Autonomy— A third choice would be "the government of Algeria by Algerians; backed up by French help and in a close relationship with France, for economy, teaching, defense and foreign relations."

De Gaulle pledged that an Algerian referendum to choose one of the alternatives would be held "at the latest four years after the actual restoration of peace,....." He pledged that in the interim between pacification and the plebiscite, France would pour funds into Algeria to "give the Algerians enough to support themselves with their own work...."

Rightists Oppose De Gaulle Offer. European rightists in Algeria generally expressed opposition to the de Gaulle plan. The Algiers Public Safety Committee denounced the plan September 18 and demanded "integration" and a "French Algeria." The formation of a French group in metropolitan France dedicated to Algerian integration with France — the Rally for a French Algeria (RAF) — was reported from Paris September 20. Leaders included ex-Premier Georges Bidault and Colonel Henri Thomazzo and Jean-Baptiste Biaggi, rightist members of the Gaullist UNR party.

Rebels Offer Talks. A communique issued September 28 in Tunis by Ferhat Abbas, Algerian rebel premier, said the provisional government was "ready to enter into conversations with the French Government ... to discuss the political and military conditions of a cease-fire and the conditions and guarantees of the application of self-determination." The communique rejected de Gaulle's contention that an Algerian solution could be found without negotiation with "the Provisional Government of the Algerian Republic."

New French Cease-Fire Offer. A French offer to negotiate a cease-fire with representatives of the Algerian National Liberation Front (FLN) was made public Oct. 11, 1959 by Foreign Minister Maurice Couve de Murville. In a taped interview for CBS-TV's "The UN in Action," Couve de Murville said France was "prepared to discuss a cease-fire with all those who fight [in Algeria], and that means ... the people of the FLN." Couve de Murville made it clear, however, that France would not negotiate with the FLN on Algeria's "political future," a matter which, he said, was "to be decided by all the Algerians."

Parliament Votes "Self-Determination." President de Gaulle's program for Algerian peace and self-determination was approved by the French National Assembly October 16 by a 441-23 vote (28 abstentions). Nine rightist Gaullists resigned from the UNR Parliamentary group October 14 in protest against Premier Debre's blocking of their efforts to lead Assembly opposition to the de Gaulle program and to support total integration of Algeria with France. Among the dissidents were Leon Delbecque, Pascal Arrighi and Jean-Baptiste Biaggi, leaders of the May 1958 revolt against the 4th Republic.

De Gaulle Orders Army "Discipline." President de Gaulle called on leaders of the French army and civil administration in Algeria October 28 to show devotion and discipline to his efforts to end the Algerian rebellion. The message was considered a rebuke to Marshal Alphonse-Pierre Juin, General Maxime Weygand and General Andre Zeller, leading military opponents of de Gaulle's offer of Algerian self-determination.

UNR Backs Algerian Program. The first national congress of the Gaullist Union for the New Republic Nov. 1, 1959 affirmed its "total confidence" in de Gaulle and his efforts to end the Algerian rebellion. The indorsement of de Gaulle's domestic and foreign policies came after Premier Debre and UNR Secretary General Albin Chalandon had defeated attempts of rightists led by Sahara Minister Jacques Soustelle to win a declaration of UNR support for the total integration of Algeria and France. The congress' final motion, voted with Soustelle's backing, pledged the UNR to support de Gaulle's offer of Algerian self-determination but declared that the party would work against Algerian secession and for a close union between Algeria and France.

War Casualties Announced. The Algerian rebellion entered its sixth year November 1, 1959. The semi-official Agence France Presse October 31 listed the following casualty figures for five years of Algerian fighting: rebels — 120,000 killed, 60,000 captured; French Army — 10,000 killed, 22,000 wounded; French civilians — 1,700 killed, 4,500 wounded, 300 missing; Moslem civilians — 12,000 killed, 9,000 wounded, 10,000 missing.

Communists Support "Self-Determination." The French Communist Party Central Committee reversed its previous opposition to de Gaulle's Algerian plans November 3, presumably to conform with Soviet Premier Nikita Khrushchev's praise of the program in an October 31 statement to the USSR's Supreme Soviet. A Central Committee resolution said a September 17 Politburo denunciation of the de Gaulle plan had been erroneous and had "deviated" from the party's past views on the Algerian problem.

De Gaulle Renews Peace Bid. In his second press conference as president, de Gaulle November 10 repeated his September 16 offer of Algerian self-determination. The Algerians, he declared, "will have to decide their destiny themselves." The rebel leaders, he said, could, if they desire, "discuss with the [French] authorities the conditions for an end to the fighting...." He charged that his rightist opponents in Paris and Algiers were attempting to "obscure what is perfectly clear," the need for self-determination.

Rightists Oppose De Gaulle. The rightist Rally for a French Algeria (RAF), led by ex-Premier Bidault, declared its opposition to de Gaulle's Algeria program November 11. The RAF appealed to "the European and Moslem French of Algeria" to oppose any "secret conversations" between the French government and Algerian rebels on conditions for the political plebiscite promised by de Gaulle when Algerian fighting ceased.

Rebels Name Captives Envoys. The rebel Algerian government accepted President de Gaulle's offer of cease-fire talks Nov. 20, 1959 but angered the French and posed insurmountable conditions by naming as true delegates five rebel leaders held prisoner in France since 1956. Named to the rebel peace delegation were these members in absentia of the Algerian Provisional Government's cabinet: Vice Premier Ahmed Ben Bella; State Ministers Mohammed Khider, Mohammed Boudiaf, Hocine Ait-Ahmed and Rabah Bitat. Ben Bella, Khider, Boudiaf and Ait-Ahmed had been captured in October 1956 when their Moroccan airliner, flying from Rabat to Tunis, was diverted to Algiers by its French pilot. The rebels were imprisoned in a French fortress on the Ile d'Aix, off the Atlantic coast of France.

De Gaulle Rebuffs Bid. The rebel designation of the five prisoners as cease-fire envoys was rejected by de Gaulle November 20 as a political maneuver. De Gaulle made clear that his offer to negotiate applied to "those who are fighting," not "those who are out of the fight."

THE SECOND ALGIERS UPRISING
January 1960 — February 1960

De Gaulle's liberal Algerian policy offering the choice of "self-determination" was severely challenged in January 1960 by a rightist rebellion in Algiers. The rebels, demanding that Algeria remain under French rule, were led by elements which had participated in the May 1958 Algiers insurrection bringing about de Gaulle's return to power.

The Jan. 24, 1960 uprising followed de Gaulle's dismissal of Major General Jacques Massu, popular hero of the 1958 coup, and reaffirmation by the Debre cabinet of de Gaulle's Algerian policy.

Massu Dismissal. Massu was fired as military and civil commander of the Algiers region January 22 after he had been summoned to Paris to explain statements he made to a West German newsman that the French army was opposed to de Gaulle's policies. The Massu interview, published January 18 by Munich's *Sueddeutsche Zeitung*; asserted that French army leaders "no longer understand the [Algerian] policies of President de Gaulle ... [and] never expected any such policy." Asked if the army could impose its views on the Algerian situation, Massu warned: "The army has the power. It has not shown it so far. ... In a particular situation, however, the army will bring its power into play."

Ordered to Paris January 19, Massu was replaced as Algiers region commander January 22 by Lieutenant General Jean Crepin, commander of the southern Oran district. In a private interview with de Gaulle January 23, Massu reportedly reaffirmed his submission to government orders.

De Gaulle Stand Reaffirmed. Premier Debre's cabinet met with de Gaulle January 20 and issued a statement reaffirming its intentions of carrying out de Gaulle's liberal policies on Algeria despite the opposition of Algerian dissidents. Orders issued January 21 by Paul Delouvrier, delegate general in Algeria, barred ex-Premier Georges Bidault, leader of the nationalist Rally for a French Algeria, from entering Algeria for a campaign of speeches against de Gaulle's Algerian policy.

Algiers Rightists Rebel. Algiers rightists clashed with police and security forces January 24. Fighting began when 2,500 persons, the remnants of an earlier anti-de Gaulle government demonstration by 20,000 persons, apparently fired on security forces attempting to clear them from Algiers' Forum area. At least 24 persons were killed, eight of them members of security forces.

The armed insurgents were led by Joseph Ortiz, head of the neo-Fascist French National Front, and Pierre Lagaillarde, National Assembly deputy and Algiers student leader prominent in the May 1958 revolt. The rebels occupied several buildings within their barricades, established command posts and began a buildup of arms, supplies and men. Their numbers grew to an estimated 5,000 by January 26. Thousands of civilians gathered at the barricade to demonstrate support for the rebels. A communique issued January 26 by a coordinating committee of Algiers extremist groups declared that "the committee, grouping war veterans organizations with the national movements..., have engaged themselves in a struggle that will only cease with the nullification of self-determination."

Siege Declared. A state of siege was declared in Algiers January 24 by General Maurice Challe, who charged the mob with firing the first shots. Troops and tanks sealed off the Algiers region from the rest of Algeria January 25, and 3,000 parachutists, backed by reinforcements from other areas, surrounded the barricaded area of the city, establishing a no-man's-land between it and government forces.

In a special broadcast to Algeria January 25, de Gaulle denounced the Algiers uprising as "a bad blow against France in Algeria ... [and] before the world." He warned the rebels that "I will do my duty" in upholding the republic.

Debre Mission. Premier Debre flew to Algiers January 25-26 to confer with Challe, Delouvrier and other French commanders and to transmit de Gaulle's orders for putting down the rebellion. Debre reportedly was told that the rebellion was more widespread than believed, that many French army units sympathized with the rebels and would be unreliable if ordered to fight them. The *New York Times* reported that army leaders had informed Debre that they could not or would not order their troops to attack the insurgents.

In meetings with de Gaulle January 26 on his return from Algeria, Debre reportedly refused to order a French army attack on the Algiers rebels. Debre reportedly told de Gaulle of his sympathy for the insurgents and warned that he would resign if they were attacked by loyal troops. Sahara Minister Jacques Soustelle and other cabinet members were said to have supported Debre with threats of a mass cabinet resignation.

Support for de Gaulle. National Assembly groups including the Gaullist UNR, Radicals, Catholic Popular Republicans (MRP) and Socialists issued declarations of support January 27 for de Gaulle's stand against the Algiers rebellion. The Communist-led General Confederation of Labor and Socialist and Catholic labor federations condemned the uprising January 27 and offered to support government action against it.

Army Waivers. Faced with the rebels' apparent determination to defend their barricaded Algiers positions and evidence that many French soldiers and officers in the city sided with the rebels, Delegate General Delouvrier and General Challe moved their Algerian headquarters January 28 from Algiers to the former U.S. Air Force base at Reghaia. The headquarters move came amid reports that Lieutenant General Crepin, Massu's successor, was undecided whether to act against the insurgents.

De Gaulle Calls for Order. In a stirring radio-TV address from Paris' Elysee Palace, de Gaulle called on "all Frenchmen" January 29, "wherever they are and whoever they are, to reunite with France" and end the uprising. Wearing his World War II brigadier general's uniform and speaking "as General de Gaulle as well as chief of state," he denounced as "usurpers" the rebellious Algiers rightists and emphasized that he would not withdraw his pledge of self-determination for Algeria's Moslems — "the only policy worthy of France."

Warning that "the unity, the progress, the prestige of the French people are at stake and ... its future is blocked as long as the Algerian problem is unsettled," de Gaulle said:

"I have taken in the name of France this decision: The Algerians shall have the free choice of their fate. . . . it will not be dictated to them.

"Certain Frenchmen . . . demand that I give up self-determination. . . . In order to impose their claims on the nation . . . [they] have entered into insurrection." "They are in arms against the authority of France."

Certain French army elements believe they are "entitled to a policy that is not the policy of France. I say to all our soldiers: Your mission does not carry with it any equivocation or interpretation. . . . I am the supreme responsible one. It is I who bear the destiny of the country. I must therefore be obeyed by all French soldiers." "No soldier, under pain of grave infraction, must associate himself . . . even passively, with the insurrection. . . . Public order must be restored. I give the order for it."

"By virtue of the mandate the people have given me and the national legitimacy that I have embodied for 20 years, I call on everyone to support me whatever happens." Despite the rebellion against the policy of self-determination, "let everyone know . . . and know well that I shall not go back on this decision." To yield to the uprising would be to ruin French chances in Algeria and to "abase the state before the outrage being done to it. Immediately, France would become no more than a poor, dislocated toy on the sea of unknown peril."

Army Moves to Contain Rebels. The de Gaulle address strengthened the position of loyal officers and apparently swayed army factions that had been undecided or favorable to the rebels. The army's first steps to contain and halt the rebellion were taken immediately following the de Gaulle message. Reservists behind the rebel barricades were ordered by the Army January 29 to leave the rebel positions and report to their unit assembly points. When the guardsmen, backbone of armed rebel strength, failed to respond immediately to the order, the parachutist cordon surrounding the rebel barricades was reinforced and soldiers occupied rooftop positions overlooking the enclave.

An army ultimatum for a rebel surrender was rejected January 30 by Lagaillarde. He appealed to unarmed rebel-sympathizers and mothers to assemble before the barricades between the insurgents and army troops. A mob of 2,000 men and women who responded to the call were permitted to pass the parachutist cordon but returned to their homes at nightfall.

French Workers Back de Gaulle. "The first unified work stoppage called by France's Communist, Socialist and Catholic labor federations since World War II was staged nationwide for one hour Feb. 1, 1960. The demonstration, involving 12 million workers, was to show that labor supported de Gaulle in the Algerian crisis and would paralyze the country in the event of a right-wing attempt to overthrow him.

Insurgents Surrender, Uprising Ends. The uprising collapsed February 1. Rebels left their barricades to return unarmed to their homes or with their arms to volunteer for service with the Foreign Legion's First Paratroop Regiment. The surrender had been negotiated January 31-February 1 by Colonel Henri Dufour, commander of the paratroop regiment.

Lagaillarde was arrested February 1, flown to Paris and held for trial on charges of attacking the security of the French state. Ortiz fled the rebel area and disappeared January 31. The barricades were levelled by French troops later February 1. Delouvrier and Challe moved their headquarters back to Algiers later that day.

Decree Powers Voted. De Gaulle summoned the French National Assembly February 1 to request a special delegation of powers enabling him to rule by decree for one year. The request, technically from Premier Debre, invoked Article 38 of the French constitution authorizing Parliament to delegate to the government for a limited period powers to decree "measures which are normally in the domain of law."

The transfer of legislative powers to Debre and through him to de Gaulle was approved February 3 by the National Assembly 441-75 and by the Senate 225-39. The bill authorized the government to decree "measures necessary to assure the maintenance of order, the safety of the state and the administration of Algeria."

Addressing the Assembly late February 3 Debre said de Gaulle alone had prevented what might have become "civil war." "National legitimacy has spoken," he said "but it was one man and one man alone who embodies this legitimacy."

Soustelle Dismissed. Minister Delegate Jacques Soustelle was dropped from Premier Debre's cabinet February 5 on de Gaulle's orders. Soustelle, a political leader of the 1958 coup, had been responsible for Saharan and atomic energy affairs and was dismissed for his overt support of the latest Algiers insurrection. In a statement issued after his dismissal, Soustelle charged that he had been fired for his attachment "to the cause of French Algeria." (Soustelle April 25 was expelled from the UNR for his refusal to support de Gaulle's Algerian policies.)

Cabinet changes announced with the dismissal: Armed Forces Minister Pierre Guillaumat assumed Soustelle's post of minister delegate for atomic affairs; Lieutenant Colonel Pierre Messmer was named armed forces minister; Information Minister Roger Frey became state minister for French Community relations; Robert Lecourt became state minister for the Sahara and overseas departments; Interior State Secretary Michel Maurice-Bokanowski replaced Bernard Cornut-Gentille as post and telegraph minister. Two new ministers, both UNR deputies, were named to the cabinet: Louis Terrenoire as information minister and Jean Foyer as French Community state secretary.

Algiers Rightists Purged. Armed Forces Minister Messmer, Interior Minister Pierre Chatenet and Justice Minister Edmond Michelet arrived in Algiers February 8 to investigate military and political leaders' collusion with the insurrection as a prelude to reorganization of the army and civil administration in Algeria. They carried out intensive questioning of army and civil administrators, ordered arrests of leading rightists and replaced some key police and security officials before ending their mission February 9 to report to President de Gaulle.

Six rightist groups were ordered dissolved February 4 by Delegate General Delouvrier. They included the Committee for Understanding Among Algiers Nationalist Movements (liaison group for 16 leading rightists groups), the French National Front of Joseph Ortiz, the Nationalist Students Movement of Pierre Lagaillarde and the Popular Movement of May 13, led by chiefs of the 1958 Algiers rebellion. The 20,000-man home guard, which had supported the insurrectionists against de Gaulle, was relieved of all military duties February 7.

In France, arrests of rightist leaders followed the collapse of the Algiers uprising. Jean-Baptiste Biaggi of Paris and Mourad Kaouah, an Algiers Moslem, both National Assembly deputies, were among those arrested in Paris February 2.

FIRST TRUCE MOVE FAILS
February 1960—July 1960

Rebel Cabinet Revised. A cabinet reorganization announced in Tunis Feb. 19, 1960 by the rebel Algerian government dropped extremists opposed to a negotiated peace with France. Eliminated from the cabinet were Foreign Minister Mohammed Lamine-Debbaghine and Cultural Affairs Minister Ahmed Tewfik el-Madani, both known to favor pan-Arab support against the French, and Social Affairs Minister Ben youssef Ben Khedda and State Secretary Omar Oussedik, leaders of a rebel mission to Communist China believed to have urged acceptance of Communist aid and arms. The ousted ministers were replaced by moderates.

De Gaulle Orders Reforms. Moves to break the power of Algerian rightists and their supporters in the French army and civil administration were ordered by President de Gaulle February 10 with the approval of the Debre cabinet.

Acting under his new special decree powers, de Gaulle:

(1) Suppressed the army's 5th Bureau, responsible for psychological warfare, which had backed groups seeking to keep Algeria French and had become a lever for rightist influence in the army.

(2) Dissolved the Algerian home guard organization. (Members of the 100,000-man home guard, composed largely of veterans, had joined the insurrectionists behind their Algiers barricades.)

(3) Dismissed three leading French army commanders in Algeria. (The three — Major General Jacques Faure, Brigadier General Henri Mirambeau, Brigadier General Andre Gribius — reportedly had backed the Algiers insurgents against de Gaulle.)

(4) Reorganized police and judicial administration in Algeria and removed the police from army supervision, placing it under the civilian control of Delegate General Delouvrier.

(5) Ordered new local elections to be held in the spring 1960.

The French Appeals Court February 16 approved a government request to transfer to Paris the trials of Algerian extremists jailed for acts against state security.

Rebels Ask "Self-Determination" Guarantees. Premier Ferhat Abbas of the rebel Algerian government February 29 reaffirmed rebel acceptance of an Algerian settlement based on self-determination. But he expressed rebel fears that Algerian rightists and their military supporters might prevent an honest referendum. Abbas declared: "it remains for the French government to accept talks on the guarantees for a free consultation [referendum]." He asserted that Algeria's Moslems "no doubt" would choose freedom from France in an honest referendum. He asserted, however, that "this choice...does not exclude a free cooperation between Algeria and France, with respect for their mutual interests."

De Gaulle for "Algerian" State. Back from a three-day inspection of the French army in Algeria, President de Gaulle March 7, 1960 publicly declared his hopes for the establishment of an "Algerian Algeria" uniting its Moslem and European populations and linked closely to France. The phrase "an Algerian Algeria" marked a further contrast between de Gaulle's liberal policy and the demands of rightists for "a French Algeria" meaning the integration of Algeria with metropolitan France.

French Military Command Revised. A program for the staffing of key Algerian military posts with officers personally loyal to President de Gaulle was largely completed with the replacement April 23 of General Maurice Challe, Algerian commander-in-chief, by Lieutenant General Jean Crepin. Challe became NATO commander for central Europe. French commanders in Algeria closely associated with the Algiers rightist revolt were transferred to new posts outside Algeria.

Gaullists Win Algerian Elections. Moderate candidates pledged to support President de Gaulle's program for Algerian self-determination won an overwhelming victory in elections May 27-30 for general councils in Algeria's 13 departments. They defeated European rightists favoring Algeria's integration with France. The pro-Gaullists won 298 council seats, integrationists won 87, and candidates running on purely local issues won 67. About 56% of Algeria's registered European and Moslem voters cast ballots. Moslems living in rural areas were trucked to the polls by the French army, but most urban Moslems abstained from voting. (Rebel reprisals had been threatened against Moslem voters.)

De Gaulle Appeals to Rebels. In a radio-TV address to the French nation June 14, 1960 President de Gaulle renewed and extended his appeal for leaders of Algeria's Moslem revolt to come to Paris and open negotiations on "an honorable end to the fighting." De Gaulle asserted: "We have never been closer to a real solution." He made it clear that France would not negotiate with the rebel leaders as the exclusive representatives of Algeria's Moslems, but it would guarantee their freedom to participate, with other Moslem groups, in the Algerian political consultation to follow a cease-fire.

New Algiers Rightist Group. The formation of a Front for French Algeria, linking all Moslem and European groups favoring the total integration of Algeria within France, was announced June 16 in Algiers. The Front, headed by Vice President Bachaga Boualem of the French National Assembly, declared that it would use force if necessary to prevent the carrying out of de Gaulle's pledge of Algerian self-determination.

Rebels Accept Peace Talks. Negotiations for settlement of the Algerian rebellion under de Gaulle's offer of self-determination were accepted June 20 by the rebel Algerian Provisional Government. A communique read to a Tunis news conference by Ferhat Abbas, rebel premier, declared that the rebels would "send a delegation presided over by...Abbas to meet General de Gaulle" in Paris. It said that a rebel leader would precede Abbas to Paris "to organize the details of the journey." Citing de Gaulle's pledge that "the final decision belongs to the Algerian people," the rebels asserted their confidence that "if the ... referendum is surrounded by all the indispensable guarantees, ... the choice of the Algerian people will be ... independence."

Rebel Mission in France. Emissaries of the Algerian Provisional government met with French representatives June 25-29 in Melun, near Paris, in an unsuccessful attempt to fix conditions for proposed cease-fire talks between the de Gaulle government and the rebel mission to be headed by Premier Ferhat Abbas. The rebel envoys—Ahmed Boumendjel and Mohamed Ben Yahia—landed at Paris' Orly Airfield June 25 and were flown by helicopter to Melun, where they met with Secretary General Roger Moris of the Algerian Affairs Office and General Hubert Mace de Gastines, deputy commander of the Paris Military Region, representing French Premier Debre. The rebel envoys were returned to Orly by helicopter and flew to Tunis July 1.

Rebels Reject French Terms. A communique issued by the rebel government July 4, 1960 in Tunis rejected French conditions for the proposed cease-fire talks. The rebels said their emissaries had been given conditions that made it clear that France intended "to organize unilaterally ... the meeting between the Algerian and French delegations." France was said to have presented "unalterable" conditions under which a mission by rebel Premier Ferhat Abbas would be forbidden contact "under any form" with any person or group, including the five rebel ministers held prisoner by France. The Abbas mission, it declared, "would have much less freedom in France than political prisoners." The French conditions were rejected as a "refusal to negotiate."

In a radio address to the Algerian people via Tunisian and Moroccan radios, Abbas appealed July 5 for a strengthening of "our armed combat" against France "while striving for negotiations." Abbas charged that French conditions for the talks were "so humiliating that any free negotiation becomes illusory for the moment." Declaring that it was only "by combat that the Algerian people won recognition of their right to self-determination," Abbas warned that "the war may still be long."

De Gaulle Renews Appeal. De Gaulle called on rebel leaders July 6 to "put an end to the last engagements" and to join France in a "great Algerian work." He asserted that despite the failure of preliminary talks "we are moving toward peace" in Algeria. "One cannot resolve in a few months a drama which has lasted six years and a problem which has existed for 130 years," he said.

THE "SELF-DETERMINATION" REFERENDUM AND
THE GENERALS' COUP
November 1960 — April 1961

War Casualty Reports. French military sources in Paris and Algiers reported Nov. 1, 1960 that an estimated 172,000 persons had been killed in Algerian fighting since the rebellion began October 31, 1954. The French estimates: 145,000 rebels killed, 40,000 captured, surrendered or deserted for service with the French; 13,000 French soldiers killed and 26,000 wounded; 12,000 Moslem civilians and 2,000 European civilians killed in rebel attacks.

(Agence France Presse, the semi-official French news agency, reported December 1 that 2,998 persons had been killed and 7,287 had been wounded in Algerian terrorist attacks in France from January 1956 to September 1960. 2,871 Moslems, 88 European civilians and 39 French soldiers and policemen were killed in the attacks; 6,506 Moslems, 508 European civilians and 273 soldiers and police were wounded.)

New De Gaulle Offer. A French pledge to respect the formation of an independent Algerian republic if it were desired by a majority of Algerian Moslems was broadcast November 4 by President de Gaulle.

In a nationwide radio-TV address, de Gaulle declared that France hoped for "an emancipated Algeria, ... in which the Algerians themselves will decide their destiny, an Algeria in which the responsibilities will be in the hands of the Algerians, an Algeria which, ... will have its own Government, its institutions and its laws." He again called on rebel leaders to "agree [with France] to stop killing each other" as a preliminary to talks on an Algerian referendum. The recent Melun talks had failed because the rebels posed insurmountable terms, among them withdrawal of "the army back to... France" and recognition as "the government of the Algerian Republic, a republic which will one day exist, but... has never yet existed."

Rightist Opposition to New Offer. De Gaulle's new Algerian statement was denounced November 6 by the rightist Algerian Front for French Algeria as a virtual pledge that the Moslem rebels would achieve their aim of independence from France. The Front claimed a membership of 1,000,000.

Thousands of youths staged Armistice Day demonstrations in Algiers November 11 in favor of a French Algeria. The rioters stoned police, wrecked buses and sacked the downtown Algiers cultural center of the U.S. Information Service (USIS). The demonstrations began after Delegate General Delouvrier had been jeered by a mob of 10,000 at the Algiers war memorial.

Referendum Planned. The French cabinet announced November 16 that President de Gaulle would "consult the French people" in a national referendum "on a bill for organizing of the administration in Algeria pending self-determination." The government disclosed November 23 that the referendum would be held throughout France and Algeria early in January 1961.

(The Debre cabinet informed Parliament December 8 that the referendum on Algeria would be held January 8, 1961 to seek approval for (1) reforms to increase the Moslem role in Algeria's administration, (2) the holding of a second, purely Algerian, referendum on self-determination.)

Opposition to Referendum. Ex-Gaullist supporter Jacques Soustelle attacked the referendum November 17 on grounds that it would lead to the "unconstitutional" question of withdrawing Algeria "from French territory" and of depriving Frenchmen of their nationality.

A rebel Algerian government communique issued in Tunis November 19 condemned de Gaulle's planned reorganization of the Algerian administration as a "decisive new step in denying the principle of self-determination." It accused France of attempting to "blackmail" Algeria's Moslems with threats of the "territorial partition" of the country.

French Algerian Officials Changed. The leadership of the French administration for Algeria was revised November 22-23. A Presidential decree issued by de Gaulle November 22 appointed Education Minister Louis Joxe as state minister for Algerian affairs. Jean Morin, "superprefect" for southwestern France, was named November 23 to replace Paul Delouvrier as delegate general in Algeria.

Rightists Flee Trial. Algiers rightist leaders, among them Pierre Lagaillarde, on trial before a Paris tribunal for their roles in the January rebellion against President de Gaulle's Algerian policies, failed to appear in court Dec. 5, 1960 and were reported to have crossed into Spain en route to Algeria. The trial of the five escapees had begun in Paris November 3. All of the accused had been granted provisional liberty, requiring them to remain in France and appear for court sessions.

De Gaulle in Algeria. De Gaulle flew December 9 to eastern Algeria to begin a six-day tour planned to avoid Algeria's large cities, the centers of his European opposition. He was greeted in Ain Temouchant by 5,000 Moslems who shouted their support for his pledge of an "Algerian Algeria" and who waved pro-de Gaulle banners despite European's attempts to intimidate them. De Gaulle, who mingled unguarded with the Moslem crowd here and elsewhere on this trip, told local officials that "this Algeria, your Algeria, is in the process of being transformed."

De Gaulle delivered addresses to cheering Moslem crowds in Orleansville, Tizi-Ouzou and Bougie December 11. Cutting short his tour by one day, he flew from Bone to Paris December 13 after reports of unrest in major Algerian cities.

Algerian French, Moslems Riot. De Gaulle's trip touched off severe rioting in major Algerian cities December 11-15. The riots were begun by Europeans opposed to de Gaulle's policies; they provoked counter-demonstrations and violence by Moslems demanding Algerian independence. French security police, regular troops, and paratroops eventually put down the violence.

The demonstrations began December 9 when European extremists staged a general strike protesting de Gaulle's policies and his visit. Moslem counter-demonstrations started the next day in Algiers, where Moslems fought with European rightists and shouted a mixture of anti-French and pro-de Gaulle slogans. The Moslem riot was the first reported in an Algerian city in four years. Seven hundred persons were injured.

The violence reached its high point December 11 when 61 persons were killed in Algiers and four in Oran as paratroops fired on demonstrating Moslems. More shootings in Algiers, Oran, and Bone December 12 through 15 brought the reported death toll to over 120, mostly Moslems. The general strike in major cities ended December 14.

Cabinet Acts Against De Gaulle's Opponents. The Debre cabinet announced Dec. 15, 1960 that it had approved actions against certain opponents of de Gaulle's policies. It disclosed that "administrative sanctions" had been ordered against General Raoul Salan for refusing to return to France from Spain. (Salan had left France for Spain October 31 following a Defense Ministry decision barring him from Algeria for publicly opposing de Gaulle's policy. He was reported December 11 to have been placed under Spanish police surveillance, together with Pierre Lagaillarde and three other Algerian rightist leaders who had fled to Spain.)

In other actions taken December 15, the cabinet announced that the rightist Front for French Algeria had been dissolved and that 40 officials of the French administration in Algeria had been dismissed for joining the rightist strike protesting de Gaulle's Algerian tour.

De Gaulle Asks New Talks. In a TV address to France and Algeria, delivered December 20 in Paris, de Gaulle called on Algerian rebel leaders to accept new peace negotiations and on Frenchmen to support the planned referendum on his proposals for Algeria, including a second, purely Algerian referendum on self-determination.

Rebel Premier Ferhat Abbas had described the referendum as a "sinister masquerade" December 16 in a speech broadcast from Tunis.)

Referendum Campaign. The political campaign for the referendum on de Gaulle's Algerian policies began December 26 in France and Algeria and ended Jan. 6, 1961 with a radio-TV address in which de Gaulle appealed to Frenchmen and Algerians to give "a sincere and massive yes" vote to his Algerian reform and self-determination plans.

During the campaign appeals for defeat of the de Gaulle proposals had been issued by rightists and conservatives. At a Paris news conference January 4 Jacques Soustelle, ex-Premier Georges Bidault and ex-Defense Minister Andre Morice denounced the referendum.

At least 27 persons — most of them Moslems — were killed in clashes in Algeria during and after the referendum, despite the arrival of security reinforcements including 6,000 marine commandos ordered to Oran January 2. In France the campaign proceeded without violence.

Referendum Backs Algerian Self-Determination. President de Gaulle's planned Algerian reform program was supported by 72.2% of the French voters participating in a special referendum carried out January 6-8 in France, Algeria and all French overseas departments and territories.

Voters were asked to approve or disapprove a draft law proposed by de Gaulle to permit reform of the French administration in Algeria and eventual Algerian self-determination as steps toward ending the six-year old Algerian rebellion. The draft law's provisions: (1) The Algerian administration would be reformed to create deliberative and executive bodies to govern all Algerian affairs except defense, finance and education; (2) "the Algerian populations should make known by...direct and universal suffrage the political destiny they choose with respect to the French Republic."

The referendum was carried out January 6-8 in Algeria and January 8 in France. Complete official returns January 9 showed that of the 31,600,948 registered voters in France and Algeria, 23,436,381 (74.2%) had gone to the polls and 16,944,217 — 72.2% of those voting — had approved the draft law. Separate returns for the 2 areas: France — 27,186,312 registered voters, 20,796,887 votes cast, 15,196,668 (75.25% of those voting) "yes," 4,995,912 "no"; Algeria — 4,414,636 registered voters, 2,639,494 ballots cast, 1,747,529 (69.1% of those voting) "yes," 782,052 "no."

In his first public comment on the outcome of the referendum, de Gaulle declared January 11 that the voting would compel him to implement his Algerian policy "without reserve in its spirit as in its letter."

Peace Talks Sought. Statements issued January 16-18 by the rebel Algerian government and by the French government affirmed that both sides were prepared to reopen negotiations. A rebel communique published in Tunis January 16 declared that "the provisional government of the Algerian Republic is ready ... to enter into negotiations with the French government." The French cabinet declared January 18 that Algerian developments had become "more favorable to the eventuality of peaceful contacts" between the opposing sides.

French Army's Powers Cut. Decrees made public March 1, 1961 by the Debre cabinet restricted the police and political powers of the French army in Algeria and returned certain of these functions to civilian control. The decrees (1) limited the army's power to detain suspected Algerian rebels and their supporters without formal charges and (2) created civilian prefects of police for the Algiers and Oran areas.

(General Jean Olie, personal aide to President de Gaulle, replaced General Paul Ely as French armed forces chief of staff March 1. General Fernand Gambiez had been named February 1 to succeed General Jean Crepin as military commander-in-chief in Algeria.)

De Gaulle Crushes Rightist Military Coup

Four Generals Lead Revolt. A rightist military coup de'etat was launched in Algeria early April 22, 1961 by four retired French generals opposed to de Gaulle's Algerian policies. The insurgent junta was led by General Maurice Challe, former commander of French forces in Algeria. Challe's coconspirators were General Raoul Salan, also a former commander in Algeria, General Andre Zeller and Air Force General Edmond Jouhaud. Active in the Algiers junta were a number of other officers who had been transferred from Algeria to France as politically unreliable but who appeared in Algiers when the coup began.

(French forces in Algeria numbered about 500,000 troops, the vast majority of them conscripts considered unsympathetic to the European rebels' cause. The insurgents' support was drawn from among the 20,000 Foreign Legionnaires and 25,000 paratroops constituting the "elite corps" of the troops in Algeria. The Foreign Legion units, composed entirely of professional soldiers — 14,000 of them Germans — were considered the rebels' basic military force.)

Insurgents Strike. Troops of the Foreign Legion's First Parachute Regiment arrested French Delegate General Jean Morin and General Fernand Gambiez, French commander in Algeria, April 22. The insurgents cut all communications out of Algeria and broadcast a manifesto in which the junta proclaimed its authority throughout the country and threatened harsh action against anyone acting in support of de Gaulle's policy of "abandonment" of Algeria. The rebel manifesto, broadcast in the name of the Secret Army Organization (OAS), ordered martial law imposed on

Algeria's civil population. Rebel broadcasts April 22 claimed that the rebels had won control of the military garrisons of Oran and Constantine — Algeria's second and third largest cities.

De Gaulle Acts. President de Gaulle, in his first public statement on the revolt, announced in a radio-TV speech April 23 that he had assumed near-dictatorial powers to crush the insurrection. Appearing in his World War II brigadier general's uniform, he condemned the uprising as the work of "ambitious and fanatical officers" whose rebellion "cannot but lead to a national disaster." He declared that he had centralized all state power in his hands under Article 16 of the French constitution. He declared: "In the name of France, I order that all means — I say all means — be employed everywhere to bar the route to these men until they are subjugated. I forbid any Frenchmen, and first of all any soldier, to execute any of their orders."

Civil War Threatened. Warnings of insurgent plans for an imminent invasion of France by paratroop and airborne units from Algeria were broadcast April 23 by Premier Debre. Debre said there was "reason to think that in a very brief while a surprise action will be attempted on metropolitan France, particularly in the Paris region. Aircraft are ready to drop or land paratroops on various airdromes to prepare a seizure of power."

The Debre statement was accompanied by a heavy movement into Paris of Republican Security Companies (CRS) and gendarmerie forces. Tanks and machine-gun posts surrounded de Gaulle's Elysee Palace residence and all key government buildings.

The de Gaulle and Debre appeals for popular support brought an immediate response April 23 from all political groups except rightists and the conservative Independent Party. The three major trade union confederations — Communist, Socialist and Catholic — pledged to oppose any attempt to extend the coup to France. Ten million trade union members staged a one-hour strike throughout France April 24 to demonstrate their support for de Gaulle against the insurrection. Thousands paraded in Paris shouting: "Shoot the generals!"

Revolt Collapses. The Algerian insurrection crumbled early April 26, 1961 after loyal troops and air and naval units had resisted the rebels' efforts to extend the coup to other bases and garrisons in Algeria. In a personal message transmitted to de Gaulle early April 26, Challe announced his surrender and offered to put himself "at the disposition of justice." (Zeller surrendered May 6. Generals Salan and Jouhaud remained at large.)

According to Paris dispatches, the rebellion had begun to collapse April 25 when loyal troops regained control of Oran and Constantine and messages proclaiming loyalty to de Gaulle began arriving in Paris from the commanders of 80% of the French troops in Algeria. A rebel attempt to seize the naval base of Mers-el-Kebir, near Oran, was defeated April 25, when a French cruiser lying offshore fired over a column of advancing paratroops preventing them from reaching the base. Air Force pilots flew their planes to France to keep them from falling into insurgents' hands.

A pro-government force composed of gendarmerie and army units began moving into Algiers late April 25. The loyal forces penetrated to the city's center and began reoccupying key government buildings. Algiers radio was heard to summon European rightists to the city's center for a final rally and then went off the air. When broadcasting resumed minutes later, an announcement said the station no longer was under rebel control.

Insurrection Aftermath. The French government took strict political and security measures against military personnel and civilians involved in the April 22-26 Algiers military insurrection. Over 200 military officers were arrested in France and Algeria for complicity in the insurrection. Four hundred rightist activists were arrested in France and a similar number in Algeria on the same charges. Special security regulations, including a curfew, were imposed on Algiers and other Algerian cities. All military units that had taken part in the insurrection were disbanded by the French government April 29. The units dissolved included the First Paratroop Regiment of the French Foreign Legion and the 14th Battalion and 18th Regiment of Paratroops. The command divisions of the disbanded units — the French army's 10th and 25th Parachute Divisions — were dissolved May 4.

Generals' Trials. A special military tribunal was created by French government decree April 28 to judge the military leaders of the insurrection. (The French government had announced April 24 that the leaders of the Algiers junta had been stripped of their military rank by the Defense Ministry.)

The first to be tried were former generals Maurice Challe, the leader of the uprising, and Andre Zeller. Both were convicted and each was sentenced to 15 years' imprisonment May 31. Challe testified that he had agreed to lead the uprising only after he became convinced that de Gaulle's program of Algerian self-determination would cause the loss of Algeria, first to the rebels and then to communism.

EVIAN PEACE TALKS AND OAS VIOLENCE
May 1961 — December 1961

New Peace Talks Scheduled. French and Algerian rebel communiques issued in Tunis May 10, 1961 said that formal negotiations on conditions for an Algerian cease-fire would begin May 20 in Evian-les-Bains, a French resort on Lake Geneva. The agreement to begin peace talks on the basis of de Gaulle's offer of Algerian self-determination had been worked out in meetings between French and rebel envoys in Tunisia and in Switzerland.

The rebels' readiness to accept peace talks was attributed largely to de Gaulle's successful suppression of the April 22-26 Algerian military coup, the apparent powerlessness of Algeria's European rightists who backed the coup, and his demonstration of control over the French army.

French Command Revised. Lieutenant General Charles Ailleret was appointed June 7 to replace General Fernand Gambiez as French commander-in-chief in Algeria. Gambiez was assigned to a staff post in Paris. His replacement was part of a major revision of the Algerian command in the wake of the insurrection.

Evian Peace Talks. Representatives of France and of the rebel Algerian government met in Évian-les-Bains, France May 20-June 13 to begin negotiations toward settling the 7-year-old Algerian rebellion. The talks were recessed with no settlement in sight. The Évian meetings were held at a heavily-guarded hotel on the shore of Lake Geneva. For political and security reasons, the Algerian negotiators resided in Geneva and commuted by helicopter across the lake to attend conference sessions. France was represented in the negotiations by Algerian Affairs Minister Louis Joxe and the rebels were represented by Foreign Minister Bolkacem Krim. The negotiations were closed to the press, but news conferences were held by delegation chiefs or spokesmen.

Krim told a Geneva news conference May 23 that the rebels would not accept any settlement based on partition of Algeria. He thereby rejected French threats to form French enclaves in Algeria and to sever the oil-rich Sahara from an independent Algeria.

Joxe said at a news conference May 26 that France did not seek the division of Algeria into French and rebel zones but that "in the case where fear and anguish seized the population, we would be led to partition and we would accept it."

Talks Deadlock. The French and rebel delegations reached a virtual deadlock in two meetings June 7 and 10, 1961. A French statement issued June 10 said that "the Algerian nation can be born only after a vote of all the Algerian populations and according to the will they express." A rebel statement replied: "After nearly seven years of war ... we know our nation is a fact...."

The French delegation broke off the Evian negotiations June 13. Joxe told the Algerians that France wanted "a time of reflection for each side to look for a way out of the impasse." Krim said at a Geneva news conference June 14 that the rebels had opposed the suspension of the talks. He confirmed that the deadlock had resulted from the rebels' views that an agreement was possible only if it specified that the Sahara was to remain part of Algeria. A rebel cabinet communique, issued in Tunis June 20 after Krim had returned to report on the talks, called on France to resume the negotiations.

Rightist Violence. The Evian truce talks were preceded and accompanied by a wave of bombings and shootings attributed to the Secret Army Organization (OAS) and other rightist political and paramilitary groups opposed to halting the war against the rebels.

Ten persons were wounded in the explosion of four bombs in Paris May 13, the third anniversary of the 1958 Algiers rebellion. More than 20 bombs in Algiers and Oran May 20 wounded several other persons. A rightist mob sacked and burned the Swiss consulate in Oran to protest Swiss willingness to permit the rebel delegation to Evian to stay in Geneva. The Algiers Police Commissioner was stabbed to death May 31 by unknown Europeans. Six persons were killed in Oran June 12. Eleven persons were wounded in Paris in bomb explosions June 16 and 19.

Coup Leaders Condemned. Ex-General Raoul Salan and seven other former generals and colonels were sentenced to death in absentia July 11, 1961 by a special military tribunal set up in Paris to try leaders of the Algiers military coup staged in April. The seven others condemned: ex-Generals Edmond Jouhaud and Paul Gardy; ex-Colonels Yves Godard,

Antoine Argoud, Jean Gardes, Joseph Broizat and Charles Lacheroy. (All eight of the condemned had fled after the collapse of the April revolt.)

De Gaulle Announces Troop Withdrawal. In a radio-TV report to the French people July 12, de Gaulle declared that the French army's pacification of Algeria had succeeded to the point where it was possible to recall one division and prepare a second for duty elsewhere. France's 27-month conscription term would be cut and the manpower and money savings would be used to modernize the army, he said.

New French-Rebel Talks Fail. French Algerian Affairs Minister Joxe and Foreign Minister Krim of the Algerian Provisional Government met near Evian, July 20 to resume negotiations on conditions for a cease-fire and a negotiated end of the Algerian rebellion. The talks, a continuation of the negotiations held in Evian May 20-June 13, were suspended July 28 in a deadlock over claims to the Sahara and its oil and mineral resources.

Krim July 28 requested suspension of the talks after Joxe reportedly had refused any concession to rebel claims that the Sahara become part of a future Algeria. Krim, at a Geneva news conference July 31, called on France to end the "myth" of a French Sahara. The desert, he asserted, constituted "4/5 of our national territory."

Soustelle in Exile. The *New York Times* reported August 24 that Jacques Soustelle, former de Gaulle cabinet member, had chosen voluntary exile in an undisclosed foreign country rather than face the threat of arrest.

Ben Khedda Replaces Abbas. The relatively "moderate" Algerian rebel government of Ferhat Abbas was ousted August 27 and replaced by one headed by Benyoussef Ben Khedda. The announcement came at the end of a three-week secret meeting in Tripoli, Libya, of the policy-making rebel National Council.

Ben Khedda, in his first public speech since taking office, said at the conference of non-aligned nations in Belgrade September 4 that the Algerian rebels would continue the fight for independence. He said that he was ready to negotiate with "the French people" but that the rebels would never give up their claim to the Sahara.

French Division Withdrawn. The French government announced Sept. 3, 1961 withdrawal of the 7th Light Armored Division from service in Algeria and assigned it to a new base in Alsace, near the German frontier.

De Gaulle Assassination Fails. An attempt to assassinate de Gaulle failed September 9 when a bomb, laid to blow up a car carrying The President and his wife from Paris to their country home in Colombey-les-Deux-Eglises, did not fire properly. The car drove through a sheet of flame, but neither de Gaulle nor members of his party were hurt.

The man who set the bomb, Martial de Villemandy, said to be a member of the OAS, was arrested in a nearby cafe a half-hour after the incident.

OAS Riot in Algiers. Bomb explosions and anti-government demonstrations by Europeans opposed to French withdrawal from Algeria continued in Algiers and increased in tempo in September 1961.

Members of the OAS seized the Algiers TV station during the evenings of September 21 and 22 and blew up the transmitter. The TV station's frequency was then used by OAS leaders broadcasting with another transmitter. Broadcasts by men identifying themselves as ex-Generals Raoul Salan and Paul Gardy, called on Algerians to demonstrate against the government, "show" the forbidden OAS flag September 26 and "prepare for the final assault" against President de Gaulle.

Massu Assumes New Post. Major General Jacques Massu, a leader of the 1958 Algerian army revolt, was returned to active duty September 6. He was appointed military governor of Metz, 175 miles east of Paris, and commander of the surrounding 6th Military Region.

De Gaulle Ends Powers. The special decree powers assumed by President de Gaulle April 23 to suppress the military coup in Algeria were relinquished September 30. De Gaulle retained the power to order detention without trial of persons plotting against the state and to order censorship of news.

De Gaulle, Rebels Call for New Talks. De Gaulle in a radio-TV address Oct. 2, 1961 declared that France stood ready to reopen negotiations with the Moslem rebels. "We are prepared," he said, "once again to seek an agreement with the leaders of the rebellion, to bring peace once and for all to Algeria, to settle the conditions for self-determination and to decide upon the basis of a Franco-Algerian cooperation...."

Premier Benyoussef Ben Khedda of the Algerian rebel regime called on France October 24 to open "negotiations... on the principle, the means and the date of a proclamation of independence as well as on a cease-fire." Ben Khedda's declaration, issued in Tunis, said that de Gaulle's reiteration of the need for Algerian self-determination meant that "France agrees that our cause is well-founded and that independence is not only possible but that it constitutes the clear, worthy solution to the conflict."

OAS Violence Mounts. Rightist opposition to de Gaulle and a negotiated peace in Algeria continued its campaign of bombings and unrest in all Algerian cities during October. The bombings, carried out daily, were attributed to the OAS, led by ex-General Salan. A Salan speech attacking de Gaulle's Algerian policies was broadcast by the OAS "pirate" transmitter October 9 after the Algiers radio had been forced off the air by sabotage.

Seventeen French rightist leaders in exile in Spain were arrested by Spanish police October 7, reportedly for plotting a new rebellion against the de Gaulle government. Four of them prominent in the May 1958 and January 1960 Algiers rebellions — Pierre Lagaillarde, Joseph Ortiz, ex-Colonel Antoine Argoud and ex-Colonel Charles Lacheroy — were exiled to the Canary Islands October 26.

Moslems Riot in Paris. Thousands of Algerian Moslems clashed with police in the Paris area October 17-20, demonstrating against curfew regulations barring them from the street after 8:30 p.m. The demonstrations were considered an index of pro-rebel sentiment among the 400,000 Moslems living and working in France.

The Paris police reported October 27 that 14,394 Moslems had been arrested during the demonstrations but that all had been released except 2,300 considered to be active rebels and liable for deportation.

Revolt Anniversary Riots. Eighty-three Algerian Moslems and three French soldiers were reported killed, and 150 persons, mostly Moslems, were reported injured throughout Algeria Nov. 1, 1961 during the riots and demonstrations marking the seventh anniversary of the Algerian nationalist rebellion.

Rebel Hunger Strike. Five Algerian rebel leaders held prisoner in France began a hunger strike November 1 to protest the withdrawal of special privileges accorded them as cabinet ministers in absentia of the rebel Algerian government. The five rebel leaders—Vice Premier Mohammed Ben Bella, Hocine Ait-Ahmed, Mohammed Khider, Mohammed Boudiaf and Rabah Bitat—were protesting harsher treatment allegedly given them. They ended the strike November 20 after a Moroccan cabinet delegation had interceded on their behalf for a relaxation of the conditions of their imprisonment.

Four thousand other Algerians held as prisoners in France held a parallel hunger strike ending November 20, reportedly on orders from Ben Bella, after France had agreed to recognize them as political prisoners. The settlement of the two groups' grievances was viewed as a substantial step toward the renewal of open peace negotiations between France and the rebel government.

Salan Interview. Ex-General Raoul Salan warned in a CBS-TV interview broadcast November 6 that the OAS would fight under his leadership to prevent creation of an independent Algeria. Salan was interviewed in a secret hideout in Algeria November 2 by CBS. The OAS, he said, was fighting to keep "Communism out of Algeria." It would no longer heed de Gaulle because he had "lied too much."

France to Recall Troops. De Gaulle announced Dec. 29, 1961 that starting in January two French divisions and "a number of air formations" would be brought back from Algeria. De Gaulle said France "intends to bring to an end" its "political, economic, financial and military commitment" in Algeria.

TRUCE SIGNED; OAS-MOSLEM VIOLENCE; INDEPENDENCE PROCLAIMED
January 1962 — September 1962

French Government Fights OAS Terror. The French cabinet reaffirmed Jan. 17, 1962 that it would use all means to halt the terror campaign directed against President de Gaulle's policies by the OAS.

New security measures for Algeria, announced by the cabinet, (a) sealed off Algiers, Oran and Bone with roadblocks; (b) banned civilian cars from main avenues and forbade all civil traffic after 9 p.m.; (c) ordered permanent military cordons around all terror-ridden districts; (d) authorized searchs of individuals and houses without warning or warrant; (e) authorized immediate curfews in areas subject to terrorist incidents.

OAS Paris Attacks. The OAS intensified its terrorist campaign in the Paris region. Fourteen bombs were detonated in Paris January 25, presumably to mark the second anniversary of the Algiers barricade uprising against de Gaulle. The bombings were directed against the homes of prominent Frenchmen, among them the editors of three Paris newspapers. Seventeen OAS bombs had been detonated in Paris in three hours the night of January 17-18.

OAS Algerian Terror Toll. The *New York Times* reported February 1 that unofficial tabulations showed 555 persons — 220 Europeans and 335 Moslems — had been killed during January in OAS terrorist attacks in Algeria. The *Times* reported that an additional 990 persons, 608 of them Moslems, had been wounded in the 801 attacks known to have been carried out in Algeria in January.

OAS directives mailed to Algeria's Europeans and posted publicly in its cities January 19 ordered all civilians to cooperate with OAS agents who would contact them to begin the "mobilization" ordered by ex-General Raoul Salan. The directives warned that any civilians attempting to leave Algeria without OAS permission would be considered traitors and would be tried and shot.

De Gaulle Sees Independent Algeria. President de Gaulle declared February 5 that his policy of self-determination for Algeria would eventually lead to an independent Algerian state. In a radio-TV address broadcast both in France and Algeria, de Gaulle reaffirmed his determination to settle the Moslem rebellion and to suppress the OAS terror campaign against his policies. Outlining his plans for the future, de Gaulle declared: France's energies were devoted to "achieving peace and helping Algeria take in hand its own destiny by bringing about immediately the creation of a provisional executive and by holding ourselves ready to recognize, without any restrictions, that which will not fail to emerge from self-determination, . . . a sovereign and independent state."

Moslem Rebels Hail de Gaulle. Tunis spokesmen of the rebel Algerian government hailed de Gaulle February 5 for his reaffirmation of Algerian independence in the face of violent rightist opposition. They stressed de Gaulle's mention of rapid measures to create a "provisional executive" in Algeria and his overt agreement that the proposed self-determination referendum would produce a majority for independence.

Anti-OAS Demonstrations in Paris. Five hundred thousand Parisians participated in a public funeral procession held February 13 to honor victims killed February 8 during an anti-OAS demonstration. The February 8 demonstration, held despite a government prohibition, had been called by the Communist and Catholic labor federations, the National Students' Union and teachers' groups with the support of the Communist Party; violence broke out when security police charged the crowd to disperse it. The dead included four men, a youth and three women.

The February 13 funeral procession was sponsored by nearly every major labor union and leftist political and student organization. The ceremonies were accompanied by a general strike throughout Paris.

Algerian Truce Signed; Moslem Rebellion Ended. The seven-and-a-half-year-old Moslem uprising against French rule in Algeria was ended March 18, 1962 by a truce agreement signed by French and rebel negotiators in Evian-les-Bains, France. The agreement included provisions insuring an Algerian self-determination referendum and full sovereignty for an independent, Moslem-governed Algerian state, expected to result from the referendum.

A cease-fire between French forces and the "Army of Liberation," the military arm of the Moslem rebel National Liberation Front (FLN), became effective throughout Algeria at noon March 19.

Evian Agreement. The final Evian talks were begun March 11. The negotiations were carried out in strict secrecy, and little was known of their progress until the accord was virtually complete. The French delegation was headed by Algerian Affairs Minister Joxe; the rebel Algerian government delegation was led by Deputy Premier Belkacem Krim. The terms of the truce agreement were announced simultaneously by the French and rebel delegations at separate news conferences. Summaries of the accord were issued by both sides.

The following are excerpts from the summary issued by the French government and published March 19:

1. CEASE FIRE. All armed combat both inside Algeria and on its frontiers is to cease. Prisoners of war will be released within 20 days. An amnesty will be proclaimed.

2. INTERIM PERIOD. Algeria remains under French sovereignty. The powers of the French government will be exercised by a High Commissioner.... A 12-man Provisional Executive will be named by the French government representing the different political groups in the country. It will administer the country and aid the High Commissioner in preparing... a referendum...

3. SELF-DETERMINATION. All Algerian citizens will vote in a referendum in which they may choose whether: (a) They want Algeria to remain an integral part of metropolitan France, as it now is considered. (b) Independence with all links... broken off. (c) Independence in cooperation with France.

4. SAFEGUARDING OF FRANCE'S PERMANENT INTERESTS. France will maintain its existing rights in the Sahara and in the field of military security. French oil mining rights will remain untouched. In the future, French interests will enjoy preference in granting of mining rights. French experimental rocket and nuclear testing installations in the Sahara will remain in French hands for five years. France also will keep its air field installations in the Sahara for five years. France will have the right to station armed forces in Algeria for three years.

De Gaulle Address. President de Gaulle appealed to the French people in a nationwide radio-TV address March 18 to support the peace agreement negotiated by his government. De Gaulle asked the French to give him "national approval and confidence" in a popular referendum to be held on the Evian agreement. He expressed confidence that the referendum would confirm that the accords "satisfy the mind of France."

Ben Khedda Address. Premier Benyoussef Ben Khedda of the rebel Algerian government gave rebel troops the order to lay down their arms in an address broadcast March 18 from Tunis. Ben Khedda pledged that a new Algerian state would respect the rights of all Europeans who chose to stay in Algeria.

Moslem Rebel Leaders Freed. Algerian rebel Vice Premier Mohammed Ben Bella and four other members of the rebel cabinet were released from French detention and were flown to Geneva March 18. The five—Ben Bella and State Ministers Mohammed Boudiaf, Hocine Ait-Ahmed, Rabah Bitat, and Mohammed Khider—had been French prisoners ever since their Moroccan airliner was diverted to Algeria by its French pilot during a flight from Rabat to Tunis October 26, 1956. The five leaders flew March 21 to Casablanca, where they were united for the first time with Premier Ben Khedda and other members of the rebel cabinet.

Cease-Fire Effective. Dispatches from Algeria reported March 19 that the cease-fire between French and Moslem rebel forces had been imposed effectively on all fronts. An order of the day issued March 19 by General Charles Ailleret, commander-in-chief of French forces in Algeria, lauded the French for their tenacity in trying to pacify Algeria and said that the rebels had been an "always courageous" adversary.

French Government Measures for Interim Period. Christian Fouchet, French ambassador to Denmark, was named March 19 to serve as high commissioner in Algeria during the interim period in which the self-determination referendum would be held and its results implemented. The appointment was made by the French cabinet at a meeting March 19. The cabinet also approved decrees (1) establishing the 12-member provisional executive to rule Algeria under Fouchet, and (2) fixing conditions for the amnesty to be granted the thousands of Algerians imprisoned on political or terrorist charges connected with the rebellion.

OAS Declares War. The OAS declared open warfare March 18, 1962 against the de Gaulle government and the French-Moslem peace agreement. A communique issued by ex-General Salan, OAS commander-in-chief, proclaimed the underground's "determination to carry on the fight against the Algerian [Moslem] rebellion until its complete annihilation." OAS leaflets circulated in Algiers said that Salan had been empowered to remove the de Gaulle government and restore "the sovereignty of the French people."

OAS Violence. Europeans fought French troops in Algeria's major cities March 21-26 as the OAS began open war against the French army and its efforts to impose the truce agreement signed by France and Algeria's Moslem rebels March 18.

The OAS attacks on French security forces began in Oran March 21, when European rightists began sniping and hurling grenades at military police in the city's center. The military police had been conducting a house-to-house search for a clandestine OAS radio transmitter.

The attacks on troops spread to Algiers March 22. OAS units armed with machine guns attacked gendarmes and other security forces at three points in the city. Three gendarmes were wounded and three Europeans killed in the attacks. Six Moslems were shot down by OAS gunmen in Algiers March 22.

Fighting was resumed in Algiers March 23 when residents of the European workers' district of Bab-el-Oued fired on French troops searching for hidden arms and OAS gunmen. At least 15 French soldiers were killed and 75 wounded in the fighting.

The French government announced March 23 that President de Gaulle had ordered all means used "to crush without pity the armed insurrection which is developing in the two largest cities of Algeria." Informed of the OAS Bab-el-Oued attack during a cabinet meeting, he immediately drafted and made public a letter to Premier Debre in which he declared that "everything must be done immediately to smash and punish the criminal action of the terrorist bands in Algiers and Oran."

Thousands of troops supported by armored cars sealed off the Bab-el-Oued district March 24 and prevented anyone and all traffic except ambulances and trucks moving prisoners from passing their lines. A house-to-house search was begun and 1,000 suspected OAS terrorists were said to have been arrested and transferred to a camp near Algiers by March 25. A total curfew was enforced by the troops.

At least 50 European civilians were killed and 150 were wounded in Algiers March 26 in the most serious clash between Europeans and French troops since the start of the OAS movement. The civilians were killed when the troops fired on them at point-blank range with machine guns as they attempted to march to Bab-el-Oued in a demonstration of solidarity with the district's residents.

Jouhaud Caught. The arrest of ex-General Edmond Jouhaud, second-in-command of the OAS after Raoul Salan, was announced March 26. Jouhaud was arrested in Oran March 26 with seven OAS aides during a routine search of a European apartment building. He was flown to France and placed in Paris' Sante Prison March 26.

De Gaulle Opens Referendum Campaign. President de Gaulle addressed the French nation on radio and TV March 26 to open a campaign to win a massive majority for the French-Moslem truce agreement in a popular referendum to be held April 8.

De Gaulle said that a massive "yes" vote would "demonstrate that we are capable of resolving with determination a major problem of our time" and would make certain that "the criminals, who are endeavoring by terrorist attacks to force the hand of the state and to subjugate the nation, have no future other than punishment."

Algerian Provisional Executive Named. The membership of the 12-man provisional executive, intended to rule Algeria under interim High Commissioner Christian Fouchet until the completion of self-determination, was made known in Paris March 27. It was composed of nine Moslems, five of them rebel officials, and three Europeans; all were native Algerians. It was headed by a president, Abderrahmane Fares, former speaker of the defunct Algerian Assembly. Fares was known to have close ties with the rebel National Liberation Front.

Referendum Backs de Gaulle. French voters, in a national referendum April 8, 1962, overwhelmingly declared their approval of President de Gaulle's peace agreement with Algeria's Moslem rebels. The plebiscite was carried out in France and Corsica and in overseas departments and territories. It was not extended to Algeria, which, under the Evian agreement, was to hold a referendum later to decide whether or not to become fully independent of France.

Final returns April 9 for France and Corsica showed 17,505,473 "yes" votes to 1,794,553 "no." The affirmative votes amounted to 90.7% of the valid ballots cast.

The rightist European community in Algeria generally expressed shock at the size of the affirmative vote. The vote was considered to have given de Gaulle the massive popular mandate he had asked for to carry out the Algerian peace accords and proceed with his plans for the "national renovation" of France.

OAS Terrorism Continues. The OAS continued its campaign of violence in Algeria through April 10, despite what newsmen said was a growing reaction in the European community against its terrorist methods.

OAS gunmen invaded a private Moslem clinic April 3 and machine-gunned the patients in their beds; 10 patients were killed and seven wounded. Forty persons, most of them Moslems, were killed by OAS attacks April 6. Eighteen persons were killed in daylight shootings in Algiers and Oran April 7 and 26 more were killed throughout the country the next day. Skirmishes involving the use of mortars and grenade launchers took place in Oran April 8 and again April 10 between the OAS and French soldiers.

Moslems Attack OAS. The first major Moslem rebel action against the OAS was reported April 10. Algiers sources reported that at least 30 members of an OAS commando group that had attempted to coerce Moslems in the Ouarsenis Mountains area, 60 miles from Algiers, had been killed by a rebel FLN unit holding positions in the region under the cease-fire accord.

Bidault Joins OAS. Ex-Premier Georges Bidault announced in letters to French newspapers April 12 that he had gone underground to assume leadership of the OAS' "National Council of Resistance." Bidault, who was believed to be in Switzerland, had headed the similarly named council for anti-Nazi resistance in occupied France in 1943-44. Long a supporter of the "French Algeria" movement, Bidault denounced de Gaulle for "treason" and said he would fight to save France from "dishonor and tyranny."

Jouhaud Condemned; Spared by de Gaulle. The captured OAS second-in-command, ex-General Edmond Jouhaud, was condemned to death by a Paris military tribunal April 13 after a three-day trial for insurrectionary acts against the state — participating in the April 1961 Algiers mutiny and subsequent role in OAS terrorism in the Oran region. A native Algerian, Jouhaud fully admitted his role as an OAS leader and declared that he had "abandoned everything for my native land."

(President de Gaulle November 28 commuted the death sentence of Jouhaud.)

Salan Captured, Convicted. Ex-General Raoul Salan, leader of the OAS, was captured in Algiers April 20, 1962 and was flown to Paris to face trial for insurrection against the French state. Salan was already under sentence of death for his role in the coup but was entitled to a retrial of his in-absentia conviction and was to be tried also for his leadership of the OAS terror campaign.

(Ex-General Paul Gardy, the sole remaining former general in the OAS' leadership, announced April 21, in an Oran broadcast over a clandestine radio, that he had assumed Salan's post.)

Salan was convicted by a nine-man military court in Paris May 23 on five counts of participating in the April 1961 generals' revolt in Algeria and leading the OAS terror campaign against the French government's Algerian peace settlement. The court, which had been expected to sentence Salan to death, imposed a life sentence.

Anti-OAS Campaign. Algerian High Commissioner Fouchet denounced OAS terrorism at a news conference May 11. He said: "I shall lash out without pity against those who are guilty and those who aid them, with their words, their deeds or their omissions."

Oran police May 11 arrested 500 persons on charges of being pro-OAS. Among those arrested were 14 prominent community leaders. Police chief Jacques Biget said the 14 would be imprisoned in the Sahara until they decided to aid the restoration of order in Oran. Biget disclosed that the hundreds of others arrested had been confined to the city's stadium. He denounced Oran's civil servants who did not oppose the OAS. Those who refused to work against the OAS, Biget declared, would be suspended and imprisoned in the Sahara.

Europeans Flee Algeria. French authorities in Rocher-Noir estimated May 21, 1962 that a total of 20,000 Europeans had left Algeria since the March 18 cease-fire agreement. The exodus started despite the OAS threat to "execute" any European leaving Algeria without its permission.

Fourteen hundred Europeans, camped at the airport for days, had been flown to France aboard 16 planes May 20 as French authorities established an emergency airlift that day to evacuate Europeans wishing to leave Algeria. The airlift was ordered by Algerian Affairs Minister Joxe who had arrived from Paris May 19 to confer with French military officials.

The arrival of 4,500 would-be repatriates at the Algiers airport May 25 forced the closure of the airport until they could be put aboard planes. Twenty-two planes left Algiers for France May 26 and carried a record 2,080 refugees. At least 30 large transports were on airlift duty between Algiers and Paris, and special ship services were organized between Algiers, Oran and Marseilles.

Robert Boulin, state secretary for repatriated persons, announced in Rocher-Noir May 25 that the French government would begin paying the passage of all repatriates in addition to assuring them a monthly resettlement allowance of $60-$140 on arrival in France. French officials abolished exit visa requirements May 24 for women, children under 17 and men over 65 leaving for France.

De Gaulle on Algerian Referendum. President de Gaulle predicted June 8, 1962 in a nationwide radio-TV broadcast that the self-determination referendum to be carried out in Algeria July 1 would settle the Algerian problem and would leave France free to proceed with the strengthening of its own state institutions.

He attributed France's success in dealing with Algeria to the presidential powers he had obtained as a condition of his assumption of office. This was regarded as confirmation that de Gaulle intended to seek constitutional reforms to provide for a popularly elected president.

OAS-Moslem Truce. An OAS-Moslem truce agreement was made public in Algeria June 17 in a statement issued by the Algerian Provisional Executive, and in a communique broadcast by a clandestine OAS transmitter in the name of "the high command of the Secret Army."

The agreement contained three basic Moslem concessions to European demands: (1) implied recognition of the OAS as the representative organization of Algeria's European community; (2) an amnesty for OAS terrorists; (3) a pledge of European participation in future Algerian security forces. (OAS-Moslem truce negotiations had been underway since June 1 with Abderrahmane Fares, Moslem chairman of the Provisional Executive, acting as mediator.)

OAS Algiers Cease-Fire Achieved. A cease-fire became generally effective in Algiers June 18; the city's curfew was lifted and most military roadblocks had been removed by June 19. Algiers' 250,000 Moslem workers returned to their jobs June 20 at the orders of their FLN-controlled trades unions. Many had not worked in months.

Oran OAS Rejects Truce. Leaders of the OAS terrorist campaign in Oran rejected the truce negotiated in Algiers and announced June 18 that "the fight continues." The Oran terrorists were believed to be supported by extremist OAS factions in Bone and other cities. Broadcasts from the clandestine OAS transmitter in Oran expressed contempt for the Algiers OAS faction and made it clear that the truce would not be applied in Oran.

Oran OAS commander ex-General Paul Gardy announced in a broadcast June 22 that his men had resumed their "freedom of action" to renew terrorism. Gardy said that the Moslems had refused to guarantee the safety of Europeans after July 1. (Immediately after he spoke, OAS commandos blew up and burned the Oran city hall.)

OAS bombings destroyed six schools, public health facilities and eight other public buildings June 24. Terrorists fired eight gasoline storage tanks in Oran's port area June 25, starting a blaze that covered the city with smoke. The tanks contained 2-1/2 million gallons of diesel oil.

Exodus Mounts. The continuation of terrorism provoked a near-panic exodus of Algeria's Europeans; it was reported June 25 that 280,000 of the 1,000,000-member European community had left for France and other Mediterranean countries in the previous three months, and that departures were averaging 8,000 to 12,000 daily. It was estimated that the three-month total included 60,000 of Algeria's 110,000 Jews. More than 70,000 of Oran's 200,000 Europeans were believed to have left Algeria for France.

OAS Violence Ends. The collapse of OAS terrorism became evident June 27-28; attacks had ceased entirely in Algiers and other cities in which "moderate" OAS factions had accepted a truce with Moslem authorities, and they virtually had ended in Oran and Constantine, centers of the "extremist" OAS units led, respectively, by ex-General Gardy and ex-Colonel Henri Dufour. It was reported June 27 that Gardy and his aides had fled Oran. A broadcast by Dufour, monitored the same day, called on all European terrorists in Western Algeria to halt their attacks. Jean-Jacques Susini, political leader of the OAS, and commander of its Algiers organization, declared in a broadcast June 27 that the truce was in force in all of Algeria. (Susini, in another broadcast heard June 30, called on Algeria's Europeans to vote "yes" in the referendum to "have faith in the future we have planned for you.")

Leaders of Oran's European community met with Moslem nationalist representatives June 28 to begin efforts to restore peace to the city before the referendum vote. Their efforts were successful; only one terrorist attack, an attempt to burn a public building, was reported from Oran that day.

Algiers, Oran, and Algeria's other major cities were reported calm June 29-30 as both Moslem and European communities awaited the referendum. Moslems flocked June 30-July 1 to the centers of the cities to begin a massive popular victory celebration as the voting began. No last-ditch attacks by OAS terrorists were reported.

Referendum Backs Independence. The Algerian self-determination referendum pledged by President de Gaulle was carried out July 1, 1962 after European extremists of the Secret Army Organization (OAS) had ended their terrorist campaign against Algerian independence.

The voting took place throughout Algeria at polling stations set up by the Provisional Executive and guarded largely by Moslem nationalist soldiers. The overwhelming mass of Moslem voters were joined by numbers of Europeans who explained to newsmen they hoped to insure their status in an independent Algeria by proving they had voted in the referendum. Voters were given their choice of casting white "yes" or pink "no" ballots on the following questions: "Do you wish Algeria to become an independent state cooperating with France under the conditions defined by the declarations [the French-Moslem Evian peace accords] of March 19, 1962?"

Final results of the referendum, announced July 3 by the Electoral Control Commission: 5,975,581 "yes" votes; 16,534 "no" votes.

Algerian Independence Proclaimed. An independent Algeria came into existence July 3, 1962 after 132 years of French rule, 114 of them as an integral part of France.

The new state was born in a proclamation issued in Paris by French President de Gaulle on the basis of an overwhelming vote for independence in the referendum carried out July 1. De Gaulle's proclamation stated: "The President of the French Republic declares that France solemnly recognizes the independence of Algeria."

The French government announced July 3 that Jean-Marcel Jeanneney had been named as France's first ambassador to the new Algerian republic. A Presidential decree ended the terms of the 68 National Assembly deputies and 34 senators elected from the former French departments of Algeria.

The Algerian nationalist flag was raised over Rocher-Noir, the former French administrative center near Algiers, at noon July 3.

Moslem Leaders Return. Premier Benyoussef Ben Khedda and the leaders of the Moslem rebel Algerian Provisional Government returned to Algeria July 3, within hours after proclamation of the country's independence from France.

The Moslem nationalists were welcomed by wildly enthusiastic Moslem crowds as they landed at Algiers' Maison Blanche airport in a Tunis Air jet provided by Tunisian President Habib Bourguiba.

Rebel Leadership Split. The enthusiastic welcome given Premier Ben Khedda and his cabinet did not obscure a political struggle that had split the nationalists' government and military leadership at its upper levels. The challenge to Ben Khedda's relatively moderate policies came from Vice Premier Mohammed Ben Bella and a group of high military officers.

Civil War Threatened. Fighting broke out in Algeria July 25 between two factions of the Moslem nationalist movement, each of which claimed leadership of the rebels who had won Algeria's independence.

The rival groups were headed by Benyoussef Ben Khedda, moderate premier of the nationalist Algerian Provisional Government, and Mohammed Ben Bella.

The fighting occurred when rebel troops backing Ben Bella and Colonel Houari Boumedienne, nationalist chief of staff, seized control of the cities of Bone and Constantine in eastern Algeria. No resistance was known to have opposed the Ben Bella troops that seized Bone and the surrounding countryside.

The Ben Khedda government in Algiers condemned the dissidents' move but took no coordinated countermeasures. Premier Ben Khedda, in a communique broadcast July 25, warned that it was "absolutely necessary to halt the process of deterioration" in the rebel ranks. He declared that the "bloody incidents" in Constantine had created the threat of "civil war, of foreign intervention."

Ben Bella Assumes Power. The Moslem nationalist faction led by Vice Premier Mohammed Ben Bella assumed power in Algeria Aug. 7, 1962. All authority was transferred from the Algerian Provisional Government of Premier Benyoussef Ben Khedda to a seven-member Political Bureau named by Ben Bella.

The transfer of power was the result of an agreement imposed on the Ben Khedda government by the growth of the Ben Bella victory.

Negotiations between the opposing Ben Khedda and Ben Bella factions took place in Algiers August 1, with State Minister Mohammed Khider representing Ben Bella and Vice Premiers Mohammed Boudiaf and Belkacem Krim speaking for the Ben Khedda regime. It was announced August 2 that the negotiators had reached an agreement on the following basis: the Ben Khedda regime would accept the authority and composition of the Political Bureau named by Ben Bella; in return, elections for an Algerian Constituent Assembly would be held by August 27.

Ben Bella returned to Algiers August 3 for the first time since his 1956 capture by the French. He was accorded a tumultuous welcome by thousands of Algiers Moslems on his way into the city in a motorcade from the Maison Blanche airport.

Terrorism's Toll. Algerian Affairs Minister Louis Joxe reported to the French National Assembly August 4 that 16,378 Moslems and 2,788 Europeans had been killed in terrorist attacks alone during the Moslem war for independence from November 1, 1954 to March 19, 1962. Some 13,610 Moslems and 7,541 Europeans were wounded in the attacks and 13,296 Moslems and 375 Europeans still were listed as missing. A total of 42,090 terrorist attacks were reported during the seven-year war.

French Exodus Figures. The French government reported July 31 that 498,000 persons, about half of Algeria's 1,000,000 Europeans, had fled to France since the beginning of 1962. Most of the refugees were said to be living in southern France — 160,000 in Marseilles and 70,000 in the Toulouse region — creating serious local tensions.

De Gaulle Assassination Fails. President Charles de Gaulle escaped unhurt Aug. 22, 1962 when assassins machine-gunned the car in which he was riding near Petit-Clamart, nine miles southwest of Paris. De Gaulle's wife and Colonel Alain de Boiseau, his son-in-law, were in the car but were uninjured. The attackers, described by police as Secret Army Organization (OAS) gunmen, fired on de Gaulle from a parked sedan and light truck. He was on his way to Villacoubly Air Base for a flight to his home at Colombey-les-deux-Eglises after attending a cabinet meeting in Paris on the problem of OAS terrorism. De Gaulle continued the trip to the airport and boarded a plane for his home.

Nearly all members of the assassin squad were captured by police and confessed by September 17. Those arrested were: Alain Bougrenet de la Tocnaye, army deserter and a leader of the plot, ex-paratrooper Jacques-Charles Prevost, Air Force Sgt. Alexis Ducasse, Pierre Magade, a deserter, and Pascal Bertin, a Paris high school student.

Announcing the first arrests in the case at a Paris news conference September 7, Interior Minister Roger Frey said their statements to police had confirmed that orders for the assassination came from OAS leaders outside France. He asserted that the attack had been approved also by the National Council of the Resistance (NCR), the clandestine group formed by ex-Premier Georges Bidault to coordinate extra-legal opposition to the de Gaulle regime.

Police in Paris disclosed September 15 that ex-Major Henri Niaux, one of nine additional persons arrested for complicity in the plot, had hanged himself in his Paris prison cell. The police reported that Niaux had confessed directing the assassination attack. They announced September 17 that Jean-Marie Bastien-Thiry, an Air Ministry engineer, had been arrested and had confessed to organizing the attack and to having been in contact with the National Council of Resistance.

Bidault Group Banned. The French Interior Ministry announced September 3 that it had outlawed the NCR, led by Bidault and Jacques Soustelle, former adviser to de Gaulle. Under the ministry's order, any person suspected of NCR membership was liable to prosecution. A second ordinance issued by the ministry the same day permitted the trial within 48 hours of any person arrested on suspicion of terrorist crimes.

A warrant for Bidault's arrest had been issued by the French government August 10 on the basis of charges that he had replaced imprisoned ex-General Raoul Salan as chief of the OAS. The warrant had not been served on Bidault, who was in exile. The Italian Interior Ministry announced September 8 that it had arrested Bidault and had expelled him from Italy the previous day but his country of asylum was not announced.

1961 Assassins Convicted. The five suspected OAS men accused of attempting to kill de Gaulle with a plastic explosive charge Sept. 9, 1961 were tried by a criminal court in Troyes and were convicted and sentenced to prison Sept. 7, 1962. During their trial, the five had admitted their participation in the plot and attack. All had confessed to working under OAS orders, but most claimed that the explosion had been intended to "warn" France and de Gaulle rather than to kill de Gaulle. The five defendants received sentences ranging from twenty to ten years.

THE ALGERIAN WAR AND THE UNITED NATIONS

Under de Gaulle, France consistently maintained that the Algerian war was a French domestic problem beyond the scope of UN jurisdiction. France, therefore, refused to accept UN consideration of the Algerian question through the end of the war.

At the regular sessions of the UN General Assembly in 1958, 1959, 1960, and 1961, France boycotted all UN debates on the Algerian question and refused to participate in any Assembly vote on Algeria. In 1962, with the conclusion of the Algerian war and the establishment of an independent Algerian state, the Algerian issue was removed from the agenda of the General Assembly.

De Gaulle Sept. 5, 1960, at his third presidential press conference, rejected a proposal made August 22 by the Algerian rebel government for a settlement of the rebellion by a UN-controlled referendum. De Gaulle, repeatedly referring to the UN slightingly as "the nations that are so-called united," declared that an Algerian referendum was beyond "the competence of the UN" and warned that France would "not recognize any UN resolution on Algeria."

The French UN delegation was absent from the following General Assembly votes (1958-1961):

(1) The General Assembly Dec. 13, 1958 voted not to adopt an Asian-African resolution calling for French-rebel negotiations to end the war. (2) The Assembly Dec. 12, 1959 voted down a resolution calling for a peaceful solution of the rebellion on the basis of the Algerian "right of self-determination." (3) The Assembly Dec. 19, 1960 adopted by a 63-8 vote (27 abstentions) a resolution recognizing the UN's responsibility to help bring about Algeria's independence; earlier December 19, the Assembly rejected a resolution calling for a UN-supervised referendum in Algeria to decide the nation's future. (4) The Assembly Dec. 20, 1961 voted 62-0 (38 abstentions) to call on France and the rebel government to "resume negotiations" to implement the "independence" and "integrity" of Algeria.

DECOLONIZATION

EVOLUTION OF FRENCH COMMUNITY AND TRUSTEESHIPS

The French Community came into being Sept. 28, 1958 in the referendum approving the Constitution of the Fifth Republic held in metropolitan France and in all French overseas departments and territories.* Creation of the Community from the French Union (established in 1946) marked a further step toward autonomy and self-government in what had previously been a large colonial empire comprising vast territories in Africa, Southeast Asia (Indo-China), various islands in the Pacific and Atlantic oceans, and French Guiana in Latin America.

Following the 1958 referendum, the French Community included:

1. The French Republic: metropolitan France and its nineteen overseas *departments*— Martinique, Guadeloupe, Reunion, Guiana, Algeria (13 departments), and the Sahara (two departments). In addition, five *overseas*

---

*All French overseas departments and territories with the exception of Guinea approved the September 28 referendum and thereby became members of the Community. See pages *territories*— Somaliland, Polynesia, New Caledonia, Comoro, and St. Pierre and Miquelon — voted in December 1958 to retain their status in the French Republic as overseas territories. (Constitutionally, overseas territories enjoyed greater administrative autonomy than overseas departments.)

2. Twelve *autonomous republics* following their decision in the September 1958 referendum to become members of the Community, 12 overseas territories — all African — decided to transform their status into autonomous republics in votes held October through December 1958 in their territorial assemblies. The twelve, with date in parenthesis representing date autonomous republic status was chosen: Madagascar (October 14); Sudan (November 24); Senegal (November 25); Gabon, Chad, Congo, Mauritania (November 28); Ubangi-Shari (December 1); Dahomey, Ivory Coast (December 4); Upper Volta (December 11); Niger (December 18). Upon declaration of autonomous republic status, Ubangi-Shari became the Central African Republic and Madagascar became the Malagache Republic. (*Autonomous republics* enjoyed complete internal autonomy, elected their own prime ministers, but depended on Community executive organs for foreign policy, defense, and finance.)

Outside the Community, France administered Togoland and Cameroons as UN Trusteeships. The French government announced Oct. 2, 1958 that it would terminate its Togoland Trusteeship by 1960. The government announced October 18 that the Cameroons Trusteeship would also end by 1960.

De Gaulle Tours Somaliland, Madagascar. President de Gaulle left Paris July 2, 1959 for a tour of French Somaliland and Madagascar and a two-day meeting of the French Community Executive Council in Tananarive, Madagascar. In Djibouti July 3, he warned separatists of the Greater Somalia movement that France was "here and intends to stay" and "will not abdicate her responsibilities." He flew to Tananarive July 6 and asserted that the French Community would permit France and its former colonies to "develop... in common, stay free in common, and... give the world an example of the unity of peoples."

De Gaulle presided over a meeting of the French Community Executive Council July 7-8 in Tananarive and French Foreign Minister Couve de Murville assured the Council July 7 that its 12 African members would be permitted to establish relations with foreign states and international organizations through French embassies and diplomatic missions.

De Gaulle returned to Paris July 11 following visits to Grand Comore and Reunion islands in the Indian Ocean.

Community Senate Installed. The first French Community Senate was formally installed by President de Gaulle July 15 in Paris. The inauguration of the Senate, composed of 155 members from metropolitan France and 129 from the 12 French African republics, French overseas departments and territories and Algeria and the Sahara, completed the formation of the basic institutions of the French Community. The new

Senate, limited to a consultative role, could be summoned and recessed only by the president.

Senegal, Sudan Seek Independence. The Mali Federation of Senegal and Sudan informed President de Gaulle formally November 27, 1959 of its intention to become independent while maintaining ties with France. (Senegal and the Sudan had decided January 17 to form the Mali Federation within the French Community).

African Republics Choose Independence. The French Community underwent profound transformation in 1960 as the 12 African autonomous republics chose independence while remaining within the Community. In addition, France's two UN Trusteeships in Africa also achieved independence.

Independence for each of the French Community African republics was formalized first in an agreement granting independence signed between the French government and the republic. Subsequently, each of the 12 republics proclaimed its own independence.

Agreements Signed. Agreements signed by the French government in 1960 granting independence were: Malagache Republic (March 26); Mali Federation (April 4); July 11: Ivory Coast, Dahomey, Niger, and Upper Volta; July 12: the Congo Republic, Chad, Central African Republic; Gabon (July 13); Mauritania (July 28).

Community Tie Preserved. A constitutional amendment to permit former French colonies to become independent but remain within the French Community was passed by the National Assembly May 11, 1960 by a 280-174 vote and by the Senate May 18 by a 146-127 vote.

Mali Federation Proclaims Independence, Splits. The Mali Federation of Senegal and the Sudan proclaimed its independence June 20. The Federation split August 20 when the Senegalese government issued a declaration of secession. France formalized the break-up of the Mali Federation September 11 by granting recognition to the independent Republic of Senegal. On September 22, the Sudanese Republic took the name of Republic of Mali.

Republics Proclaim Independence. Ten African republics proclaimed independence in 1960 as follows:

Malagasy Republic (formerly Malagache Republic) — June 26; Dahomey — August 1; Niger — August 3; Upper Volta — August 5; Ivory Coast — August 7; Chad — August 11; Central African Republic — August 13; Congo — August 15; Gabon — August 17; Mauritainia — November 28.

Trusteeships Independent. An independent Cameroon Republic was proclaimed January 1. An independent Togo Republic was proclaimed April 27.

WITHDRAWAL FROM MILITARY BASES IN MOROCCO AND TUNISIA

The independence of Morocco and Tunisia, former French protectorates, had been recognized by the Fourth Republic in 1956. Protocols of independence with Tunisia (March 2) and Morocco (March 26) provided for maintenance of French military bases in both countries.

During the Algerian rebellion, clashes occurred between French and Algerian forces at the Algerian borders with Morocco and Tunisia. The French military command in Algeria charged that Morocco and Tunisia provided sanctuaries and training areas for Algerian rebel troops. As a result, French relations with Morocco and Tunisia were strained; and in 1957 and 1958 the two North African countries were demanding evacuation of French military bases on their territory.

Withdrawal from Morocco. The French government informed Morocco June 14, 1958 that French troops would be withdrawn from 11 military posts in Morocco by mid-July. The withdrawal brought French forces in Morocco down 5,000 to a total of 25,000.

French troops completed their evacuation of all military bases in Morocco March 2, 1961 under the terms of a French-Moroccan agreement of Sept. 1, 1960.

Withdrawal from Tunisia (The Bizerte Crisis). Tunisian President Habib Bourguiba May 26, 1958 called for immediate withdrawal of France's 16,000 troops from Tunisia following French air attacks May 25 on Tunisian troops and civilians near Remada, southern Tunisia, on the Algerian border. Premier de Gaulle June 2 appealed to Bourguiba to help settle "difficulties between our two countries."

Agreement was reached June 17 on the withdrawal of all French troops stationed on Tunisian territory to the Bizerte enclave on Tunisia's Mediterranean coast within four months.

Bourguiba Ultimatum. President Bourguiba July 17, 1961, addressing the Tunisian National Assembly, gave France 24 hours to begin negotiations on a Bizerte withdrawal. He said that if France rejected his ultimatum he would order a blockade of the Bizerte naval and air installations.

French Warning. A French government note delivered to Tunisia July 18 warned that France would take "all measures" necessary to protect its Bizerte installations.

Blockade Begins. Tunisian forces July 19 began surrounding the Bizerte base area, manning roadblocks and building obstacles to French military traffic between sections of the base.

French Retaliate. French troops, supported by tanks and rocket-firing aircraft, broke the blockade July 20 and drove into the city of Bizerte. French air attacks also were made on other nearby towns and road centers. The attacks were coordinated with what was described as a massive artillery barrage. They drove Tunisians back from their barricades surrounding the base and demolished their artillery strongpoints. A French ultimatum to surrender the city was rejected by the Tunisians, who defended key positions for more than 24 hours. The French forces occupied most parts of Bizerte and the surrounding area by late July 22. An estimated 1,000 Tunisians and 30 French soldiers were killed in the actions.

Tunisia Breaks French Ties. President Bourguiba announced July 20 that Tunisia had severed diplomatic relations with France and had requested an immediate U.N. Security Council meeting to condemn "French agression."

Security Council Votes Cease-Fire. The UN Security Council voted July 22 by 10 — 0 (France abstaining) to call on both sides to cease firing and return their troops to positions held before the fighting began.

Second Council Session. A second session of the Security Council was convened July 28 at Tunisia's request. Tunisia urged Council action to compel France to abide by the earlier resolutions to withdraw its troops from the Bizerte area. At the session, Secretary General Dag Hammarskjold, who had made an inspection trip to Tunisia July 24 — 27, reported July 28 that France had not obeyed the UN's initial demand that it return its troops to their positions before the Bizerte attack. The French UN delegation attended the session but did not participate in the debate; a French letter to the Council July 28 made it clear that the delegation's silence was a protest against the session. Three resolutions on Bizerte were submitted to the Council July 29 but did not win sufficient votes for passage; France did not participate in these votes.

UN General Assembly Meets. A special session of the UN General Assembly was called August 10 by Secretary General Hammarskjold to meet August 21 on the Bizerte crisis. French Foreign Minister Maurice Couve de Murville announced August 10 that France would boycott the special Assembly session.

UN Vote Backs Tunisia. The Assembly August 25 approved 66 — 0 (30 abstentions) an Afro-Asian resolution upholding Tunisia in her dispute with France. The resolution called for (1) reaffirmation of the Security Council's cease-fire order of July 22, (2) recognition of Tunisia's "sovereign right" to call for the withdrawal of French troops from Tunisian territory, (3) "immediate negotiations" between France and Tunisia for a Bizerte settlement. France boycotted the August 25 session.

Bourguiba Defers Exit Demand. Tunisian President Bourguiba reversed his demand that France evacuate the Bizerte base immediately and proposed instead September 8 that French naval and air forces retain use of the base "during the present world (Berlin) crisis."

President de Gaulle had said at his September 5 Paris press conference that, while France had "never contested" the principle of Tunisian sovereignty over Bizerte, France "could not and would not" evacuate the base in view of current world tensions — an allusion to the Berlin crisis.

French Troops Draw Back. French troops began to withdraw October 1 from the section of the city of Bizerte they had occupied following the outbreak of fighting July 20. The withdrawal was completed October 3, with the French troops returning to the military bases located at Bizerte.

Bourguiba Threatens "Battle." President Bourguiba warned in a National Assembly speech October 12 that Tunisia would fight another "battle of Bizerte" if France refused to evacuate its military base there.

CHAPTER IV

GOVERNMENT, POLITICS AND THE ECONOMY

Gaullists Win Legislative Elections. Gaullists and conservative candidates won control of the Fifth Republic's first National Assembly in elections held in two rounds, Nov. 23 and 30, 1958. Communists, non-Communist leftists, and moderates were virtually eliminated as a political force in the Assembly.

Candidates of the Gaullist Union for the New Republic (UNR), led by Information Minister Jacques Soustelle, won 188 of the 465 seats allotted France in the Assembly and were assured of nearly all of the 71 Assembly seats filled in Algerian elections held November 28-30. The Communist Party retained France's largest popular vote bloc (18% of the electorate) but won only ten Assembly seats.*

Party standing in the new Assembly (compared with seats held in the outgoing Assembly): Union of the New Republic — 188 (13); Independents, Conservatives and Peasants — 132 (107); Popular Republican (MRP) and Christian Democrats — 57 (71); Socialists — 40 (91); Centrists and dissident Radicals — 22 (35); Radicals — 13 (42); Communists and Progressists — 10 (144); minor leftists — 5 (0); Poujadists — 1 (30).

President Coty to Retire; Presidential Election Set. President Rene Coty informed Premier de Gaulle December 1 that he (Coty) would not seek reelection in indirect presidential balloting scheduled for December 21. French municipal and departmental general councils met December 7 to choose most of the 75,000 presidential electors for the December 21 balloting. The councils elected their share of the 75,000 "grand electors" empowered to choose a new French president. Assembly deputies, senators, territorial deputies and municipal councillors automatically were designated as "grand electors."

De Gaulle formally announced December 13 his candidacy for the presidency of the Fifth Republic.

De Gaulle Elected President. Premier de Gaulle was elected Dec. 21, 1958 to a seven-year term as first president of the Fifth Republic. (He did not relinquish the premiership until Jan. 8, 1959, when he was proclaimed

---

*The two-round system worked to the disadvantage of the Communists because non-Communist candidates trailing after the first round (November 23) withdrew from the second round to permit their supporters to vote for allied non-Communist candidates in the decisive second round (November 30). Communist candidates were unable to form alliances with other groups for the second round elections.
(Under the two-round system, candidates receiving an absolute majority of votes in round one gained an Assembly seat; only 41 seats were decided in the November 23 round. The remaining seats were decided in the second ballot among leading candidates in the first round, the candidate receiving a plurality of votes winning a seat in the Assembly.)

president.) Final returns December 22 for the indirect presidential election gave de Gaulle 62,395 (78.5%) of 79,414 ballots cast by a special roll of grand electors in France and the French Community. Georges Marrane, Communist mayor of a Paris suburb, received 10,354 votes and Professor Albert Chatelet, candidate of the liberal Union of Democratic Forces, 6,722.

Economic Reforms Announced. In a major effort to restore economic and financial stability to France, the de Gaulle cabinet December 27-30 announced a series of measures embracing monetary devaluation and convertibility, import liberalization, and increased taxation and austerity. Details of the measures:

Devaluation and Convertibility: The exchange value of the franc was fixed at the rate of 493.7 to the U.S. dollar instead of the 420-$1 rate in effect since August 1957. Plans were also announced December 27 for the gradual replacement of the present franc with a "heavy franc" valued at 100 old francs. This move, to be accomplished in 1959, would align the franc with more stable European currencies, such as the West German Deutsch mark and Swiss franc. The franc was made freely convertible for persons resident outside the franc zone for the first time since before World War II. This move towards convertibility was made jointly with nine other West European nations.

Import Liberalization: Quota restrictions and licensing controls on 90% of France's imports from other European countries were abolished. The French government removed import quotas from more than 50% of its imports from the United States and Canada December 31.

Taxation and Austerity: Premier de Gaulle appealed to the French people in a radio-TV address December 28 to accept a "great sacrifice" to aid French efforts "in the great national enterprise of financial and economic recovery." He warned that taxes would be increased on corporations, persons with high incomes and luxury items. He urged war veterans "to renounce their pensions" to aid French recovery. He pledged, however, that low-paid workers, aged pensioners and the unemployed would receive increased aid.

Finance Minister Antoine Pinay disclosed December 29 that the 1959 French budget deficit would be kept within $1.36 billion by the withdrawal of $543 million in subsidies for nationalized industries and the imposition of $626 million in new taxes. Pinay made clear that France's economic reforms would not permit wage rises for any but the lowest paid workers, who were pledged a 4% increase in February 1959. The wage and price policies of the new economic program were attacked bitterly December 29 by all major labor unions.

(Price decrees issued under plans for the new French austerity budget raised railway fares January 5, postage January 6 and prices of tobacco, meat, gasoline, gas and electricity January 15. Most increases ranged from 15% to 20%.)

De Gaulle Becomes President. De Gaulle was proclaimed first president of the Fifth Republic Jan. 8, 1959. In a brief speech, he made clear that he would revitalize the presidency under provisions of the new constitution. De Gaulle said that he would "have the duty to represent, to achieve, even to impose" the "national interest in the nation" and "the common interest in the community" if "the public good should demand it."

Debre Cabinet Formed. In his first official act January 8, President de Gaulle appointed Michel Debre, a leading member of the Gaullist Union for the New Republic (UNR), as premier at the head of a 27-member cabinet. Debre's cabinet included members of the UNR group in the Assembly, Independents, Catholic Popular Republicans (MRP), Radicals, a member of the Algerian bloc in the Assembly and a member of the African Democratic Rally. Socialist leaders refused to serve in the Debre cabinet despite appeals for their participation by de Gaulle during a meeting January 2 with Guy Mollet, Socialist party leader.

Debre's cabinet took office January 10 when it formally was presented to President de Gaulle at the Elysee Palace. The new cabinet (party affiliation in parentheses):

> *Premier*—Michel Debre (UNR); *Minister-Delegate to the Premier*—Jacques Soustelle (UNR); *State Ministers*—Felix Houphouet-Boigny (African Dem. Rally), Louis Jacquinot (Independent), Robert Lecourt (MRP), Andre Malraux (no party); *Justice*—Edmond Michelet (UNR); *Foreign Affairs*—Maurice Couve de Murville (no party); *Interior*—Jean Berthoin (radical); *Armies*—Jean Guillaumat (no party); *Finance and Economic Affairs*—Antoine Pinay (Independent); *National Education*—Andre Boulloche (no party); *Public Works, Transport and Tourism*—Robert Buron (MRP); *Industry and Commerce*—Pierre Jeanneney (no party); *Agriculture*—Roger Houdet (Independent); *Labor*—Paul Bacon (MRP); *Public Health*—Bernard Chenot (no party); *Construction*—Pierre Sudreau (no party); *Veterans*—Raymond Triboulet (UNR); *Communications*—Bernard Cornut-Gentille (UNR); *Information*—Roger Frey (UNR); *State Secretaries*—Miss Nefissa Sid Cara (UNR Algerian bloc), Victor Chatenay (UNR); Max Flechet (Independent), Joseph Fontanet (MRP), Valery Giscard d'Estaing (Independent), Michel Maurice - Bokanowski (UNR).

Parliament Opens. The National Assembly and Senate of the Fifth Republic convened for the first time January 15 for Premier Debre's presentation of his cabinet and policies. Deputies, summoned to confirm the Debre cabinet, voted January 16 by 453-56 (Socialists and Communists opposed, 29 rightists abstaining) to approve the cabinet and its policies.

Foreign Debt Drops. Paris dispatches reported April 12, 1959 that French foreign credits exceeded debts for the first time in 10 years. French credits were reported to total $1.4 billion ($590 million of it in gold held by the Bank of France, the rest in French holdings in the Exchange Stabilization Fund). French foreign debts were said to total $1.226 billion owed to the International Monetary Fund, the European Payments Union, the United States and various European nations.

Gaullists Lose in Senate Elections. Moderates and conservatives, many of them Fourth Republic political leaders, outpolled Gaullist UNR candidates April 26 to win control of the first Senate (total number of seats, 307) of the French Fifth Republic. Final returns for the 255 Senate seats from metropolitan France showed the following distribution of seats among parties: Communists 14; minor leftists 1; Socialists 48; Radicals and moderates 51; UNR Gaullists 27; Independents and Peasants 85. Thirty-two Algerian senators—20 Moslems and 12 Europeans—were elected in separate balloting May 31. Twenty more seats were allocated to senators representing the Sahara (2), Overseas Departments (7), Overseas Territories (5), and French citizens living in foreign countries (6).

Mendes-France Heads New Party Grouping. The Autonomous Socialist Party, ending a three-day congress in Paris May 3, voted to merge with the non-Communist Socialist Left Party and continue its participation in the anti-Gaullist Union of Democratic Forces led by ex-Premier Pierre Mendes-France.

Assembly Power Reduced. The Gaullist controlled National Assembly voted June 4, 1959 by 434 to 94 to adopt permanent rules of procedure that barred Assembly votes on resolutions approving or disapproving cabinet policies. The rules also forbade any resolutions to increase government expenditures or decrease revenues. They granted the cabinet full power to decide when the Assembly would vote on government policies and restricted the opposition to one weapon—a censure motion signed by at least 1/10 of the Assembly and passed by an absolute majority.

1960 Budget Adopted. Finance Minister Antoine Pinay, presenting an $11.6 billion 1960 French budget to the National Assembly November 6, pledged that France would end all special restrictions on U.S. trade in "the shortest possible time" and all quota limitations on European and U.S. imports within two years. Pinay announced that French gold and dollar reserves had grown from $600 million in 1957 to $1.911 billion October 31, due, in part, to a favorable trade balance. He said the increased liberalization of trade would be "the best of stimulants and... most effective of disciplines" for the French economy.

The 1960 budget was automatically passed by the French National Assembly November 28 whan a Socialist-Radical censure motion against the Debre cabinet was given only 109 of the 277 votes required to reverse the government on a matter of confidence. Under the new constitution, only affirmative censure votes were counted, and a bill was considered passed without vote when the motion failed. The censure motion, presented November 25 by a coalition of 60 Socialists and Radicals led by ex-Premiers Guy Mollet and Felix Gaillard after Debre had refused to restore cuts in veterans' pensions, was the first attempted under the Fifth Republic.

Civil Servant Strike. An estimated 60% of France's civil servants struck for 24 hours Dec. 2, 1959 to protest limited pay increases accorded them in the 1960 budget. Ignoring President de Gaulle's appeals for labor discipline, they paralyzed water, postal and telephone systems, air traffic and other public services.

New Franc Issued. A new franc, equivalent in value to 100 old francs, was put in circulation Jan. 1, 1960 by the Bank of France. The new currency, valued at nearly 20 cents (U.S.), realigned the franc with other European currencies of similar valuation.

Pinay Quits Cabinet. Finance Minister Antoine Pinay, author of financial austerity measures credited with French economic recovery under the Fifth Republic, resigned from Premier Michel Debre's cabinet January 13 and was replaced by Wilfrid Baumgartner, governor of the Bank of France.

Pinay was said to have opposed de Gaulle's policy of increasing state control over the French economy and his rejection of integration of NATO armed forces. A presidential communique issued January 13 said Pinay's

conservative economic program "will be pursued." Baumgartner, a career
civil servant, told newsmen the same day that he had accepted the post on
condition that Pinay's hard money policies continue.

In a statement to reporters January 13, Pinay, a leader of the con-
servative Independent Party, asserted that he was "withdrawing from all
public life." Independent Secretary General Roger Duchet declared
January 16 that the party would assume "aggressive opposition" to the
Debre government. The Independents controlled 118 of the 552 seats in the
National Assembly.

(Louis Joxe, a state secretary in Debre's cabinet, was named January
15 to replace Andre Boulloche as education minister.)

(The Independent Party's National Council January 29 adopted a
resolution calling upon de Gaulle to support the aims of the European
rightists in Algeria. Three Independent Party cabinet members who
opposed the resolution — Agriculture Minister Henri Rochereau, State
Minister Louis Jacquinot and State Secretary for Finance Valery Giscard
d'Estaing — announced that they take no further part in Independent
Party deliberations.)

Amiens Farmers Riot. Some 122 persons, 53 of them policemen,
were injured in Amiens Feb. 11, 1960 when 25,000 to 30,000 farmers,
gathered to protest government agricultural policies, rioted and clashed
with police. The meeting had been organized by the National Federation of
Agricultural Producers to protest removal of farm produce from the
mobile index tying farm prices to those of other basic commodities. It was
the first major anti-government demonstration reported in France since
the 1958 Algiers coup.

Farm Price Supports Announced. Farm price supports were established by government decree March 4 to meet growing rural unrest caused
by the gap between stable agricultural prices and rising production costs.
In a farm message broadcast the same day, Premier Debre pledged long-
term credits to reduce farm debt and finance modernization.

De Gaulle Rejects Special Assembly Session on Farm Problem. A
demand presented March 16 by 287 National Assembly deputies for a
special Assembly session to deal with growing unrest among French
farmers was rejected March 18 by President de Gaulle.

De Gaulle's rejection of the request, made by 11 more deputies than
the Assembly majority required by the French constitution*, was protested
by many political parties as an unconstitutional attempt to curtail Assembly powers. In a letter to Assembly Speaker Jacques Chaban-Delmas, de
Gaulle said he had refused the special session because (a) pressure for the
session primarily came from farm groups with no political responsibility; (b) deputies were forbidden to introduce measures raising expenditures or lowering revenues, hence could not present farm aid
bills; (c) government farm measures were under preparation.

Decree Cuts Assembly Power. Cabinet decrees published April 18
transferred from the National Assembly to the cabinet the sole power to
declare states of emergency. But prolongation of an emergency for more
than 12 days would require Assembly approval.

---

*Article 29 of the constitution stated that a special Assembly shall be called if requested by a majority of depu-
ties. But Article 30 said such a session was to be summoned by a presidential decree, refused by de Gaulle.

Censure Motion Fails. A censure motion presented April 28 by Socialist and Radical deputies to protest de Gaulle's refusal to honor constitutional demands for a special Assembly session on the farm problem won only 122 of a required 276 votes May 5. About 300,000 French farmers staged protest rallies against low prices and de Gaulle's agricultural policies April 7 in Tours and 17 other provincial centers. Police used clubs and tear gas to disperse the meetings in Sens, near Paris, and Quimper, Normandy.

Payments Surplus. A $1.15 billion French balance of payments credit during 1959 was reported May 1, 1960 by Finance Minister Wilfrid Baumgartner. There had been deficits of $98 million in 1958, $1.7 billion in 1957 and $1 billion in 1956.

Labor Unrest. Ninety per cent of France's railwaymen struck for 24 hours May 31 in a demand for a speed-up in a 16% wage increase offered by the government in steps over two years. The strike was observed by Communist and Socialist (but not by Catholic) railway unions.

Nearly 1,000,000 French civil servants struck for 24 hours June 10 to protest the inadequacy of a promised 5% pay increase. The strike slowed and halted air and land transportation, mail and communications and closed public schools and state offices.

Auriol Resigns. Ex-President Vincent Auriol announced his resignation from the French Constitutional Council July 2, 1960 in protest against President de Gaulle's alleged efforts to create "a system of personal and arbitrary power" in France. Auriol charged that de Gaulle had violated the constitution by his refusal to recall Parliament despite a request by a majority of deputies and his amendment of the constitutional structure of the French Community.

(The Constitutional Council, responsible for determining the constitutionality of disputed legislation, came into existence Feb. 20, 1959. Auriol and ex-President Rene Coty automatically became ex-officio Council members for life.)

Budget Presented. A $13.93 billion fiscal 1961 budget was presented to the National Assembly September 29 by State Secretary for Finance Valery Giscard d'Estaing, principal deputy to Finance Minister Baumgartner. The budget, based on an anticipated 5.5% rate of economic expansion in 1961, provided $3.36 billion for defense expenditures, among them the cost of Algerian military operations and initial funds for a French nuclear striking force. Revenues of $12.51 billion and a deficit of $1.35 billion were foreseen.

Farmers Riot. French farmers in Brittany and other parts of France staged violent anti-government demonstrations June 4-30, 1961 to protest falling farm prices.

Among the major developments:

Morlaix (15,000 population) was besieged early June 8 by farmers, who forced the sub-prefect from his office, seized his headquarters and blocked off entries to the town and streets. The farmers lifted the blockade later June 8 after the local farm federation denounced its members' tactics.

Security forces in Pontivy, Brittany used tear gas June 16 in repelling a farmers' attack on the town's central government building. Farmers blocked town roads with tractors and paraded in the streets.

Some 500-600 tractor-riding farmers blocked all approaches to Carhaix June 18 while hundreds of others staged a protest demonstration there.

One thousand farmers used tractors June 19 to block off the prefecture of the Vendee Department. Prefecture employees, with the exception of Vendee mayors, were barred from entering the building until the demonstration ended at noon.

The government, in a move to alleviate Brittany's economic plight, announced June 16 that the Brest region would get priority for economic development. Measures announced by Premier Michel Debre June 17: (1) government purchase of potatoes, butter and other dairy products at support prices; (2) opening of slaughter houses to increase the farmers' share of the price of meat animals; (3) electrification of a rail line and extension of existing roads to facilitate farm-to-market transportation.

Despite the government measures announced June 16-17 and a radio-TV appeal by Debre June 23 urging the farmers to end their rioting, farm violence continued through June 30.

About 2,500 farmers gathered around the Montauban prefecture June 24 and hurled bottles and stones at security forces who broke up the demonstrations with tear gas grenades. Two policemen were injured. About 7,000 farmers in other parts of southwestern France used tractors to block roads and besiege prefectures June 24.

Calais roads were blocked for two hours June 28 by farm tractors. Farmers near Narbonne in the south used tractors and mule carts June 28 to block the main road to Perpignan, Barcelona and the Spanish coast. Tractor-driving wine growers June 28 blocked the Toulouse-Marseilles rail line near Courson and Lezignan.

The French government June 29 agreed to provide emergency price supports for cereals, meat, poultry, milk products, wine, fruit and vegetables. The concessions were agreed to after a meeting in Paris of Premier Debre and other government officials with leaders of the National Federation of Farm Unions and nine other farm groups. The June 29 agreement brought almost a month of farm violence to an end.

Cabinet Shuffled. President de Gaulle Aug. 24, 1961 announced these cabinet appointments (former posts in parentheses):

Information— Christian de la Malene, replacing Louis Terrenoire; *Agriculture*— Edgard Pisani, replacing Henri Rochereau; *Sahara and Overseas Departments*— Jean de Broglie, replacing Robert Lecourt; *Justice*—Bernard Chenot *(Health)*, replacing Edmond Michelet; *Health*— Joseph Fontanet *(Internal Commerce)*; *Internal Commerce*— Francois Missoffe; *State Secretary for Repatriation* (new post to deal with French returnees from North Africa)— Robert Boulin.

Assembly Deputies Protest vs. de Gaulle. A special session of the National Assembly, called to discuss the farm problem, was boycotted by Socialist and right-wing deputies and about 50% of the 206 Gaullist deputies September 12 in protest against President de Gaulle's retention of rule by decree powers since April, when he had assumed the powers in response to the Algiers' generals' coup.

Premier Debre retaliated September 13 by canceling briefing sessions, scheduled for that day, by himself, Foreign Minister Maurice Couve de Murville and Defense Minister Pierre Messmer before the Assembly's Foreign Affairs and Defense committees.

A Socialist motion to censure Debre's (in effect, de Gaulle's) government was introduced September 12. National Assembly Speaker Jacques Chaban-Delmas ruled September 19 that the Assembly could vote the government out of office only in the regular Assembly session, which was to open October 3. The censure motion had been submitted at the beginning of a special session on farm problems and was meant specifically to condemn the government's agricultural policies. De Gaulle had told Debre in a letter August 31 that the Assembly had the right to convene the special session for discussion only, not legislation.

Anti-Gaullist Parties Attempt Unity. A new session of the National Assembly was convened Oct. 3, 1961 amid indications that center and left parties were studying the possibility of forming a non-Communist opposition bloc. The conservative Independent Party's directing committee attacked de Gaulle's policies October 4 and demanded a return to Parliamentary rule as specified in the 1958 constitution. The Radical Party's annual convention voted October 8 to participate in a center-left coalition opposed to the Debre government and de Gaulle's alleged "systematic violation" of the constitution.

Ex-Premiers Guy Mollet and Pierre Mendes-France met in Paris September 29 to open discussions on the possible regrouping of their two Socialist parties and other center-left groups.

Economic Plan. A four-year economic and social progress plan envisaging a 24% increase in private consumption was announced by the government's State Planning Commission Ocotber 16. The plan called for: (a) Large investment increases — about 50% for education, town planning, health and sports facilities; 28% for industry and agriculture; 25% for housing. (b) Reduction of the length of military service from the current 28 months to provide enough civilian workers to help meet production goals. (c) Creation of about 1,000,000 new jobs to satisfy an expected increase in the working population.

Budget Approved. The French National Assembly Dec. 2, 1961 approved by a 261 — 234 vote a 70-billion franc ($14 bilion) 1962 budget.

Nationwide Strike. About 500,000 employees of France's government-owned transport, gas and electric power industries staged a one-day nationwide strike November 28 — 29 for higher wages. Many shopkeepers joined the walkout to protest government plans for price freezes. Transportation in Paris was at a virtual standstill, and many factories in the city were forced to close.

Giscard d'Estaing Finance Minister. Wilfrid Baumgartner resigned as finance minister Jan. 18, 1962 and was replaced by his principal deputy, Valery Giscard d'Estaing.

Pompidou Becomes Premier. Georges Jean Raymond Pompidou, a banker and close personal associate of President de Gaulle, was named by de Gaulle April 14 to succeed Michel Debre as French premier. Debre, whose three years and three months in office were a record for a French republican premier, resigned to make possible a change in government after the completion of action on the Algerian truce accords.

Pompidou retained most key members of the Debre government in the new French cabinet made public April 15. Of the 29 ministers named, 19, among them Foreign Minister Maurice Couve de Murville, Interior Minister Roger Frey, Finance Minister Valery Giscard d'Estaing and Armed

Forces Minister Pierre Messmer, were retained in their old posts. A majority of Pompidou's ministers were members of the Gaullist Union for the New Republic group in Parliament, although five were members of the moderate Catholic MRP group and a few were Independents. Pompidou, director general of the Rothschild Freres banking house, was not himself a member of Parliament.

The April 15 French cabinet (* denotes holdover):

Premier— Georges Pompidou; *Ministers of State*— Pierre Pflimlin *(Cooperation with African States);* Louis Joxe* *(Algerian Affairs);* Andre Malraux* *(Cultural Affairs);* Gaston Palewski *(Scientific Research); Ministers Attached to Premier's Office*— Maurice Schumann *(Regional Planning)* Roger Dusseaulx *(Parliamentary Relations); Foreign Affairs*— Maurice Couve de Murville*; *Interior*— Roger Frey*; *Armed Forces*— Pierre Messmer*; *Finance and National Economy*— Valery Giscard d'Estaing*; *Justice*— Jean Foyer*; *National Education*— Pierre Sudreau*; *Public Works*— Robert Buron*; *Commerce and Industry*— Michel Maurice-Bokanowski*; *Agriculture*— Edgard Pisani*; *Labor*— Paul Bacon*; *Veterans Affairs*— Raymond Triboulet*; *Posts and Telecommunications*— Jacques Marette; *Construction*— Jacques Maziol; *Overseas Territories*— Louis Jacquinot*; *Health*— Joseph Fontaret; *Secretaries of State*— Alain Peyrefitte *(Information),* Georges Gorse* *(Foreign Affairs),* Robert Boulin* *(Repatriation),* Pierre Dumas *(Public Works),* Gilbert Grandval *(External Commerce),* Francois Missoffe* *(Internal Commerce),* Jean de Broglie* *(Civil Service).*

Pompidou Cabinet Confirmed. Premier Georges Pompidou's new French cabinet was confirmed in office April 27 by a 259—128 National Assembly vote (119 abstentions.) The weak majority—86 votes less than the lowest vote accorded the Debre cabinet during its three years in office—was attributed to parliament's resentment at its loss of powers and President de Gaulle's reported plans to transform France still further toward a presidential republic. The vote came after Pompidou, in a two-day investiture debate, had pledged to "pursue (the Secret Army Organization) without letup" in order to enforce the French-Moslem peace in Algeria and turn France's energies toward an economic program designed to increase production by 5.5% in 1962.

MRP Ministers Resign over de Gaulle's European Policies. Five cabinet ministers—all members of the Catholic Popular Republican Movement party (MRP)—resigned from the Pompidou government May 16, 1962 in protest against de Gaulle's European policies. (De Gaulle had outlined his opposition to European political integration May 15 at his semiannual press conference.) The ministers were: Pierre Pflimlin, state minister for cooperation with the African states; Maurice Schumann, regional planning minister; Robert Buron, public works minister; Paul Bacon, labor minister; Joseph Fontanet, public health minister.

(Premier Pompidou in a cabinet revision announced later May 16, assumed the regional planning post and named Raymond Marcellin to the public health post. Parliamentary Relations Minister Roger Desseaulx was named public works minister and his portfolio was taken by Pierre Dumas, whose post of state secretary for public works was abolished. Pompidou abolished the portfolios of two other ministers to name them to the remaining vacancies left by the MRP resignations: Foreign Affairs State Secretary Georges Gorse became state minister for cooperation with the African states, and External Commerce State Secretary Gilbert Grandval became minister of labor.)

Independents Oppose de Gaulle on Europe. National Assembly members of the Independent Party voted May 22 by 57 — 31 to condemn de Gaulle's European views and to withdraw support from the government. The four Independent Party ministers in the Pompidou cabinet — Finance Minister Valery Giscard d'Estaing, State Minister for Overseas Territories Louis Jacquinot, Public Health Minister Raymond Marcellin, and Civil Service State Secretary Jean de Broglie — refused, however, to obey the parliamentary group's demand. Their decision was made public May 23.

Parliamentary "Walkout" in Support of European Unity. The MRP-Independent opposition to de Gaulle's European policies was given the formal support of the Socialist and Radical parties June 13, when 293 of the National Assembly's 553 deputies walked out of the Assembly after their request for a vote at the conclusion of a foreign affairs debate was denied by the Gaullist government. The 293, members of the four leading center parties, had signed a "European Manifesto" in which they affirmed "our will to see France direct herself toward European unity, which we conceive as a democratic community of people and not as a series of old-style conferences between governments." The manifesto demanded "the fusion of communal organisms, the election of the European Assembly with universal suffrage and the progressive institutions of majority vote within the [European] council of ministers."

U.S. Debt Prepaid. French repayment to the United States ahead of schedule of a debt installment totaling $293,400,000 was announced July 12, 1962 in a letter sent by French Finance Minister Valery Giscard d'Estaing to U.S. Treasury Secretary Douglas Dillon. The installment included $210 million in Marshall Plan repayments of a 1946 Export-Import Bank reconstruction loan. France simultaneously announced conversion of part of its dollar holdings into gold by the purchase of $112-1/2 million worth of U.S. gold. This prepayment reduced France's foreign indebtedness (all long-term) to $1.179 billion.

CONSTITUTIONAL CRISES: DE GAULLE VS. PARLIAMENT

DeGaulle Asks Popular Vote for President; Bypasses Constitution. President de Gaulle announced Sept. 20, 1962 that he would submit to a national referendum a plan for amending the French constitution to permit popular election of his successors in office. (The constitution required parliamentary approval of constitutional amendments. It provided for the indirect election of the president by a special college of "grand electors," made up of about 75,000 electors representing local and national institutions.)

De Gaulle, in a September 20 radio-TV address, said: "I believe ... I must put the following proposal before the country: when my own seven-year term of office comes to an end, or if death or sickness should interrupt it before the seven years are up, the president of the republic shall hence-forth be elected by universal suffrage."

De Gaulle, recounting the events that had led to his return to power, pointed out that his successors might not possess "the same national distinction" for which he had been recalled to office. He asserted that they would be certain of their mandate to uphold a strong executive only if they "receive their mandate directly from all the citizens."

De Gaulle brushed aside criticism of his plan to amend the constitution without parliamentary assent. He declared that a referendum would be the "most democratic way" to consult the nation. "It is also the most justified way," he said, "for national sovereignty belongs...to the people first and foremost with regard to the constitution." He conceded that the constitution provided a parliamentary process for its amendment, but he maintained that it also (a) gave the president the right to submit to referendum "any bill concerning the organization of public powers" and (b) specified that "the people shall exercise their sovereignty either through their representative or through referendums."

Pompidou Cabinet Overthrown on de Gaulle's Popular Vote Plan. The National Assembly forced the resignation of Premier Pompidou's cabinet Oct. 6, 1962. This was the first time since the founding of the Fifth Republic in 1958 that Parliament had succeeded in ousting a government.

Pompidou's reversal came on a motion adopted by the Assembly October 5 to censure his government for its acceptance of President de Gaulle's plan for national referendum on direct, popular election of his successors to the presidency. The censure motion was approved by 280 votes — 39 more than the majority required — drawn from every opposition party, from the Communists to the right-wing Independents. Only 21 non-Gaullists joined the 179 members of the Gaullist UNR party in abstaining from the vote.

The censure motion declared that the Fifth Republic's constitution "prescribes formally...that a proposal to revise the constitution must be: 1. Voted by the two houses of Parliament; 2. Approved by a referendum after the French people has been informed by the parliamentary debates." It charged that de Gaulle, in proposing that the method of presidential election be changed by referendum, without the approval of the Assembly, "violates the constitution of which he is the guardian" and was "opening a breach through which an adventurer might pass some day to overthrow the Republic and suppress its liberties."

The censure motion, signed by representatives of the Socialist, Catholic Popular Republican (MRP), Radical and Independent parties, had been presented to the Assembly October 2 when it reconvened after the summer recess. De Gaulle's plans for a presidential election referendum October 28 had been submitted to the Assembly the same day; the referendum was to take place despite the Pompidou government's reversal. (Gaston Monnerville, who had attacked de Gaulle September 29 for "outrageous violation of the republic," was reelected October 2 by a vote of 212 to 3 [29 abstentions] to his seventeenth consecutive term as Senate president.)

Pompidou formally submitted his resignation to de Gaulle October 6. He was asked to remain in office on a caretaker basis until a new cabinet could be formed. De Gaulle then met October 6 with Senate President Monnerville and Assembly Speaker Jacques Chaban-Delmas for mandatory consultations preliminary to dissolving the Assembly and ordering new general elections.

De Gaulle Speech. The nature of the conflict between de Gaulle and Parliament had been made clear by de Gaulle in a radio-TV address delivered October 4, before the vote censuring Pompidou. Ignoring the parliamentarians' objections that his plan for a referendum on popular election of the president was unconstitutional, de Gaulle called on the French to give him a massive "yes" vote in the October 28 plebiscite. His appeal contained the implication that he would resign if the electorate failed to give him this "direct proof" of its confidence.

De Gaulle conceded that "from the very beginning, I knew that, before the end of my seven-year term of office, I would have to put it to the country to decide that it be so." His decision to call for the referendum immediately was due, he said, to "the attempts perpetrated or planned on my life," which obliged him "to make sure...that after me there shall be a strong republic."

Asserting that France had been transformed from the "'sick man of Europe'" into a nation whose "weight and influence are recognized throughout the world," de Gaulle warned that these achievements would disappear if "the state, after de Gaulle, [were] delivered up once again to political practices that would lead it to a shameful catastrophe. A catastrophe, this time, without recourse."

Parliament Dissolved. A de Gaulle decree dissolving the National Assembly was published in the French Official Journal October 10. The decree ordered elections held for a new Assembly in two rounds of balloting Nov. 18 and 25, 1962.

De Gaulle Wins Referendum. President de Gaulle's plan for the direct popular election of future French presidents was supported by more than 62% of the voters participating in a national referendum held October 28.

De Gaulle, whose proposal had been opposed as unconstitutional by every party except his Union for the New Republic, had threatened in an October 18 radio-TV address to resign unless the plebiscite produced massive support for the plan. In the address, de Gaulle's warning was clear. Party corruption, he said, "had almost hurled France into the abyss" during the Fourth Republic. He asserted that, with the direct support of the French people, "I have been able, for four years,...to ensure the leadership of the country toward progress, prosperity and grandeur, to suppress one by one the criminal threats that were raised against the state to prevent a return to the shortcomings of the condemned regime." He warned French voters: "If your answer (in the referendum) is 'no,'...or even if the 'yes' majority is weak, mediocre, uncertain....my task will be immediately and irretrievably terminated."

Final referendum results reported October 29 by the Agence France-Presse news agency gave de Gaulle's presidential election plan 62.1% of the valid votes cast in France and the French overseas territories. This was a 46.5% plurality of the total number of registered voters, almost 23% of whom had abstained from voting. "No" votes accounted for 37.9% of the valid votes cast and for 28.4% of the registered electorate.

Total registered electorate in France and its territories: 28,059,124. Referendum votes cast: 21,598,591. "Yes" votes: 13,053,234. "No" votes: 7,964,478. Invalid ballots: 580,879.

A French cabinet communique issued October 31 had reported de Gaulle to be satisfied with the resuts of the October 28 referendum. The communique said that de Gaulle considered the referendum results to be "a capital element of solidity and continuity."

Gaullists Win Parliament Control. Candidates pledged to support President de Gaulle won an absolute majority in the French National Assembly in a two-round general election November 18 and 25.

Gaullists won 275 of the 482 seats in the new Assembly. This was the first time in modern French history that one political party or an alliance pledged to one political leader had won such a victory.

Official Gaullist candidates were grouped in two parties: the Union for the New Republic (UNR), the party formed in conjunction with de Gaulle's return to power in 1958, and the Democratic Union of Labor (UDT), a new grouping of left-wing Gaullists. To these were added candidates of a new Independent Republican Party, composed of former members of the anti-Gaullist Independent Party, and several members of the Radical Party running with Gaullist support.

Ninety-six candidates, 63 of them Gaullists or Gaullist-indorsed, were elected in the first balloting Nov. 18, 1962. The Gaullist candidates won 31.9% of the votes cast in the first round, a record plurality for any single French political group. Communist candidates received 21.78% of the first-round total, to elect nine deputies and become France's second party in terms of popular vote. Right-wing and conservative parties suffered heavy losses in the first round as did the center parties — the Socialists, Radicals and Catholic Popular Republican Movement (MRP).

This trend in the popular vote was reinforced by the second-round balloting held November 25 in the remaining 360 districts where no candidate had been elected November 18. In spite of the losses in votes, however, the Socialist and Radical Parties gained seats through second-round electoral alliances with other center-left groups.

Final results for the popular vote cast in the second-round balloting: Registered voters, 21,957,468. Valid ballots cast, 15,208,101. Abstentions, 27.9%. UNR-UDT, 6,165,929 (40.5%). Communists, 3,243,041 (21.3%). Extreme Left, 183,844 (1.2%). Socialists, 2,304,330 (15.2%). Radicals and Center Left, 1,068,101 (7%). MRP, 806,908 (5.3%). Independents, 1,361,853 (9%). Republican Center, 51,164 (0.4%). Extreme Right, 16,943 (0.1%).

Strength of each party in the new and old Assemblies (figures in parentheses indicate deputies pledged to support the UNR-UDT Gaullists):

Description	1958	1962
UNR-UDT	171	234
Communists	10	41
Extreme Left	2	5
Socialists	43	67
Radicals & Left Center........	43	44(9)
MRP	57	38
Independents	136	50(32)
Republican Center	3	1
Extreme Right	12	0

The overwhelming Gaullist victory was won largely at the expense of the extreme right and the traditional conservative parties. The rightest Unity of Republic party failed to elect a single deputy; the conservative Independent Party lost more than one-half its strength in the Assembly, and 32 of its elected deputies were pledged to support the Gaullist majority.

Of the non-Gaullist parties, only the Socialists and Communists made substantial gains in the new Assembly. This was due to the fact that Communist and Socialist candidates had observed a form of electoral alliance by withdrawing in each others' favor in those districts where the combined leftist vote was large enough to prevent the election of a Gaullist.

Forty-one of the 67 Socialists elected to the Assembly, including party leader Guy Mollet, owed their victories to the withdrawal of Communist candidates and the transferring of Communist support to their candidacies in the second balloting. Mollet, appearing in a radio debate November 12, had pledged that Socialists would withdraw in favor of Communist candidates wherever ths would make possible the defeat of a Gaullist. Considered a strong anti-Communist, Mollet had declared that France faced a greater danger from the election of a Gaullist majority than from the election of a few more Communist deputies.

Pompidou Renamed Premier. Premier Pompidou, whose resignation October 6 following a vote of censure had led to the dissolution of the Assembly and the elections, was reappointed premier by de Gaulle Nov. 27, 1962.

Cabinet Formed. De Gaulle December 6 announced the formation of a new cabinet. The cabinet, much the same as the previous one (only three new members were added while several other ministers changed portfolios), emphasized the government's desire to retain a continuity of policy, which de Gaulle believed the voters had indorsed in National Assembly elections.

The new cabinet was made up of sixteen UNR members (including the three new ministers), three Independent supporters of de Gaulle, one ex-Radical (Edgar Pisani, agriculture minister) and six non-political pro-de Gaulle "technicians." Roger Dusseaulx had been dropped from the cabinet as public works minister to become president of the UNR in the Assembly; Georges Gorse had been relieved as minister of cooperation with African states to become ambassador to Algeria.

The Algerian Affairs Ministry, formerly headed by Louis Joxe, was downgraded to that of a secretariat of state. Joxe was shifted to the post of administrative reform minister.

The new cabinet:

Premier— Georges Pompidou; *Ministers of State: Cultural Affairs*— Andre Malraux; *Overseas Departments and Territories*— Louis Jacquinot; *Administrative Reform*— Louis Joxe; *Scientific, Atomic and Space Questions*— Gaston Palewski. *Ministers: Foreign*— Maurice Couve de Murville; *Justice*— Jean Foyer; *Interior*— Roger Frey; *Armed Forces*— Pierre Messmer; *Finance and Economic Affairs*— Valery Giscard d'Estaing; *Cooperation with African States*— Raymond Triboulet, *National Education*— Christian Fouchet; *Public Works and Transport*— Marc Jacquet; *Industry*— Michel Maurice-Bokanowski; *Agriculture*— Edgar Pisani; *Labor*— Gilbert Grandval; *Public Health and Population*— Raymond Marcellin; *Housing*— Jacques Maziol; *Veterans and War Victims*— Jean Sainteny; *Postal Services and Telecommunications*— Jacques Marette; *Information*— Alain Peyrefitte; *Repatriates (from North Africa, including Algeria)*— Francois Missoffe. *Secretaries of State: Algerian Affairs*— Jean de Broglie; *Relations with Parliament*— Pierre Dumas; *Foreign*— Michel Habib-Deloncle; *Budget*— Robert Boulin.

Assembly Elects Speaker. The National Assembly December 6 elected Jacques Chaban-Delmas, a UNR leader, as speaker.

CHAPTER V
FRANCE AND WESTERN DEFENSE

ATOMIC POLICY AND NATO

De Gaulle's determination to equip France with an independent nuclear striking force and his demand that French influence in NATO be increased by French participation in a three-power NATO directorate clashed with U.S. and British efforts to create an integrated nuclear-armed NATO command.

Creation of an independent French nuclear striking force had been under discussion in France in the years prior to de Gaulle's return to power. France's first plutonium-producing atomic power plant began operation January 1956 at Marcoule in the Rhone Valley. The Saclay nuclear center (near Paris) announced construction of a nuclear powered submarine March 1957. Defense Minister Jacques Chaban-Delmas declared Nov. 20, 1957 that France might be forced to begin unilateral nuclear arms production to avert "its abdication as a world power."

U.S. Refuses Aid to French A-Weapons Program. U.S. Secretary of State John Foster Dulles flew to Paris July 4, 1958 and in a meeting with de Gaulle July 5 informed him that the United States would not be able to fulfill French requests for direct aid in development of French nuclear weapons. A French statement issued July 5 said that de Gaulle had "let no doubts remain as to the intention of his Government to raise France to the rank of the nuclear powers" and had "underlined the primary importance of this question."

Dulles, who had told newsmen in Washington July 3 that the United States would offer to sell France a nuclear submarine propulsion unit, made clear July 5 that liberalizing amendments to the U.S. Atomic Energy Act still would not permit the supply of U.S. nuclear weapon components to France. French cabinet spokesmen confirmed July 11 that Dulles and de Gaulle had reached agreement on supply of the nuclear submarine unit under the Mutual Security Program.

De Gaulle Urges NATO Triumvirate. Reports Oct. 25, 1958 said that the formation of a U.S.-British-French political directorate to coordinate NATO policies and extend NATO responsibility into new areas had been suggested by French Premier de Gaulle in personal messages September 14 to U.S. President Dwight D. Eisenhower and British Prime Minister Harold Macmillan.

De Gaulle's suggestion was said to have been formulated in reaction to the U.S. landing in Lebanon in July 1958 and U.S. support in the fall and winter of 1958 for the Chinese Nationalists regarding the offshore (Pecscadores, Matsu and Quemoy) islands in the Formosa Strait without prior consultation with other NATO powers. Although the French Foreign Minister asserted October 28 that de Gaulle had urged only formal and continuous U.S.-British-French consultation on policies affecting NATO, informants insisted that his plan centered on creation of a Big Three triumvirate above the NATO Council to oversee all Western foreign and defense policies.

U.S. Opposes De Gaulle Plan. NATO foreign ministers, attending a NATO ministerial council meeting in Paris December 16-18, failed to take any action on French proposals for establishment of a NATO political directorate after Secretary of State Dulles had met with Premier de Gaulle December 15 but had been unable to resolve French-U.S. differences over the plan. Dulles refused to commit the United States to support the directorate proposal, reportedly on grounds that it would lead to U.S.-British-French domination of NATO and was designed primarily to increase French prestige and power within the alliance.

France Cuts Navy Role. The NATO Permanent Council in Paris was informed by France March 11, 1959 that French Mediterranean Fleet units earmarked for NATO use in war would remain under French control. The French decision March 13 revoked a standing agreement to turn over 1/3 of the fleet for operation by the NATO Mediterranean Command in case of war.

De Gaulle March 25 at his semiannual Paris press conference explained the withdrawal of the Mediterranean Fleet from NATO control in wartime on grounds that NATO's "zone of action" did "not extend south of the Mediterranean" to areas of the Middle East, Africa and the Red Sea in which major French defense commitments were situated. He noted that Britain and the United States had maintained their principal naval and nuclear bomber forces outside NATO.

U.S. to Provide A-Fuel to French Sub Program. The White House announced May 7 the signing of an agreement providing for the sale of 440 kilograms of enriched uranium over a 10-year period for use as fuel in France's development of a land-based prototype of an atomic submarine power plant. No supply of U.S. secret atomic weapon information to France was called for in the agreement because of a Congressional prohibition against giving such data to any nation that did not have a substantial and proved atomic weapon capability.

(An agreement was also announced May 7 under which the United States would help Great Britain develop and produce atomic warheads and the missiles to deliver them; in addition, the United States would deliver non-nuclear parts of atomic warheads and design information on atomic submarines to Great Britain.)

France Demands A-Role. The French Foreign Ministry confirmed June 8, 1959 that France had refused to make any "new commitments with NATO" until settlement of "an ensemble of problems," including the stockpiling of nuclear weapons on French territory and aid in development and manufacture of a French nuclear weapons arsenal.

U.S. State Department officials told the Joint Congressional Atomic Energy Commission July 1 that they had no intention of seeking changes in the Atomic Energy Law to permit nations such as France a greater share in the American nuclear secrets or control of American nuclear weapons.

A-Bomb Program Advances. Defense Minister Pierre Guillaumat predicted in a TV address July 3 that France "soon will be able to have its atomic experiments" and "atomic bombs and thus become the fourth power to enter the nuclear club." He said that plutonium needed for a nuclear bomb was under production by nuclear reactors in the Marcoule atomic center.

U.S. Jets Moved from France. The NATO Permanent Council in Paris was informed July 8 that 200 U.S. Air Force jet fighter-bombers based at NATO airfields in France would be transferred to Britain and West Germany. The decision to remove the NATO jets from French bases stemmed from French refusal to permit the stockpiling of U.S. nuclear weapons or the construction of missile launching sites on French territory unless France was granted a share in control over the nuclear weapons and an increased role in NATO policies.

De Gaulle–Eisenhower Meeting. Following two days of talks in Paris, Presidents de Gaulle and Eisenhower Sept. 3, 1959 issued a communique indicating they had achieved fuller comprehension of each others' views without formal resolution of French demands for a greater voice in NATO affairs. Both leaders "stressed their devotion to the Atlantic alliance" and discussed "means of assuring a more efficient functioning of NATO."

De Gaulle vs. Military Integration. French intentions to withdraw from NATO's integrated military forces and to reconstitute national command of France's armed forces were made clear by President de Gaulle November 3. Addressing the French military Staff College, he declared that "if your country is forced to make war, it must be its war. It must defend itself by itself." De Gaulle warned that "the conception of defense in which France will no longer be itself is clearly unthinkable."

French plans to acquire nuclear warheads and missiles were defended by de Gaulle despite current international efforts to limit such weapons: "When one can destroy France from any part of the world, we must also be able to attack any point in the world."

A-Budget Presented. A $3.37 billion 1960 defense budget presented in the French National Assembly November 18 provided $308 million for the development of nuclear weapons and a French nuclear striking force. Eighty-five million dollars was earmarked for nuclear programs associated with weapons production, $81 million for production by 1966 of 50 Dassault Mirage IV long-range nuclear bombers, $122 million for 100 supersonic Mirage III jet fighters and $20 million for basic research and development of a French Intermediate Range Ballistic Missile.

French Role Attacked. A NATO Ministerial Council meeting convening in Paris Dec. 15, 1959 was presented with American charges that France's refusal to integrate its armed forces within NATO was weakening the alliance and could endanger European security.

The charges were made by General Nathan F. Twining, chairman of the U.S. Joint Chiefs of Staff, at a meeting of the NATO Military Committee in Paris December 9-10. Twining said France had hobbled NATO defenses by its refusal to implement 1957 agreements to accept U.S. nuclear missile bases and to integrate their air forces into a unified European air defense system by 1963.

Eisenhower–de Gaulle Meeting. A Paris meeting between Presidents Eisenhower and de Gaulle December 19-20 failed to resolve the Western military and political rift stemming from France's refusal to accept integration of NATO armed forces until the United States, Britain and France formed a NATO political directorate. Eisenhower was reported to have stressed his belief that integrated command of the armed forces of NATO states was essential if the alliance was to function effectively under modern warfare conditions.

De Gaulle reportedly defended the view that France must independently control its armed forces to meet military requirements in Africa and other areas beyond the NATO defense area. The de Gaulle-Eisenhower discussions officially were termed "inconclusive."

France Detonates A-Bomb. French scientists successfully detonated France's first atomic bomb — a plutonium device — Feb. 13, 1960 atop a 350-foot tower 28 miles south of Reggan, in the Sahara Desert. The test site was located 750 miles south of Algiers and 650 miles east of Casablanca.

The bomb, according to the French Armed Forces Ministry, produced an explosive force equivalent to 60,000-70,000 tons of TNT. The successful test made France the world's fourth nuclear power after the United States, the Soviet Union, and Great Britain.

De Gaulle Statement. President de Gaulle, in a jubilant message February 13 to Armed Forces Minister Guillaumat at the Reggan site, declared that as a result of the test, "France, thanks to her own national effort, can reinforce her defensive potential, that of the [French] Community and . . . of the West." France, he said, was in a "better position to further its actions toward the conclusion of agreements among the atomic powers with a view to achieving nuclear disarmament."

Test Criticized. News of the Sahara Atest brought a wave of criticism of France for carrying it out despite a 1959 UN General Assembly resolution opposing tests and the U.S.-British-Soviet test moratorium in effect since November 1958. African states expressed fears of the health danger from test-caused fallout.

De Gaulle declared February 26 in Narbonne that foreign criticism of the February 13 French nuclear test was "hysterical" and that some countries "which said nothing about the 199 preceding [nuclear] explosions accuse us of wanting to poison humanity."

Second A-Test. A "limited power" plutonium bomb described as compact and capable of being modified for military use was detonated by French technicians April 1, 1960 at a test site near Reggan in the Sahara Desert.

The bomb, reportedly of an explosive force equal to 19,000 tons of TNT, was exploded 13 miles south of the point at which the first French nuclear device was tested February 13. The government announced that the test was carried out under precautions to insure that "fallout presents no danger to the population."

First U.S. A-Fuel Shipment Set. A U.S. agreement to make available to France "something less than 30 kilograms" of enriched uranium-235 for research on an experimental nuclear submarine engine was disclosed in Paris April 15 at the end of a tour of French atomic installations by U.S. Atomic Energy Commission Chairman John A. McCone. The nuclear fuel shipment would be the first under a May 7, 1959 agreement for the supply of 440 kilograms of fission material. The agreement implied continuation of the U.S. position that France had not made "substantial progress" in its nuclear research and hence was not entitled to receive classified U.S. data or materials for direct use in building a nuclear submarine power plant.

France Rejects NATO A-Missiles. NATO Secretary-General Paul-Henri Spaak met July 21 with French President de Gaulle in a renewed effort to win agreement for the deployment of Polaris Intermediate Range Ballistic Missiles in France under NATO control. Spaak was said to have offered to place other missiles under exclusively French control. De Gaulle was said to have rejected the compromise.

H-Bomb Program Presented. A four-year, $2.3 billion program to equip France with an independent hydrogen and atomic bomb striking force was presented to the National Assembly's Finance Commission by Premier Michel Debre July 23 with the warning that modern states were faced with the choice of becoming nuclear powers or "satellites."

De Gaulle Calls for NATO Revision. President de Gaulle Sept. 5, 1960 called for a major reshaping of the NATO alliance into a political and military association that would preserve its member states' "national character." Addressing French cabinet members and 650 newsmen at his semi-annual Paris news conference, de Gaulle said the NATO treaty must be revised on two basic points: "The first, the limitation of the alliance to the zone of Europe: We consider that, at least between the world powers of the West, something should be organized from the point of view of the alliance as to their political and...strategic behavior elsewhere than in Europe, and particularly in the Middle East and in Africa, where these three powers [the United States, Britain and France] are continually implicated. The second point...is that of integration as regards the defense of Europe. It appears to us that the defense of a country, while certainly being combined with that of other countries...must have a national character."

A-Bomb Veto Demanded. De Gaulle declared October 7 that France would demand the right to veto the use of nuclear weapons by any NATO member state in any future conflict. Speaking in Grenoble, de Gaulle made clear the French position in the deadlocked NATO effort to base nuclear missiles in France under joint French-U.S. control. He said: "France intends that if, by misfortune, atomic bombs were to be dropped in the world, none would be dropped by the free world's side unless she [France] should have accepted it, and that, from her soil, no atomic bomb should be launched unless she herself should have decided it."

French A-Force Voted. A 1961 military budget providing $1.2 billion through 1964 for initial development of a French nuclear striking force was passed on second reading by the French National Assembly November 22, when a censure motion opposing the measure received only 214 of the 277 votes required for adoption. The bill, which had been rejected by the French Senate November 10 by a 186-83 vote, was sent to the Senate again November 22. The Senate could delay but not prevent adoption of the measure on its third and final reading in the Assembly.

U.S. Proposes Joint NATO A-Control. U.S. proposals to grant NATO political authority over nuclear weapons assigned to European defense tasks were announced Nov. 21, 1960 in Paris by General Lauris Norstad, NATO supreme commander. Norstad, speaking to the annual advisory conference of NATO parliamentarians, declared that the establishment of joint NATO control over allied nuclear weapons would be "a great and dramatic new step."

Norstad asserted that measures to give NATO control over the nuclear weapons used in NATO defense would (a) calm European fears that the weapons might be launched by the United States for objectives not shared by the alliance's European members, (b) make impossible a U.S. withdrawal of its nuclear weapons from Europe or a U.S. hesitancy to use them in Europe's defense for fear of provoking Soviet nuclear attack directly against the U.S., (c) "lead certain nations (France) to give up their desire to create their own nuclear force" under purely national control.

French A-Force Enacted. President de Gaulle's plans for establishing an independent French atomic striking force were enacted into law December 6. The measure, rejected for the second time by the French Senate November 30, became law when it came before the National Assembly for the third reading and a censure motion opposing it received only 215 of the 277 votes required for adoption.

Third A-Test. France set off its third nuclear explosion above the ground Dec. 27, 1960. The test — of a compact device reported to be a prototype of an operational atomic weapon — was carried out at the Sahara test site near Reggan, in southwestern Algeria. It was reported from Paris December 27 that the device tested was a plutonium bomb with an explosive force equivalent to 10,000 to 14,000 tons of TNT.

De Gaulle Reaffirms Opposition to A-Integration. President de Gaulle restated France's policies toward NATO nuclear strategy at his semiannual Paris news conference held April 11, 1961. De Gaulle said:

> It is the duty and the right of . . . European powers to have their own national defense. It is intolerable to a great nation that its destiny be left to the decisions . . . of another nation, however friendly. The question of the use of nuclear weapons by the two nations [a reference to U. S. and British nuclear armed missiles] that have them . . . must be clarified, for the continental European powers who are much more vulnerable must know exactly with what weapons and in what conditions their overseas allies will take part in the common battle.

De Gaulle's request for clarification was a clear reference to changing concepts of nuclear strategy advanced by the Kennedy Administration. In a series of statements issued in April, the Kennedy administration had made clear that it was studying a new and more flexible nuclear strategy that would avoid involving the world in general nuclear war in response to any Soviet attack on NATO, however limited. The new Administration's strategic proposals, in contrast to the Eisenhower-Dulles strategy of "massive retaliation," would involve a substantial increase in NATO conventional forces to strengthen NATO's ability to meet a non-nuclear attack with non-nuclear forces and a decision not to order the use of nuclear weapons unless a Soviet conventional attack was of a greater intensity than NATO conventional forces previously had been able to withstand. In an address April 10 at a Washington meeting of the NATO Military Committee, President Kennedy said: "NATO needs to be able to respond to any conventional attack with conventional resistance which will be effective at least long enough...to force a pause." "In our studies we have found a serious need for a sensitive and flexible control of all arms, and especially over nuclear weapons...."

Fourth A-Test. France's fourth atomic device was detonated April 25 at Reggan in the Sahara. The French Atomic Energy Commission announced Oct. 7, 1961 that its series of nuclear tests in the atmosphere had been completed.

French-U.S. A-Agreement. U.S. President John F. Kennedy October 4 signed a resolution authorizing the U.S. government to train French military forces in the use of and defense against atomic weapons. The resolution, implementing a Franco-American agreement, also permitted the transfer to French NATO forces of non-nuclear parts of atomic weapons systems (but not parts of atomic weapons). Similar agreements had been negotiated with six other NATO nations.

U.S. Commits A-Armed Subs; France Derides Action. The United States informed its NATO allies May 5, 1962 that it had committed five nuclear-powered submarines and their complement of 80 Polaris missiles, each presumably equipped with a nuclear warhead, to operational command of NATO Supreme Allied Headquarters, Atlantic.

The announcement was made by U.S. Defense Secretary Robert S. McNamara at a closed session of the NATO Council's spring ministerial meeting, convened May 4 in Athens, Greece. The commitment was made subject to the same terms under which other U.S. nuclear forces were assigned to NATO: the submarines would remain vessels of the U.S. Navy but would receive orders through Admiral Robert C. Dennison, NATO Atlantic commander; the submarines' complement of nuclear warheads would remain under the exclusive control of the U.S. president.

McNamara was reported to have presented the Council with a U.S. pledge to eventually assign all 41 planned Polaris nuclear submarines to the NATO command. In addition, the United States agreed to provide all NATO states with detailed information on U.S. nuclear deterrent forces and the standing criteria for their potential use to defend the alliance.

French Foreign Minister Maurice Couve de Murville was quoted as telling the Council May 5 that it was "intellectually dishonest" to "pretend" that the U.S. statement of nuclear intent was a new policy. The French delegation contended that as long as the exclusive right to order use of the Polaris weapons remained in the hands of the U.S. president, there had been no basic alteration of Western nuclear policy. It was made clear that France would continue its program for creation of its own nuclear striking force.

First Underground A-Test. The French government confirmed May 8 that it had carried out its first underground nuclear test explosion in the Sahara Desert May 1. The test took place in the Hoggar Mountains, 500 miles south of the usual French atomic test site at Reggan, in the central Sahara.

De Gaulle Reaffirms Nuclear Independence. France's determination to become a nuclear military power so that "whatever happens," Frenchmen would "have our own share of our own destiny," was proclaimed by President de Gaulle May 15 at his semi-annual Paris news conference.

The French leader's words were considered an open challenge to the U.S.' past predominance — both politically and in terms of nuclear armaments — within the NATO alliance. They were viewed as a warning that France no longer would accept dependence on U.S. pledges, however sincere, for the nuclear defense of Europe.

In his review of the reasoning behind France's demand for reshaping of the Western alliance, de Gaulle said: NATO had been founded and built during a period when the U.S.' virtual monopoly of nuclear armaments made it in fact the guarantor of Europe's security against Soviet aggression; but the Soviet Union had succeeded in building an "enormous nuclear armament" and thus both East and West now were "in a position to strike each other . . . and even to put each other to death, or something close to it"; the Soviet-American nuclear monopoly had subjected all nations to the danger of annihilation and had made it impossible to achieve purposeful solution of the world's major problems; within this situation, France intended to "achieve what appears to be possible to her and what is within her reach" and to assure a share in its own destiny by construction of a national nuclear striking force; this "modest" French force is going to change "the conditions of long-range intervention and the conditions of the aid we can give our allies."

JFK Opposes de Gaulle. The United States' rejection of de Gaulle's formula for revision of the NATO alliance and of Europe's post-war ties with America was made clear by U.S. President Kennedy May 17. He told a Washington news conference: "We do not believe in a series of [atomic] deterrents. We believe that the NATO deterrent . . . provides very adequate protection. Once you begin, nation after nation . . . feeling that it is necessary as an element of independence to develop a separate deterrence, it seems to me that you are moving into an increasingly dangerous situation. First you have France and then another country and then another, until a very solid and, I think, effective defense alliance may be weakened."

French Leaders and Rusk Confer on A-Force. U.S. Secretary of State Dean Rusk conferred in Paris June 19-21, 1962 with President de Gaulle and Foreign Minister Couve de Murville.

It was reported from Paris June 20 that Rusk had delivered a U.S. proposal for study of coordination of a future French nuclear force with the U.S.-British nuclear deterrent committed to NATO. Couve de Murville was said to have replied that the French force inevitably would be coordinated with those possessed by other Western powers, but that the matter still was premature.

French sources were said to have expressed satisfaction at the implication, basic to the Rusk proposals, that the United States had accepted the inevitability of a nuclear armed France.

Assembly Approves Uranium Plant. A government appropriations bill providing $40 million for the start of a $900 million isotope separation plant in Pierrelatte in the Rhone Valley was approved by the National Assembly without vote July 25. The plant was needed to supply fission materials for France's planned nuclear arsenal. An opposition motion censuring the Pompidou government for its plans to provide France with an independent nuclear force had been defeated July 17 when it won only 206 votes, 35 short of a majority.

Nuclear Strategy Disclosed. A Defense Ministry report made public September 21 revealed that France planned a radical reshaping of its armed forces into three nuclear war commands by 1970. These would be a nuclear strategic force, a force of intervention and a force of defense. The strategic force would be equipped with nuclear weapons and a small fleet of Mirage IV jet bombers by 1964; this would be supplemented by nuclear-armed strategic missiles in 1964-70. This force, the report said, would be "a major instrument of the policy of the government, freed of any external dependence, but capable of employment within the framework of the (NATO) alliance; it can act at any moment, any place." (The establishment of a French Strategic Air Command had been announced February 24.)

U.S.-French A-Sub Pact Reported. The *New York Times* reported Oct. 16, 1962 that the United States was planning to sell France a nuclear-powered submarine, an action promised by the Eisenhower Administration in July 1958 but dropped due to Congressional opposition. The report was confirmed by the French government October 17 but not by the United States.

According to the *Times*, the submarine was to be one of the Nautilus-type attack craft, not a missile-launching type. The agreement for the sale of the submarine was said to have been negotiated in September at a meeting of U.S. Deputy Defense Secretary Roswell Gilpatric and French Defense Minister Pierre Messmer.

Representative Chet Holifield (D. Calif.), chairman of the Joint Congressional Atomic Energy Committee, assailed the reported agreement October 17. Holifield said: His committee had not been informed of the plan; he opposed the transfer of nuclear weapons and secrets to "nations whose political structure is unstable and whose security capability is questionable."

NATO Ministers Deadlocked on A-Policy. The NATO Ministerial Council, at its annual winter meeting in Paris Dec. 13-15, 1962, debated but failed to settle a mounting controversy over proposals for reshaping the West's U.S.-controlled nuclear deterrent forces. The Council took no action in the disputes generated by the French decision to build an independent nuclear striking force.

The Council instead affirmed — without making precise its commitment — its support of the United States' contention that the primary task of the alliance's European members should be the strengthening of the NATO conventional forces promised by these nations.

Nassau Pact: U.S. and Britain Agree on Unified NATO A-Force. President Kennedy and British Prime Minister Macmillan announced December 21 that they had reached agreement on steps toward creating a unified Western nuclear force. The Kennedy-Macmillan accord, produced during a meeting December 18-21 in Nassau, the Bahamas, pledged that U.S. and British atomic weapons and military units would be assigned to "a multilateral NATO nuclear force (to be formed) in the closest consultation with other NATO allies."

Although the United States previously had offered to assign Polaris missile submarines to NATO control, this was the first time that the two major Western nuclear powers had agreed to commit units jointly from their nationally-controlled atomic forces to form the core of a NATO nuclear force.

The agreement was based on British acceptance of a U.S. offer to provide Polaris missiles for a future British nuclear force which, together with equivalent U.S. units, would be merged into the proposed NATO force. The agreement was viewed as the first step toward a new effort to persuade France to abandon its planned national nuclear force and to join in the new unified striking force, or eventually to accept a similar pact for the provision of Polaris missiles under terms that would subject France to NATO control of its nuclear arms.

De Gaulle Rebuff Predicted. French government sources reported December 27 that President de Gaulle had decided to reject President Kennedy's offer to supply Polaris missiles for a French nuclear force integrated within NATO.

(President de Gaulle was informed of the terms of the Kennedy-Macmillan agreement December 21 by the U.S. and British ambassadors in Paris. De Gaulle conferred with Premier Pompidou, Foreign Minister Couve de Murville and Defense Minister Messmer December 22 on the implications for France of the agreement. The AP reported that the United States had invited France to accept Polaris missiles on the same basis as had been offered Britain. The AP said the offer had been made in a letter transmitted from President Kennedy to de Gaulle December 21.)

De Gaulle was said to have informed his senior aides that the offer was unacceptable because: (1) NATO integration of French atomic units would end their role as an independent national nuclear force; (2) although the planned French nuclear bomber force would be less effective than a Polaris missile-armed submarine fleet, the bomber fleet could be operational by the end of 1963, whereas France could not build an effective Polaris fleet or the missile warheads required for it before 1970.

In a New Year's eve TV address to the French people, de Gaulle made no mention of the U.S. offer but emphasized that France's planned nuclear force was intended to insure its security and contribute to that of the West.

EAST-WEST RELATIONS: BERLIN AND THE GERMAN PROBLEM

USSR Reopens Berlin Question. Soviet Premier Nikita Khrushchev, in a Moscow speech Nov. 10, 1958, called on the United States, Britain and France to "give up the remnants of the occupation regime in (West) Berlin and thus make it possible to create a normal atmosphere in the (East German) capital." The USSR, said Khrushchev, would hand over its occupation functions in East Berlin to the "sovereign" East German regime. In what was an apparent effort to obtain Western recognition for the Soviet supported East German regime, Khrushchev suggested that the Western powers "form their own relations with the...(East

German government)...if they are interested in certain questions connected with Berlin," presumably those involving Western road, railway, and air access to West Berlin.

The United States, Britain, and France rejected Khrushchev's call for a Western evacuation of Berlin. A French Foreign Ministry statement November 21 said France was "determined to stay in Berlin...to guarantee the will to freedom of the West Berliners."

USSR for "Free City"; Six-Month Ultimatum. The Soviet government proposed November 27 that West Berlin be made into a "free city" independent of either East or West Germany. Soviet notes handed to the U.S., British, French and West German ambassadors in Moscow by Foreign Minister Andrei A. Gromyko proposed that West Berlin be made "an independent political entity—a free city"—demilitarized and separate from "either of the existing German states."

The USSR warned that it would turn all Soviet occupation functions over to the East German government at the end of the six-month period if the Western powers had not accepted the free city proposal. It specifically renounced Allied agreements signed Sept. 12, 1944 and May 1, 1945 providing for four-power occupation and control of Greater Berlin. It made clear that Soviet military authorities would cease their Berlin duties at the end of six months and that the East German government then would "fully control...its sovereignty on land, on water and in the air."

West Rejects Soviet Demand. The Soviet demand for liquidation of the postwar military occupation of Berlin and for creation of a free city of West Berlin were formally rejected Dec. 31, 1958 by the United States, Britain and France in notes delivered to the Soviet Foreign Ministry. The Western powers instead proposed renewed East-West efforts to settle the Berlin dispute as part of broad negotiations for a reunified Germany, a German peace treaty and a European security settlement.

France and West Germany Adopt Tough Line. West German Chancellor Konrad Adenauer and President de Gaulle conferred near Paris March 4, 1959 to align French-West German opposition to any substantial concession to the USSR on Germany. The meeting resulted in what was described as a French-West German "axis" opposed to flexibility in East-West talks and to proposals, primarily advanced by Britain, for the disengagement of NATO and Warsaw Pact forces in Europe. De Gaulle was said to have backed Adenauer's rejection of any proposed East-West agreement on Germany which depended on revision of the current status of Berlin, recognition of East Germany or the withdrawal of West Germany from NATO.

De Gaulle States Views on Germany. Addressing his first presidential press conference, General de Gaulle expressed his support March 25 for an East-West summit conference to settle the German problem. He made clear, however, that French participation in a summit meeting depended upon "the elements of an accord on important points" by a prior East-West foreign ministers' conference. In so doing, he ranged France with West Germany against British views that a summit meeting should be held even if the foreign ministers' conference failed to show progress toward agreement on major East-West problems.

Other major French policies were stated by de Gaulle in these terms:

● France was "not prepared to recognize this (East German) regime as a sovereign and independent state because it could not...exist except by virtue of the Soviet occupation and...an implacable dictatorship." France would support the "reunion of the two parts into a single Germany which would be entirely free...provided that they do not call into question their present frontiers in the west, the east, the north and the south and that they move toward integrating themselves...in a contractual organization of all Europe."

● France was opposed to proposals for "disengagement" or for "turning Germany into a neutralized territory." An acceptable disarmament plan must extend over "an area deep enough and large enough for France to be covered and not [left militarily]...exposed." An effective East-West disarmament zone must reach "as near to the Urals as it is to the Atlantic" to maintain the existing strategic balance between NATO and Warsaw Pact forces.

Western Foreign Ministers' Berlin Accord. The foreign ministers of the United States, Britain, France and West Germany announced April 30 that they had reached complete agreement on Western strategy to be followed in East-West Geneva talks on Germany and Berlin. Ending two days of talks in Paris, U.S. Secretary of State Christian Herter and Foreign Ministers Selwyn Lloyd of Britain, Maurice Couve de Murville of France and Heinrich von Brentano of West Germany reaffirmed "their willingness to enter into negotiations with the Soviet Union with a view to establishing a just and durable peace in Europe." But they made clear that until an agreement was reached with the USSR on Germany and Europe, the West was determined "to maintain the freedom of the people of West Berlin and the rights and obligations there of the Allied powers."

EAST-WEST GENEVA CONFERENCE

Foreign Ministers Convene. The foreign ministers of the United States, Britain, France and the USSR met in Geneva May 11, 1959 to begin East-West talks on the problems of Berlin, German reunification, an all-German peace treaty and European security. The conference was intended as a preliminary to a possible meeting of East-West heads of government.

French Position Stated. Foreign Minister Couve de Murville declared May 13: the "present conference has been convened...to try to dispel" the crisis caused by "measures taken by the Soviet Government over the past six months." "The concern which the Soviet Government states that it feels today in regard to Berlin merely corroborates what we have been saying...for...15 years—namely, that there can be no real security and stability in Europe until there is an overall settlement of the German problem," which remained "the responsibility of the four powers represented around this table."

Conference Deadlocked on Western, Soviet Plans. The conference reached a deadlock May 18 after the presentation of conflicting Western and Soviet plans for resolving German and European security problems.

The two proposals made to the conference:

●*A Western plan,* presented May 14 by U.S. Secretary of State Herter for the reunification of Berlin and Germany and the establishment of a European security system. The Western plan envisioned a four-stage plan for a "permanent settlement in Europe": Stage I — East and West Berlin to be reunited through free elections held under four-power or UN supervision; Stage II — A "mixed German committee" composed of members from both East and West Germany would work to expand contact between both parts of Germany and would prepare for ratification by plebiscite in both parts of Germany a draft law providing for general free and secret elections; Stage III — Elections would be held for an all-German assembly in both parts of Germany. The assembly would draft an all-German constitution and establish an all-German government on the basis of the constitution; Stage IV — A "final peace settlement" would be concluded with "a government representing all Germany."

●*A Soviet plan,* submitted May 15 by Foreign Minister Gromyko calling for the negotiation of separate World War II peace treaties with the East and West German governments before the unification of Germany or a Berlin settlement.

Both the Western and Soviet plans were rejected May 18 by Soviet Foreign Minister Gromyko and U.S. Secretary of State Herter. Gromyko said the Western plan was "utterly unacceptable," particularly in its suggestions for rapid reunification of Berlin. Herter said that the Soviet plan would lead to the permanent division of Germany. French Foreign Minister Couve de Murville May 19 reiterated the West's rejection of the Soviet plan.

Berlin Deadline Passed. The six-month Soviet ultimatum for the dissolution of the Allied occupation regime in Berlin expired May 27 without any overt Soviet attempts to force Western troops to withdraw from the city or to close Western military access routes to Berlin from West Germany.

Deadlock Persists; Talks Recess. The conference was reported to be near a breakdown June 10 following Western and Soviet rejection of each others' proposals for a Berlin settlement. The conference was recessed June 20 until July 13.

Conference Resumes; Deadlocked; Recessed Indefinitely. In a concluding statement to the conference, U.S. Secretary of State Herter said Aug. 5, 1959 that it had succeeded in isolating a number of specific differences which, if reconciled by future negotiations, "should lead to an agreement which will give real hope for a secure position for … West Berlin" and for "overcoming the continued division of Germany." Final addresses by British Foreign Secretary Lloyd and Soviet Foreign Minister Gromyko stressed that forthcoming Eisenhower-Khrushchev talks could prepare the way for a German settlement. (President Eisenhower had announced August 3 that Soviet Premier Khrushchev would make an official visit to the United States in September.) French Foreign Minister Couve de Murville reiterated the view that "the German people must have the last word" on any agreement to unify Germany:

French Oppose U.S.-Soviet Deal. French Premier Michel Debre warned August 16 that France would "make herself heard" in order to "avoid being crushed by agreements between very great powers." Debre made clear that he was referring to the danger posed by "visits by chiefs of state...carefully organized between Moscow and Washington." Debre asserted that increasingly independent French policies represented a reaction against alliances leading France into "bondage" to foreign powers.

Paris dispatches August 14 reported that President de Gaulle, at a recent cabinet meeting, had criticized Mr. Eisenhower's invitation to Khrushchev to visit the United States as that of a "lone horseman" seeking talks with the enemy camp. (A Soviet government memorandum delivered to de Gaulle August 17 by Soviet Ambassador to France Sergei A. Vinogradov was said to have expressed sympathy with French demands for greater world recognition but was known to be critical of French-West German political cooperation.)

De Gaulle Seeks East-West Summit Delay. In a cabinet statement said to have been written by President de Gaulle, the French government Oct. 21, 1959 called for postponement of a projected East-West summit conference until the spring of 1960.

(At the conclusion of Khrushchev's visit to the United States, Eisenhower September 28 declared that his talks with Khrushchev had "removed many of the objections that I have heretofore held" against an East-West summit meeting. A positive decision to go to the summit was, he said, "a matter for negotiation and consultation with our allies.")

The French statement urged delay of the talks to "preserve all the chances for a confrontation...that could be decisive for peace." It held that "before such a conference there should be...an effective reduction of tension." It indicated de Gaulle's view that a summit conference should be "preceded by meetings among them (the Western powers)...without haste."

Paris dispatches reported October 21 that Khrushchev had agreed to meet de Gaulle in Paris before a summit meeting. Khrushchev's acceptance of a French invitation to Paris was said to have been conveyed to de Gaulle October 20 by Soviet Ambassador to France Vinogradov. The French proposal to delay a summit meeting was attributed to (1) de Gaulle's desire to have personal contact with Khrushchev and to achieve an Algerian settlement in advance of summit talks, and (2) French hopes to test a nuclear weapon early in 1960 and to attend the conference as a full nuclear power.

U.S. Opposes Delay. President Eisenhower indicated his disappointment October 21 at the French attempt to postpone a summit meeting. Eisenhower's displeasure was implied in a White House statement, issued after learning of the French statement, that he was ready to attend "a Western summit meeting with our allies...any time from now on."

France Presses Summit Delay. French demands for delay of an East-West summit meeting were reiterated October 27 in statements made to the Senate by Premier Debre and to the National Assembly by Foreign Minister Couve de Murville.

The statements stressed that France was awaiting "favorable signs" that would indicate that an East-West meeting would have "fruitful perspectives." It asserted that the Eisenhower-Khrushchev meetings were only a "first step" toward the "improvement of the world climate" that France considered "necessary...for a meeting at the supreme level." It reiterated that preparations for a summit meeting would take "time and care" and that France would favor holding the conference "next spring."

French demands for a summit postponement were supported by West German Chancellor Adenauer. Adenauer October 25 called for a delay in the East-West summit to permit careful Western preparation.

De Gaulle Delays East-West Summit. The East-West summit meeting was considered to have been delayed until April or May 1960 following the disclosure by President de Gaulle Nov. 10, 1959 that Soviet Premier Khrushchev would arrive in Paris March 15 for a pre-summit visit to France.

De Gaulle, at his second presidential press conference, welcomed plans for a Western summit meeting in December but made clear that "it would be desirable for us to meet again" (presumably after Khrushchev's French visit) before the East-West talks.

Acknowledging that "some signs of an easing of the [East-West] situation are visible on the part of the Soviet world," de Gaulle laid down these three conditions for summit talks:

●The "improvement in international relations must continue during the coming months, so that heads of state may be able to talk in an atmosphere of relaxation and not of crisis."

●The "Western heads of state...should have reached understanding beforehand on the questions to be dealt with and the common position they will take up on each item."

●There must be "personal contact between...Khrushchev and myself...and our Government" to enable "Russia and France...to exchange (views) on the world problems which beset both countries."

Western Summit Meeting; East-West Summit Set. In a three-day Western summit meeting held in Paris Dec. 19-21, 1959, Eisenhower, British Prime Minister Harold Macmillan, de Gaulle and Adenauer agreed that an East-West Big Four summit conference (Germany excluded) should be held in Paris beginning April 27, 1960.

Separate but similar summit invitations from Eisenhower, Macmillan and de Gaulle were delivered to Khrushchev in Moscow December 21. The messages made clear that the Paris meeting was intended to be the first of a series of East-West summit conferences to seek solution of major disputes between the West and Soviet bloc.

An agreement to convene an East-West summit meeting in Paris May 16, 1960 was reached in an exchange of notes December 25-30 by the United States, Britain, France and the USSR.

KHRUSHCHEV VISITS FRANCE

Arrival in Paris. Soviet Premier Khrushchev flew to Paris March 23, 1960 for a visit to France. Khrushchev, accompanied by a government delegation headed by Foreign Minister Gromyko and Deputy Premier Alexei N. Kosygin, was greeted at Paris' Orly Airport by President de Gaulle, Premier Debre and his cabinet and the heads of government of most French Community states. Khrushchev received a polite but not enthusiastic welcome from an estimated 80,000 persons as he drove with de Gaulle into Paris through its Communist-dominated working class suburbs.

At least 16,000 special police and security guards had been mobilized in Paris and along Khrushchev's route into the city to prevent anti-Soviet incidents. Anti-Communist East European refugees had been rounded up and sent to Corsica for the duration of the Khrushchev visit, and police March 22 had arrested twelve extremists and leaders of a campaign protesting the visit.

Warnings About Germany. In a series of speeches on his arrival March 23, Khrushchev sounded the major political theme of his French visit — that a rebirth of German militarism threatened France and Europe and could be stopped most effectively by a French-Soviet alliance based on principles of peaceful coexistence.

In a toast to de Gaulle and France at an Elysee Palace state dinner March 23, Khrushchev said: "We know that in France you are aware... of the threat of a [German] revenge... and want to prevent the growth of this threat by different methods from ours." "We are of the opinion that, so that militarism and aggression should no longer threaten the peace of Europe, it is necessary to finish with the last traces of the second World War and to conclude a peace treaty with Germany.... All the former partners of the anti-Hitler coalition would gain from it, as well as the German people."

Political Talks Begin. Khrushchev and de Gaulle held formal political discussions March 24-25 at the Elysee Palace.

Khrushchev told a meeting of the French Diplomatic Press Association March 25 that he and de Gaulle were at "opposite poles" in their views on politics and social organization. Khrushchev expressed admiration for de Gaulle and support for his Algerian self-determination policy but implied his disagreement with most French foreign policy. French spokesmen told newsmen the two leaders' views on Germany were so conflicting that no real negotiation had been possible.

Meeting later March 25 with French National Assembly deputies who were members of various French-Soviet friendship groups, Khrushchev denounced Chancellor Adenauer's efforts to create a French-West German partnership, which, he said, was directed primarily against the USSR. "The courtship that West Germany is making toward France does not fill us with joy," he declared. Khrushchev admitted that he had come to France with the hope that he could prevent the total rearmament of West Germany. He asserted that if he succeeded in preventing the repetition of pre-World War II history, "I will have fulfilled my duty toward the Soviet people."

Provincial Tour. Khrushchev left Paris March 26 for a six-day tour of the French provinces. As in Paris, Khrushchev devoted his time to carrying Soviet warnings against German militarism to the greatest possible number of Frenchmen. He returned to Paris March 31 for final talks with de Gaulle.

Talks End Without Accord. Khrushchev ended his 12-day visit to France and returned to Moscow April 3 after failing to agree with de Gaulle on any major East-West problems. Khrushchev and de Gaulle held two days of talks April 1-2 at de Gaulle's presidential chateau in Rambouillet, 35 miles southeast of Paris. Parallel talks were carried out in Paris April 1-2 by Foreign Ministers Gromyko and Couve de Murville and other French and Soviet officials on trade and cultural and scientific exchange accords announced by Khrushchev and de Gaulle April 2.

A joint communique issued by de Gaulle and Khrushchev April 2 disclosed that de Gaulle had accepted an invitation to visit the USSR but made clear that no accord had been reached on the key problems of disarmament, Germany or European security.

The French-Soviet trade accord outlined by the communique provided for negotiations on a "long-term commercial agreement" for "a substantial increase in trade between the two countries during the coming years." French and Soviet trade experts were to meet during 1960 to plan expansion of the current French-Soviet agreement (1960-62) and to prepare a continuing accord for trade through 1965. (French-Soviet trade during 1959 was valued at $100 million.)

De Gaulle in Britain, Canada; East-West Summit Discussed. President de Gaulle and Foreign Minister Couve de Murville visited England April 5-8, 1960 and held talks with Prime Minister Harold Macmillan and Foreign Secretary Selwyn Lloyd centering on Khrushchev's visit to France and on Western policy at the scheduled May summit meeting.

De Gaulle and Couve de Murville arrived in Ottawa April 18 to begin a 17-day visit to Canada, the United States and French possessions in the Caribbean and South America.

In a televised address at an Ottawa luncheon, de Gaulle said April 19 that France favored postponing a final effort to solve the German problem in order to concentrate, at the Paris summit meeting, on disarmament. The West, he said, must avoid any "insoluble" debate or "threat in connection... with the problem of the German people."

De Gaulle met with Prime Minister John Diefenbaker and the Canadian cabinet April 19 for political talks centering on the Paris summit meeting. He flew to Quebec April 20 and to Montreal and Toronto April 21 to complete the four-day Canadian visit.

DE GAULLE VISITS UNITED STATES

Greeted in Washington. De Gaulle flew to Washington from Toronto April 22. He was welcomed by President Eisenhower and enthusiastic crowds estimated at 200,000. Eisenhower, greeting de Gaulle as the president of both France and the French Community, said that the United States was as eager "for the development of those countries under the sponsorship of France as is France herself."

At a news conference at the National Press Club April 23, de Gaulle outlined French hopes for an East-West "detente." His major points:

● "It does not seem possible" to solve either "all the German problems or ... the Berlin problem in particular" at the Paris summit meeting. "It is highly possible ... after the passage of time" that an acceptable "modus vivendi will appear."

● "It seems to me that the efforts to reach a detente should focus on nuclear weapons and ... (should) be limited to reciprocal control of rockets, strategic aircraft and ships capable of carrying nuclear weapons." In this area "I think it is still possible to do something practical."

● "Germany, as it stands today, threatens no one. France in particular does not feel the least bit threatened by the Germany of Chancellor Adenauer ... And I do not think that Soviet Russia has any reason to feel threatened by the Germany of today."

Camp David Talks. De Gaulle and Eisenhower flew April 24 to Eisenhower's Camp David retreat for private talks. A statement issued April 24 by the two presidents asserted that they had reached agreement "as to how we should proceed at the summit meeting." They returned to Washington later April 24 and renewed their discussions at the White House April 25. Parallel pre-summit talks were held in Washington April 24-25 by Secretary of State Herter and Foreign Minister Couve de Murville. A final communique was issued April 25 but did not mention matters discussed by de Gaulle and Eisenhower.

Addresses Congress. In an address April 25 before a joint session of Congress, de Gaulle reiterated his belief that "there is no other hope for the future of our species" than "to destroy these [nuclear] weapons by common consent, ... not to manufacture any others [and] to open up all territories to reciprocal supervision." De Gaulle warned that "failing the renunciation of atomic armaments by those states who are provided with them," France "will be obliged to equip itself with such armaments ... [And] how many others will attempt to do the same?"

Applauded enthusiastically by Congress, de Gaulle declared: "What a sigh of relief would pass across the globe if, ... above their rivalries, these great states [of East and West] establish practical cooperation" to aid "development of the unfavored masses of Asia and ... Africa."

De Gaulle paid a farewell visit to President Eisenhower at the White House April 26 before beginning a tour of the United States.

U.S. Tour. New York: De Gaulle was given an enthusiastic welcome by an estimated 1,000,000 onlookers as he arrived in New York April 26 and rode along the traditional Broadway parade route. In two addresses April 26 — at a New York civic luncheon and at a dinner given by French-American organizations — de Gaulle repeated his pleas for nuclear disarmament and a world aid program.

San Francisco: De Gaulle flew to San Francisco April 27. More than 250,000 San Franciscans gave de Gaulle what he termed "an unforgettable lesson" in Franco-U.S. amity.

New Orleans: De Gaulle was given a floodlit welcoming parade and military review, attended by 100,000 persons in New Orleans April 28.

(De Gaulle ended his Western Hemisphere visit with stops in Cayenne, French Guiana April 30, Fort-de-France, Martinique May 1 and Pointe-a-Pitre, Guadeloupe May 2. He flew to Paris May 3.)

Western Pre-Summit talks. The Western foreign ministers met in Washington April 12-14, 1960 to seek unified positions on the problem of Berlin and Germany and for the East-West summit meeting scheduled to open in Paris May 11.

The talks were conducted by U.S. Secretary of State Herter and Foreign Ministers Lloyd of Britain, Couve de Murville of France and von Brentano of West Germany, who joined the talks April 13. No communique on Berlin was issued, but newsmen reported that agreement had been reached on a plan for phased reunification of Berlin and then East and West Germany.

U-2 Incident; East-West Summit Collapses

USSR Downs U.S. Spy Plane; Krushchev Threatens Summit. A U.S. U-2 high-altitude jet reconnaissance plane was shot down near Sverdlovsk, in the central USSR, May 1 while on a military intelligence mission.

The mission, initially denied by the United States, was admitted after the USSR announced the capture of the U-2 pilot, ex-U.S.-AF First Lt. Francis Gary Powers, 30, of Jenkins, Ky. Powers was described as a civilian pilot employed by the Lockheed Aircraft Corp. for the U.S.' National Aeronautics & Space Administration (NASA), ostensibly to fly the U-2 for a weather research project. Powers was believed to have been flying intelligence missions for the Central Intelligence Agency (CIA).

Disclosure of the U.S. reconnaissance mission and of its interception in "the interior of the Soviet land" was made by Soviet Premier Khrushchev May 5 in an address to the USSR's Supreme Soviet in Moscow. He declared angrily that the flight was "an aggressive provocation aimed at wrecking the summit conference..." Krushchev reported to the Supreme Soviet May 7 that the U-2 pilot had been captured, had confessed his intelligence mission, and would be brought to trial.

The United States admitted May 7 that the plane had been on a spying mission. A statement cleared by President Eisenhower and released by the State Department declared that "in endeavoring to obtain information now concealed behind the Iron Curtain, a flight over Soviet territory was probably undertaken by an unarmed civilian U-2 plane."

Spy-Plane Apology Demanded. The East-West summit conference collapsed at its opening session in Paris May 16 when Soviet Premier Khrushchev refused to begin talks unless President Eisenhower formally apologized for the sending of U.S. aircraft on military intelligence missions across the USSR.

The heads-of-government meeting began May 16 in Paris' Elysee Palace. It adjourned indefinitely three hours later after Khrushchev had delivered a denunciation of U.S. policy and had refused to continue unless President Eisenhower made amends for the U-2 incident.

Khrushchev withdrew his invitation for the President's scheduled June visit to the USSR and suggested that the summit talks be postponed for "approximately six to eight months." For a summit meeting to have a chance of success, the United States would have to confess "that it has committed aggression and admits that it regrets it," Khrushchev said.

De Gaulle Fails in Attempt to Save Summit. De Gaulle May 17 invited Eisenhower, Macmillan and Khrushchev to meet "to ascertain whether it is possible for the summit conference to begin the study of the questions which we agreed should be taken up." Eisenhower and Macmillan accepted the invitation, but Soviet aides replied that Khrushchev would attend only if given assurances the meeting was considered preliminary to and not part of a summit conference.

The meeting summoned by de Gaulle was begun by the three Western leaders at 3 p.m. without Khrushchev. A statement issued by Khrushchev an hour later and conveyed to the Western leaders said that he would be ready to "participate in the summit conference" only if the United States had "come to the decision to condemn the treacherous incursion ... into the airspace of the Soviet Union, publicly express regret over these incursions, punish those who are guilty and give assurances" they "will not be repeated."

A final conference statement was drafted by de Gaulle with the approval of Eisenhower and Macmillan and was issued before the end of their meeting at 5 p.m. It said that the Western leaders had met to discuss whether "the summit conference could begin" but that in "the absence of Mr. Khrushchev," the "planned discussions could not take place."

French UN Vote Opposes U-2 Condemnation. The United Nations Security Council voted May 26 by 7-2 (two abstentions) to reject a Soviet resolution to condemn the United States as an aggressor for U-2 flights over the USSR. The resolution, supported by only the USSR and Poland, was opposed by the United States, Britain, France and four other Security Council members.

De Gaulle Declaration on Summit. In a televised address to the French people, President de Gaulle May 31, 1960 reviewed the failure of the summit conference and outlined proposals to create conditions for an East-West accommodation.

Conceding that the United States' May 1 U-2 flight over the USSR had been "ill-timed," de Gaulle held that "this was not sufficient reason for refusing to open the discussion of the affairs of the world at the summit." He said the division of the world into two rival camps, either of which was capable of wiping out "a large part of humanity ... in a few hours," made "exorcising this monstrous peril" more important than any "territorial disagreement or ideological dispute." To accomplish this he proposed the world act to meet these three conditions:

●"The first is a detente, ...the bettering of international relations, putting a stop to provocative actions and speeches, and increasing trade and cultural exchanges..."
●"The second condition is a specific degree of controlled disarmament, preferably aimed at the devices capable of carrying bombs to strategic distances."
●"The third condition is a beginning of organized cooperation between East and West devoted to the service of man by helping in the progress of under-developed peoples."

Within this framework, France intended to remain "ready to defend herself," de Gaulle declared. He said: "She shall remain an integral part of the Atlantic alliance"; "she too must acquire a nuclear armament"; but France also would work "to build Western Europe into a political economic, cultural and human group, organized for action, progress and defense," foreseeing "the probable evolution of [a] political regime" and a "European entente from the Atlantic to the Urals."

De Gaulle Meets Adenauer on Berlin. President de Gaulle flew to Bonn May 20, 1961 for a one-day meeting with Chancellor Adenauer on Western policies to be discussed at forthcoming meetings between de Gaulle and U.S. President John F. Kennedy in Paris and Kennedy and Soviet Premier Khrushchev in Vienna.

The results of the de Gaulle-Adenauer talks were reported at a Bonn news conference held May 20 by State Secretary Karl Carstens of the West German Foreign Ministry. Carstens said de Gaulle and Adenauer had reached agreement on the West's continued position in Berlin. This comment was taken as a reiteration of de Gaulle's belief that the current Berlin situation was preferable to any revision of the city's status acceptable to the Soviet Union.

Kennedy Visit, Agreement on Berlin. President and Mrs. Kennedy arrived in Paris May 31 to begin a three-day state visit to France. Mr. Kennedy was to hold extensive personal talks with French President de Gaulle before proceeding to Vienna June 3 for his first meeting with Soviet Premier Khrushchev.

The Kennedys were greeted by de Gaulle and other leading French and Western officials and by crowds of Parisians variously estimated to number from 500,000 to 1-1/2 million.

The two leaders rode through enthusiastic crowds from Paris' Orly Airport to the Quai d'Orsay, where the Kennedys were to stay. Mr. Kennedy and de Gaulle then drove to the presidential Elysee Palace, where their political discussions began. A report on their initial talks said that the two leaders had discussed Berlin and had expressed a "complete identity of view" on the readiness of France and the United States to meet with force any Soviet threat to the city.

(U.S. newsmen reported from Paris May 31 that the two leaders' swift accord on Berlin implied President Kennedy's acceptance of de Gaulle's belief that the West should be prepared for open military action — apparently including limited nuclear war — to counter any Soviet move deemed a major threat to the city.)

Following further talks June 1 and 2, de Gaulle and Kennedy June 2 issued a joint communique that paid tribute to the "fundamental agreement" that existed between them and the "deep solidarity" that bound their two nations but contained little mention of specific policy agreements or disagreements. The sole exception was its reference to the two leaders' "identity of ... views on the commitments and responsibilities toward Berlin."

Kennedy flew to Vienna June 2 for his meeting with Khrushchev.

Soviet Ultimatum. Soviet Premier Khrushchev in a June 15, 1961 radio and TV address to the Russian people reported on his June 3-4 Vienna meeting with President Kennedy. His report contained a new ultimatum on Berlin and Germany. Khrushchev, reviewing the USSR's proposals for a "free city" of West Berlin and for a World War II German peace treaty, said: "The conclusion of a peace treaty with Germany cannot be postponed any longer. A peaceful settlement in Europe must be attained this year."

Concerning the problem of Western access to West Berlin, Khrushchev declared:

(1) When we suggest signing a peace treaty with Germany and turning West Berlin into a free city we are accused of wanting to deprive the Western powers of access to this city. But that is . . . wrong . . . . All countries of the world wishing to maintain . . . ties with this city would have the right.

(2) Of course, agreement would have to be reached with the country (East Germany) across whose territory pass the communications that link West Berlin with the outside world. This is normal. Otherwise the sovereignty of the state within which West Berlin is situated would be jeopardized.

(3) The Soviet Union and our friends do not want war and we will not start it. But we will defend our sovereignty, will fulfill our sacred duty to defend our freedom and independence. If any country violates peace and crosses the borders—ground, air or water—of another it will assume full responsibility for the consequences of the aggression and will receive a proper rebuff.

De Gaulle on Khrushchev Threat. President de Gaulle declared July 12, 1961 in a radio-TV report to the French people that there was "no chance" that the West would accept Soviet terms for settlement of the Berlin crisis. De Gaulle, who accused Khrushchev of invoking "the peace of the world while posing demands that risk . . . it," warned the Soviet leader that his German policy could have serious consequences. De Gaulle emphasized that a Berlin settlement was possible only if the USSR halted its threats as a first step toward a relaxation of tensions.

West Rejects Khrushchev Terms. The United States, Britain and France informed the Soviet government July 17 that Premier Khrushchev's terms for settlement of the Berlin and German questions were unacceptable to the West and could not be the basis for any negotiations on these problems.

The West's position was set forth in three separate but similar notes delivered in Moscow July 17. In their messages, the three Western powers categorically rejected the Soviet threat to sign a separate peace treaty with East Germany and to impose the status of a "free city" on West Berlin. They made it clear that they would defend their rights in Berlin, with force if necessary.

The Western powers expressed agreement with the USSR that a German settlement would enhance world peace. They declared, however, that such a settlement would be possible only on the basis of self-determination and free elections in all parts of Germany and Berlin.

Communists Seal Border Between East and West Berlin. The border between the Western and Soviet sectors of Berlin was closed to East Germans August 13 by troops, police and factory militia of the Soviet-backed East German government. The border closure effectively stopped the mass exodus of East German refugees, more than 16,000 of whom had registered at West Berlin centers since August 1.

West Blames Moscow. The United States, Britain and France August 17 sent identical notes to the Soviet government blaming the USSR for the Berlin border closings and demanding that the Soviet government "put an end to these illegal measures." The USSR, in an unprecedentedly quick reply August 18, rejected the Western protest.

The Western notes, delivered by the ambassadors of the three protesting countries, said: The Western powers had "never accepted that limitations can be imposed on freedom of movement within Berlin"; the boundary between the two sectors of Berlin "is not a state frontier"; the Western powers did "not accept the pretension that the Soviet sector of Berlin forms a part of the so-called 'German Democratic Republic' and that Berlin is situated on its territory"; the Western powers "cannot admit the right of the East German authorities to authorize their armed forces to enter the Soviet sector of Berlin."

France Readies Troops. French President de Gaulle August 17 ordered an undisclosed number of French ground and air units shifted from Algeria to France because of the Berlin crisis.

Berlin Air Access Debated. The USSR charged in nearly identical notes to the United States, British and French embassies in Moscow Aug. 23, 1961 that the three Western powers were abusing their air access to West Berlin by flying "extremists, saboteurs and spies" and West German officials and politicians to West Berlin for "subversive activity" against East Germany "and other Socialist countries."

The three Western powers August 26 rejected the Soviet allegations as "false" and, in virtually identical notes delivered in Moscow, warned that "interference by the Soviet government or its East German regime with free access to Berlin would have the most serious consequences for which it would bear full responsibility."

De Gaulle Threatens War. President de Gaulle declared Sept. 5, 1961 that the West should be prepared to defend with force its positions in Berlin and Germany even if this led to general war.

De Gaulle, at his semiannual Paris news conference, said: " .... If the Soviets want, by force, to reduce the positions and cut the communications of the allies in Berlin, the allies must maintain (these) by force .... Clearly one thing leads to another, ... and ... we may end up with a general war. But then, this would be what the Soviets deliberately wanted." "Admittedly the Soviets possess terrible nuclear weapons, but also the Western powers also possess some formidable ones. If the world conflict were to break out, ... (it would bring) the complete disruption of Russia and the countries which are a prey to Communism" and would destroy the Soviet regime.

De Gaulle specifically suggested that any Soviet interference with Allied traffic to Berlin be resisted in Berlin and be answered with Western attacks on Soviet air and sea traffic anywhere in the world.

French Position Remains Firm. French and West German opposition to any Western concessions on Berlin or the German problem was conveyed to President Kennedy in personal letters from President de Gaulle October 23 and Chancellor Adenauer October 24. De Gaulle's message was said to have reiterated his objection to entering any Berlin negotiations under Soviet threats and to have warned that the West weakened its position by repeated declarations of willingness to participate in such negotiations. West German Ambassador to the United States Wilhelm Grewe said that "the German evaluation of the situation is very close to the French position" but that Bonn was not opposed to exploratory talks seeking "common ground" for possible negotiations.

De Gaulle Opposes Negotiations. President de Gaulle, in a radio-TV address to the French people October 2, said France's duty was "to stand firm and erect in the face of demands from the totalitarian bloc and to urge our allies to do the same." He added: " ... Nothing would be more dangerous to our cause ... than to retreat step by step before those who are menacing us. But, should the threats stop ... and should relations between East and West return to normal, then France will be ready to enter into constructive negotiations ... on world problems."

De Gaulle had said at a rally in Rodez, France September 21 that the West would be risking "disaster" if it sought hasty negotiations on Germany. He said that to negotiate on Soviet terms, "you start out giving your hat, then you give your coat, then your shirt, then your skin, and finally your soul."

De Gaulle-Adenauer Talks. France's refusal to negotiate on Berlin was made clear by President de Gaulle during a five-hour meeting with West German Chancellor Adenauer in Paris Dec. 9, 1961.

It was generally believed that Adenauer had gone to Paris to urge de Gaulle to accept some of the terms for Berlin negotiations worked out by Adenauer and President Kennedy in their November 19-22 Washington talks. A joint communique issued by de Gaulle and Adenauer December 9 declared their agreement on the need for Western solidarity, but it contained no hint that de Gaulle had yielded on the question of a negotiated Berlin settlement. Bonn sources claimed, however, that Adenauer at least had persuaded de Gaulle to accept continued Western diplomatic probing of the USSR's position.

France Divides West on Berlin. French Foreign Minister Couve de Murville, U.S. Secretary of State Dean Rusk, British Foreign Secretary Lord Home, and West German Foreign Minister Gerhard Schroeder conferred in Paris December 11-12 but failed to agree on a unified Western position on negotiating with the USSR on Berlin. The major obstacle to Western agreement was France's refusal to accept such negotiations as wise or necessary. The French held that the Berlin crisis was solely a Soviet creation and that the West's position was not negotiable.

No joint communique was issued but Western officials reported that the four ministers had agreed only to continue exploratory diplomatic talks with the Russians to find out whether a reasonable basis existed for full negotiations on Berlin. France refused to join in the diplomatic soundings, under way in Moscow, but it agreed not to disavow them publicly. It did not promise to join in any East-West negotiations resulting from the Moscow soundings.

Couve de Murville reiterated France's refusal to enter into direct Berlin negotiations with the USSR at the semi-annual ministerial session of the NATO Council held in Paris December 13-15.

West Resists Berlin Air Curbs. France, the United States and Britain announced Feb. 9, 1962 that they had rejected Soviet demands that parts of the three air corridors to West Berlin be reserved for the use of Russian aircraft on military maneuvers.

The Soviet demands were followed by a series of incidents in which Russian planes sought to harass Western flights in the Berlin air lanes by "buzzing" and other menacing tactics.

The three Western powers protested to the USSR February 15 against the harassment of Western flights to Berlin. The protests were made in three separate but parallel notes delivered to the Soviet Foreign Ministry in Moscow.

De Gaulle Position Stays Firm. At his semi-annual press conference President de Gaulle May 15, 1962 declared that "in the present international situation... it is vain to wish for a satisfactory settlement of the German problem." He conceded that "France cannot object to her ally, America, resuming on her own behalf talks [on Berlin] with Moscow which by euphemism are called soundings," but it insisted that "the status of Berlin... should not be changed."

The United States had been maintaining contact with the USSR on the Berlin question. An agreement to continue East-West contacts on the Berlin problem and to expand them into substantive negotiations had been announced in Washington April 23 by Secretary of State Rusk and Soviet Ambassador to the United States Anatoly F. Dobrynin.

Tensions Grow in Berlin. A marked increase in East-West tensions in Berlin occurred in June following a growing number of incidents in which East Berlin police fired on persons attempting to escape to the West through the wall between East and West Berlin. The incidents brought an exchange of protests in which the USSR and the Western Allies accused each other of deliberately provoking shootings along the city's borders.

The Soviet notes, delivered to the United States, Britain and France June 7, accused the West of responsibility for several incidents in which West Berlin police were alleged to have fired on East German frontier guards and "Fascist elements" were said to have blown gaps in the East Berlin wall.

Talks Asked on Wall Terror. The United States, Britain and France called on the USSR June 25 to join in four-power talks to explore the ending of the current wave of violence along the Communist wall dividing Berlin.

The Western proposal was made in separate but similar notes replying to Soviet messages June 7 protesting recent shootings involving East German border guards and refugees attempting to escape to West Berlin.

West Renews Call for Talks on Incidents. The three Western occupation powers in Berlin renewed their appeals to the USSR August 24 and 27 for a four-power meeting to discuss measures to halt the growing number of shootings along the Berlin wall.

Soviets Reject Talks. The Soviet government Sept. 6, 1962 rejected Western appeals for four-power talks on the curbing of violence along the Berlin wall. It said that such violence could be stopped effectively only by a Western agreement "to abolish the occupation regime in West Berlin through the signing of a German peace treaty, to liquidate the NATO military base, to withdraw the troops of the three powers from West Berlin."

USSR Accuses Paris&Bonn of "Collusion." The Soviet news agency Tass September 18 issued a statement accusing President de Gaulle and West German Chancellor Adenauer of entering into "collusion" to delay a German peace settlement. The statement warned that the USSR would not permit this to delay progress toward a German peace treaty.

West vs. Soviet Tension. The three Western Allies charged the Soviet government September 25 with "unreasonable" refusal to negotiate a lessening of tension and violence in Berlin. The charges were made in separate, parallel Western notes in reply to the September 6 message in which the USSR had rejected proposals for four-power talks on measures to reduce violence along the border between East and West Berlin.

Foreign Minister Couve de Murville met October 7 in New York with Secretary of State Rusk and told him that France had not abandoned its opposition to East-West talks on a Berlin settlement as long as the USSR maintained its pressure on the West's position in the city.

EAST-WEST RELATIONS: DISARMAMENT

De Gaulle's goal to arm France with nuclear weapons led him to steer clear of efforts by the world's three nuclear powers (the United States, the Soviet Union, and Great Britain) to reach agreement banning the testing of such weapons. French disarmament proposals centered on limitation of delivery systems for nuclear weapons.

After France achieved the status of a nuclear power by successfully completing its series of nuclear tests (1960-61), de Gaulle in 1962 called for French participation in four-power disarmament negotiations with the other nuclear powers. Following Soviet refusal to hold four-power nuclear disarmament negotiations, de Gaulle ordered French abstention from the wider disarmament negotiations held by the United Nations Eighteen-Nation Disarmament Commission (ENDC) in Geneva.

U.S., USSR, UK Seek Nuclear Test Ban; France Opposes. The world's three nuclear powers — the United States, the Soviet Union, and Great Britain — agreed in August 1958 to begin negotiations toward conclusion of a treaty to end the testing of nuclear weapons. U.S. President Dwight D. Eisenhower and British Prime Minister Harold Macmillan August 22 proposed the three-power test ban talks with the Soviet Union in similar statements and official notes to Soviet Premier Nikita Khrushchev. Krushchev accepted the proposal August 29.

French policy toward the three-power talks, which began in Geneva Oct. 31, 1958, was made clear October 20 by Jules Moch, French delegate to the United Nations. Moch told the UN General Assembly's Political Committee that France would not be bound by an East-West agreement to ban nuclear tests. France abstained November 4 when the General Assembly adopted a resolution urging the United States, Britain and the USSR to suspend nuclear testing during their negotiations on an international test ban.

France Opposes Soviet Plan for Total Disarmament. Soviet Premier Khrushchev Sept. 18, 1959 called on all the nations of the world to disband their armed forces as part of a plan to achieve "general and complete disarmament" within four years. Addressing the UN General Assembly, Khrushchev appealed for Western cooperation with the USSR to eliminate the possibility of war by destroying all armaments and denying "military advantage" to any bloc.

French Foreign Minister Maurice Couve de Murville told the Assembly September 30 that genuine world disarmament was inconceivable without the reduction of East-West tension. Couve de Murville attacked the Khrushchev plan on grounds that control and inspection "will not actually function until after the agreed measures of disarmament have already been implemented." He said only settlement of "the (political) conflicts that arise, whether in Europe, Asia or elsewhere," would make "everything...possible, starting with effective disarmament."

Moch Plan on A-Delivery Systems. French delegate Jules Moch October 22 presented a plan to the United Nations calling for elimination of "all vehicles for nuclear devices."

The plan called for "measures prohibiting first the development, then the manufacture and possession" of these potential "vehicles" for nuclear weapons: "satellites, rockets, supersonic or long-range aircraft, submarines, aircraft carriers and launching pads." Moch told the General Assembly that "past refusals to compromise" had made impossible "any effective control over stockpiles of nuclear weapons" or certainty "of a total reconversion of these stockpiles to peaceful ends." He suggested that "elimination of the most dreaded vehicles for...universal destruction" still was feasible and would be more effective than a first-stage disarmament plan limited "only (to) declarations."

Moch Vs. Three-Power Test Ban. Moch Nov. 4, 1959 affirmed France's intentions to proceed with nuclear weapons tests in the Sahara desert unless the United States, Britain and the Soviet Union "renounce their nuclear armament."

Moch told the General Assembly's Political Committee that France would carry out the planned test even if the three present nuclear powers signed an agreement to suspend their tests. France would "forego all military tests" only on condition that the United States, Britain and the USSR renounce testing and give up their atomic arms.

UN Resolution Condemns French A-Tests. The UN General Assembly Nov. 19, 1959 adopted by a 51-16 vote an Asian-African resolution expressing "grave concern" at French plans to test a nuclear device in the Sahara desert and calling on France to cancel the test. The resolution was opposed by the United States, Britain and France. The resolution was voted after French representative Moch had warned that France would proceed with its test plans despite the General Assembly's action.

France Shuns Test Ban Talks. The French Foreign Ministry announced Feb. 16, 1960 that France would not request admission to the United States-British-Soviet conference in Geneva on a treaty to ban nuclear tests. The announcement came three days after the successful testing of France's first atomic bomb in the Sahara. It reiterated the French disarmament plan including the elimination of current stockpiles of nuclear weapons.

France In Ten-Nation East-West Arms Talks

Geneva Meeting. The first full-scale East-West disarmament negotiations in 2-1/2 years were convened in Geneva March 15, 1960 by Western and Soviet delegations to a ten-nation Committee on Disarmament. Jules Moch led the French delegation at the talks.

(East-West disarmament talks had been dormant since a five-nation subcommittee of the UN Disarmament Commission recessed deadlocked sessions in London Sept. 6, 1957. Other aspects of the East-West arms race had been considered in diplomatic exchanges with the United States, Soviet Union and Britain banning nuclear tests, but no general disarmament talks had taken place since the London talks. The ten-nation committee had been proposed and explored at the 1959 Big Four foreign ministers' Geneva conference on Germany and was sanctioned by a joint U.S.-Soviet resolution voted Nov. 20, 1959 by the UN General Assembly.)

The new group recognized past Soviet demands for parity with the West in disarmament negotiations. Membership was fixed at ten nations — five Western powers (the United States, Britain, France, Canada and Italy) and five Soviet-bloc states (the USSR, Poland, Czechoslovakia, Rumania and Bulgaria).

Western Disarmament Plan. A draft Western disarmament plan contained in a working paper transmitted to Soviet bloc delegations was made public in Geneva March 14.

The unified three-stage Western plan had been worked out in Paris March 7-10 by the U.S., British, French, Canadian and Italian delegations. The plan provided for conventional and nuclear disarmament under strict controls designed to lead to elimination of all means of mass destruction. It was to be supervised by an international disarmament organization.

France Opposes Test-Ban Treaty. French delegate Moch March 22 told the ten-nation committee that France would not join in the test-ban treaty under discussion by the United States, Britain and USSR. Moch said that the proposed treaty meant "perpetuating discrimination for the benefit of the powers which have already made a sufficient number of tests." Moch called for nuclear disarmament through rigid control and limitation of missiles and other means of delivery of nuclear weapons.

West Vs. Khrushchev Plan. A formal rejection of Soviet Premier Khrushchev's proposal for total world disarmament was delivered April 5, 1960 by Western delegates led by French delegate Moch. (Khrushchev's plan, first presented to the UN General Assembly in 1959, was repeated March 12 in a message to the ten-nation committee.)

Moch declared that the total disarmament theme "does not offer a basis of acceptable compromise...." Rejecting proposals for disarmament without inspection within the four-year period called for by Khrushchev, Moch made it clear that the West would not negotiate on the basis of the Soviet plan and awaited specific East bloc suggestions for gradual verified disarmament.

De Gaulle For Destruction of A-Weapons. President de Gaulle April 7, in an address to the British Parliament, called for the destruction of all nuclear weapons to remove "the general fear of sudden annihilation" and as a step toward attainment of peace. France, he declared, wished all "stocks of nuclear weapons to be destroyed, the installations where they are made to be used for different purposes, the rockets and aircraft capable of carrying them... and the fixed or floating bases from which these vehicles of death can be launched, to be placed under surveillance." France then would "give up the [atomic] tests and the capital expenditures" necessary to create a French nuclear arsenal, he pledged.

Moch Presents West's "Principles." The West's basic principles and conditions for general disarmament were presented to the ten-nation conference April 26 by French delegate Moch:

(1) Disarmament measures must be formulated "progressively," beginning with the least difficult, and be applied in stages without a time limit.

(2) Conventional and nuclear disarmament must be interrelated and balanced so that neither East nor West would be given military superiority.

(3) Disarmament must be supervised by an international agency linked with the United Nations and must provide for an international force to keep peace.

(4) An arms pact must provide for preservation of outer space for peaceful purposes and for elimination of mass destruction weapons and their vehicles.

The Western principles were immediately rejected by Soviet delegate Valerian Zorin as "disappointing" and unrelated to the problem of total disarmament.

Arms Talks Recessed. The ten-nation Geneva disarmament talks recessed April 29 until June 7 after failing to agree on a communique summarizing the conference's 32 sessions. The adjournment was intended to permit consideration of the disarmament problem at the Paris East-West summit meeting in May.

Ten-Nation Committee Resumes; New Soviet Plan. New Soviet disarmament proposals were presented to the ten-nation disarmament committee when it resumed meeting in Geneva June 7, 1960 following the collapse of the summit meeting. Chief Soviet delegate Zorin June 7 called for simultaneous abolition of foreign bases and means of delivering nuclear weapons as the first step towards disarmament. His proposal was attacked by the U.S., British and French delegates.

French delegate Moch, who had originally proposed Oct. 22, 1959 at the United Nations a plan for elimination of the nuclear weapons danger by controlling their means of delivery, warned the Soviet Union June 13 that the Western powers remained united in their disarmament position "even if some (i.e., France)... felt at certain times closer to certain Soviet concepts... than did others." He stated June 15 that the Soviet proposal for elimination within a brief period of all means of delivering nuclear weapons were impractical.

Soviets Quit Ten-Nation Talks. Negotiations of the ten-nation Committee on Disarmament were suspended June 27 when Soviet delegate Zorin led the five Communist nations in a walkout from the conference. Zorin announced that the USSR and its allies were withdrawing because the West had refused to negotiate seriously on the revised Soviet plan for total world disarmament. French delegate Moch and other Western representatives denounced the Soviet action June 28 and adjourned when the Soviet bloc representatives failed to appear.

In a note Soviet Foreign Minister Andrei Gromyko delivered June 27 to UN Secretary General Dag Hammarskjold, the Soviet Union asked that the disarmament question be placed on the agenda of the UN General Assembly session beginning in September. The note, reiterating Soviet charges that the Western powers were responsible for the breakdown of the ten-nation negotiations, cited as an indication of Soviet readiness to compromise that the revised Soviet arms plan had "unreservedly accepted France's view that the means of delivering nuclear weapons should be prohibited and destroyed first."

De Gaulle Opposes UN Debate, Calls for Resumption of Ten-Nation Talks. A note from President de Gaulle to Soviet Premier Khrushchev July 2, 1960 opposed the USSR's intention to return the disarmament problem to the 82-nation UN General Assembly. De Gaulle warned that "such problems cannot be discussed in a practical manner except in a narrow circle of countries [that are] principally interested and technically competent."

(De Gaulle also denied that the Soviet plan for "destruction" of missiles and other means of delivering nuclear weapons was a reasonable variation of the French plan for "control" of such "vehicles." He said that "to destroy all the rockets and all the airplanes and prevent construction of others would appear to be...inapplicable in our century, which is essentially that of airplanes, rockets and...satellites.")

De Gaulle, in a message sent to Premier Khrushchev August 15 and made public August 24, urged a resumption of disarmament talks in the ten-nation Committee on Disarmament rather than in the General Assembly. De Gaulle said fruitful arms negotiations could not take place in the "strange, impassioned and tumultuous proceedings" of the United Nations.

Three-Power A-Test Ban Talks Resume, French Tests Attacked. The U.S.-British-Soviet negotiations on a treaty to ban nuclear weapons tests were reconvened in Geneva March 21, 1961 after 3-1/2-month recess. The talks, underway since Oct. 31, 1958, had been recessed at U.S. request Dec. 5, 1960 to permit a review of policy on the nuclear test question by the Kennedy Administration.

In an address to the conference March 21, Soviet delegate Semyon K. Tsarapkin warned of the possible effect on the talks of continued French nuclear tests. He told newsmen later that reports of planned French nuclear tests seemed to indicate "an artificial division of labor under which the United States and Britain stop testing while France continues to test" and "then pass[es] on the results to her allies."

Soviets Threaten A-Test Resumption. The USSR threatened May 15, 1961 to resume its nuclear test program unless the United States and Britain took steps to insure that France halted its atomic tests. Tsarapkin told the three-power Geneva meeting that if France carried out any new nuclear tests in defiance of the Soviet warning, its action would "free the Soviet Union to resume testing of nuclear and hydrogen bombs." Tsarapkin accused the United States and Britain of having encouraged the continued French test program in order to obtain new weapons research data without resuming their own nuclear test programs. The United States and Britain rejected the Soviet charge.

Soviets Resume A-Testing. The Soviet Union announced Aug. 31, 1961 that it had decided to resume the testing of nuclear weapons. It asserted in a statement made public by Tass that it had been forced to end the voluntary moratorium on atomic tests because of war threats from the United States and its allies. The Soviet announcement, made through the official news agency Tass was followed by the detonation in quick succession of four Soviet nuclear devices September 1, September 4, September 5 and September 6.

A French government statement August 31 called the Soviet decision to resume testing "a deliberate menace designed to bring the free world around to its way of thinking."

Soviet Premier Khrushchev September 7 in a statement given to the *New York Times* declared the USSR would not resume its moratorium on nuclear weapons testing. "We already declared in the past," he said, "that if France conducts tests, we shall also be compelled to start testing." The United States and Britain "want us to stop ... while France is left complete freedom of action" to test — with United States and British aid — "not only for herself" but for NATO.

U.S. Resumes A-Tests. The United States ended its three-year self-imposed ban on atomic tests by detonating two underground nuclear weapon devices September 15 and 16, 1961. President Kennedy September 5 had ordered the resumption of U.S. nuclear tests; "we have no other choice," he said.

France Named to 18-Nation UN Committee. The UN General Assembly voted unanimously December 20 to adopt a joint U.S.-Soviet resolution creating an Eighteen-Nation Disarmament Committee (ENDC) that would renew negotiations toward an "agreement on general and complete disarmament under effective international control." The committee replaced the ten-nation Committee on Disarmament which had adjourned June 28 in Geneva following the Soviet walkout. France was elected to membership in the new committee.

De Gaulle for Four-Power A-Missile Talks. President de Gaulle Feb. 19, 1962 called for a conference of the world's four nuclear powers that would have as its "immediate goal the destruction, the banning and the control of all means of delivery of nuclear weapons."

De Gaulle's proposal, made in a note to Soviet Premier Khrushchev, rejected Khrushchev's own proposal announced February 10 that the first meeting of the ENDC should be convened at the summit level. De Gaulle expressed doubt that the 18-nation committee would achieve any agreement.

He said that it was necessary that negotiations be held by, and limited to, "the powers that possess nuclear weapons or will possess them in the near future." The "essential question," he said, was "not the halting of tests, but rather ... the destruction of existing weapons and the banning of the manufacture of new ones." Since it was "easy to conceal" nuclear weapons, "no one could ... be certain that they would be destroyed, even if all conceivable methods of control were employed." For this reason, de Gaulle said, France repeated its proposal that "the destruction, the banning and the control should first be applied to the means of delivery of nuclear weapons — launching pads, planes, submarines, etc."

France Boycotts Talks. The French government announced March 5 that it would not be represented at the projected ENDC meeting in Geneva. The government announcement followed Soviet Premier Khrushchev's rejection February 28 of de Gaulle's proposal for four-power nuclear disarmament negotiations.

The ENDC conference was convened March 14. It was the first major international meeting to be devoted to disarmament since the collapse of a ten-nation disarmament conference in Geneva in June 1960. France's decision to boycott the ENDC reduced its effective membership to 17. An empty chair was reserved for a French delegation.

Soviets Vs. French Boycott, A-Tests. The question of France's refusal either to participate in the 18-nation committee or to halt its nuclear weapons test program was raised May 9, 1962 by Soviet Deputy Foreign Minister Valerian Zorin, who made French participation a condition for Soviet acceptance of a test-ban agreement. Zorin said: "There is another power now testing nuclear weapons. This power is refusing to take part in the negotiations and has never said it would adhere to a nuclear test ban treaty. The Soviet Union will not sign any treaty on banning nuclear tests unless France is a party to it."

France Abstains on UN Disarmament Votes. France abstained twice Nov. 6, 1962 in votes on two UN General Assembly resolutions on nuclear disarmament. Both resolutions called for the drafting of a treaty to halt further nuclear testing and for the reconvening of the ENDC, which had recessed September 7.

CHAPTER VI
FRANCE AND WESTERN EUROPE
EUROPEAN ECONOMIC INTEGRATION AND RAPPROCHEMENT WITH GERMANY

Treaties establishing the European Economic Community (EEC, or Common Market) and the European Atomic Energy Community (Euratom) were ratified July 9, 1957 by the National Assembly of the Fourth Republic.

France had joined West Germany, Italy, Holland, Belgium, and Luxembourg in signing treaties creating EEC and Euratom March 25, 1957 in Rome. The Common Market treaty provided for abolishment of custom duties in trade among the six nations during a 12-year transitional period, commencing Jan. 1, 1959. Common tariffs on goods imported from outside the six-nation area would be established within 12 years also.

Under de Gaulle, France maintained a strong commitment to economic cooperation within the EEC but simultaneously opposed the development of "supranational" political institutions in EEC. De Gaulle sought regular political consultation among the EEC member governments. A major goal of his West European policy was to achieve improved relations with Germany, France's enemy in two world wars.

France Renews Pledges on EEC, Euratom. In messages to the West German and Italian governments June 6, 1958 the French government promised that the new de Gaulle regime would carry out France's commitments under the EEC and Euratom treaties.

French-British Trade Rift. During a brief meeting with British Prime Minister Harold MacMillan in Paris June 29, President de Gaulle refused to make a commitment on British proposals for a 17-nation European free trade zone in industrial goods.

Talks on establishment of a 17-nation European free trade zone to parallel the six-nation European Economic Community were suspended indefinitely November 17 in Paris following an open rift between France and Britain as leaders of the EEC and non-EEC European nations respectively. The suspension in talks came after French Information Minister Jacques Soustelle November 14 rejected British plans for extension of tariff cuts and increased import quotas among the six Common Market nations to the eleven other members of the Organization for European Economic Cooperation (OEEC). The OEEC had been established in 1948 comprising the 17 nations participating in the European Recovery Program (the Marshall Plan).

(Observers reported that the split was due to British fears that France sought to use the six-nation Common Market to extend the French protectionist system to the Common Market's tariffs and quotas and thus discriminate against non-market nations. France was said to view British proposals for a 17-nation European free trade zone, members of which would fix their own tariffs, as an attempt to undermine the six-nation EEC and protect British exports to Europe. France had urged the 17 nations to agree to fixed tariffs as part of a "common commercial policy" against all outside nations.)

De Gaulle-Adenauer Opposition to British Plan. President de Gaulle and West German Chancellor Adenauer met in Bad Kreuznach, West Germany, Nov. 26, 1958 and agreed to oppose the British European free trade zone proposal in favor of a looser "multilateral association" of the six EEC nations with Britain and other OEEC countries.

French-British Split Continues. The French-British dispute was carried over into a December 15 session of the OEEC. French Foreign Minister Couve de Murville rejected the proposed European free trade zone on grounds that France's EEC commitments had priority. He made clear that France considered major EEC tariff and trade benefits applicable only to EEC states and that creation of the six-nation Common Market necessarily would bring discrimination against non-members.

EEC, Euratom Pacts in Effect. The six-nation Common Market and Euratom treaties became effective Jan. 1, 1959. The pacts were designed to weld France, West Germany, Italy, Holland, Belgium and Luxembourg into a single trade unit and a commonly operated nuclear power program over a 12-year period.

Measures put into effect January 1 by France and the other five EEC members included a 10% reduction in tariffs and a 20% increase in import quotas on EEC goods.

De Gaulle Hails West Germany. At his first presidential press conference, de Gaulle March 25 spoke of France and West Germany as "two old adversaries who have given up fighting and destroying each other...have resolved to cooperate." "Germany as she is in no way threatens us;" on the contrary, "with her capabilities, her energy, her resources, she constitutes an essential element of the life and progress of Europe and the whole world."

British-Led Trade Group Established. A convention establishing a European Free Trade Association (EFTA) was signed in Stockholm Nov. 20, 1959 by ministers of Britain, Austria, Denmark, Norway, Portugal, Sweden and Switzerland. Negotiations to form the EFTA had begun after the collapse of British-led efforts in 1958 to create a European free trade zone to include all member states of the Organization for European Economic Cooperation, including the six EEC nations. A communique issued by the EFTA founders at the end of their November 19-20 meeting expressed hopes that the seven-nation accord be temporary and a "step toward an agreement" to extend the trade association to the other OEEC states. It called on the EEC nations to agree to renew free trade zone negotiations within the OEEC.

France Backs Quota Cut Extension. France supported an EEC Ministerial Council decision announced November 24 in Strasbourg that import quota liberalizations planned for EEC states Jan. 1, 1960 would be extended to other Western nations, not members of EEC. All import quotas were to be enlarged by at least 10%, most by 20%.

De Gaulle Visits Britain; Statement on Rift. President de Gaulle was greeted by Queen Elizabeth II, Prince Philip, and Prime Minister Macmillan as he arrived in London April 5, 1960 for his first visit to Britain since his return to France June 14, 1944 with the Allied armies.

Responding to the Queen's toast at a palace banquet April 5, de Gaulle emphasized that France and Britain remained "side by side" in the postwar world. De Gaulle said the two nations were working for the "necessary slackening of international tension,... the limitation and the control of armaments [and restoration of]... the peace and balance of Europe."

Alluding to the potential trade rift between the British-led proposed free trade zone and the EEC, de Gaulle conceded that "differences" existed between France and Britain because of "the largely continental character of France's economy" and "the nature" of Britain's, "which is based essentially on overseas exchanges."

In an address April 7 to both houses of Parliament, de Gaulle expressed gratitude for the British role in the liberation of France from Nazi occupation. He appealed, however, for understanding of "the German people, who were yesterday our enemies but who are today a vital part of the West and our common ally."

De Gaulle-Adenauer Talks on EEC. President de Gaulle and West German Chancellor Adenauer held talks July 29-30, 1960 at Rambouillet near Paris on ways to give political direction to the Common Market. The talks took place in secret, and no final communique was issued, but French and West German spokesmen reported July 30 that agreement had been reached on the broad outline of an EEC political secretariat or "European cabinet" to coordinate policies of the six EEC nations.

De Gaulle Opposes "Supranational" Europe. At his semiannual Paris press conference, de Gaulle September 15 said that European cooperation and unity must be based on the "reality" of the nation-state: It was "true that it has been possible to institute certain organisms [i.e., the EEC] more or less extra- or supranational; these organisms have their technical value, but have not and cannot have authority and... political efficacity." Effective European cooperation in the political, economic, cultural and defense domains must be guided by "an organized, regular concert of the responsible governments."

EEC Tariff Cut. The six EEC nations, carrying out an accelerated program for reducing internal tariffs, cut them 10% for industrial imports from member states and 5% for imports of certain agricultural products, both reductions effective Jan. 1, 1961. This brought to 30% the total of EEC internal tariff cuts since Jan. 1, 1958.

EEC "Summit" on Political Unity. The heads of government and foreign ministers of the six EEC nations — French President de Gaulle, West German Chancellor Adenauer, Italian Premier Amintore Fanfani, Belgian Premier Gaston Eyskens, Netherlands Premier Jan E. deQuay and Luxembourg Premier Pierre Werner — met in Paris February 10-11 to discuss French proposals for a confederation that would coordinate the six countries' economic and political policies without subordinating their sovereignties to a new supranational institution.

The six nations failed to reach agreement on the French plan. A communique issued February 11 disclosed that a second European "summit" meeting would be held to consider recommendations to be prepared by a working committee.

France for Quick Extension of EEC Market to Agriculture. French Agriculture Minister Henri Rochereau announced June 6, 1961 that France would halt all EEC tariff reductions after 1961 unless the Common Market adopted a Europe-wide farm policy. The French farm economy produced at the cheapest prices in Europe and would gain the most from such a policy. Other EEC nations, especially West Germany, had highly protected agricultural economies which would be threatened by freer trade in farm products.

Second EEC "Summit" on Political Role. The heads of government of the six Common Market states met in Bonn July 18 and reached agreement on establishment of a system of regular political consultation and cooperation.

The six leaders — French President de Gaulle, West German Chancellor Adenauer, and Premiers Fanfani of Italy, Theo Lefebre of Belgium, de Quay of the Netherlands and Werner of Luxembourg — issued a declaration in which they announced their decision to "give form and body to the will of political unity" expressed in the organization of the EEC, the European Coal and Steel Community and Euratom. The declaration said that the six leaders had agreed to "organize their cooperation and assure its regularity" and to meet regularly to "coordinate policy...to further Europe's political unity and thus strengthen the Atlantic alliance." It disclosed that a committee had been designated to study "ways and means of giving a statutory character to the unity of their peoples."

The committee established at the meeting (known as the Fouchet committee, after its chairman, Christian Fouchet of France) was charged with preparing a draft treaty for a European political union comparable with the European institutions existing in the economic fields. Negotiations in the committee began in July 1961. Throughout the year the negotiations in the committee were divided between those countries (mainly France, with increasing West German support) favoring institutions limited to facilitating the development of common policies by consultation among the sovereign European states, and those (chiefly Belgium and the Netherlands) favoring the development of genuinely supranational European institutions providing for majority rule and representation of the peoples involved.

Britain Applies to EEC. Britain's application for membership in the European Economic Community was submitted to the EEC Council in Brussels Aug. 10, 1961. The application was a necessary preliminary to the opening of negotiations on the special conditions posed by Britain for its membership in the six-nation European trade group. The application did not commit Britain to EEC membership if the conditions were not met.

A British delegation led by Edward Heath met with representatives of the six EEC countries in Brussels November 22-25 to begin negotiations on conditions for Britain's entry into the EEC.

EEC Enters Second Stage. The Council of Ministers of the European Economic Community announced Jan. 14, 1962 that it had reached agreement for the Common Market's second stage to start, effective retroactively to January 1.

Under the treaty's second stage, all EEC Council decisions would by the end of 1966 be taken by simple majority (during the first stage, unanimous agreement of Council members was required for EEC actions). Minimal tariff and trade measures to be accomplished during the second stage (by 1966): (1) an additional 10% reduction on tariffs on industrial goods traded within the EEC; (2) steps toward building a common tariff on imports from non-EEC countries; (3) free movement, within the EEC, of member states' labor forces, capital and industry. Completion of these goals would be required for the start of the "third stage," under which a European customs union and partial economic integration would be achieved in 1966-69.

Paris Opposes UK Terms on EEC Entry. Edward Heath, British minister responsible for negotiating Britain's entry into EEC, proposed February 22 that Britain be given a four-year exemption from Common Market agricultural policies to enable it gradually to accustom British consumers and farmers — as well as Commonwealth nations — to the new farm trade and price patterns of the EEC. Heath's proposal, made to the EEC Ministerial Council in Brussels, was opposed by French Foreign Minister Couve de Murville who stated that the EEC's agricultural policy had been achieved only with great difficulty and that Britain, if it joined the Common Market, would have to adhere to the timetable under which a common EEC farm production and trade pattern would be fully established by 1970.

EEC Meeting on Political Unity Fails. The foreign ministers of the six EEC states met in Paris April 17, 1962 to examine a compromise political draft submitted by France, Italy and West Germany. The meeting, which had been expected to produce agreement on submitting the compromise draft to a later European summit meeting, ended in a disagreement when Foreign Ministers Paul-Henri Spaak of Belgium and Joseph M. A. H. Luns of the Netherlands made clear that their governments would refuse even to consider signing a European political treaty until Britain had been granted membership in EEC and had become a participant in the negotiations. A French Foreign Ministry statement said "it has been impossible to agree on the principle of a European political union" because of the position taken by Belgium and the Netherlands.

Paris-Bonn Coordination. A growing French-West German agreement to force acceptance of de Gaulle's European plans to prevent Britain's rapid entry into the EEC and the political negotiations was reported in May. West German sources reported May 9 that Chancellor Adenauer had said at a closed meeting of the Berlin Senate May 7 that he now opposed full British participation in EEC and would favor some form of associate EEC membership that would keep Britain outside the projected European political union. Adenauer's reported shift in position was attributed to the increasing French-West German political entente and to his dissatisfaction with the continued readiness of the Macmillan and Kennedy governments to negotiate an interim Berlin settlement with the USSR.

De Gaulle Rejects "Supranationalism." President de Gaulle May 15 at his semiannual presidential press conference set forth his views on the political organization of Europe. De Gaulle specifically rejected any movement toward creating supranational European political institutions. He instead proposed a periodic consultation among European leaders to coordinate their nations' separate policies.

Major points of his statement:

> To organize ourselves politically, let us begin at the beginning. Let us organize our cooperation, let our heads of state or government meet periodically to examine our problems together and to make decisions . . . which will be those of Europe. Let us set up a political commission, a defense commission and a cultural commission, just as we already have an economic commission. . . .
> . . . These opponents (of the French proposals) tell us: You want to make a Europe of the fatherlands; we want to make a supranational Europe—as if a formula were enough to mix together these powerfully established entities which are called peoples and states.
> I have already said, and I repeat, that at the present time there is not and cannot be any other possible Europe than a Europe of states, apart of course from myths, fictions, parades.

De Gaulle's statement stressed the view that the only "hope of uniting Europe in the political and defense fields" depended on the growing "solidarity between France and Germany."

De Gaulle & Macmillan Meet on UK Entry. Prime Minister Macmillan and President de Gaulle held talks in Paris June 2-3, 1962 on the Common Market problem. French sources reported that the talks had reduced the mistrust that had grown between Britain and France during the Common Market negotiations. In a communique issued June 3, the two leaders affirmed that a "community of interests" existed between France and Britain and would guide their future negotiations.

Despite the reports of strengthened Anglo-French amity, the British and French governments later expressed disagreement over the positions taken by de Gaulle and Macmillan in their discussions. French spokesmen reported June 3 that Macmillan had given the impression that he was determined to bring Britain into the EEC without reservations and without special conditions. British spokesmen rejected the French view June 5 and told newsmen that Macmillan had emphasized his determination to negotiate a settlement that would fulfill Britain's pledges to the Commonwealth.

Adenauer Visits France. West German Chancellor Adenauer traveled through France July 2-8 in the first major tour of the country made by a German head of government since World War II.

Adenauer's visit was planned to demonstrate the success of his efforts toward a French-West German reconciliation and the integration of West Germany within the new European community. It also apparently was intended by the French to advance President de Gaulle's plans to make the growing Bonn-Paris political alliance the foundation stone of a revived and more powerful Europe.

Adenauer was greeted warmly by de Gaulle at Paris' Orly Airport July 2; his welcoming speech expressed "honor" and "joy" at receiving the man who, he said, had led Germany back to the path of reason and cooperation within Europe. De Gaulle's demonstration of respect for Adenauer was repeated publicly throughout the chancellor's four-day official visit to Paris. The public response to his visit was courteous but unenthusiastic.

The two leaders conferred privately and with French Premier Georges Pompidou and their foreign ministers, Maurice Couve de Murville and Gerhard Schroeder, July 2-5. A joint communique issued July 5 disclosed that they had agreed on the need "to bring the discussions on the creation of a (European) political federation...to a conclusion as soon as possible, in agreement with their partners." It expressed "the hope that...negotiations...will allow the problems arising from Great Britain's request for entry into the European community to be solved in the spirit of strengthening the reconstruction of Europe."

Adenauer returned to West Germany July 8. He said at a Bonn press conference July 10 that his French visit had cemented the two countries' political reconciliation, which he termed the keystone of a political dam "against the spread of communism in Europe." He added that his visit had made it impossible that either country ever would combine with Russia against the other.

France Deadlocks UK-EEC Negotiations. A crucial negotiating session on British entry into the EEC was held August 1-4, 1962 in Brussels. The session ended in a deadlock when the French delegation demanded as a condition to its acceptance of a British-EEC agreement that first a final settlement be reached on the disposition of duties to be imposed on farm imports coming into the EEC from non-EEC nations. The French demand made it impossible to reach agreement on Britain's position that agricultural goods coming from British Commonwealth nations be assured access to Common Market trade. (Agricultural products from Commonwealth nations entered the United Kingdom duty-free.)

De Gaulle in Germany. French President de Gaulle made a six-day state visit to West Germany September 4-9. His trip, intended to cement publicly the growing Franco-German reconciliation and the two nations' political alliance in Europe, was viewed as an unqualified success.

De Gaulle's visit was the first made to Germany in modern times by a French chief of state. Given an enthusiastic welcome by the West German public, de Gaulle was considered to have won popular support for the plans he and Chancellor Adenauer were known to have formulated for the political and economic organization of Western Europe under Franco-German leadership.

De Gaulle, accompanied by Foreign Minister Maurice Couve de Murville, was greeted by West German President Heinrich Luebke and Adenauer on his arrival September 4 in Cologne. Speaking at a state dinner given there later in the day, de Gaulle reaffirmed his hopes for Franco-German construction of a European community in which Britain apparently would be limited to a secondary role.

De Gaulle declared that there must exist "on the old continent a pillar of power and prosperity of the same order as that which the United States constitutes in the new world." Referring to the current British negotiations for admission to the European Economic Community (EEC), he said: "Certain...prejudices inside the community, joining themselves with certain influences on the outside, have, momentarily, been able to keep the conclusion in suspense. But France and Germany, which are in agreement on the principles and the methods of this vital construction, have every reason...to reinforce their own solidarity without delay."

The only purely political talks held by de Gaulle during his visit were carried out with Adenauer September 5. Spokesmen said that the two had reached broad agreement on close French-West German political cooperation in Europe.

De Gaulle began his tour of West Germany September 5 with addresses in German to enthusiastic crowds in Bonn and Cologne. His Cologne speech, in which he referred to "the great German people" and to Adenauer as "my friend," brought an unusually emotional response both from his listeners and Adenauer.

A call for creation of "organic cooperation" between the French and West German armed forces was issued by de Gaulle in Hamburg September 7, in an address to the West German War College. De Gaulle declared that such cooperation was necessary to face the continuing Soviet threat and to provide a military basis for "the union of our two countries."

De Gaulle flew from Hamburg to Munich September 8 and Stuttgart September 9 for the final stops of his tour. In each city he addressed crowds (150,000 persons in Hamburg) that were described as the largest and most enthusiastic to be seen since World War II. He returned to Paris by air September 9. (A communique issued by the French and West German governments on his departure sought to reassure other European nations that the two leaders' European plans did not exclude them; it said France and West Germany would "promote with their partners European unification for which the foundation stone has been laid.")

De Gaulle-Macmillan Deadlock. The stalemated negotiations for British entry into the EEC were the central subject of two days of talks held Dec. 15-16, 1962 by President de Gaulle and British Prime Minister Macmillan at de Gaulle's presidential estate in Rambouillet, near Paris. A communique issued by the two leaders December 16 conceded that "difficulties... have been encountered" in the British-EEC negotiations. Reports from Paris made it clear that Macmillan had not won the support he sought from de Gaulle for Britain's effort to join the EEC.

French-West German Links. The French and West German governments announced December 17 that Foreign Ministers Maurice Couve de Murville and Gerhard Schroeder had reached agreement on the establishment of "systematized" cooperation between the two governments in politics, defense, and culture. The agreement was reached at a meeting in Paris December 16-17.

CHAPTER VII

FRANCE AND THE UNITED NATIONS
THE CONGO CRISIS AND THE PROBLEM OF UN FINANCE

Following the proclamation of Congo independence July 1, 1960 and the Congo army mutiny and political rebellion which ensued, France July 14 abstained when the UN Security Council voted voted 8-0 (Britain and China also abstaining) to send a UN military force to the Congo to restore order. Throughout the Congo crisis France, the USSR, Soviet-bloc nations and other member states expressed continued disapproval of UN intervention in the Congo by refusing to pay their share of UN special assessments to cover the cost of the UN Force sent to the Congo.

Major French actions 1960-1962:

● Abstained Aug. 9, 1960 in Security Council vote to send UN troops into secessionist Katanga Province.

● Abstained September 17 in Security Council vote to summon General Assembly into special session to deal with Congo crisis.

● Abstained September 20 in General Assembly vote on resolution calling for "vigorous action" by Secretary-General Dag Hammarskjold to carry out Security Council orders to restore "law and order" and "safeguard" the Congo's "territorial integrity and political independence."

● Abstained December 20 in an Assembly vote on a U.S.-British sponsored resolution calling on Hammarskjold "to continue to discharge the mandate entrusted to him by the United Nations." The resolution failed to win a required two-thirds majority; most French-speaking African states of the French Community joined France in abstaining.

● Abstained Feb. 21, 1961 in Security Council vote to authorize UN troops to resort to force of arms in order to prevent civil war in the Congo.

● **Refuses Payment of Congo Costs.** Andre Ganem, French delegate to the UN, said April 4 that France had taken no steps to pay its share of 1960 Congo costs and would not commit itself to pay the 1961 Congo assessment. (France's share of special UN assessments for the Congo operation was set at $3,099,642 — 6.4% of the 1960 Congo costs.)

● **De Gaulle Vs. UN Role.** A virtual boycott by France of UN operations with which it did not agree was announced by President de Gaulle at his fourth presidential news conference April 11.

De Gaulle, who declared that the UN had been transformed into a body inconsistent with the wishes of its original founders, said that France "did not wish to participate either by her men or her money in any present or possible enterprise of this organization — or this disorganization." He confirmed that France would not pay its share of the cost of UN opera-

117

tions in the Congo or of any future UN military operations. French Foreign Ministry spokesmen said later the same day that de Gaulle's statement had been meant to refer to UN "military" enterprises, rather than all UN enterprises.

● **France Vs. UN Attack on Katanga.** A UN Force September 13 landed an attack on the secessionist state of Katanga in an attempt to overthrow Premier Moise Tshombe's regime and restore central Congolese government authority.

The French Foreign Ministry asserted September 15 that UN officials had exceeded their mandate and possibly violated the UN Charter by ordering "offensive" operations in the Congo.

● **Maintains Katanga View.** A Foreign Ministry statement declared December 8 that France maintained "complete reserve" toward UN actions in Katanga. It described them as contrary to the UN Charter. France December 15 closed French airspace to planes carrying men or supplies to the UN forces in Katanga.

● **UN Vote on Finance.** The General Assembly voted December 20 by 52 to 11 (France and the Soviet bloc opposed, 32 abstentions) to ask the International Court of Justice for an advisory opinion on whether member states were bound legally by the UN Charter to pay their assessments for UN "peace-keeping" operations that had been voted by a majority of UN members.

● **Court Backs Peace Costs.** The International Court of Justice at The Hague handed down the opinion July 20, 1962 that all UN member states were legally obliged to share financial support of the UN peace forces in the Congo and the Middle East.

PART II

THE FOREIGN POLICY YEARS

(1963-1967)

CHAPTER VIII

GOVERNMENT, POLITICS AND THE ECONOMY

De Gaulle Death Plot Thwarted. Five persons were arrested in Paris Feb. 15, 1963 for allegedly plotting to assassinate President Charles de Gaulle that day during his visit in Paris to the Ecole Militaire, France's army staff college. The plotters, linked to the OAS, were arrested several hours before de Gaulle arrived at the Ecole Militaire.

Argoud Seized. Ex-Colonel Antoine Argoud, self-proclaimed leader of the terrorist National Council of Resistance, formerly the Secret Army Organization (OAS), was found by Paris police February 26, bound and beaten in a small truck a few feet from police headquarters.

Argoud, sought by police for two years on rebellion charges, told the police he had been kidnapped from a hotel in Munich, West Germany by three men and brought to Paris. He had rebelled against de Gaulle's Algerian policy. Argoud was indicted in Paris February 27 on charges of plotting against the government.

Miners Strike. French coal miners walked out March 1, 1963 in what originally was intended as a 48-hour nationwide strike for higher wages. Potash, iron and uranium miners joined the strike in sympathy. The coal miners, whose average daily wage was $3.60, demanded an 11% raise. The government had offered a 5-3/4% raise over a 12-month period.

De Gaulle Return-to-Work Order Fails. President de Gaulle March 3 signed a requisition order, effective March 4, requiring the strikers to return to work or face dismissal, fines and imprisonment.

The requisition order was largely ignored March 4 as almost all of the 30,000 miners in the northeast Lorraine region stayed away from the pits. Miners in smaller mines in south and central France reported to their posts but refused to work.

The full impact of the strike was felt March 5 as more than 100,000 miners in the Nord and Pas-de-Calais Departments, who had been on a normal two-day work holiday, joined the 50,000-70,000 mine strikers in the Lorraine, central and southern districts.

Sympathy Strikes. Thousands of other workers throughout the country, in response to a March 3 mine union appeal, staged work stoppages March 5 for 15 minutes to several hours. The sympathy walkouts temporarily halted trains, electric service, newspaper presses, teleprinters and factories. College students sympathetic to the miners left their classes.

Pompidou Plea Fails; Strikes Spread. A government appeal for an end to the strike was made by Premier Pompidou in a TV-radio address March 8. Pompidou said the government had conceded that miners' wages

121

had not kept pace with those of workers in other private and government-owned industries. But he said the raise offered the miners was not negligible and that to offer more would raise the spectre of inflation.

Workers at a natural gas plant in the Pyrenees town of Lacq, which supplied much of the Paris region, extended their 48-hour strike to March 11 and then voted March 11 to prolong the strike indefinitely. Their demands: an 11% wage increase, a shorter work week, a month's paid vacation. The gas plant strike forced the Paris subway March 8 to stop service for two hours and severely reduced suburban electric train service.

Railroad workers staged short spot strikes throughout the country March 12 in support of the miners. The walkouts, ranging from 15 minutes to two hours, affected suburban and longline service.

Strike Talks Collapse. Negotiations to end the nationwide strike of 170,000 coal miners collapsed in Paris March 24 as union officials rejected a new wage offer by the government's coal board. The negotiations had resumed on order of President de Gaulle after he and other ministers had studied the report of a three-man fact-finding committee formed to study the wage gap between workers in nationalized industries and those in private employ.

The fact-finders had conceded that coal industry pay was 10% below (the unions claimed 11%) private industry figures. The committee recommended that the government increase its previous 5.7% raise offer to 8%, 6.5% of which was to be granted April 1, the remainder by the end of the year. The mine unions approved the increase but insisted that all of it be granted April 1. The coal board also opposed the miners' demand for immediate discussion of their request for a 40-hour work week and a fourth week of paid vacations.

Striking miners clashed with police March 26 at a mine entrance in Carling in Lorraine. Several miners and some women were injured.

Nationwide Strikes Continue. While the miners remained on strike, France was plagued by a series of nationwide walkouts of other government workers demanding higher wages. Employees of the nationalized railroads staged a 24-hour strike March 15-16 that almost completely paralyzed rail traffic throughout France. Some 140,000 gas and electric power station workers went on strike for four hours March 20. The walkout caused gas supplies to drop to a dangerously low level. The lack of electricity forced the Paris subways and suburban railroads to halt service; stores and factories could not operate; movie houses were closed; traffic lights were out. The electric power workers went on strike again March 22. Airline ground personnel struck March 20 and caused several flight cancellations and delays. Postmen went on strike March 21.

Workers at the natural gas plant in the Pyrenees town of Lacq signed an agreement March 26 to return to work March 27. They accepted government assurances that they would be given the same concessions granted the coal miners.

Mine Strike Ends. The coal mine unions April 3, 1963 accepted a government wage offer to end their nationwide walkout. The accord provided for an immediate 6.5% wage increase and an additional 6% raise by April 1964. Most of the miners began returning to the pits April 4.

Wage agreements also were reached in the government-owned road, gas and electricity industries, which had been plagued by strikes since March 1. The railroad men April 4 accepted an 8.2% pay increase for 1963. The gas and electric workers April 5 agreed to a 7.35% pay increase for the same period.

Plotters Sentenced. Six members of the National Council of Resistance were convicted March 4, 1963 and sentenced to death for the Aug. 22, 1962 attempt to assassinate President de Gaulle. Three of the six were sentenced *in absentia*. Six others received prison sentences. The trial, conducted by the Military Court of Justice, had started January 28.

Sentenced to death in court: Lt. Colonel Jean-Marie Bastien-Thiry, an air force engineer who had organized the plot; Lt. Alain Bourgenet de la Tocnaye, Bastien-Thiry's deputy; Jacques Prevost, who had directed the machine-gun fire at de Gaulle's car as he drove through Petit-Clamart on his way from Paris to an airport.

Bastien-Thiry was executed by firing squad in Paris March 11. De Gaulle commuted to life in prison the death sentences of two other defendants: Bourgenet de la Tocnaye and Prevost.

Bidault Found in Germany. Georges Bidault, leader of the National Council of Resistance, was detained by Bavarian (West German) police March 10 in Steinebacham-Worthsee, 20 miles west of Munich. Bidault had been in hiding since his expulsion from Italy Sept. 8, 1962.

Bavarian Interior Minister Heinrich Junker said that Bidault, who had asked for West German asylum, was taken from his home. Bidault was returned to his home and, at his request, was given police protection, pending the outcome of his plea for asylum.

Bidault left Germany March 25 by plane for Lisbon, Portugal after the Bavarian state government announced March 19 that he could remain in Bavaria only if he refrained from all political activity, including the granting of political interviews. He had declared March 15: "I will certainly not trade political activity for security. I am the leader of the National Council of Resistance. I am the boss of it all."

A Portuguese Foreign Ministry official said March 27 that Bidault would have to leave Portugal because he had illegally entered the country with false identity documents.

Bidault Seeks Exile in Brazil. Bidault arrived in Rio de Janeiro, Brazil April 9 from Lisbon. Brazil granted Bidault a renewable 90-day tourist visa on condition that he refrain from anti-Gaullist politics. The Brazilian Foreign Ministry emphasized that Bidault was not getting political asylum.

On his arrival in Rio de Janeiro, Bidault said: "I have accepted the Brazilian terms for my entry here.... I will not make political statements while in Brazil, but someday I will return to France."

Plotter Jailed. Serge Bernier was arrested in Paris April 19, 1963 on charges of participating in the Aug. 22, 1962 plot to assassinate President de Gaulle. Bernier, who had been sentenced to death *in absentia* March 4, was seized as he and a companion were trying to steal a car.

Bernier was convicted and sentenced to life in prison by a Paris military court June 25. Another man involved in the de Gaulle assassination plot, Gyula Sari, a Hungarian who had fled his country during the 1956 revolt, also was convicted and received a 20-year sentence. The two convictions brought to 11 the number of persons captured and sentenced for the crime.

Debre Elected to National Assembly. Ex-Premier Michel Debre was elected to the French National Assembly May 5 as a representative of the Indian Ocean island of Reunion, a French department. Debre, a Gaullist, received 30,830 votes to 7,406 for his Communist opponent, Paul Verges. The balloting was in one of four by-elections (one other in Reunion and two in France) held May 5 as a result of the invalidation of those four districts' results in the Nov. 18 and 25, 1962 Assembly elections. Debre, defeated in those elections, was forced to run in the Reunion race when none of the Gaullists elected in November would give up his Assembly seat to permit him to run in France.

Farmers Riot. Farmers in Britanny and southern France staged violent anti-government demonstrations in June and July, 1963 to protest falling fruit and vegetable prices and foreign competition from North Africa, Spain and Italy. The low farm prices resulted from surpluses, particularly of potatoes, tomatoes, apricots and peaches.

The disturbances broke out in late June in Britanny, where farmers used tractors to cover the streets with potatoes. Farmers in Perpignan threw tomatoes at police June 29.

Avignon police July 1 used rifle butts and tear gas in battling farmers who tried to storm the city's prefecture; at least 12 persons were injured. Farm demonstrators July 2 sacked market places in Avignon and Chateau-Renard and forced mayors of 13 towns in the Vaucluse Department to resign.

In a move to ease the farmers' plight the government July 1: (a) ordered a halt in the import of tomatoes and apricots; (b) arranged for special trains to handle the huge apricot crop that had reached the market; (c) granted special subsidies for exporting apricots or processing them into jam. The government July 4 granted wheat farmers a 2% price increase and expanded its wheat price-support program.

Anti-Inflation Plan. The French government announced Sept. 12, 1963 a stabilization plan in a drive for price and financial stability. (Consumer prices had risen 16% in the previous three years.)

Among the plan's features: (a) The prices of manufactured goods would be frozen at the August 31 level; any modifications would require government authorization. (b) A reduction in the budget deficit would be made by cutting public spending by 1,340 million francs ($73,469,551), increasing taxes on sales of land for buildings and putting a 6% sales tax on race track betting. (c) A $408,163,265 bond issue, with tax benefits allowed for 10 years of its 20-year maturity period, would be floated (September 23) to carry off excess credit. (d) Installment buying would be discouraged by raising minimum down-payment requirements and reducing payment duration.

Premier Georges Pompidou said September 12 that the government would discourage wage increases for a year.

Budget. The government announced September 19 that its 1964 budget would be a record $18-1/2 billion, a 7-1/2% increase over 1963. With revenues of $17.58 billion, France's deficit would be $450 million less than in 1962 and would be the lowest deficit since 1952.

De Gaulle Assassin Arrested. Paris police disclosed September 19 the arrest of Lajos Marton, a Hungarian sentenced to death *in absentia*, March 4 for participating in the attempt to assassinate President de Gaulle in August 1962.

Amnesty to Rightists. De Gaulle Dec. 15, 1963 pardoned about 100 persons who had been jailed on charges of subversion in connection with attempts by the Secret Army Organization (OAS) to prevent him from ending the Algerian war. Pardons were also granted to three French youths who had supported the Algerian rebels. None of the amnesties applied to the major OAS leaders, who were serving long prison terms.

Presidential Candidates. Marseilles Mayor Gaston Deferre, a Socialist, announced December 18 that he was a candidate for the French presidential elections scheduled to be held in the fall of 1965. Jean-Louis Tixier-Vignancour, a right-wing lawyer, had announced November 17 that he would run in the presidential election. (This was to be the first election of a French president by popular vote under the system adopted in 1962 by referendum.)

Argoud Sentenced. Ex-Colonel Antoine Argoud, leader of the National Council of Resistance, was convicted of treason and sentenced to life in prison December 30. Argoud was convicted and sentenced in Paris by the Court for the Security of the State.

De Gaulle Assassin Arrested. Swiss police were reported Jan. 18, 1964 to have arrested Georges Watin, who had been sentenced to death *in absentia* by a French court in March 1963 on charges of participating in the August 1962 attempt to assassinate de Gaulle.

Ex-French cabinet minister Jacques Soustelle was arrested by Swiss police in Lausanne February 29 and expelled to an undisclosed country of his choice March 1. Soustelle had been sought by France ever since he fled in 1962 to escape prosecution for his OAS activities.

Defferre Nominated. Gaston Defferre was nominated February 2 as the Socialist Party candidate for the 1965 presidential elections. During sharp debate at the party meeting in Paris February 1-2, Defferre persuaded the conference to permit him to direct his campaign toward a wide sector of left and center opinion. The party also accepted Defferre's program, which included a 15-year social-and-economic plan, abandonment of France's atomic force and endorsement of the Atlantic Alliance as the mechanism of collective security.

De Gaulle Undergoes Surgery. President de Gaulle underwent successful surgery on a diseased prostate gland in a Paris hospital April 17, 1964. Premier Georges Pompidou assumed control of the government pending de Gaulle's resumption of his official duties.

Thorez Replaced as CP Boss. Maurice Thorez was replaced May 17 as secretary general of the French Communist Party by Waldeck Rochet. The announcement came at the close of the party's Seventeenth Congress in Paris. The Congress stressed the party's unity with the French Socialists against President de Gaulle.

Budget Surplus Announced. The French government September 16 announced a 92.08 billion franc ($18-1/2 billion) budget for 1965. Anticipated revenues were estimated at 97.72 billion francs ($19-1/2 billion). Most of the surplus was to be used for public works programs. It was the first time in 36 years that the budget had not shown a deficit.

Expenditures were to rise by 6.9%, increases going for new military equipment, schools, roads, old-age pensions and family allowances. Twenty billion francs were budgeted for defense and foreign aid. Slight income tax cuts were planned.

Economic Plan Approved. The National Assembly November 27 approved, 353-120, the goals of the de Gaulle government's five-year plan (1966-70) for economic and social development: Increases of 27% for overall production, 24% for private consumption and 39% for public consumption, including emphasis on thermonuclear arms development.

Government Employees Strike. Two million government employees and public service workers went on strike for 24 hours Dec. 10-11, 1964 as the major unions protested against government wage restraints. Electricity was cut off at most power stations. Trade, communications, transportation and government and municipal services were disrupted. The state and municipal-operated industries and services returned to normal by December 12.

Municipal Elections. Municipal council elections were held in over 37,000 French cities and towns March 14, 1965. Results showed little change in council control by the Gaullist UNR party or the non-Gaullist parties. Particular interest centered on Marseilles, where Socialist Mayor Gaston Defferre's candidacy in the scheduled 1965 presidential elections was bolstered by a success in run-off balloting held March 21. Defferre's coalition of Socialists, centrists and conservatives won 41 of 63 council seats.

Center, Left Parties. The Popular Republican Movement (MRP), the Catholic center party, voted overwhelmingly in Vichy May 28 to back Defferre's proposal to establish a Federation of the Socialist Left. But the MRP specified these three reservations: (1) that no agreement with the Communists be made; (2) that the goal of the federation be the formation of a single party; (3) that it not become a mere satellite of the Socialist Party.

Nearly all of the 1,500 delegates to the Socialist Party's National Congress, meeting in Clichy near Paris, voted June 6 to accept presidential candidate Gaston Defferre's proposal for a federation of center and left political forces. Socialist Party Secretary Guy Mollet and other party leaders had opposed Defferre's plan but dropped their opposition when it became obvious that most of the delegates were prepared to accept it.

Rightists Nominate Marcilhacy. A political convention of several rightist groups, held in Paris April 25, nominated Pierre Marcilhacy, an independent senator from southwest France, to run against President de Gaulle in the fall's presidential elections. Marcilhacy defeated Jean-Louis Tixier-Vignancourt, an extreme rightist candidate, by 310-167 vote.

Defferre Withdraws Candidacy. Socialist presidential candidate Gaston Defferre withdrew his candidacy June 25, 1965 after his attempts to form a coalition of center and non-Communist left parties had collapsed. The parties—principally the Socialists, Popular Republicans (MRP) and Radicals—had failed to reach an agreement at an all-night meeting held in Paris June 17.

Information Minister Alain Peyrefitte announced July 1 that the planned presidential elections would be held December 5. A second round of balloting would be held December 19 if none of the candidates obtained a clear majority.

Ben Barka Disappears. Mehdi Ben Barka, exiled leader of the opposition to the government of Morocco, disappeared while in Paris Oct. 29, 1965. French Information Minister Alain Peyrefitte said November 10, after a meeting of the French cabinet, that an investigation of the affair had been ordered and that France had informed the Moroccan government that the matter would be followed until its conclusion. (Ben Barka, founder of the leftist National Union of Popular Forces, had been in exile from Morocco for two years. In 1963, he was sentenced to death *in absentia* for allegedly participating in a plot against Moroccan King Hassan and for supporting Algeria in its border conflict with Morocco.)

PRESIDENTIAL ELECTION

First Round Setback for De Gaulle. In a stunning political upset, President de Gaulle failed to obtain an absolute majority of votes in the French presidential election, held Dec. 5, 1965. (This was the first election of a French president by popular vote since 1848. Popular election by a two-round ballot system had been adopted in 1962, by referendum.) As a result, a runoff election was scheduled for December 19 between de Gaulle and his closest competitor on the first ballot, Francois Mitterand, who had campaigned on an independent leftist program and had received the indorsement of the Communist Party.

Complete election returns for metropolitan France, as announced December 7: De Gaulle — 10,504,007 votes, or 43.97%; Mitterand — 7,655,042, 32.04%; Senator Jean Lecaneut, former head of the Popular Republican (MRP) Party — 3,770,771, 15.78%; Jean-Louis Tixier-Vignancour, a right-wing extremist — 1,269,095, 5.31%; Sen. Pierre Marcilhacy, who ran as an independent conservative — 414,056, 1.74%; Marcel Barbu, a former Assembly deputy who backed low cost housing — 278,420, 1.16%. Partial results from France's overseas departments and territories, which backed de Gaulle heavily, pushed his percentage of the vote to at least 44.61%. A record 85% of the registered voters in metropolitan France participated in the vote.

De Gaulle's failure to obtain a majority on the first ballot surprised practically all political observers. In mid-October, an opinion poll by the French Institute of Public Opinion had indicated that he would win about 68% of the vote.

The Campaign. De Gaulle announced his candidacy in a nationwide radio-TV address Nov. 4, 1965. He asked the voters to give him a frank and massive indorsement. Such a vote "would assure the future of the new republic indefinitely," he declared. Without it, "no one can doubt that she [the Fifth Republic] will soon crumble and that France — this time without any hope of recourse — will be reduced to confusion more disastrous than she has ever known."

During the official campaign period (November 19-December 3) the five opposition candidates were permitted equal time (four hours) with de Gaulle on the state controlled radio-television system. Not counted in the equal time were talks by Gaullist ministers before or after the campaign began. For example, Finance Minister Valery Giscard d'Estaing November 18 gave a radio-TV address on the healthy state of the French economy. Supporters of the opposition candidates could not use the state radio-TV system; as a result, ex-Premier Pierre Mendes-France, who backed Mitterand, twice debated former Gaullist Premier Michel Debre, who backed de Gaulle, from a Luxembourg radio station which could be heard in France. The radio-TV addresses by the five opposition candidates were taped in advance and submitted to a five-man government commission before being cleared for broadcast.

De Gaulle, who had originally planned to make a single radio-TV address December 3, the final night of the campaign, decided, however, to speak November 30 when it became apparent that Lecanuet and Mitterand were making a favorable impression on TV and opinion polls showed de Gaulle's percentage dropping. In his November 30 speech, he sharply criticized U.S. domination of NATO and termed the Vietnam war absurd.

Lecanuet, 45, a relative unknown before the election, conducted a vigorous campaign and became known as a "Kennedy" type candidate. In his November 25 TV address he declared: "Don't worry General, France will continue!" Throughout the campaign he sharply criticized de Gaulle's Common Market and NATO policies and opposed France's independent nuclear force.

Mitterand, 49, a member of the small Democratic and Socialist Union (UDSR) party and eleven times minister during the Fourth Republic, also criticized de Gaulle's foreign policy. In a Bordeaux address December 1, he said education and domestic economic progress were more important than an independent atomic weapons program. In a reference to charges that he would be controlled by the Communists, he pledged December 1 that he would be "dominated by no single party, however friendly."

The French Communist Party had indorsed Mitterand September 23 in a central committee statement issued by party chief Waldeck Rochet. The declaration referred to Mitterand as the sole candidate of the left and termed its union with Mitterand a popular front. Although no common program had been agreed on, the party said it backed Mitterand because he opposed personal power and was acceptable to all democrats. "The party", said Rochet, "takes it for granted that the Common Market exists."

De Gaulle, in his December 3 TV address, made what were reported as concessions to the critics of his foreign policy. He pledged to work for the economic union of the Common Market, and he avoided all references to the anti-American stand he had taken in the November 30 speech. Speculation that de Gaulle might withdraw from the second ballot was ended December 8 when Information Minister Alain Peyrefitte said after a cabinet meeting that de Gaulle would naturally be a candidate in the December 19 ballot.

De Gaulle Wins Runoff. De Gaulle was reelected president of France Dec. 19, 1965 by defeating leftist candidate Francois Mitterand in the run-off election.

Complete election returns, including France's overseas territories, were released December 20 by the Interior Ministry. De Gaulle received 13,085,407 votes, or 55.2% of the valid ballots. Mitterand received 10,623,247 (44.8%). Some 661,791 ballots (2.34% of those in metropolitan

France) were marked blank and were void. Of France's registered voters 23,864,586 (84.5%) cast ballots, compared with the record 24,002,093 (85%) December 5.

Mitterand conceded his defeat at 9 p.m., about an hour after the polls closed. He said: "We are faced with a dying regime, a reborn Left and a republic which will be rejuvenated some day. When we see how shaky Gaullism is with de Gaulle, what will it be without de Gaulle? I shall resume the struggle against Gaullism tomorrow."

De Gaulle returned to Paris from his country home December 21 and released a statement saying he had received "a direct mandate from the whole French people" that had "decidedly confirmed" his regime "before the nation and the world."

During the official runoff campaign period December 11 - 17, de Gaulle and Mitterand spoke on radio and TV under equal-time regulations. De Gaulle changed his TV style from that used during the campaign for the first ballot by permitting himself to be interviewed on TV by a reporter. In what was regarded as his first public statement about the problem of choosing his successor, de Gaulle, 75, said December 15: "Naturally a day will come... when de Gaulle will pass away"; France would then have to select a man "faithful to the line it has pursued at my calling." But he described himself as "still, for the moment, a national necessity," and he warned that repudiating him in favor of a "regime of the parties would be an immense disaster." In his final TV appeal (December 17), he said: "I am not saying that I am perfect or that I am younger than my age. I know, better than anyone, that I will have to have successors and that the nation will choose them so that he will follow the same line. But I am in the process of working to assure progress.... This is why I am ready to assume again the highest duty."

Mitterand December 13 said de Gaulle's foreign policy was "anti-American with the Russians; anti-Russian with the Americans; anti-British with the Germans; anti-German with the British; anti-Chinese with the Russians, and anti-Russian — I want to stop here." He declared December 17 that he offered the voters a "fundamental choice between authoritarianism and a republic of citizens." "Who can pretend," he said, "that France is nothing without him [de Gaulle]?"

All the candidates eliminated on the December 5 ballot (Jean Louis Tixier-Vignancour, Sen. Pierre Marcilhacy, Marcel Barbu and Jean Lecanuet) opposed de Gaulle. Lecanuet urged his supporters December 16 not to vote for de Gaulle, but he did not indorse Mitterand.

De Gaulle Revises Cabinet. De Gaulle was inaugurated Jan. 8, 1966 for his second seven-year term as president of the Fifth French Republic. He immediately renamed Georges Pompidou as premier, and a new French cabinet was announced later in the day. The incoming Pompidou cabinet included 11 newcomers.

A major cabinet change was the replacing of Finance Minister Valery Giscard d'Estaing with ex-Gaullist Premier Michel Debre. Debre became minister of economy and finance. The second major change was the appointment of ex-Fourth Republic Premier Edgar Faure as agriculture minister. Faure replaced Edgard Pisani, who became public works minister. (The Radical Socialist Party January 10 issued a communique expelling Faure from the party. The statement said Faure had stepped out of the party by supporting de Gaulle's candidacy in the presidential election.)

The new cabinet (asterisks indicate new cabinet members):

> *Premier*—Georges Pompidou.

> *Ministers of State: Cultural Affairs*—Andre Malraux; *Administrative Reform*—Louis Joxe; *Overseas Territories and Departments*—General Pierre Billotte*.

> *Ministers: Justice*—Jean Foyer; *Foreign Affairs*—Maurice Couve de Murville; *Interior*—Roger Frey; *Armed Forces*—Pierre Messmer; *Education*—Christian Fouchet; *Public Works*—Edgard Pisani; *Agriculture*—Edgar Faure*; *Industry*—Raymond Marcellin; *Social Affairs (health and labor)*—Jean-Marcel Jeanneney*; *Minister—Delegate for Scientific, Atomic & Space Research*—Alain Peyrefitte; *Veterans' Affairs*—Alexandre Sanguinetti*; *Postal and Telecommunications*—Jacques Marette; *Youth and Sports*—Francois Missoffe*; *Economy and Finance*—Michel Debre*.

> *Secretaries of State: Parliamentary Relations*—Pierre Dumas; *Foreign Affairs*—Jean de Broglie; *Information*—Yvon Bourges; *Foreign Affairs for Cooperation with Former Colonies*—Jean Charbonnel*; *Interior*—Andre Bord*; *Budget*—Robert Boulin; *Foreign Trade*—Charles de Chambrun*; *Education*—Michel Habib-Deloncle; *Housing*—Raymond Nungesser*; *Transportation*—Andre Bettencourt*.

Ben Barka Affair

Gaullist Intelligence Officials Implicated. During testimony Jan. 14, 1966 before Judge Louis Zollinger, who was investigating the disappearance and presumed kidnapping of Moroccan leftist Mehdi Ben Barka, several high French officials were implicated in the case. Police Inspector Louis Souchon testified that three officials were involved. Souchon, being held on suspicion of participating in the kidnapping, said he had been informed by another defendant, Antoine Lopez, a French secret agent, that the abduction of Ben Barka had been cleared in advance with (1) Jacques Foccart, head of President de Gaulle's secretariat; (2) Major Marcel Le Roy of the SDECE (France's counter-intelligence agency, Service de Documentation Exterieur et de Contre-Espionage); and (3) Jacques Aubert of the Interior Ministry.

Witness Found Dead. Georges Figon, a key witness in the disappearance of Ben Barka, was found dead January 17 in a Paris apartment. According to Agence France-Presse, Figon had shot himself just as the police were about to arrest him. Figon, an ex-convict and underworld figure, had been suspected of persuading Ben Barka to come to Paris in October 1965, immediately prior to his disappearance October 29.

SDECE Shakeup. President de Gaulle January 19 discharged air force General Paul Jacquier as SDECE director following testimony before Judge Zollinger that SDECE officials had been involved in the Ben Barka abduction. Judge Zollinger had heard testimony from Major Marcel Le Roy, one of Jacquier's subordinates, that Le Roy had been fully informed by Antoine Lopez, an SDECE agent under arrest in the case, of the Ben Barka kidnapping. Le Roy admitted having waited from Oct. 30, 1965 (the day after Ben Barka disappeared) to November 2 to report to Jacquier on the information Lopez was giving him. Le Roy was dismissed from the SDECE January 18 following the disclosure of his testimony.

Moroccan Officials Accused; Arrest Warrant Issued. Judge Zollinger January 20 issued an international arrest warrant for Moroccan Interior Minister General Mohammad Oufkir. French officials said the warrant made Oufkir subject to arrest in countries with which Paris had bilateral judicial and extradition agreements.

The warrant was for Oufkir and two of his close aides, Major Ahmed Dlimi, head of Moroccan security services, and Larbi Miloud Chtouki, head of the secret police. Witnesses testifying before Zollinger had asserted that all three men were in Paris Oct. 30, 1965, the day after Ben Barka's disappearance.

According to testimony given to Zollinger by SDECE agent Lopez, Lopez had met Oufkir, Dlimi and Chtouki October 30 at Paris' Orly Airport and had driven with them to a suburban Paris villa owned by Georges Boucheseiche, an ex-convict and underworld figure. Lopez and French police Inspector Souchon had previously testified that they had driven Ben Barka to Boucheseiche's villa October 29. The villa was cited in testimony as the last place Ben Barka had been seen alive. Georges Figon, the witness found dead January 17, had stated in an interview published in the news weekly *L'Express* January 10 that he had watched Oufkir torture Ben Barka in the villa October 30.

French-Moroccan Diplomatic Rift. France and Morocco recalled their ambassadors from each other's capitals January 23-24 in a growing dispute stemming from the probable murder of Ben Barka.

French Ambassador-to-Morocco Robert Gillet was recalled January 23 following a Moroccan government announcement January 23 that it had rejected the warrants for Oufkir, Dlimi and Chtouki. Gillet presented the Moroccan government with a French Foreign Ministry note stating that Judge Zollinger was convinced that "the Moroccan interior minister organized the kidnapping and that (Oufkir) and several of his direct collaborators participated personally in the final phase of the operation." The note said Gillet had been recalled because the Moroccan government had failed to take any adequate action in reply to French demands for action against Oufkir, Dlimi and Chtouki.

At a diplomatic reception in Rabat January 23, King Hassan II declared his support of Oufkir and his aides in the face of the French government's charge.

Moroccan Ambassador-to-France Prince Moulay Ali was recalled January 24. (The Moroccan and French embassies in Paris and Rabat were left under the direction of *charges d'affaires*.)

Economic Plan. Information Minister Yvon Bourges announced Feb. 16, 1966, following a cabinet meeting presided over by President de Gaulle, that the government had approved measures to implement the fifth economic plan (1966-1970).

Economy and Finance Minister Michel Debre told a news conference February 16 that the measures approved, to cost $180 million, would provide for expansion with stability and social progress. Debre also said the minimum wage would rise 2.12%, government allotments to families and the aged would increase, and 15,000 new housing units would be built in Paris. Businesses were to receive a 10% tax credit for spending on new equipment. Railway passenger and freight rates were to increase by an average of 5%. A new cabinet committee was to be created to study the problem of foreign investment in France.

De Gaulle Accuses Morocco on Ben Barka. President de Gaulle, at his thirteenth semiannual press conference February 21, directly charged Moroccan Interior Minister Mohammad Oufkir with responsibility for the abduction (and presumed murder) of exiled Moroccan leader Mehdi Ben Barka. "Oufkir has never, and with reason, explained his comings and goings in and around Paris," de Gaulle declared. "A member of the Moroccan government (Oufkir) has intervened directly on French territory, and . . . (Morocco) has done nothing . . . to justify, or to make amends for the infringement made on our sovereignty. It is therefore inevitable . . . that French-Moroccan relations are suffering the consequences."

Amnesty Bill Passed. The National Assembly June 3, 1966 passed an amnesty bill granting freedom to about 3,200 persons sentenced for crimes committed during the Algerian War. The bill also empowered President de Gaulle to pardon by decree four former generals — Raoul Salan, Edmond Jouhaud, Maurice Challe and Andre Zeller — who had led an abortive Algiers uprising in April 1961. De Gaulle July 13 pardoned Zeller, who had served five years of a 15-year sentence, and 11 other political prisoners, including Jean-Marie Vincent, who had been serving a life sentence for a 1961 bombing attack on the President.

Ben Barka Suspect Surrenders. Lt. Colonel Ahmed Dlimi, head of the Moroccan state security service, voluntarily surrendered to French officials in Paris Oct. 19, 1966. He had arrived from Morocco under an assumed name the previous day. A communique issued October 18 by King Hassan II's office in Rabat had said that Dlimi had gone to Paris to exonerate himself and the Moroccan government of any complicity in the probable murder in France of Mehdi Ben Barka.

Besides Dlimi, twelve others were implicated in the Ben Barka affair: General Oufkir, Moroccan interior minister; Larbi Miloud Chtouki, Moroccan police official; El Ghali El Mahi, Moroccan student; Antoine Lopez, auxiliary agent in the French counter-intelligence service, the SDECE; Maj. Marcel Le Roy, a former member of the SDECE; Philippe Bernier, a French journalist; Louis Souchon and Roger Voitot, French police officers; and four French underworld figures — Georges Boucheseiche, Julien Le Ny, Pierre Dubail and Jean Palisse.

Dlimi's surrender brought to a halt the Paris trial of the above 13 persons accused of complicity in the kidnapping and presumed murder of Ben Barka.

The preliminary investigation into Ben Barka's disappearance had been concluded in March but was reopened April 27 at the request of the French Ministry of Justice. The investigation was completed June 8, and trials were ordered for the 13 defendants. Seven of them, including Oufkir, Dlimi, Chtouki, and the four French underworld figures mentioned above, were to be tried *in absentia.*

The trial began September 5. The jury was scheduled to hand down a verdict October 19 on the six persons being tried in court and October 20 on Dlimi, General Oufkir and the five others tried *in absentia.* With

Dlimi's arrival, however, the trial was suspended indefinitely to permit the presentation of new evidence.

Record Budget. The National Assembly Nov. 10, 1966 approved by a 295-142 vote a record budget of $22 billion for fiscal 1967. Finance Minister Michel Debre had said at a news conference July 13 that the budget adhered to the price stabilization program and was based on the assumption that prices would rise by only 2.3% in 1967 while the gross national product would increase by 11%.

Challe Pardoned. President de Gaulle pardoned ex-General Maurice Challe December 23. Challe had served five years of a 15-year sentence for his involvement in the military uprising in Algiers in April 1961. De Gaulle also reduced or remitted the sentences of 33 other persons who had been imprisoned on subversive charges.

Leftist Election Pact. The French Communist Party and Francois Mitterrand's Federation of the Democratic-Socialist Left agreed December 20 to form a loose coalition for the 1967 spring parliamentary elections. The agreement would end the Communist Party's 20 years of virtual isolation in French politics.

The agreement provided that, although the Communist Party and the Federation would run separate candidates in the first round of balloting March 5, the candidate having the lower number of votes, if more than one remained in the running, would be withdrawn on the second balloting a week later to increase the left's chances of defeating a Gaullist candidate. (French elections were decided in two stages unless one of the candidates received a majority on the first ballot. Any candidate receiving less than 10% of the vote on the first ballot was required to withdraw.)

The withdrawal agreement was limited to constituencies "where the left is in a position to win." The Communist Party indicated that it would withdraw its candidate only in favor of another leftist, while the Federation indicated that it might throw its support behind a non-leftist if it felt the Communist candidate had no chance of winning.

French Communist Party Congress. The French Communist Party, holding its eighteenth Congress in Levallois Jan. 4-8, 1967, mildly indorsed President de Gaulle. A resolution adopted January 8 praised de Gaulle "without hesitation" for the improvement of Franco-Soviet relations and for his opposition to United States policy in Vietnam. It noted, however, de Gaulle's "negative aspects," including his record on disarmament.

PARLIAMENTARY ELECTIONS CUT GAULLIST MARGIN

Left Makes Big Advance. The Gaullist majority in the French National Assembly was reduced to the bare minimum — one seat — in a two-round general election held March 5 and 12.

Candidates pledged to support de Gaulle won 244 of the Assembly's 487 seats; the combined opposition won 241 seats. In the outgoing Assembly elected in 1962, the Gaullists had controlled 269 seats, the opposition 213.

The big winners in the election were the French Communist Party (PCF) headed by Waldeck Rochet, and the non-Communist Federation of the Democratic-Socialist Left, headed by Francois Mitterrand. The PCF won 73 seats, a gain of 32, and the Federation won 116 seats, a gain of 25.

The leftist gains resulted from the successful implementation of a coalition agreement worked out in December 1966 by the PCF and the Federation and joined by ex-Premier Pierre Mendes-France's Unified Socialist Party (PSU). The announced aim of the agreement was to defeat as many Gaullist candidates as possible.

Official Gaullist candidates were grouped in the Democratic Union for the Fifth Republic, which consisted of the Union for the New Republic (UNR) of Premier Georges Pompidou, the Independent Republicans (R1) of ex-Finance Minister Valery Giscard d'Estaing and the Democratic Workers Union (UDT). The Federation comprised the Socialist Party (SFIO) of Guy Mollet, the Radicals and a number of small political clubs. The remaining candidates were grouped in the PCF, the PSU, the Democratic Center Party (PCD) of Senator Jean Lecanuet and a small rightist group headed by Jean-Louis Tixier-Vigancourt; several leftists and moderates ran independently.

Eighty-one candidates, 68 of them Gaullist, were elected in the first-round balloting March 5. The Gaullist candidates won 8,453,512 (37.75%) of the 22,392,317 votes cast. (The total vote represented 80.9% of the registered voters.) The PCF received 5,029,808 votes (22.46%), the Federation 4,207,166 (18.79%), the PCD 2,864,272 (12.79%), moderates and leftists 1,330,967 (5.95%) and the PSU 506,592 (2.26%).

In a hard round of bargaining following the March 5 voting, the Federation, PCF and PSU March 7 forged a single slate of candidates to contest the Gaullists in the second-round balloting March 12. The PCF sacrificed 15 of its candidates by dropping them in favor of a non-Communist leftist, although these PCF candidates actually had received more votes in the first-round balloting. The successful implementation of the pre-election agreement meant that, for the first time since the Popular Front in 1936, French politics was polarized in two broad coalitions. In the second-round voting, a Gaullist faced a leftist in each of about 300 of the 405 constituencies being contested.

Second-Round Round Totals. The popular vote in the second round March 12: Valid ballots cast, 18,572,261 (about 80% of the registered voters); Fifth Republic (UNR, UDT, RI), 7,985,381 (43%); Federation (SFIO, Radicals), 4,460,612 (24%); PCF, 4,002,506 (21.5%); PCD, 1,647,287 (8.8%); Moderates and leftists, 302,999 (1.6%); PSU, 173,476 (1%).

Composition of the 1962 and 1967 Assemblies:

1962		1967	
UNR-UDT-RI	269	UNR-UDT-RI	244
SFIO	66	Federation	116
PCD	55	PCF	73
PCF	41	PCD	27
Democratic Rally	39	Various moderate	15
Nonaligned	12	Various left	5
		PSU	5

In a bid to strengthen the Gaullists in the election, de Gaulle had instructed all but two of his cabinet ministers to run in the election. Premier Georges Pompidou and five other ministers were elected in the first-round balloting March 5. But in the runoff elections March 12, Foreign Minister

Maurice Couve de Murville, Armed Forces Minister Pierre Messmer, Veterans' Affairs Minister Alexandre Sanguinetti and State Secretary for Foreign Assistance Jean Charbonnel were defeated.

Although French law stipulated that a cabinet minister could not simultaneously hold a legislative seat, the defeat of the ministers did not necessarily mean that they would be dropped from the cabinet. Elected deputies who were named to cabinet posts were replaced in their Assembly seats by substitutes [suppleants].

Mendes-France Elected. Ex-Premier Mendes-France made a political comeback after nine years by defeating his Gaullist opponent in Grenoble in the second-round balloting March 12. His election had been practically assured by the withdrawal of the PCF candidate after the March 5 voting. Federation leader Mitterrand, PCF Secretary General Rochet and RI leader Giscard d'Estaing had all been reelected in the March 5 voting.

Jacques Soustelle, former Gaullist leader who turned against de Gaulle during the Algiers rebellion, lost to his Gaullist opponent in Lyons in the March 12 voting. Soustelle had conducted his campaign from exile since he was subject to arrest in France.

Communists Hail Advance. In a statement issued after the election March 13, the Communist Party leadership committee declared: "the dominant fact of the second round" was the Gaullist "set-back" and the electorate's "massive approval" of the left; the alliance of the Federation, PCF and PSU could soon become a majority and could "assure a genuinely democratic replacement of the Gaullist regime."

Pompidou Heads New Cabinet. President de Gaulle renamed Georges Pompidou as premier April 6, 1967. On Pompidou's recommendation, de Gaulle announced the formation of the new cabinet April 7. Seven former members were dropped from their posts, and five others changed portfolios; there were eight new members.

Foreign Minister Maurice Couve de Murville, Defense Minister Pierre Messmer, and Economic and Finance Minister Michel Debre all retained their posts.

The major changes: Christian Fouchet, former education minister, became interior minister, replacing Roger Frey, who was named minister of state in charge of relations with parliament; alain Peyrefitte, former minister of state in charge of scientific research, became education minister; Louis Joxe, former minister of state for administrative reform, succeeded Jean Foyer as justice minister; Foyer was dropped from the cabinet, as were Alexandre Sanguinetti, war veterans minister, and Jacques Marette, post office and telecommunications minister.

The new cabinet (asterisk denotes new member):

> *Premier*—Pompidou; *Ministers of State: Cultural Affairs*—Andre Malraux; *Civil Service*—Edmond Michelet*; *Overseas Departments and Territories*—Pierre Billotte; *Scientific Research, Atomic and Space Affairs*—Maurice Schumann*; *Relations with Parliament*—Roger Frey.

> *Minister Delegate to the Premier: Economic Planning and Town and Country Planning*—Raymond Marcellin.

Ministers: Justice—Louis Joxe; *Foreign*—Maurice Couve de Murville; *Interior*—Christian Fouchet; *Armed Forces*—Pierre Messmer; *Economic and Finances*—Michel Debre; *Education*—Alain Peyrefitte; *Equipment and Housing*—Edgard Pisani; *Agriculture*—Edgar Faure; *Industry*—Olivier Guichard*; *Social Affairs*—Jean-Marcel Jeanneney; *Transportation*—Jean Chamant*; *War Veterans*—Henri Duvillard*; *Post Office and Telecommunications*—Yves Guena; *Youth and Sports*—Francois Missoffe; *Information*—Georges Gorse.

Secretaries of State: Attached to the Premier (Tourism)—Pierre Dumas; *Attached to the Foreign Affairs Minister*—Andre Bettencourt; *Attached to the Minister of Foreign Affairs (cooperation with developing nations)*—Yvon Bourges; *Attached to the Interior Minister*—Andre Bord; *Attached to the Economy and Finance Minister*—Robert Boulin and Roland Nungesser; *Attached to the Social Affairs Minister (Employment)*—Jacques Chirac.

Assembly Elects Chaban-Delmas Speaker. In the first test of Gaullist strength following the parliamentary elections, the National Assembly April 3 reelected Gaullist Jacques Chaban-Delmas to his third term as speaker. Chaban-Delmas, by a 261-214 vote, defeated Gaston Deferre, a Socialist and parliamentary leader of the Federation of the Democratic and Socialist Left. In contrast to its policy in previous speaker elections, the French Communist Party did not put up its own candidate but threw its support to Deferre.

De Gaulle Seeks Special Economic Powers. President de Gaulle announced April 26 that he would ask the National Assembly to grant him executive authority to decree economic and social legislation during the six-month period ending October 31. He said measures so decreed would go into effect immediately and would be subject to ratification by the Assembly no later than December 31. De Gaulle declared that the urgency of social and economic reform precluded extensive parliamentary debate. The proposed executive-powers bill, which would bar the Assembly from debating and voting social legislation during the six-month period, came under heavy attack from the Communist Party and non-Communist Federation of the Democratic-Socialist Left. Both indicated April 27 that they would introduce a censure motion when the bill was presented to the Assembly May 17. In a statement issued April 27, the Communist Party denounced the measure as undemocratic and reactionary.

Equipment and Housing Minister Edgard Pisani, a "left Gaullist," resigned from the cabinet April 28 in protest against the measure. Francois-Xavier Ortoli, director of France's five-year economic development plan, was appointed to succeed Pisani.

France's four major labor federations May 3 issued a call for a one-day general strike May 17. The four unions: the Socialist-dominated Workers Force, the Communist-led General Confederation of Workers, the Catholic-oriented French Democratic Confederation of Workers and the Federation of the National Education, the national teachers' union. All four federations published almost identical statements charging that the special powers sought by de Gaulle would endanger union liberties and social advancement.

Ben Barka Trial Ends; Eight Found Guilty. Eight persons were convicted and five defendants acquitted June 5, 1967 at the conclusion of a trial of 13 persons accused of complicity in the Oct. 29, 1965 abduction and probable murder in France of Moroccan opposition leader Mehdi Ben Barka. The Paris trial had been resumed April 17 after having been in recess since Oct. 19, 1966 following the sudden arrival in Paris of Lt. Col. Ahmed Dlimi, head of the Moroccan state security service and one of seven defendants in the case being tried *in absentia.*

Besides Dlimi, the other defendants in the Ben Barka affair were: Gen. Mohammed Oufkir, Moroccan interior minister; Larbi Chtouki, Moroccan police official and deputy of Oufkir; El Gahli El Mahi, Antoine Lopez, Maj. Marcel Le Roy, Philippe Bernier, Louis Souchon, Roger Voitot; George Boucheseiche, Julien Le Ny, Pierre Dubail and Jean Palisse. Those tried *in absentia* in the resumed trial: Oufkir, Chtouki, Boucheseiche, Le Ny, Palisse and Dubail.

The three judges and the jury June 5 sentenced Lopez and Souchon to prison terms of eight years and six years, respectively, for illegal arrest (of Ben Barka) and acquitted Dlimi, El Mahi, Bernier, Voitot and Le Roy. Sitting without the jury, the judges then convicted Oufkir, Chtouki, Boucheseiche, Le Ny, Palisse and Dubail and sentenced them to life prison terms *in absentia.*

Special Economic Powers Granted. The special Enabling Law authorizing the government to rule France's economy and social welfare system by decree-laws up to October 31 was passed by the National Assembly June 16. According to the government, the legislation was to enable it to take measures to assure that the country's economy was made more competitive by July 1, 1968, the date when all tariffs among the Common Market countries would be removed. Under the provisions of the bill, the government was empowered to legislate, without submitting to debate or vote in the parliament, measures (1) to give workers a share in the profits and ownership of industry; (2) to implement reforms in the social security system and employment practices, and (3) to modernize industry.

The four major labor federations, which had previously stated their opposition to the granting of the decree powers, staged a 24-hour strike May 17, causing severe disruptions in public services such as transportation, gas and electricity and schools. The same day, a protest march was held in Paris by about 100,000 participants. Earlier May 16, printers and newspaper workers struck in Paris, preventing President de Gaulle's press conference remarks from reaching the public that day.

The bill, first introduced in the Assembly May 5, faced a joint motion of censure May 20 by the Federation of the Left, led by Francois Mitterrand, and the Communist Party. The censure motion was defeated the same day, receiving 236 votes, only 8 short of the 244 necessary for it to pass in the 487-seat Assembly. (In accordance with the French constitution, defeat of the censure motion was formally regarded as a vote of adoption for the enabling bill.) The Senate, composed mostly of opposition members, rejected the bill June 2 and again June 13. The Senate's rejection allowed the Assembly to reintroduce the censure motion twice more: the second time June 9 and before the third and final reading of the bill June 16. Both times the motion was defeated by a narrow margin, and the bill became law June 16.

Special Laws Decreed. The government decreed 35 ordinances between July and the end of September 1967 in the fields provided for by the Enabling Law. Among the major ordinances were:

Employment: (1) Creation of a National Employment Agency with special powers to aid regions facing severe unemployment; (2) extension of the powers of the National Employment Fund to retrain workers; and (3) a raise in minimum unemployment benefits.

Profit-sharing: (1) Measures making profit-sharing compulsory for all firms employing 100 or more workers (optional for smaller firms), effective Jan. 1, 1968. The law provided three formulas for implementing the plan: (a) issuance of shares to employees, (b) creation of an employee-owned investment fund, which was to be at the firm's disposal, or (c) participation in a national investment fund which could invest only in private enterprise (if no agreement was reached between management and labor, the second formula would automatically apply); (2) special rules governing the establishment of investment funds by individual firms; and (3) exemption of sums paid to workers under profit-sharing plans from personal income taxes.

Social security: (1) Creation of three new national funds to cover sickness, retirement and family benefits; (2) increased health contributions by both employers and workers and a cut in medical benefits; (3) extension of maternity and sickness insurance to foreign nationals residing in France; and (4) financial and administrative measures to offset a social security deficit of approximately $800 million.

Agriculture: (1) Measures to aid the transformation of agricultural cooperatives into "companies of commercial type" already existing in other Common Market countries; and (2) financial incentives aimed at the retirement of older farmers.

Trade & finance: (1) Measures to stimulate investment through savings and to enable firms to buy their own shares; (2) creation of a strong Stock Exchange Commission (to upgrade the international role of the Paris Bourse); (3) fiscal and other incentives aimed at company mergers; and (4) protective measures for a limited period to reduce company bankruptcies.

Modernization: Financial incentives to induce Paris-based firms to transfer to less-developed provincial areas. (A total of $60 million was made available to private business for this purpose.)

(As part of the new economic policy, the government increased Paris transit fares effective July 15 and freight rates on the national railways October 1. Gas and electricity rates also were raised.

Farmers Riot. Thousands of farmers demonstrated throughout France Oct. 2 and 12, 1967 in protest against the government's agricultural policies. The demonstrations were the first conducted at the national level since the farmer riots in 1963.

Demonstrations were staged October 2 in response to a call by the National Farmers Union for a nationwide "action day" to press farmer demands, particularly for higher prices and greater government protection. While the majority of the demonstrations were orderly, violence broke out in more than a dozen cities and towns.

In Quimper, Britanny, a crowd of 6,000-10,000 farmers clashed with police in the most serious incident of the day. Some 179 policemen and more than 100 farmers were injured in the clash.

President de Gaulle met with his cabinet October 3 to discuss the farmer unrest. In a statement issued after the meeting, de Gaulle noted that small farmers had experienced difficulties because of "unavoidable economic changes," but he asserted that these were changes that "the government has tried to direct and whose worst consequences it has tried to alleviate."

The leftist opposition (Communist Party and Federation of the Democratic and Socialist Left) introduced in the National Assembly October 3 a censure motion charging that the government had to bear the basic responsibility for "pushing the farmers to demonstrations and revolt." The motion was defeated October 10 when it received only 207 of the 244 votes necessary for adoption.

Farmers staged further demonstrations October 12. The demonstrators barricaded major roads throughout the country, harrangued motorists and handed out leaflets stating their case against the government.

Budget Approved. The National Assembly voted by 252 to 234 November 11 to approve a $25.6 billion government budget for 1968. Military expenditures were increased by 5% over 1967 and science outlays by 17%. The deficit was expected to total $360 million.

Gaullist Congress. The Union for the New Republic (Gaullist party) held its fourth national congress in Lille November 26-28. The major task of the congress was to prevent the slow deterioration of the party in the face of growing opposition from the Federation of the Democratic-Socialist Left as well as the Communist Party. Premier Georges Pompidou November 26 asserted the government's "firm will to oppose the seizure of the power by the Communist Party under any mask whatever." The congress approved a new name for the party — the Union of Democrats for the Fifth Republic.

Jouhaud Pardoned. President de Gaulle Dec. 22, 1967, pardoned ex-General Edmond Jouhaud, who had served five years of a life sentence for attempting to overthrow the French government during the Algerian War.

CHAPTER IX
FRANCE AND WESTERN DEFENSE

ATOMIC POLICY AND NATO

President de Gaulle's commitment to the development of an independent French nuclear striking force continued to clash with the efforts of the United States to create an integrated NATO nuclear force. Two major U.S.-supported proposals for NATO nuclear integration were under discussion and negotiation throughout 1963. The first, which originated from the Anglo-American agreement reached in Nassau in December 1962,* was referred to as the "multinational" force — or MNF. The second, proposed by the Kennedy administration in March 1963, was referred to as the "multilateral" force — or MLF. France rejected the Nassau Pact, but participated in the negotiations for the establishment of MNF and joined in a compromise agreement, announced May 24 in Ottawa by the NATO foreign ministers. France boycotted MLF negotiations because de Gaulle viewed the proposal as an American challenge to his plan for a French national nuclear force.

Under the concept of MNF, existing national nuclear striking forces were to be assigned to a joint NATO command. These forces — three U.S. Polaris missile submarines, a number of envisaged British Polaris missile submarines, the entire RAF "V" bomber force, and the nuclear-armed tactical jet fighter-bomber units of eight other NATO nations including France — were to be subject to NATO operational control but were to retain their national identity and be subject to withdrawal in the event of overriding national emergencies.

Non-nuclear NATO nations, including France, had demanded at a Nov. 13, 1957 Paris meeting of the NATO Parliamentary Military Committee that their NATO-committed forces be armed with U.S. tactical atomic warheads. Secretary of State John Foster Dulles Nov. 19, 1957 confirmed that the United States would establish nuclear warheads for NATO nations' use at strategic points throughout the NATO perimeter. At a Dec. 16, 1957 Paris meeting of the NATO foreign ministers, Dulles announced the U.S. proposal to establish nuclear warhead stockpiles in NATO countries. The stockpiles would remain under U.S. custody. In the event of war, U.S. crews would arm the NATO nations' missiles or aircraft with the nuclear warheads. Firing of the missiles would require full agreement of both the United States and the recipient NATO nation. A bill, authorizing this method of sharing U.S. nuclear weapons (known as the "double key" system) with NATO nations, was passed by the U.S. Congress in June 1958 and signed by President Eisenhower July 2, 1958. Under the authorization of this legislation, U.S. nuclear warheads were assigned to the NATO-committed units of eight NATO members. The eight: France, West Germany, Greece, Canada, Belgium, the Netherlands, Italy, and Turkey.

The MLF proposal envisaged the joint construction and operation of a Western fleet of 25 warships, each equipped to fire eight Polaris missiles. The vessels would be manned by mixed crews, each representing at least three participating nations and each to include a United States contingent. The fleet would be a self-contained force with a commander operationally responsible to NATO's Supreme Allied Commander, Europe. The United States would supply the Polaris missiles and their nuclear warheads and guidance system.

The MLF, according to its proponents, would be a genuinely integrated force, organized so as to make it impossible for any unit to be identified nationally or to be diverted to national use. Although the United States would be the only member to have its nationals aboard all of the 25 vessels planned, each major participant would have to give its assent to the launching of the fleet's nuclear-armed missiles. One of the main objectives of the MLF proposal was to counter West German pressures for independent acquisition of nuclear weapons.

Each major participant thus would retain veto power over the fleet's use. It was estimated that MLF would cost $4 to $6 billion and would take eight years to complete.

De Gaulle Rejects Nassau Plan. President de Gaulle Jan. 14, 1963 rejected the U.S.-British proposal for a multi-national NATO nuclear force, as formulated by President Kennedy and Prime Minister Macmillan at their Nassau meeting in December 1962. De Gaulle's rejection of the plan was linked with his simultaneous rebuff to Britain's application for membership in the European Common Market.

De Gaulle's statement, made at a formal Paris presidential press conference, his seventh since resuming office, made it clear that France would proceed with the building of its own independent nuclear force. He argued that Western Europe could depend on the U.S. nuclear deterrent only so long as the United States remained the sole world nuclear power. The Soviet Union's development of nuclear weapons, said de Gaulle, had confronted the United States for the first time "with the possibility of direct destruction." As a result, de Gaulle argued, France was required in its own defense to construct its own nuclear force. De Gaulle conceded that France would be unable to build a nuclear striking force equivalent in strength to that of the United States or the Soviet Union, but he maintained "that the French atomic force... will have the somber and terrible capability of destroying in a few seconds millions and millions of men. This fact cannot fail to have at least some bearing on the intents of any possible aggressor."

French A-Force Plans Announced. Defense Minister Pierre Messmer predicted January 22 that the first elements of France's planned nuclear force would be operational by the end of 1963. Messmer said that this first unit of the striking force would consist of three Mirage IV supersonic bombers armed with atomic bombs three times more powerful than a Hiroshima-type bomb. The completed force was to consist of 50 nuclear-armed Mirage IV's by 1966. Messmer added that France's H-bomb and strategic missile programs were ahead of schedule.

JFK Rebuts de Gaulle. The United States response to the challenge issued by de Gaulle at his January 14 Paris press conference was delivered by President Kennedy January 24. Kennedy referred specifically to de Gaulle's contention that France needed an independent nuclear force because the United States could not be trusted to employ its nuclear strength — and thus risk Soviet nuclear retaliation — to defend Western Europe. Mr. Kennedy said: "I think the United States over the last 15 years... has given evidence that its commitments are good. Some in some parts of Europe may not believe that commitment, but I think that... Khrushchev does, and I think he is right."

Seven Nations Back A-Force; Paris Opposes. It was reported from Paris Feb. 27-28, 1963 that seven NATO nations — Britain, Italy, West Germany, Greece, Belgium, the Netherlands and Turkey — had expressed support for the Anglo-American plan to establish a unified Western nuclear striking force.

The proposal had been submitted to the NATO Permanent Council in Paris February 27 by Livingston T. Merchant, U.S. special envoy for the proposed NATO nuclear force. Although the Council's session was closed to newsmen, it was reported that the United States and Britain had reaffirmed their Nassau Pact offer to assign units of their existing nuclear forces to NATO control and to aid in creating a multilateral NATO force of surface vessels armed with nuclear warhead-bearing Polaris missiles.

French representatives to the Permanent Council were reported to have assailed the U.S.-British plan immediately after its submission at the meeting February 27. The French charged that the proposal was intended to preserve U.S. control of the West's existing nuclear forces and of any such force that might be raised in the future by West European nations. French delegates reportedly warned that the dual Anglo-American proposal — providing for development of multinational (MNF) and multilateral (MLF) nuclear forces — was illogical and was opposed by prominent members of the Kennedy Administration and the U.S. Congress.

Rusk, Couve de Murville Meet on A-Plans. U.S. Secretary of State Dean Rusk conferred with French Foreign Minister Maurice Couve de Murville in Paris April 7 and was reported to have been encouraged by Couve de Murville's interest in nuclear force proposals. Rusk was said to have conceded that the MNF offered the most rapid progress toward a Western nuclear force, but he stressed that the plan for an MLF surface fleet was more essential to satisfy European demands for nuclear representation.

Addressing the NATO Permanent Council in Paris April 10, Rusk declared that elements of the MNF already were in existence. Rusk, who spoke at a closed session of the Council, reportedly stressed that U.S. Polaris submarines already had been assigned to NATO command and that eight members of the alliance had strike forces equipped with U.S. nuclear weapons. The forces due to be at the service of the MNF already were co-ordinated and pre-targeted by NATO, he said.

(According to Paris sources April 10, under a U.S.-French agreement, in the event of war the French tactical fighter squadrons in West Germany were to be armed with U.S. nuclear weapons and assigned to predeter-mined NATO targets; this, according to U.S. sources, constituted a form of de facto French participation in MNF.)

De Gaulle Visits Greece, Hails NATO. President de Gaulle visited Greece May 16-19, 1963. He arrived in Athens May 16 and was greeted at the airport by King Paul.

In an address to the Greek Parliament May 18, de Gaulle declared: "if both Greece and France belong to the Atlantic alliance, which binds our Europe to America, it is with the conviction that in this dangerous state of the world there is no other guarantee for the free peoples but peace and, failing this, no other chance to regain it except by being completely united . . . and by being organized to act all together immediately . . . ."

France Approves Compromise MNF Plan. The NATO foreign ministers, meeting in Ottawa, announced May 24 their approval of mea-sures intended to lead to the creation of an inter-allied nuclear striking force. The projected force would include Britain's 180-plane V-bomber fleet, three U.S. Polaris missile-firing atomic submarines and the nuclear-armed tactical air squadrons assigned to NATO by eight member states, including France. The seven other members states, whose NATO-assigned aircraft had been armed with U.S.-supplied nuclear weapons, were West Germany, Greece, Canada, Belgium, the Netherlands, Italy, and Turkey.

The announcement, which came at the end of the NATO Council's spring ministerial meeting, was cloaked in vague language, reportedly to satisfy French demands that the decision be minimized and made to appear as a routine reorganization of NATO's existing nuclear forces. In defer-ence to French wishes the communique stipulated that the units composing the MNF were to remain national in identity despite their assignment to NATO command. They were to be financed and manned by the individual governments concerned, and were to remain subject to national authority. The United States and Britain were to retain ultimate authority over the nuclear weapons used by the force under the "double key" system requiring the assent both of the unit's tactical commander and of the U.S. or British "war-head commander" for the launching of a nuclear weapon.

The purposely vague meaning of the agreement was stressed by French Foreign Minister Couve de Murville in his address to the opening session. He said that France had assented to the modified MNF because it was clear that it had not altered NATO's agreed mission or goals.

Following a visit by Couve de Murville to Washington May 25 it was reported that he had told Secretary of State Rusk that the Ottawa agree-ment still had not dealt with French demands for nuclear status; according to reports, Couve held that the United States and Britain had not relin-quished their veto over use of the weapons involved in the Ottawa agreement.

West Europe Divided on MLF. The MLF (multilateral force) plan, a jointly operated fleet of 25 warships equipped with Polaris missiles, was taken up with European leaders by President Kennedy during his tour of

West Germany, Ireland, Britain and Italy June 22-July 2, 1963. Kennedy and West German Chancellor Adenauer were reported June 25 to have affirmed their governments' commitment to the proposal, but Adenauer was said to have urged and to have obtained Kennedy's agreement to postponement of further action on MLF in view of reluctance by Britain and Italy to commit themselves to the plan.

French Naval Units Withdrawn. It was reported from Paris June 20 that the French government had informed NATO that, beginning Jan. 1, 1964, its naval units earmarked for British Channel service would no longer be available for NATO use in the event of war. Agence France-Presse reported the next day that official sources in Paris had disclosed that "the French government had decided to withdraw from the NATO fleet in the north Atlantic." The decision was described as a logical sequence to France's 1959 withdrawal of its Mediterranean fleet from NATO control. Washington military officials reported June 21 that the withdrawals left only a few French submarines at the disposal of NATO naval commanders in the event of war.

De Gaulle Reaffirms French A-Plans. President de Gaulle July 29, at his eighth presidential press conference, reasserted France's intention to equip itself "with the means of immeasurable destruction possessed by the other powers" despite the recent Moscow treaty curbing nuclear tests. He made clear his view that:

> the fact that the Russians also now have the wherewithal to destroy the world..., [makes] it...quite natural that America [sees] its own survival as the principal objective in a possible conflict and is not considering the...terms and conditions of its nuclear intervention for the defense of other regions,...except in relation to this...necessity. This, moreover, is one of the reasons that France is equipping herself with her own atomic weapons. The result of this is that, as far as the French Government is concerned, important modifications are necessary with regard to the terms and conditions of our participation in the Alliance, since this organization has been built on the basis of integration, which today is no longer valid for us.

French A-Force Operational. Recurring reports that the first element of France's planned nuclear striking force was operational were confirmed elliptically Oct. 9, 1963 by a French cabinet communique in which it was announced that French forces were completing their withdrawal from the Bizerte naval and air base in Tunisia. The statement said that the Bizerte withdrawal was permissible militarily because "the creation of new means that the armed forces are beginning to have at their disposal permits... this regrouping without compromising the defense of France in the Mediterranean basin." Press and diplomatic interpretations of this as an announcement of the nuclear force's initial readiness were not denied by the government. Defense Minister Pierre Messmer November 1, in an address to the French National Assembly, stated that French nuclear facilities had been manufacturing atomic bombs since the middle of the year and that the first operational bombs and Mirage-IV jets were a reality. Messmer said that France would have 15 to 20 of its planned 50 Mirage-IV's in service by the end of 1964. (He said that the planes were able to carry bombs up to 60 kilotons in power.) Messmer asserted that France's "second generation" nuclear force, to consist of medium-range ballistic missiles and three Polaris missile-type nuclear submarines, all armed with hydrogen warheads, would begin to be delivered in 1968-69 but would not be completed for 12 years.

MLF Talks Continue; France Abstains. A seven-nation NATO Paris conference on the formation of a multilateral force (MLF) of missile-armed surface vessels received assurances November 28 that the new Johnson Administration in the United States would continue to support the MLF proposals made to European nations by the Kennedy Administration. (U.S. President John F. Kennedy had been assassinated Nov. 22, 1963 and was succeeded in office by Vice President Lyndon B. Johnson.) The *New York Times* reported from Paris that these assurances were directed particularly at one of the most controversial aspects of the MLF plan — the proposed manning of the vessels with crews of mixed nationalities. It also was reported that the European states involved in the Paris negotiations, especially Britain, Italy and West Germany, had shown increased interest in rapid creation of the fleet despite French opposition to the project. France boycotted the conference.

De Gaulle at JFK Rites. President Johnson, in a personal message sent to de Gaulle December 2, expressed his gratitude for de Gaulle's November 25 trip to Washington to attend the Kennedy funeral and said that "I look for more thorough conversations with you next year." (Johnson spoke briefly to many of the foreign leaders in Washington following the Kennedy funeral. De Gaulle, the first foreign leader to confer privately with Johnson, met with him for about 15 minutes during a Presidential reception for the foreign visitors at the State Department.) The letter, made public December 3, did not mention a possible date or site for a meeting. De Gaulle was to have come to Washington for talks with President Kennedy in February 1964.

De Gaulle Restates Nuclear Goals. The French government's intentions to press ahead with completion of an independent national nuclear striking force were reaffirmed by President de Gaulle in two major statements in 1964. The first of these was a radio-TV address delivered to the French people April 16; the second was at a formal presidential press conference (de Gaulle's tenth) held in Paris July 23.

In his radio-TV address de Gaulle said: "So long as the ambition of the Soviets and the nature of their regime brings a threat of terrible conflict to bear on the free world,... France is in danger of destruction and invasion without having any certainty that her American allies, themselves directly exposed to death, would know how to prevent this for her."

Speaking to an audience of newsmen, diplomats and French officials at his July press conference, de Gaulle asserted:

... France ... [has] judged it necessary ... to become an atomic power.... And ... we are reaching results. Our first atomic air unit becomes operational this year. In 1966 we will have enough Mirage IV's and refueling planes to be able to carry at one time, over a distance of thousands of miles, bombs with a total power exceeding that of 150 Hiroshima bombs. Furthermore, we are working on moving on from series A fission bombs to series H fusion bombs, the latter launched from either atomic submarines, surface vessels or land.... We are in a position to think that, six years from now, our deterrent means will reach a total instantaneous power of 2,000 Hiroshima bombs. This is what certain, obviously unthinking, opponents call France's "little bombs." The field of deterrence is thus henceforth open to us. For to attack France would be equivalent, for whomever it might be, to undergoing frightful destruction itself.

Rusk Opposes French Stand. U. S. Secretary of State Rusk challenged de Gaulle's opposition to NATO nuclear integration in an address delivered in Brussels May 9, 1964. Rusk declared that absolute national sovereignty had become outmoded in the nuclear era; he said that the United States "simply cannot understand the revival of the notion of absolute independence in dealing with affairs within the free world." America, he continued, accepted the fact that postwar events had led it to assume commitments that rigorously circumscribed its sovereignty and freedom of action.

French Foreign Minister Couve de Murville replied to Rusk's views May 13 at a NATO ministerial meeting in The Hague. He declared that France opposed further integration of NATO military commands and forces, and he contended that the alliance's system of political consultation had failed to work in cases where member states' interests differed.

Bonn Backs MLF. West German Chancellor Ludwig Erhard indicated Oct. 6, 1964 that West Germany would support construction of the MLF even without the participation of France or other NATO powers. Speaking at a news conference in West Berlin, Erhard had said that "We hope ... the doors will stay wide open for other European countries to join," but "a beginning has to be made." Asked specifically if West Germany would take such action without the support of the other European members of NATO, Erhard replied: "I cannot give you a flat 'yes,' but I cannot deny it."

U. S. Presses MLF. The United States' intentions to press ahead with formation of the MLF were reaffirmed October 20 by Secretary of State Rusk in ceremonies marking the visit to Washington of a U.S. guided missile destroyer that had been manned with a mixed international crew as a demonstration ship for the MLF project. Rusk, speaking aboard the vessel to an audience made up of representatives of the eight nations involved in the MLF project, said that the ship was tangible evidence of the United States' intentions to carry out the project. "Instead of developing ... nationally manned and owned forces, eight nations have been discussing a single force to be available to NATO," he asserted.

The vessel, the *Claude V. Ricketts,* was operated under U.S. Navy regulations. It was manned by a crew composed 50 per cent of Americans and 50 per cent of contingents from the navies of Britain, West Germany, the Netherlands, Italy, Greece, and Turkey. The *Ricketts,* when fully manned, would have a crew of 18 officers and 316 enlisted men; it was expected to provide training for handling the Polaris missiles with which MLF vessels would be equipped.

France Pressures Bonn about MLF. French Premier Georges Pompidou, addressing a Paris meeting of the French Parliamentary Correspondents Association November 5, declared that if West Germany agreed to join the MLF it would be violating the French-German Treaty of Reconciliation (signed Jan. 22, 1963). Pompidou asserted that the MLF was incompatible with the creation of a united Europe and was directed politically against France. He said that the differences generated by the MLF proposal had strengthened France's view that it would be necessary to reorganize NATO to maintain it as an effective alliance.

Bonn Delays MLF Decision. West Germany's ruling Christian Democratic Union voted in caucus November 11 to delay the Bonn government's commitment to the MLF project. A CDU spokesman, announcing the party's decision, stressed that West Germany had not abandoned support for the MLF concept, but saw no special need to speed completion of the negotiations.

The CDU's decision stemmed from France's strong opposition to the step and was taken immediately after ex-Chancellor Konrad Adenauer, chairman of the CDU and leader of its pro-French "Gaullist" faction, had reported to the caucus on talks he had held with President de Gaulle in Paris November 9. Adenauer had conferred with de Gaulle during a visit to Paris for his installation as an associate foreign member of the French Institute's Academy of Moral and Political Sciences. Adenauer confirmed to newsmen that his Paris visit had been undertaken as a personal mission to end the growing French-West German rift within NATO and the Common Market.

De Gaulle Warns Germany. President de Gaulle, speaking in Strasbourg Nov. 22, 1964, warned West Germany that it would "inflict a deep wound on a great hope" if it abandoned the French-West German alliance to become an auxiliary of the United States. Although de Gaulle did not mention the current negotiations for formation of an MLF nuclear force, it was clear he was referring to West Germany's increasingly close alignment with the United States on the question. De Gaulle asserted that the transformation of France's relations with Germany had been made possible only by both nations' commitment to construction of a Europe that was "independent, powerful and influential in the free world." He declared that if West Germany renounced this aim it would be repudiating the basis of its alliance with France and would be turning its destiny over to "a power [the United States] assuredly friendly, but situated in a different world, whose destiny by nature cannot be identified with that of Europe."

Johnson Sees MLF Without France. President Johnson Dec. 3, 1964, at Georgetown University, stressed that the United States and other interested nations would proceed with the formation of the MLF despite the opposition of France. "Those of us," he said, "who are ready to proceed in common ventures must decide to go forward together... with due respect for the interests of others and with an open door for those who may join later." Alluding to one of the major motives for the MLF proposal, the hope that it would negate whatever pressures existed for the independent acquisition of nuclear weapons by West Germany, President Johnson hailed Bonn's leadership for having "rejected all separate adventures — especially and, I think, most wisely, in the field of nuclear weapons."

NATO Debates A-Fleet; France Opposes. The North Atlantic Council convened in Paris December 15 for a ministerial-level meeting devoted primarily to the U.S. proposal for establishment of a joint Western multilateral nuclear force (MLF).

United States determination to seek a resolution of the differences raised by the MLF proposal was made clear by Secretary of State Rusk in his address December 15 to the opening session. Rusk reiterated that the United States had advanced the proposal in good faith and in the hope that it would satisfy European demands for a share in NATO's nuclear defense. Strong support was expressed for Rusk's position by West German Foreign Minister Gerhard Schroeder and British Foreign Secretary Patrick Gordon Walker.

The attack on the MLF concept was led by French Foreign Minister Couve de Murville, who assailed the plan as confused and contradictory. Either, he said, it would place effective nuclear power in the hands of several more nations, thus violating the United States' professed opposition to proliferation of such weapons, or it would not; in this case, the European nations would not have obtained what was promised them. He warned that, if carried out, the MLF plan could endanger the NATO alliance and make it impossible to negotiate with the USSR on the eventual reunification of Germany.

The Council reached no decision on MLF in its three days of debate. The final communique simply contained a pledge for continued talks on MLF.

LBJ Acts to Ease MLF Rift. It was reported from Washington December 20 that President Johnson had issued policy instructions moderating the U.S. campaign for establishment of the MLF nuclear fleet in view of the differences generated within NATO by the proposal.

Johnson was reported to have issued a National Security Council memorandum outlining the Administration's policy on the matter and instructing Secretary of State Rusk and Secretary of Defense Robert S. McNamara to see to it that all diplomatic and military officials conformed to it. The memorandum was attributed to the President's concern at reports that U.S. officials had been guilty of "pressure tactics" to force European acceptance of the MLF proposal. It was said to contain these key points: (1) the West's defense was indivisible, both in planning and execution, and required the greatest possible consultation among NATO allies on nuclear power; (2) no nuclear defense system was acceptable unless it had been approved by Britain and West Germany and had been discussed fully with France; (3) no U.S. proposal for NATO should be construed as in any way hostile to European economic and political integration; (4) no deadlines were to be imposed for the MLF proposals, nor were special arrangements to be made with any single European nation to obtain its acceptance for the project; (5) any MLF agreement would have to remain open for the participation of any NATO ally, especially France, at any time in the future.

Although reports of the President's memorandum were hailed December 29 by French officials as a vindication of President de Gaulle's views on the MLF, officials in Washington stressed that it did not mean the United States had abandoned its proposal for formation of the nuclear fleet.

Paris for NATO Revision. French Foreign Minister Couve de Murville called May 20, 1965 for the reform of NATO before 1969. He told the French National Assembly Foreign Affairs Committee that the alliance was bulky and costly and that it infringed on French rights in defense questions.

U.S. Proposes NATO A-Committee. U.S. Secretary of Defense McNamara proposed May 31 that NATO establish a "select committee" of four or five NATO powers to study ways to improve consultation on the use of nuclear weapons. McNamara, who presented the project at a Paris meeting of NATO defense ministers, said the committee's dual purpose would be to study ways (1) to improve and extend allied participation in any decision to use nuclear forces, strategic or tactical; (2) to "improve communications to insure that agreed consultations concerning a decision to use nuclear forces can take place as expeditiously as possible." The committee, according to McNamara, would be composed of the defense ministers of the four to five governments represented. He emphasized that the projected committee was not related to the MLF.

France Rejects A-Committee. The U.S. proposal for creation of a select committee on nuclear planning of four or five NATO defense ministers was rejected by France at a Paris meeting July 7, 1965 of the NATO Permanent Council.

Jacques Schricke, a member of the French delegation, told the Council that the proposal concerned a technical matter that did not merit the attention of the defense ministers. He also said that if other NATO powers wanted to proceed with the proposal without French participation, Paris would raise no objection.

New A-Bomb Disclosed. The annual report of the French Atomic Energy Commission, made public July 12, said that France had developed a new nuclear explosive device. The *New York Times* reported July 13 that the new weapon was smaller and more powerful and could be more easily carried by France's Mirage IV jet bombers than its 12-foot predecessor, which had to be mounted outside the bomber.

The commission's report added that: (1) research continued on an atomic warhead for strategic ballistic missiles; (2) construction of new test sites in the South Pacific (in the Tuamotu Islands) was proceeding as scheduled; (3) the transfer from Algerian bomb testing sites to the Pacific in mid-1967 would cause no delays in tests of atomic and hydrogen bombs; (4) the commission's manpower had reached 26,231 and its budget about $1 billion by the end of 1964.

Paris Quits NATO Exercise. French Defense Minister Pierre Messmer July 21 ordered French military personnel at NATO's Supreme Headquarters, Allied Powers Europe, not to participate in preparations for NATO military exercises scheduled for the fall.

U.S. Apology for Flight over A-Plant. The United States apologized July 22 to France for a July 16 incident in which a U.S. Air Force jet made four photo-reconnaissance passes over the French nuclear production plant at Pierrelatte, near Lyon.

A French Defense Ministry statement July 19 had reported that a U.S. RF-101 reconnaissance jet had been detected by radar and then intercepted by a French fighter during the second of four passes over Pierrelatte July 16. According to the statement, the U.S. plane broke away from the French fighter to make two more passes over Pierrelatte before returning to its base at Ramstein, West Germany. The United States, said the statement, had turned over to France 175 undeveloped photographs taken by the plane from an altitude of 2,000 feet. They showed, according to the statement, that the "restricted zone had been systematically photographed."

A U.S. embassy statement released July 22 in Paris said that "after a thorough investigation by United States military authorities," the United States had expressed regrets "at the inadvertent violation of French flight regulations that occurred during a routine training flight." "Steps are being taken," the statement said, "to prevent such violations in the future."

De Gaulle Hints NATO Exit. President de Gaulle indicated Sept. 9, 1965 that France would withdraw from the integrated NATO defense structure by 1970.

Speaking at this twelfth presidential press conference, de Gaulle said France would continue to follow an independent foreign policy and would oppose further integration within NATO. He declared: "...so long as the solidarity of the Western peoples appears to us necessary for the eventual defense of Europe, our country will remain the ally of her allies, but, upon the expiration of the commitments formerly taken—that is, in 1969 by the latest—the subordination known as 'integration' which is provided for by NATO and which hands our fate over to foreign authority shall cease, as far as we are concerned." (The 20-year North Atlantic Treaty provided that any member could withdraw after April 4, 1969 on one year's notice.)

LBJ Backs NATO. A strengthening of the NATO alliance was urged by President Johnson in a statement released in Washington September 9 several hours after the de Gaulle press conference. "Naturally, each member of NATO sees the alliance...from its own perspective," Johnson said. "But this alliance...is bigger than any of its members. We must maintain its strength and...update it to serve the common aspirations of all of us."

Missile Silos Planned. French Defense Ministry sources confirmed October 12 that France planned to build 30 underground silos for strategic missiles in Haute Provence (southeastern France). The silos would be dispersed over a 220-square-mile area of the Albion Plateau. Construction would begin in 1966 and take three years.

Defense Minister Messmer told the French National Assembly October 21 that France's independent atomic armament is an accomplished fact. Two squadrons (12 planes each) of Mirage IV supersonic bombers were almost combat ready, Messmer said, and 50 of the 62 bombers would be largely operational in 1966. In 1966, he said, the strategic nuclear force would absorb 26% of the $4.4 billion defense budget.

French Rocket Orbits Satellite. France's first earth satellite, a 92-1/2-pound capsule, was put into orbit Nov. 26, 1965 by means of a 62-foot three-stage Diamant rocket launched at Hammaguir in the Algerian Sahara. The satellite was designed to emit a radio signal for two weeks and carried no sophisticated scientific equipment. The French Armed Forces

Ministry reported November 27 that the A-1 had stopped sending radio signals because of a defective transmitter.

The Diamant was scheduled to serve as the basis for French military rockets carrying nuclear weapons that were to start replacing France's Mirage-IV atomic bombers in about two and a half years. France was the third country to launch a satellite of its own. The first two: the USSR and the United States.

France Abstains from A-Committee. Defense ministers of 10 NATO nations (Belgium, Britain, Canada, Denmark, Greece, the Netherlands, Italy, Turkey, West Germany and the United States) met in Paris November 27 and set up a 10-nation NATO "Special Committee on Nuclear Consultation." The special meeting had been convened to discuss U.S. Defense Secretary McNamara's May 31 proposal for a NATO select committee for consultation on nuclear strategy. France, which had rejected McNamara's proposal, did not attend the meeting.

United States spokesmen in Paris November 27 emphasized that the newly created committee was not to be understood as a substitute for a multilateral nuclear force (MLF) or the Atlantic nuclear force (ANF), both of which were still under consideration.

Paris Opposes Permanent A-Committee. French Foreign Minister Couve de Murville December 14, addressing a Paris meeting of the NATO Council of Foreign Ministers, warned against permitting the 10-nation committee on nuclear consultation to assume a permanent NATO status. He suggested that the committee last no longer than May 1966, when it would present its recommendations at the next NATO Council meeting. U.S. Secretary of State Rusk said the committee should be allowed to decide on its own future.

De Gaulle to End NATO Bases. President de Gaulle announced Feb. 21, 1966 that France would assume control of all foreign military (NATO) installations on its territory by April 4, 1969, the date after which any North Atlantic Treaty member could withdraw on one year's notice.

Speaking at his thirteenth presidential press conference, de Gaulle asserted that new conditions had reduced the necessity for integration under NATO. He said:

> For it is quite clear that, owing to the internal and external evolution of the countries of the East [i.e., the USSR and its European satellites], the Western world is no longer threatened today as it was at the time when the American protectorate was set up in Europe under the cover of NATO. But, at the same time . . ., there was also a reduction in the guarantee of security. . . . For Soviet Russia has since that time equipped itself with nuclear power capable of striking the United States directly, which has made the decisions of the Americans as to the eventual use of their bombs at least indeterminate. . . .
>
> On the other hand, while the prospects of a world war breaking out on account of Europe are dissipating, conflicts in which America engages in other parts of the world— . . . in Korea, . . . in Cuba, . . . in Vietnam—risk, . . ., being extended so that the result could be a general conflagration. In that case Europe—whose strategy is, within NATO, that of America—would be automatically involved in the struggle, even when it would not have so desired. . . .

Consequently, without going back on her adherence to the At-lantic Alliance, France is going—between now and the final date set for her obligations, which is April 4, 1969—to continue to modify successively the measures currently practiced, insofar as they concern her. . . . [France] will hold herself ready to arrange with . . ., [her allies] the practical relations for cooperation that will appear useful on both sides. . . . In sum, it means reestablishing a normal situation of sovereignty, in which that which is French as regards soil, sky, sea and forces, and any foreign element that would be in France, will in the future be under French command alone. . . . It in no way means a rupture, but a necessary adaptation.

France to Quit NATO Force. The French government March 9, 1966 formally announced its intention to withdraw all its armed forces from the 15-nation North Atlantic Treaty Organization's integrated military command. It simultaneously announced that all NATO commands and installations located on French territory would either be required to come under French military authority or be asked to leave French soil. The decisions on withdrawal from NATO's defense framework and removal of NATO units from France were announced by Information Secretary Yvon Bourges March 9 following a meeting of the cabinet at which President de Gaulle presided.

President de Gaulle had written to President Johnson March 7 about France's decision to withdraw from NATO's integrated defense organization. De Gaulle wrote similar letters March 9 to British Prime Minister Harold Wilson, West German Chancellor Ludwig Erhard and Italian President Giuseppe Saragat. None of the four letters, all reportedly written in longhand by de Gaulle, was made public. The letters reportedly restated de Gaulle's February 21 press conference arguments against continuing NATO's defense organization in its current form.

President Johnson replied to de Gaulle's letter March 7. His reply reportedly said that the issues raised by de Gaulle struck at the heart of the alliance and posed serious questions for relations between France and the United States. Johnson insisted that all NATO states had to be consulted and that no bilateral negotiations with France would be possible.

The French decision was formally communicated to the other 14 NATO members in Foreign Ministry memos made public March 12. They were identical except for those to the United States, Canada and West Germany — the only treaty members with military installations in France. These three nations received separate notes on the status of their facilities on French territory. Neither the March 9 government statement nor the March 12 memos stipulated a deadline for implementation of the decisions; both documents insisted that France's action did not constitute a denunciation of the 1949 North Atlantic Treaty and that France had no intention of denouncing it later.

The memos to all 14 nations cited these reasons for dismantling NATO's integrated command: (1) Conditions existing "at present . . . are fundamentally different from those of 1949." Western Europe no longer faced an "immediate and menacing" threat from Eastern Europe. (2) France's "atomic armament . . . by its very nature is excluded from integration." (3) "The [U.S.-USSR] nuclear balance . . . [had] transformed the general conditions of defense of the West." (4) Europe was "no longer the center of world crisis.... All countries in the Atlantic alliance obviously are not involved [in disputes in Asia]."

The memos said:
France would not "challenge" the 1949 North Atlantic Treaty. France "considers that the alliance should continue for as long as appears necessary." But "there arises the problem of organization,...[i.e.,] the agreements...and decisions taken following the signing of the treaty in either multilateral or bilateral form."

Regarding all French forces under NATO's integrated command, "France proposes to bring an end to such assignments. This decision will produce as a consequence the simultaneous withdrawal...[from] the two integrated [NATO] commands to which its forces belong and in which it participates...that is, the Supreme Headquarters, Allied Forces Europe [SHAPE] and the Central European Command [a NATO command subordinate to SHAPE] and, by the same token, the transfer out of French territory of the headquarters of these two commands."

France would be willing to discuss the "problems" posed by the "application of...these measures" and could "examine the liaison" that might be established between French forces and "NATO commands, as well as to determine the conditions in which those [French forces] in Germany would participate in time of war...."

French forces in Germany "will be kept there in the framework of the conventions of Oct. 23, 1954." (Agreements signed Oct. 23, 1954 in Paris restored sovereignty to West Germany and joined the Bonn government to the North Atlantic Treaty. The agreements provided that the three wartime occupying powers—the United States, Britain and France—could retain troops in West Germany for the "defense of the free world.")

The separate memo to the United States pointed out that "bilateral accords" concerning U.S. military installations in France "do not fulfill present conditions," which require that "no foreign units, bases or installations coming under control of authorities other than the French authorities" can be "accept[ed]" on "French territory." France remained "ready to...settle with...the United States...the consequences" resulting from its decision to "reclaim the complete exercise of its sovereignty...." France would also be "disposed" to discuss arrangements whereby French facilities would be placed "at the disposal...of the United States" in the event of "a conflict in which both countries might participate by virtue of the Atlantic alliance." (The United States had about 26,000 military personnel in France. Including dependents and civilian employees, approximately 60,000 U.S. citizens were attached to military units in France.)

The separate memo to Canada, similar to the U.S. note, discussed Canada's two air bases in France. The note to West Germany, about the West German use of training facilities in France, said France was ready, "if necessary," to discuss future use of the facilities.

14 Allies Back NATO. The United States and 13 other NATO members issued a joint statement March 18 declaring their continued support of the 1949 North Atlantic Treaty and of the principle of military integration as embodied in the NATO defense structure. The declaration, released in the capitals of the 14 nations, constituted a reply to France's decision to withdraw from NATO's integrated defense system and to require all NATO installations and commands to leave French territory.

LBJ-de Gaulle Exchange. President Johnson March 22 wrote his second letter in less than two weeks to President de Gaulle about de Gaulle's decision to withdraw from NATO's defense system. *Excerpts from President Johnson's March 22 letter to de Gaulle:*

> ... We continue to believe that if the [NATO] treaty is to have force and reality members of the alliance should prepare the command structures, the strategic and tactical plans, the forces in being, and their designation to NATO in advance of any crisis and for use in time of crisis.... Readiness to fight instantly under agreed plans and procedures, worked out and practiced in peacetime, adds immeasurably to our common strength....
>
> The other 14 member nations of NATO do not take the same view of their interests as that taken at this moment by the government of France. The United States is determined to join with them in preserving the deterrent system of NATO — indeed, in strengthening it in support of the vital common purposes of the West.... We find it difficult to believe that France... will long remain withdrawn from... common affairs and responsibilities.... Her place will await France whenever she decides to resume her leading role.

Following publication of President Johnson's letter to de Gaulle March 23, the French government March 24 published de Gaulle's original March 7 letter to Johnson. De Gaulle's letter reiterated France's loyalty to the 1949 North Atlantic Treaty. "This means," said de Gaulle, "that unless there are changes in the fundamental bases of relations between East and West during the next three years,...[France] will in 1969 and later be resolved, as she is today, to fight on at the side of her allies in case one of them is the object of unprovoked aggression."

France Sets Withdrawal Dates. The French government March 31, 1966 published a timetable for the withdrawal of its military forces from NATO and for the forced departure of all NATO headquarters and installations from French territory. Copies of the memo had been delivered in Paris to the United States, British, West German and Italian embassies March 29 and to the embassies of the remaining ten NATO members March 30.

The French memo contained an identical message to all 14 nations. The documents addressed to the United States, Canada and West Germany, however, contained additional paragraphs concerning United States, Canadian and West German military units and installations on French territory.

The memo's main points:

● By July 1, 1966, France would withdraw from NATO's command its "land and air forces stationed in Germany." France, however, intended that these forces could remain in Germany "by virtue of the convention of Oct. 23, 1954, concerning the presence of foreign forces on the territory of the Federal Republic of Germany." (France had 75,000 men in West Germany.)

● By July 1, 1966, France would withdraw its "personnel" from NATO's "integrated" commands. "This involves the Supreme Command of the Allied Forces in Europe [SHAPE], the Central Europe command, the Southern Europe command and commands subordinated to them as well as the NATO defense college."

• By April 1, 1967, the two NATO headquarters currently in France—SHAPE and the Central European command—must be transferred out of French territory.

The separate notes to the United States and Canada established April 1, 1967 as the deadline for the removal of their military installations from France. The note to West Germany set no deadline terminating West German use of training facilities in northeastern France under a 1960 agreement.

U.S. Asks Delay on Bases. The United States asked France April 12 to postpone for one year its requirement that U.S. bases and NATO headquarters leave French territory. The United States simultaneously notified France that as of July 1, 1966, the date France had set for withdrawing its forces from NATO command, the United States would terminate a Sept. 6, 1960 agreement under which the United States supplied atomic weapons to French forces stationed in West Germany and assigned to NATO command. The United States request and decision were contained in a formal reply to France's March 29 memorandum. The reply said: "...the United States cannot...understand" why France "has concluded, without consulting the other parties to the treaty, that it is impossible to amend the NATO arrangements and that it must act unilaterally." As for U.S. installations in France, "precipitate" withdrawal would threaten the security of all alliance members.

Paris Insists Talks Start. The French government April 22 formally replied to the April 12 U.S. request for a one-year delay in removing its military installations from French territory. The reply "proposed to begin conversations now on the practical provisions that should be taken concerning the... bilateral agreements referred to" in the earlier communications (of March 29 and April 12) between the French and U.S. governments. The French reply also took "note of the fact" that the United States has decided to terminate, as of July 1, 1966, the 1960 agreement on stockpiling atomic weapons with French forces in West Germany. A U.S. State Department spokesman said April 25 that the French reply was "unresponsive" to the U.S. note.

Pompidou Criticizes U.S. NATO A-Strategy. In what was regarded as the most comprehensive explanation of France's withdrawal from the NATO command, French Premier Georges Pompidou told the French National Assembly April 20 that NATO's nuclear strategy was dictated by the United States. Pompidou said:

> The North Atlantic Council had at one time "unanimously . . . approved what is generally called the 'strategic concept' of NATO." Under this concept, supported by France, NATO was committed to all-out nuclear retaliation should any NATO nation suffer a conventional or nuclear attack. This strategy was that of massive and immediate atomic retaliation. Officially it remains the NATO doctrine. . . . But, in actual fact, this strategic concept approved by the NATO Council unanimously, still theoretically in effect, has been abandoned by the Supreme Command in favor of the concept

of the flexible response [under which NATO would measure its military response to that used by the attacker in an attempt to avoid all-out nuclear war]. It sufficed for Mr. McNamara to renounce Mr. Dulles' concepts for a strategy that the NATO Council had never approved to become, in fact, that of the [NATO] command. Certainly, we protested; we refused to take part in the exercises that were too obviously based on that new theory; we discussed—'negotiated'—throughout conferences of military leaders and diplomatic representatives our theses conforming to the official NATO doctrine. The entire apparatus, nonetheless, obeyed the directives of the American government. And I affirm, without violating secrets, that a large part, perhaps even a majority of allied military leaders, share our viewpoint. But as soon as the discussion becomes public, not one of our allies contradicts the sovereign thesis of the United States.

What we criticize about the flexible response doctrine is its being specifically conceived on the basis of America's geographical location . . . limiting the atomic battlefield by sparing the territory of the Soviet Union, and therefore the territory of the United States, and thereby creating a psychological risk, that of making it believed that the war could remain localized between the Atlantic and the Polish frontier in the East, that is to say, in Europe, but a Europe doomed to destruction.

The Cuban missile crisis of 1962 was an example of the nuclear risks that NATO presented to France: "Faced with the threat, . . . President Kennedy took immediate steps. He did not consult us, but informed us, quickly, although after the fact. . . . We agreed with President Kennedy. But, even before we announced our position— while the NATO forces were supposed to be outside the conflict, and while, even if they had been advised to take precautionary measures, no coded alert system had been set up—the American forces in Europe, including those in France, had been placed in a state of alert and, I might add, alert of the highest degree." France could, therefore, even if it did not "declare war," become a "target for atomic bombs."

A-Fuel Denied France. The *New York Times* reported April 17 that for more than a year the United States had been refusing to supply France with enriched uranium fuel that it had promised to furnish under a 1959 agreement. According to the *Times*, French diplomatic officials in Washington had revealed the U.S. refusal to fulfill the agreement, and U.S. officials confirmed their refusal without discussing reasons. France was dependent on the United States for the enriched uranium fuel for the development of a submarine reactor being built at Cadarrache.

Bonn Calls for New Agreement on Troops. The West German government May 3, 1966 rejected the French proposal, made March 29, that the 75,000 French troops stationed in West Germany and assigned to NATO command could remain in Germany without negotiating a new agreement defining their legal status. Paris had suggested that after July 1, the date France had set for terminating their assignment to NATO, the troops could remain in Germany under the provisions of the Oct. 23, 1954 convention on foreign forces in Germany. The West German note said: French troops in Germany under the Oct. 23, 1954 convention were there legally only within the framework of NATO. "The member states of the alliance... [had] expressly engaged themselves... to place under the supreme allied command in Europe their forces stationed on the European continent"; therefore, the French decision to terminate the "subordination of the French forces on... [German] territory to the supreme allied command [NATO] in Europe... affect[ed] equally their right to be stationed in Germany.... The German government is, however, desirous of concluding with the French government new arrangements permitting maintaining French forces on the federal territory...."

Paris-Bonn Troop Talks. Negotiations between France and West Germany on the legal status of France's forces in West Germany began June 13 in Bonn. As a condition for opening the talks, the French government had demanded May 18 that the West German government first answer the "political" question of whether it wanted French forces to remain on its territory after France's July 1 withdrawal from NATO. West German Chancellor Erhard replied affirmatively May 25 to the French demand. Erhard rejected, however, the French position that the 1954 convention provided a legal basis for the continued presence of French troops. He said that "all questions arising in connection with the presence of these troops [would have to] be renegotiated." "Interim solutions" would be possible, he said, if "by July 1... no new agreement... [had] been reached."

A Bonn note delivered June 30 to French Ambassador Francois Seydoux stated that West Germany was "agreed on a temporary basis" to the "maintenance starting July 1, 1966 of French forces stationed in federal territory...." Germany, said the note, reserved its "juridical point of view" and would appoint a "delegate" to represent German "sovereignty vis-a-vis French forces on the territory of the Federal Republic."

U.S. Units Quit France. The United States began its withdrawal of military forces from France June 30, 1966 when a C-130 Hercules troop carrier flew from Evreux to its new base in Mildenhall, England. Defense Secretary McNamara had announced in Washington June 15 a program for all U.S. Air Force units and some ground support supplies to be removed from France by September 1.

The moves announced June 15 involved about 12,700 U.S. military and civilian personnel and 10,700 dependents. McNamara said the remaining 17,000 military and civilian personnel and 26,300 dependents would remain at their current posts until further U.S.-French negotiations determine the status of the U.S.-built facilities in France. Further negotiations would also determine whether France would be required to pay a share of the removal costs, McNamara said.

French Forces Quit NATO Command. France July 1 withdrew to national control all its armed forces assigned to NATO. The July 1 date had been set in the French government announcement of March 31.

The immediate consequence of the French action was the departure of French personnel from SHAPE, NATO's military headquarters located at Rocquencourt, near Paris, and from AFCENT (Allied Forces, Central Europe), SHAPE's major subordinate command, located at Fontainebleau. In addition, 75,000 French air force and army personnel stationed in West Germany under AFCENT command reverted to French command July 1. The French forces remained in Germany after July 1 on an interim basis granted by the Bonn government, pending further negotiations between France and West Germany and the 13 other members of NATO.

France's withdrawal from NATO military commands did not involve a renunciation of the North Atlantic Alliance; as a result, France continued after July 1 to participate in the weekly Paris meetings of the North Atlantic Council, the alliance's highest political organ.

U.S. Units Quit France. The Defense Department announced Aug. 3, 1966 that the withdrawal from France of six U.S. Air Force reconnaissance squadrons would begin immediately and be completed by October. About 90 aircraft, 4,400 Air Force personnel and 7,000 dependents were involved. Three squadrons were to be moved to England; two others were to be returned to the United States, and one was to be disbanded.

U.S. Publishes Data on French Rift. The State Department August 13 published two documents on the origins of the U.S.-French dispute over NATO:

The first, the text of a letter sent by President Eisenhower Oct. 20, 1958 to French President de Gaulle, rejected de Gaulle's proposal for a three-power (France, United States, Britain) global directorate to determine military and nuclear strategy.

The second, a State Department memo summarizing certain events before and after the Eisenhower letter, argued that major responsibility for the dispute rested with the French government. It said that on occasions when the United States had attempted to meet de Gaulle's demands with counterproposals, the French government either rejected them or did not reply.

According to the State Department memo, de Gaulle had told Secretary of State John Foster Dulles in Paris July 5, 1958 that France "intended to become a nuclear power" and had "emphasized" that U.S. or NATO nuclear weapons could be stationed on French territory only if they remained "under French control.... The political functioning of NATO," de Gaulle told Dulles, "would be facilitated by close cooperation at the summit between France, the United Kingdom and the United States." In a letter to Eisenhower, de Gaulle September 17 "called for a tripartite organization on the level of world policy and strategy" for the purpose of taking joint decisions on political-strategic issues, "notably with regard to the employment of nuclear weapons." Eisenhower replied in the October 20 letter: "We cannot afford to adopt any system which would give to our other allies, or other free world countries, the impression that basic decisions affecting their own vital interests are being made without their participation." (The substance of the 1958 de Gaulle-Eisenhower correspondence had been widely reported at the time. The text of the de Gaulle letter remained classified in Washington and Paris.)

Following the de Gaulle-Eisenhower exchange, the State Department memo said, the French government refused to consider a series of U.S. proposals to give France some form of global tripartite consultation. According to the document:

●France did not reply to a joint U.S.-British proposal in April 1959 for three-power military talks on African problems.

●De Gaulle never responded to a proposal by Eisenhower Aug. 2, 1959 for talks among military staff officers on strategic issues of interest to France outside the NATO geographical area.

●When Eisenhower asked de Gaulle to circulate his views on NATO, de Gaulle responded "only in his press conference of Sept. 5, 1960." Eisenhower and Dulles went "as far as possible to meet the French request."

●When President Kennedy in Paris June 2, 1961 proposed to de Gaulle that the three powers appoint military representatives to study strategic commitments and prepare common positions, de Gaulle agreed; but when the United States later asked France to name a military representative for the proposed joint study group, the French government did not reply.

(The *New York Times* said August 28 that the State Department memo had excluded material that would have made the French position more understandable. According to *Times* reporter Robert Kleiman, an unpublished State Department "compilation of the facts" [prepared in 1964], "made available to the *Times* in its entirety," indicated that "responsibility" for the U.S.-French split "was more evenly divided.")

France to Cut NATO Payments. French Ambassador-to-NATO Pierre de Leusse notified the North Atlantic Council September 7 that, beginning Jan. 1, 1967, France would cease paying its share — about 12% — of NATO's military expense, except for certain activities it wanted to support. The latter included Nadge (NATO Air Defense & Ground Environment System) and existing air-warning and missile-defense networks.

SHAPE Site Selected. The North Atlantic Council September 14 ratified a decision to accept an undeveloped tract of land near Casteau, Belgium, about 30 miles southeast of Brussels, as the new site for SHAPE (Supreme Headquarters, Allied Powers Europe).

Council to Move to Brussels. The North Atlantic Council Oct. 26, 1966 unanimously endorsed a resolution calling for the transfer of the Council from Paris to Brussels. The resolution stated that "the proper functioning of the alliance requires the Council to be located near... [its military] headquarters," (SHAPE) scheduled to be relocated near Casteau, Belgium. (Fourteen of the alliance members, meeting without France, said later that France would continue to participate in the Council meetings at the new site.)

Paris-Bonn Troop Accord. France and West Germany reached agreement December 12 on the legal status of the 75,000 French troops stationed in West Germany. The agreement was made in letters of intent exchanged by French Ambassador to West Germany Francois Seydoux and West German Foreign Minister Willy Brandt. The West German letter asked France to maintain its troops in West Germany; the French reply stated that the troops would remain as long as West Germany agreed to their presence. The letters did not replace the Oct. 23, 1954 convention, but they redefined it to the extent that West Germany could demand the removal of the French troops whenever it wanted to.

NATO A-Committees Set Up without France. The foreign and defense ministers of all NATO members except France met in Paris December 14 and agreed to the formation of two permanent committees for NATO nuclear planning. (The 14 nations were meeting for the first time as the newly established Defense Planning Committee. The committee, under the chairmanship of NATO Secretary General Manlio Brosio, had been constituted as an official body October 10 to deal with most practical aspects of the alliance so that France could continue to participate in regular North Atlantic Council meetings without having to withdraw whenever military or other matters not of concern to it were discussed; the Council assumed a primarily political consultative role.) The committees formed December 14 were an outgrowth of the 10-nation "Special Committee on Nuclear Consultation" that had been established in November 1965.

The two committees were:

(1) A seven-member Nuclear Planning Group, consisting of four permanent members — the United States, Britain, West Germany and Italy — and three rotating members, to serve 18-month terms and to be selected from among Canada, Belgium, the Netherlands, Denmark, Greece and Turkey.

(2) A 12-member Nuclear Defense Affairs Committee, consisting of all NATO members except France, Luxembourg and Iceland. The functions of the committee: (a) to supervise the Nuclear Planning Group and (b) to serve in a broad advisory role.

French Missile Tested. France completed the first stage of its missile-testing program March 2, 1967 with the launching of a solid-fueled rocket from the Landes firing range in southwestern France. While French defense officials said they were satisfied with the results of the first series of tests, they admitted that they had encountered difficulties in the use of solid fuels.

Nuclear Submarine Launched. France March 29 launched its first nuclear-powered submarine, *Le Redoutable.* The submarine was to begin its sea trials in 1968 and was to become fully operational by 1970, the date set for final development and installation of its nuclear armament system — 16 sea-to-land ballistic missiles, each with a range of 1,700-2,000 miles and an atomic payload of 500 kilotons. The submarine, entirely French-built, was lauded by de Gaulle as a major milestone for "our navy, our defense and our independence."

NATO Plans "Flexible Response." NATO defense ministers met in Paris May 9, 1967 and agreed to a policy of countering aggression with a "flexible response." France, in line with its withdrawal from NATO's integrated military command, sent a liaison officer in lieu of its defense minister. The meeting was the first the defense ministers had held without the representation of France.

At the meeting, the ministers formally discarded the policy of "massive retaliation" as official NATO policy and adopted in its stead the "flexible response" policy. Although the "massive retaliation" policy had been defunct for years, it had remained official NATO policy until the meeting. U.S. officials defined "flexible response" as reacting to aggression with an appropriate reprisal, ranging from political pressure to nuclear attack.

Commands Transferred. Anticipating the April 1 deadline for the removal of all NATO headquarters and military installations from France, these commands were transferred in March: U.S. European Command Headquarters, from Camp des Loges, Saint Germain-en-Laye, to Patch Barracks, Stuttgart, West Germany, March 14; Allied Forces, Central

Europe (AFCENT), from Fontainebleau to Brunsum, the Netherlands, the week of March 19; Supreme Headquarters, Allied Powers Europe (SHAPE), from Rocquencourt to Casteau, Belgium, March 30.

Submarine Missile Tested. The French Armed Forces Ministry announced April 19 that the French navy had successfully conducted its first test-firing of the M-122 sea-to-land intercontinental ballistic missile intended for use by the French nuclear submarine fleet. The missile was fired from a submerged submarine in the Mediterranean.

Nuclear Striking Force Plans Announced. French Armed Forces Minister Pierre Messmer announced Aug. 3, 1967 that France's first hydrogen bomb, to be tested at the Mururoa test site in July 1968, would be in the 500-kiloton range. Messmer outlined this timetable for development of the nuclear force:

(1) The first stage of atomic weaponry had already become operational. It consisted of 62 Mirage IV bombers, each of which carried one 60-kiloton atomic bomb. (The Mirage IV had a top cruising range of 2,500 miles but could be refueled in flight.)

(2) The second stage, to be completed by 1969, would consist of 25 medium-range ground-to-ground ballistic missiles, each of which would carry a 240-kiloton atomic warhead. The missiles would be installed in "hardened" underground silos in Provence in southeastern France. (Estimates on the range of the missile: 1,800-2,600 miles.)

(3) The third and last stage would comprise "at least three" nuclear-powered submarines, each of which would be outfitted with 16 intermediate-range (1,700-2,000 miles) ballistic missiles designed to carry a 500-kiloton hydrogen warhead. The submarines would become operational in 1970, 1972 and 1974 respectively. Messmer also noted that by 1972 France would have tactical nuclear weapons, to be delivered by planes or rockets, that could repel any conventional (non-nuclear) attack. (The French government December 7 announced plans to build a fourth nuclear-powered submarine, to be completed in 1975 or 1976.)

Council Moves to Belgium. The North Atlantic Council, NATO's highest political body, moved from Paris to its new headquarters in the suburb of Evere outside Brussels Oct. 13, 1967. The Council had approved the move in October 1966 in order to remain near its military headquarters (SHAPE), which had moved from the Parisian suburb of Rocquencourt to Casteau, Belgium March 3.

EAST-WEST RELATIONS: THE GERMAN PROBLEM AND RELATIONS WITH THE SOVIET UNION AND EASTERN EUROPE

De Gaulle Reported Seeking European Settlement with USSR. Newspaper reports in the United States and West Europe in January 1963 said that de Gaulle had sent Soviet Premier Khrushchev a secret message proposing a European settlement based on the withdrawal of both U.S. and Russian troops from Europe proper and on some form of association between the USSR and the nations of Western Europe. The reports were given further weight by a lengthy private meeting held by de Gaulle January 29, at his request, with Soviet Ambassador-to-France Sergei Vinogradov. Although the subject of their talk was not divulged, the meeting was followed immediately by reports that de Gaulle planned to visit Moscow to discuss East-West policy with Khrushchev.

Denials of all these reports were issued January 30 by Information Minister Alain Peyrefitte. Peyrefitte declared that there was no question of a de Gaulle trip to Russia. He recalled France's persistent refusal to accept Communist proposals for the demilitarization of central Europe or to agree under threats to enter East-West negotiations on Berlin, disarmament or a nuclear test ban. He said there had been no change in these policies.

The reports were revived February 1 with the announcement that a new Franco-Soviet trade agreement had been signed in Moscow. The pact, covering 1963-65, set an annual goal of $100 million for Franco-Soviet trade. The accord had been under negotiation since 1962.

De Gaulle Rejects U.S., UK Talks with USSR. President de Gaulle July 29, 1963, at his eighth presidential press conference, rejected U.S. and British efforts to discuss with the USSR an East-West nonaggression pact and a lessening of tension in Germany and central Europe. De Gaulle emphasized that "France would not subscribe to some [political] arrangement that would be carried out above her head and which would concern Europe and notably Germany."

Bonn Urges East-West Talks on Reunification. West German Foreign Minister Gerhard Schroeder in a meeting with French Foreign Minister Couve de Murville September 17 called for inclusion of the problem of German reunification as an integral part of the issues — largely limited to disarmament — under discussion by the United States and the Soviet Union.

Rusk Seeks Accord on East-West Talks. U.S. Secretary of State Dean Rusk conferred with other Western leaders, including President de Gaulle Dec. 16, 1963, during his trip to Europe for the Paris meeting of the NATO Council. Rusk's talks were devoted primarily to the U.S. view that the time had come for new negotiations with the USSR.

The matter was discussed by Rusk at a meeting December 15 with French Foreign Minister Couve de Murville, British Foreign Secretary Richard Butler and West German Foreign Minister Schroeder. The four ministers reportedly agreed that no one of them would initiate any radical change in Western conditions for negotiations with the USSR and that all would be kept fully informed of the Soviet contacts attempted by any of their governments, particularly as they related to Berlin or proposals for a nonaggression pact between the NATO and Warsaw Treaty powers.

At the NATO Council meeting December 16, Couve de Murville expressed France's reservations on the Soviet Union's intention to enter meaningful East-West negotiations on German reunification and the problem of Berlin.

French-Soviet Contacts. A marked increase in diplomatic activity, both official and unofficial, occurred between Paris and Moscow in January, February, and March 1964. Coming in the wake of President de Gaulle's repeated declarations that he would forge a new and independent French foreign policy, the diplomatic exchanges were widely presumed to foreshadow a major Franco-Soviet accord on economic matters.

French Finance Minister Valery Giscard d'Estaing announced in Moscow January 28 that he and Soviet Foreign Trade Minister Nikolai S. Patolichev had reached agreement for the convening of talks on a new five-year Franco-Soviet trade accord to cover 1965-69. According to members of the French delegation that accompanied Giscard d'Estaing to Moscow January 21, Franco-Soviet trade would be increased.

Nikolai V. Podgorny, a member of the Soviet Communist Party Presidium, conferred with de Gaulle in Paris March 2. Podgorny, the leader of a Soviet parliamentary delegation on a goodwill visit to France, said at a news conference before his departure March 6 that his government had an ardent desire for closer relations with France. Podgorny praised what he described as the de Gaulle government's realistic attitude on international questions. He asserted that a parallel development of the French and Soviet industrial structures had created favorable conditions for a mutually advantageous cooperation between the two countries. Former Premier Edgar Faure conferred with Soviet Premier Khrushchev in the Kremlin for more than two hours March 28. Although Faure denied that he had been given any mission in Moscow by de Gaulle, it was widely rumored that he had met with Khrushchev to ascertain informally his views on French-Soviet relations.

West Denounces Moscow-East German Pact. The United States, Britain and France June 26, 1964 issued a public denunciation of the Soviet Union's signing of a 20-year friendship treaty with East Germany June 12. The Allied statement described the pact as another attempt to keep Germany divided and to restrict efforts for a peaceful settlement of European problems.

The three Western powers reaffirmed their dedication to the principle of a Germany unified by self-determination as soon as possible. They declared that no treaty signed by Moscow and the East German regime could alter the Soviet Union's legal obligations to respect Western access rights to Berlin. They stressed that West Berlin was not, as described in the Soviet-East German treaty, an independent political unit and that it had close ties with West Germany.

French-Rumanian Accord. A French-Rumanian agreement on scientific and technical cooperation was signed in Paris July 31. The pact, signed by Deputy Premier-Foreign Minister Cornelius Manescu and French Foreign Minister Couve de Murville, provided for an exchange of students and publications. Premier Ion Gheorhe Maurer, who headed the Rumanian delegation, had conferred with President de Gaulle and Premier Pompidou during his Paris stay.

French-Soviet Trade Agreement Signed. France and the USSR Oct. 30, 1964 signed a five-year trade agreement under which France extended $356 million in credits to the Soviet Union for a term of seven years. The agreement had been set up by talks held in January in Moscow by Finance Minister Giscard d'Estaing.

Bonn Presses East-West Talks. West German Foreign Minister Schroeder was reported December 8 to have suggested to U.S. Secretary of State Rusk in Washington in late November that the United States, Britain and France press the Soviet Union to participate in a four-power conference to sound out Soviet intentions toward Germany and possibly to reach a solution to the German reunification question. Schroeder and

French Foreign Minister Couve de Murville conferred on the plan in Paris December 9.

The U.S., British, French and West German foreign ministers conferred at a four-power meeting in Paris December 14. France reportedly balked at Schroeder's plans for East-West talks that would reopen the German question.

De Gaulle on German Reunification. President de Gaulle Feb. 4, 1965, at his eleventh presidential press conference, set forth his views on German reunification. He said that solution of the German question was primarily of concern to Germany's European neighbors. This clashed with U.S. policy which viewed solution of the German question as the responsibility of the Big Four World War II allies—the United States, the Soviet Union, Great Britain, and France. De Gaulle said:

> ... The German problem is, indeed, the European problem... for France, everything can be reduced to three closely linked questions; to see that Germany henceforth becomes a definite element of progress and peace; on this condition, to help with its reunification; to make a start and select the framework that would make this possible.... What must be done will not be done... except by the understanding and combined action of the peoples who have always been, who are and who will remain principally concerned by the fate of the German neighbor—in short, the European peoples.

U.S. Opposes de Gaulle Plan. Washington officials, discussing de Gaulle's proposals on German reunification, indicated U.S. opposition to any Europe-only solution. They pointed out February 4 that any German peace settlement would have to be approved by the Big Four.

De Gaulle indicated February 5, in the form of a clarification circulated by Agence France-Presse, that in his view the ultimate responsibility for German reunification still remained with the United States, Britain, France and the USSR.

French-Soviet Color TV Agreement. In Paris March 22 the USSR and France signed a pact to coordinate efforts to develop the French color TV SECAM system for use throughout Europe in preference to the U.S. or West German systems.

USSR Deputy Foreign Minister Named to Paris Post. Valerian A. Zorin, a USSR deputy foreign minister for 22 years, presented his credentials as the new Soviet ambassador to France April 10, 1965. He replaced Sergei A. Vinogradov. French President de Gaulle assured Zorin: "Everything that can be and will be done between Soviet Russia and France in the economic, scientific, cultural and political fields will constitute a service that our two countries will render together to humanity." De Gaulle expressed confidence that France and the USSR were fundamentally in accord and had no national differences. He pledged France's cooperation with the Soviet Union above ideologies to achieve peace and progress.

Vinogradov had said at a press luncheon in Paris March 11 that the USSR backed de Gaulle's February 4 proposal that Europe alone negotiate Germany's reunification, frontiers and armaments.

French-Soviet Statement. Following talks in Paris April 26-29 between Soviet Foreign Minister Andrei Gromyko and French Foreign Minister Couve de Murville, a Franco-Soviet communique was issued in which the two nations expressed hope of agreement among all the interested parties on the question of divided Germany and European security. Before returning to Moscow, Gromyko said at a press conference April 30 that France had proceeded from the fact that there were two German states. The French Foreign Ministry the same day issued a statement that France's acknowledgment of the division of Germany did not imply any French recognition of East Germany.

French-Soviet A-Pact. A two-year agreement for cooperation in studies on peaceful uses of atomic energy was signed May 4 by the USSR State Committee for the Use of Atomic Energy and the French Atomic Energy Commission. The accord, an extension of a 1960 agreement, called for exchange visits by scientists and technicians and the exchange of data.

France Agrees to U.S. Role in German Problem. In a declaration issued at the conclusion of a May 11-12 meeting of the NATO Council of Foreign Ministers in London, the United States was assured an influential role in the German reunification question. The declaration was worked out by U.S., British, French and West German representatives May 10 before the regular semiannual ministerial session of the NATO Council. In its final communique May 12, the NATO Council "associated itself with the declaration."

French agreement to the declaration represented a change in France's position that only European nations should have a role in negotiating German reunification. According to U.S. and British officials, France had reaffirmed this stand in a draft it had submitted April 23. The final declaration, however, recognized the "obligations and responsibilities concerning Germany, including Berlin and access thereto, devolving upon" the United States, Britain and France (as a result of World War II), "which they share with the government of the Soviet Union."

French Information Minister Alain Peyrefitte said after a Cabinet meeting in Paris May 12 that "there has never been any question for France of wishing to keep the United States out of a settlement of the German problem. "It is natural," he said, that the United States "should be a party to such a settlement, but this settlement is not conceivable unless the interested peoples of Europe are associated with it ...."

De Gaulle on Relations with East Europe, German Unification. President de Gaulle Sept. 9, 1965, at his twelfth press conference, spoke out on France's growing ties with East Europe and the Soviet Union and on German reunification. De Gaulle said:

> ... our contacts and our exchanges are multiplying with the countries of the East, each of them, of course, being treated only in consideration of its national personality. In this respect, we attach great importance to the new trend of our relations with Russia. We are pleased with the results achieved on the occasion of President Maurer's visit [July 1964] with respect to French-Rumanian relations. ... We are going to receive President Cyrankiewicz [Polish Premier Jozef Cyrankiewicz arrived in Paris September 9 for a state visit], hoping that his presence will serve the practical rapprochement of the French and Polish peoples.

On German reunification, he declared:

> We... envisage that the day will come when, in order to achieve a con-
> structive entente from the Atlantic to the Urals, all of Europe will wish
> to settle its own problems, and above all, that of Germany, by the only
> means that will make it possible to do so — that of a general agreement.

Polish Premier Cyrankiewicz Confers with de Gaulle. Polish Premier Jozef Cyrankiewicz conferred with President de Gaulle in Paris September 10, 11 and 15. The talks took place during an official visit to France
made September 10-16 by Cyrankiewicz. A communique of the Cyran-
kiewicz-de Gaulle meetings, released September 15, called for a "normalization of East-West relations... with a view to progressively create an
atmosphere of detente." A five-year commercial agreement between Poland and France would be signed in Warsaw, the communique said.

The communique made no mention of the Oder-Neisse frontier of
Germany and Poland. But Cyrankiewicz was reported to have said after
his September 10 meeting with de Gaulle that Poland was grateful for
France's position on the Oder-Neisse frontier. He told reporters September 15: "The people and government of Poland strongly appreciate the attitude of General de Gaulle and the French government, which considers the
postwar frontiers of Germany as definitive and impossible to modify...."

Couve de Murville on German Reunification. French Foreign
Minister Couve de Murville September 29 addressed the UN General
Assembly. In his remarks on the German problem, he said:

> ... The German people will be reunified in accordance with the frame-
> work of a well-established European security. This will... have to take
> place in peace and by a general agreement between East and West. Since
> the division of Germany is born of the division of Europe, the pre-
> requisite condition for the elimination of one is the elimination of the
> other.... France for her part is, in our opinion, making a positive con-
> tribution to this task by gradually renewing confident relations with the
> countries of Eastern Europe....

Couve de Murville in USSR. Foreign Minister Couve de Murville
visited the Soviet Union Oct. 28-Nov. 2, 1965 and conferred with Soviet
Foreign Minister Andrei Gromyko, Premier Aleksei Kosygin, President
Anastas Mikoyan and First Secretary Leonid Brezhnev. He was the first
Western foreign minister to visit the Soviet Union since Khrushchev's fall
in October 1964, and the first French foreign minister to visit there since
1956. Throughout his stay, the Soviet press hailed the closeness of Franco-
Soviet relations.

Couve de Murville conferred at length with Gromyko in Moscow
October 29. He was received October 31 by Kosygin and Mikoyan at their
vacation estates. Tass, the Soviet news agency, reported that Kosygin and
Couve de Murville discussed "European problems as well as questions of
Soviet-French relations." Tass said Kosygin had suggested that French
President de Gaulle might "find a visit here attractive in solidifying
France's position as a completely independent European nuclear power."
Couve de Murville returned to Moscow November 1 for a second meeting
with Gromyko and met Brezhnev the same day.

A joint communique November 2 said: The two foreign ministers had placed "particular attention on European problems. [They]... noted with satisfaction that a tendency toward normalization of relations between the states of the East and West of the European continent has manifested itself for some time." Both ministers "emphasized the risks of dissemination of nuclear arms in the world." Gromyko stressed the importance of an "international conference on disarmament"; Couve de Murville said "it remained [up] to the [five] nuclear powers primarily to begin the realization [of disarmament]."

French-Polish Trade Pact. French Finance Minister Giscard d'Estaing in Warsaw October 25 signed a five-year agreement under which trade between France and Poland would rise 50 percent by 1969. Giscard d'Estaing said Poland currently provided only four percent of France's imports.

De Gaulle to Visit USSR. Soviet Ambassador-to-France Valerian Zorin announced in Paris Jan. 12, 1966, after a meeting with President de Gaulle, that de Gaulle would visit the USSR in 1966. French officials confirmed later in the day that de Gaulle would make the trip and was also planning visits to other East European nations.

The *New York Times* reported January 13 that the French government had decided January 12 to liberalize its import quotas on industrial goods from the USSR and Eastern Europe. France's trade with Eastern Europe currently accounted for two and a half percent of its foreign trade.

France Opposes East German UN Bid. East Germany March 1 formally applied, for the first time, for UN membership. The U.S., British and French delegations to the UN conferred March 2 on the East German request, then issued a joint statement March 3 that rejected the bid. The statement said: The three governments "reiterate that only the government of the Federal Republic of West Germany is entitled to speak on behalf of Germany as the representative of the German people in international affairs. Since it is not a state, the so-called German Democratic Republic has no right whatever to be admitted" to the UN.

Brezhnev Hails French Relations. Soviet Communist Party General Secretary Leonid Brezhnev March 29 declared: Relations with France had experienced a "considerable improvement," and their continued development "may serve as an important element in strengthening European security." Brezhnev made these remarks at the opening session of the twenty-third Congress of the Soviet Communist Party.

Renault to Rebuild Soviet Plant. Renault, France's largest auto manufacturer, announced in Paris May 31, 1966 that it had agreed to rebuild the Moskvich auto plant in Moscow. The $80-100 million contract would increase the plant's capacity from its current production level of 80,000-90,000 cars annually to 300,000-350,000.

De Gaulle Tours USSR. President de Gaulle toured the Soviet Union June 20-July 1. It was his first trip to the USSR since 1944, when, as head of France's wartime government, he had signed a 20-year Franco-Soviet nonaggression pact. The USSR annulled the pact in 1955.

De Gaulle's spectacularly staged visit marked another step in his plan to improve Franco-Soviet relations and end the postwar confrontation of the East and West blocs. At a Kremlin reception in his honor, he declared June 30 that the "cold war period must be ended."

The USSR's leaders conferred on de Gaulle honors never given any Western statesman. He was the first Western leader to visit the Siberian industrial city of Novosibirsk (June 23-25) and the first to witness the launching of a Soviet satellite from the space center at Baikonur (June 25). In each of the five major cities he visited, Moscow, Novosibirsk, Leningrad (June 25-26), Kiev (June 27), and Volgograd (June 28), his motorcade was welcomed by huge crowds.

Soviet CP General Secretary Leonid Brezhnev conferred with de Gaulle June 21, 22 and 29 at the Kremlin. President Nikolai Podgorny escorted de Gaulle on his trip to Novosibirsk and Premier Aleksei Kosygin escorted him to Leningrad, Kiev and Volgograd. All three Soviet leaders accompanied de Gaulle on his visit to the Baikonur space center.

A joint declaration summarizing the major discussions between de Gaulle and the Soviet leaders was signed by de Gaulle and Podgorny at the Kremlin June 30. The declaration indicated that East-West relations, European security and problems relating to Germany had been the major subjects discussed. It had been reported June 21, following three hours of talks at the Kremlin between de Gaulle, Foreign Minister Couve de Murville and the Soviet leaders, that de Gaulle had urged the USSR to accept separate negotiations between individual Eastern and Western nations and had proposed bilateral talks be held by the USSR and West Germany on German unification. Brezhnev reportedly insisted on the recognition of East Germany as a first step toward German reunification. Brezhnev also was said to have repeated his proposal, made initially March 20 at the twenty-third Soviet CP Congress, for a conference on European security attended by European states only.

French spokesmen said June 22, following the second Kremlin negotiating session, that de Gaulle had told Brezhnev that the United States and USSR each served to counterbalance the other's tendencies toward hegemony. (At a Kremlin dinner June 20 he had said that "France in no way ignored the important role the United States should play" in "the restoration of Europe into a single fruitful whole.") Replying to the Soviet demand for recognition of East Germany, de Gaulle described East Germany as an artificial Soviet creation. Following the June 29 Kremlin meeting, de Gaulle and Brezhnev were again reported deadlocked on the German question.

The declaration noted that Couve de Murville and Soviet Foreign Minister Gromyko June 30 had signed two agreements covering Franco-Soviet cooperation in space exploration and in science and technology. Direct communications between Paris and Moscow were to be established by "hot-line" teletype system. The declaration disclosed that Brezhnev, Kosygin and Podgorny had accepted de Gaulle's invitation to visit France. At the June 30 Kremlin reception, de Gaulle said the "date and terms of their visit will be settled very soon."

Major points of the joint declaration:

East-West Relations and Germany—in the first instance the attention of Soviet statesmen and General de Gaulle was drawn to European problems. . . . It is precisely on their solution that the establishment of a normal situation throughout the continent and, consequently, genuine and lasting peace depend.

Both governments agree that the problems of Europe should be first of all discussed within European limits. They believe that the states of the continent should exert efforts to create conditions necessary for the establishment of an atmosphere of detente between all countries of the West and East. . . .

In this respect the prime aim for the Soviet Union and France is normalization, then a gradual development of relations between all European countries, given that there is respect for the independence of each of them and noninterference into their domestic affairs. . . .

Soviet-French Bilateral Relations—France and Russia reached agreement on the following major bilateral questions:

1. Trade. The five-year French-Soviet trade agreement signed Oct. 30, 1964 was discussed. Both countries "expressed confidence that they have big opportunities for this agreement's implementation [and] . . . for expanding the mutual trade exchanges beyond the aims of the agreement." Both "have agreed in principle on the creation of a permanent joint Soviet-French commission" to plan trade and technical exchanges "above the envisaged volume for the fulfillment of the trade agreement."

2. Space and Scientific Cooperation. "The Ministers of Foreign Affairs have signed an agreement on cooperation in the . . . peaceful utilization of outer space as well as an agreement on scientific-technical and economic cooperation." (Foreign ministers Couve de Murville and Gromyko signed the two agreements June 30. The space agreement, of 10 years duration, called for "the launching by the Soviet Union of a French satellite" and the creation of "joint working groups" to "ensure the elaboration and fulfillment of the program of cooperation." The scientific-technical and economic agreement pledged both sides to "cooperation" in these fields and stipulated that they would "set up a Joint Soviet-French Commission" to meet at least once a year.)

3. Television. Both sides expressed firm intention to implement all the clauses of the Soviet-French agreement of March 22, 1965, on color television.

4. Cultural Ties. France and the USSR were to expand their cultural relations "and in particular . . . to teach in each country the language of the other."

5. Atomic Energy. . . . Good results have already been achieved in the cooperation between the USSR and France in the peaceful uses of atomic energy. Account has been taken of the plans drafted by each of the sides on the expansion of the basis of the current joint projects, in particular in the field of the physics of high energies.

6. Consular Relations. It was also decided to sign a consular convention between the Soviet Union and France and to begin talks with this aim in the nearest future.

7. Paris-Moscow "Hot Line." . . . [the] Soviet Union and France decided to establish a direct communication line between the Kremlin and the Elysee Palace, which may be used for exchanging views and transmitting messages whenever it is found necessary.

Following the June 30 signing of the Franco-Soviet declaration, de Gaulle attended a Kremlin reception and addressed the Soviet people in a 10-minute pre-recorded TV speech which he concluded with these words in Russian: "To everyone and each of you I wish all the best for their lives, for the lives of your relatives and your country. To all of you I say that the new France is the friend of the new Russia. Long live the Soviet Union! Long live the friendship between Russia and France!"

Couve de Murville Visits Three East European Nations. French Foreign Minister Couve de Murville visited Poland May 18-20, Czechoslovakia July 25-28 and Hungary July 28-30, 1966. In Warsaw he conferred with Communist Party First Secretary Wladyslaw Gumulka and Foreign Minister Adam Rapacki. Two five-year agreements covering scientific, technical and cultural relations were signed by Couve de Murville and Rapacki May 20. In Prague Couve de Murville conferred with Czech Foreign Minister Vaclav David, Premier Joseph Lenart and President Antonin Novotny. Couve de Murville was the first French foreign minister to visit Poland and Czechoslovakia since before World War II. In Budapest he conferred with Hungarian Foreign Minister Janos Peter, Premier Gyula Kallai and Communist Party First Secretary Janos Kadar. Three agreements covering cultural, technical and scientific exchanges and consular relations were signed by Couve de Murville and Peter July 28.

Bulgarian-French Contacts. Bulgarian CP First Secretary Todor Zhivkov visited France Oct. 10-15, 1966. Accompanied by Foreign Minister Ivan Bachev, Zhivkov conferred with President de Gaulle, Premier Pompidou and Foreign Minister Couve de Murville. A Bulgarian-French technical and cultural agreement was signed October 15. The trip was Zhivkov's first official visit to a West European country. Couve de Murville had visited Bulgaria April 28-30.

Kosygin Visits France. Soviet Premier Aleksei Kosygin visited France Dec. 1-9, 1966, conferred with President de Gaulle, and achieved agreement on closer French-Soviet collaboration in economic, scientific and technological areas.

On his arrival at Orly Airfield December 1, Kosygin received a 101-gun salute, an honor normally accorded only to visiting heads of state. His nine-day visit included a tour of southern France December 5-7 with visits to the Sud-Aviation plant outside Toulouse, to factories in Lyons and to the atomic research center in Grenoble.

A joint declaration summarizing the major discussions between de Gaulle and Kosygin was signed by the two leaders December 8. It reported that, as a result of de Gaulle's and Kosygin's reciprocal visits, "a new and important stage has... been reached to the evolution of French-Soviet relations toward closer ties of cooperation, entente and friendship, based on the broad concordance existing between the essential national interests of the French and Soviet peoples."

Major points of the French-Soviet declaration:

1. East-West Relations. Detente is the first stage necessary for the evolution that seems desirable in the relations between European countries.... The first positive results are beginning to appear in this regard.... Such a transformation in the relations between the European states could progressively create conditions favorable to the discussion of the major problems that are posed in Europe and lead ultimately to an entente as to their settlement....

2. Soviet-French Bilateral Relations. It was agreed to study and draft jointly long-term cooperation plans between the two countries in the areas of trade, economy, science and technology.... Taking note of the satisfactory implementation of cooperation in the fields of color television, of the peaceful use of atomic energy and of space research, the two parties expressed the desire to extend their cooperation... to new areas of the economy, science and technology. This cooperation... will aim at placing the laboratories, research centers and business enterprises of the two countries in contact... [and] will encourage the establishment of industrial and technical cooperation between French public and private enterprises and Soviet industrial enterprises. [It had been announced in Moscow October 11 that France and the Soviet Union had agreed to joint research on a 70 billion-electron-volt nuclear accelerator under construction in Serpukhov, 62 miles from Moscow. A hydrogen "bubble chamber" for the Soviet accelerator was being built by French engineers in Saclay, France.] With a view to promoting trade between the two countries, it was agreed to create a joint French-Soviet Chamber of Commerce.

French-Soviet Contacts on Middle East Crisis. High level French-Soviet contacts were occasioned by the Arab-Israeli war in June 1967. Soviet Premier Kosygin conferred in Paris with President de Gaulle June 16 en route to an emergency session of the UN General Assembly. Kosygin met with de Gaulle again July 1 in Paris on his return trip to Moscow. French Premier Pompidou conferred in Moscow July 4-9 with Kosygin. Throughout these meetings France and the USSR adopted parallel positions on the Middle East crisis.

De Gaulle Visits Poland. President de Gaulle toured Poland Sept. 6-12, 1967. He failed during the visit to induce the Polish leadership to adopt a more flexible attitude toward West Germany and to assume a more independent stance with respect to the Soviet Union.

De Gaulle arrived in Warsaw September 6, met with Polish Chief-of-State Edward Ochab and other government officials September 7, toured outlying areas of Poland September 8-10, conferred with Polish CP First Secretary Wladyslaw Gomulka, addressed the Polish Sejm (parliament) September 11 and returned to France September 12 after conferring once again with Ochab.

Tens of thousands of Poles greeted de Gaulle on his arrival in Warsaw September 6. At a reception held in his honor later September 6, de Gaulle reiterated his acceptance of the Oder-Neisse line as the permanent western border of Poland by saying that the borders "are and must stay, where they are now." He referred for the first time to "Western, Central and Eastern Europe," a phrase interpreted as an attempt to distinguish between the Soviet Union and the Central European countries of the Soviet bloc.

Stefan Cardinal Wyszynski, primate of the Polish Roman Catholic church and the Polish regime's chief opponent, chose the time of de Gaulle's arrival to consecrate a new church in Warsaw. Wyszynski's action was assumed to be a protest against de Gaulle's refusal to meet privately with him. De Gaulle's refusal was considered an effort to placate the Polish regime. Church authorities September 5 had accused de Gaulle of showing a "lack of character" by permitting himself to be "led by the nose" by the Polish government. It was reported September 6 that de Gaulle had invited Wyszynski to attend a reception at the French embassy but that church officials had turned down the invitation on the grounds that de Gaulle should visit the primate at his episcopal palace or Warsaw Cathedral.

De Gaulle September 7 conferred for two hours with Ochab and other Polish government officials. Speaking at the Belvedere presidential palace after the conference, de Gaulle declared that France viewed Poland as "a popular, solid, respectable and powerful reality" that must be accorded a front rank position in "a world which must be a world of equilibrium and independence." He asserted that the abnormal situation of a divided Germany "must be settled by the Germans themselves within the framework of an agreement of Western, Central and Eastern Europe." As preconditions to a settlement of the German problem, de Gaulle cited West German acceptance of the Oder-Neisse line and renunciation of nuclear weapons. Once these terms were met, he said, there could follow a "relaxation of tensions, understanding and cooperation from the Atlantic to the Urals."

In his remarks September 7, Ochab declared that a settlement of the German question depended on West Germany's acceptance of the realities of World War II, that is, the creation of two German states and the establishment of the Oder-Neisse line. Implying that West Germany had yet to meet these conditions, Ochab asserted that Poland "cannot accept as changes mere appearances and gestures" associated with Bonn's "so-called Eastern policy."

De Gaulle visited the cities of Cracow, Oswiecim (Auschwitz), Bierun, Katowice, Zabrze (Hindenburg) and Gdansk (Danzig) September 8-10. He used the occasion to stress the "Polishness" of Silesia, formerly a part of Germany, and urged the Poles to assume a larger and more independent role in world affairs.

De Gaulle conferred with Polish CP First Secretary Gomulka September 11 and then addressed the Sejm. This was the first time a Western head of state had spoken before the Polish parliament. De Gaulle's remarks were largely a reiteration of his earlier statements.

Gomulka then addressed the Sejm and flatly rejected any suggestion that Poland moderate its policy toward West Germany or assume a more independent position vis-a-vis the Soviet Union. He prefaced his remarks by saying that it was his duty to tell de Gaulle "how we ourselves see our role in the construction of European security, our duties and our place in Europe." As for diplomatic relations with West Germany, these would depend on whether Bonn recognized East Germany and accepted the permanency of the Oder-Neisse frontier, which France had been "first among Western states to recognize as definitive and inviolable."

A joint declaration issued at the conclusion of de Gaulle's visit September 12 referred to the German problem in vague terms without mentioning de Gaulle's support for the Oder-Neisse line.

French-Soviet Space Shots. Two Soviet-built rockets carrying French meteorological equipment were launched from the USSR's Heyss Island rocket base in the Arctic Oct. 9, 1967 in the first French-Soviet space project under a joint agreement signed June 30, 1966. The purpose of the shots was to measure temperatures in the upper atmosphere.

Czechoslovak-French Meeting. Czechoslovak Premier Josef Lenart and Foreign Minister Vaclav David paid an official visit to Paris October 23-27 and conferred with French Prime Minister Pompidou, Foreign Minister Couve de Murville and President de Gaulle.

De Gaulle Reaffirms Polish Frontier. President de Gaulle November 27, at his semiannual press conference, reaffirmed his view that Poland's postwar Western frontier remain the Oder-Neisse line. Alluding to his voyage to Poland and his presence in Silesia, which formerly had been a German territory, de Gaulle declared: "Finding myself on Polish territory, in a region, which in my view, can no longer be contested, must not be contested, I noted what was striking — that is, the Polish character of the city where I was. I did this without wishing, the least in the world, to offend our German friends. In order to build the Europe that must be built and that includes a West, a Center and an East, it is necessary that everyone be respected, including the great German people. I do not believe I should say more today."

EAST-WEST RELATIONS: DISARMAMENT

French Participation Demanded. Soviet Foreign Minister Andrei Gromyko said Jan. 21, 1963 that it would be impossible to sign a nuclear disarmament pact without French participation. Gromyko told reporters at an Indian embassy reception in Washington that he believed "in the long run France will sign."

Underground A-Test Reported. The Algerian government asserted March 19 that France had carried out an underground nuclear test March 18 near In-Ekker, in the Hoggar region of the Sahara. The French Armed Forces Ministry refused March 19 to confirm that the detonation had taken place.

Tahiti A-Base to Be Built. French plans to build a nuclear test center in the Tahiti island in the Pacific were reported by Agence France-Presse May 1, 1963. General Jean Thiry, chief of France's nuclear experimental operations group, was quoted in a dispatch from Papeete, Tahiti as saying that the center would be functioning in three years and that the experiments would be focused on Mururoa Atoll. Thiry said the test center was part of France's efforts to build a nuclear force and was specifically aimed at the creation of a thermonuclear (hydrogen) bomb.

Three-Power Nuclear Test-Ban Treaty. Representatives of three of the world's nuclear powers—U. S. Under Secretary of State W. Averell Harriman, British Science Minister Viscount Hailsham (Quintin Hogg) and Soviet Foreign Minister Andrei Gromyko—initialed a treaty in Moscow July 25, 1963, prohibiting nuclear weapons tests in the earth's atmosphere, in outer space or under water.

The treaty, which had been the subject of intermittent negotiations since 1958, was produced during 10 days of talks begun in Moscow July 15. Excluded from the treaty were those nuclear tests carried out underground and considered by the West to be undetectible without inspection provisions unacceptable to the USSR. The pact did not bind other nations. But hope was expressed that the treaty would serve as a step toward disarmament and eventually would be accepted by all states, among them France.

France Rejects Test Ban. President de Gaulle confirmed July 29 that France would not sign the partial test-ban treaty. Addressing his eighth presidential news conference, de Gaulle declared:

. . . this Moscow agreement . . . in no way alters the terrible threat that the nuclear weapons of the two rivals bring to bear on the world, and above all on the people who do not possess them.

It is a fact that both of them hold the means to annihilate the world and it is a fact that there is no question of their being ready to give them up.

In these conditions, the world situation in relation to this threat not being changed in any way whatsoever, it is quite natural for a country such as France, who is beginning to have the means of freeing herself to a certain degree from this permanent terror, continue along this course. All the more so since nothing prevents the two rivals, their tests having been halted, from continuing to manufacture missiles in increasing quantities and power and to equip themselves with increasingly advanced launch vehicles, rockets, airplanes, submarines and satellites. The savings they could perhaps make from halting tests will enable them to strengthen even further their means of destruction . . .

Then you ask me what France is going to do after the Moscow agreement?

I will tell you once again that if one day the Americans and the Soviets reach the point of disarmament, that is the controlled destruction and banning of their nuclear means, it is wholeheartedly that we ourselves would give up securing them. . . .

However, . . . France was only awaiting the end of this useless performance—I am speaking of the Geneva Conference—to propose to the three other atomic powers certain initial effective disarmament measures, concerning particularly space, air and naval launch vehicles for nuclear missiles . . . France . . . intends before the end of the year to invite the states concerned to study with her this essential problem, while perhaps it has not yet become insoluble in its turn. . . .

Pact Signed in Moscow. The three-power treaty forbidding atomic weapons tests in the atmosphere, in space and under water was signed in Moscow Aug. 5, 1963 by U.S. Secretary of State Dean Rusk, Soviet Foreign Minister Andrei Gromyko and British Foreign Secretary Lord Home (Alexander Douglas-Home).

U.S. Nuclear Assistance Rejected. President Kennedy disclosed August 1 that the United States had offered France increased military cooperation in an unsuccessful effort to persuade it to participate in the nuclear test-ban treaty. Mr. Kennedy said: "We have...made some suggestions recently as to how that [military] cooperation could be more satisfactorily developed if there were a test ban, but we have received no response from the French government" other than President de Gaulle's public refusal (at his press conference July 29) to adhere to the treaty.

Kennedy Administration sources reported in Washington August 6 that President de Gaulle had rejected a U. S. offer to assist directly in the development of a French nuclear striking force if France abandoned its refusal to sign the test-ban treaty or participate in East-West disarmament negotiations. The U. S. offer reportedly was made in a personal message sent to de Gaulle by President Kennedy July 24, the day before the test-ban treaty was initialed in Moscow. De Gaulle's rejection was said to have been made in a letter delivered to Kennedy August 4.

French Plan H-Tests. The French government indicated September 5 that it planned hydrogen bomb tests in the Pacific Ocean within the next few years. The Foreign Ministry announced that French ambassadors in Australia, New Zealand, Chile and Peru had been instructed to oppose the systematic campaign in these countries against the tests. The announcement noted that with the exception of New Zealand, none of the four had protested against repeated U.S. and Soviet H-tests, many of them conducted in the Pacific.

French Underground A-Tests Reported. The *New York Herald Tribune* reported Nov. 4, 1963 that France had secretly carried out a series of underground nuclear tests in October. The detonations were said to have been devoted primarily to testing an atomic trigger that presumably would be used in the hydrogen bomb scheduled to be tested by France in the Pacific in 1967. The tests were conducted at the Sahara proving grounds retained by France when Algeria became independent.

France Rejects UN Resolution. The UN General Assembly November 27 approved a resolution calling for the suspension of all nuclear and thermonuclear tests, including those conducted underground and thus permissible under the Moscow test-ban treaty of July. The resolution was approved by 104-1 vote, with three abstentions. France was among the abstainers. The resolution called on all states to adhere to the Moscow treaty and urged the 18-nation UN Disarmament Committee to begin work on extending the ban to cover underground tests.

French Boycott Continues. The opening 1964 session of the 18-nation UN Disarmament Committee was held January 21 in Geneva. At the session the United States offered to join the Soviet Union in East-West negotiations to freeze the numbers and types of nuclear-armed strategic weapons possessed by both nations and their allies. The freeze presumably would apply to all nuclear delivery systems—long-range bombers, fixed-site missiles and Polaris submarines—capable of being used for strategic purposes.

France, not represented at the January 21 session, maintained its boycott of the committee's sessions throughout 1964.

France Ends Sahara Tests. French sources in Algiers said March 15, 1964 that France would end its nuclear testing program in the Algerian Sahara during 1964. French tests in the program to develop a French nuclear strike force were being transferred to Pacific sites.

Red China's First A-Test. Communist China Oct. 16, 1964 detonated its first nuclear device. In announcing the test, Peking called for a world summit conference of all the countries of the world to outlaw atomic weapons and destroy existing nuclear stockpiles. The Chinese government October 20 released the text of a note in which Premier Chou En-lai called on world leaders to join in a summit meeting to ban nuclear weapons.

U Thant Suggests Five-Power A-Talks. UN Secretary General U Thant proposed October 22 that the United States, USSR, Britain, France and Communist China meet in 1965 to discuss the banning of nuclear testing.

U.S. Bars A-Talks With China. The Johnson Administration indicated October 23 that it was not interested in either Communist China's October 16 suggestion for a world summit conference to ban nuclear weapons or in U Thant's October 22 proposal of a 1965 meeting of the five nuclear powers.

De Gaulle Backs Five-Power Talks. President de Gaulle declared in a message to Chinese Premier Chou En-lai October 30 that France was prepared to participate at any moment in any serious negotiations among the five nuclear powers. De Gaulle promised to "study with attention" Chou's October 16 proposal for nuclear disarmament talks.

De Gaulle's message also said: "For her part, France has not ceased during all of the past years to pronounce herself in favor of genuine disarmament, which naturally means that priority should be given to nuclear disarmament. On this subject, whenever the occasion has arisen, she has made detailed propositions concerning, first, the elimination of vehicles serving, or liable to serve, in the transportation of nuclear arms. Those propositions have taken into account the existing difficulty in assessing stockpiles of such devices. It is evident that disarmament cannot be conceived and cannot be put into practice if it is not accompanied by efficient control.... The French government remained ready to participate fully in any serious negotiations that could be organized among competent and responsible powers [i.e., nuclear powers] to discuss the problems of disarmament on a constructive and practical basis."

U.S. Vs. A-Aid to France. The U.S. Atomic Energy Commission acknowledged Dec. 18, 1964 that it had warned manufacturers not to sell to other countries any equipment that might be used in the development or testing of nuclear weapons. The warning was specifically aimed at France.

UN Votes World A-Conference; France Abstains. The 114-member UN Disarmament Commission in New York June 11, 1965 proposed a world disarmament conference that would include Communist China. The commission June 15 also approved a U.S. proposal for an early resumption of negotiations by the United Nations Eighteen-Nation Disarmament Committee (ENDC), which had adjourned its Geneva negotiations in September 1964.

The vote on the resolution to call a world disarmament conference was 89-0, with the United States, France and 14 other nations abstaining. The United States proposal for a resumption of the Geneva meetings of the ENDC was approved by 83-1 vote, with 18 abstentions (including the Soviet bloc and France). The proposal asked the committee to concentrate on: (1) the writing of a new treaty to prevent the spread of nuclear weapons to states that did not have them and (2) the broadening of the 1963 limited test-ban treaty to include underground tests.

When the ENDC reconvened in Geneva July 27, 1965, France continued its boycott, its seat remaining vacant.

France Abstains in Three UN Votes. The UN General Assembly Nov. 19, 1965 approved by 93-0 vote a resolution calling on "all states to take all necessary measures to conclude... a treaty preventing the proliferation of nuclear weapons." The United States, Britain and the USSR voted for the resolution; France abstained. After the Assembly's vote, UN Secretary General U Thant told the Assembly that all members of the ENDC should renew their efforts to draft a non-proliferation treaty. Since France had boycotted the ENDC since 1962, Thant's use of the word "all" was considered an appeal to Paris to participate in disarmament negotiations. France's UN delegation took no part in the three-week deliberation by the Assembly.

By a 112-0 vote, with France abstaining, the UN General Assembly November 20 adopted a resolution calling for a world disarmament conference that would include Communist China.

France again abstained December 3 when the General Assembly adopted by a 92-1 vote a resolution which: (1) urged all nations to suspend all nuclear weapons tests; (2) called on all nations to observe the 1963 Moscow treaty banning nuclear tests in the atmosphere, under water and in outer space; (3) requested the ENDC to continue with a sense of urgency its work on a comprehensive test-ban treaty to include a ban on underground testing.

French A-Tests; World Reaction. France exploded five nuclear bombs in the atmosphere July 2-Oct. 4, 1966. This was France's first atmospheric nuclear testing since April 1961. The tests were held at the newly-developed Experimental Center of the Pacific. They were France's first tests in the Pacific, and they raised to nine the number of atmospheric tests conducted by France. About 13,000 French personnel had been brought to the test area for construction and other work involved in the tests. Preparations at the site had taken two years. President de Gaulle, on a world tour, witnessed the third test September 11.

The first three bombs, described in French communiques as "plutonium fission devices" (or A-bombs), were exploded July 2, July 19 and September 11 at the Mururoa Atoll, 750 miles southeast of Tahiti.

The first bomb was said to have produced energy within the "tactical range," or equivalent to the power produced by the explosion of less than 100,000 tons (100 kilotons) of TNT. The second bomb, dropped by parachute from a Mirage IV jet bomber, produced a force of about 60 kilotons. The third, suspended from a balloon above the lagoon, produced energy believed to have been equivalent to 100 kilotons.

De Gaulle saw the third test from a position 25 miles away aboard the command cruiser *De Grasse*. He had arrived in Tahiti from New Caledonia September 6.

The last two bombs were exploded September 24 and October 4 at Fangataufa Atoll, 800 miles south of Tahiti, and Mururoa Atoll, respectively. According to an official communique, the October 4 test, "like its predecessor, contained plutonium and thermonuclear material but in a different configuration." Authorities said the force of the October 4 explosion was equivalent to 400 kilotons.

France had announced the tests May 17 and had warned shipping companies and airlines to stay clear of the danger area, which was defined as a circle around Mururoa with a radius of 400 nautical miles. Japan, Australia and New Zealand protested the proposed tests, as did Brazil, Chile, Peru, Colombia and Ecuador. De Gaulle had said May 4 that tests were necessary for France to be able to carry out its policies of "world equilibrium" and peace. He said the tests posed no danger to countries in or around the Pacific.

Following the July 2 test, the U.S. State Department issued a statement expressing regret "that France has resumed nuclear testing in the atmosphere." The statement urged France, which was not a signatory to the 1963 Moscow test-ban treaty "to adhere to the treaty and join in the effort to extend the ban on testing to include underground nuclear tests." Britain expressed "regret that France continues to ignore the principle of the partial test ban treaty and to test nuclear weapons in the atmosphere, thus causing an increase in the level of radioactivity." The Soviet news agency Tass reported the test briefly without comment.

France July 3 dismissed the criticism as "irritatingly moralizing" and said the precautions for the test had been "particularly severe" in comparison to those taken by other nuclear powers in their testing.

In its annual report July 12, the French Atomic Energy Commission announced that France would produce enough high-quality enriched uranium in less than a year to begin construction of its first H-bomb. Defense Minister Pierre Messmer had announced July 2 that France would have nuclear-tipped missiles in operation by 1969.

France Abstains in UN Vote. France abstained Dec. 5, 1966 in votes on UN General Assembly resolutions calling for the drafting of a treaty against the proliferation of nuclear weapons and for the suspension of nuclear weapons testing "in all environments."

France Continues Geneva Boycott. France remained absent Feb. 21, 1967 when the ENDC reconvened in Geneva to work out a treaty to prevent the proliferation of atomic weapons.

French Tests. France exploded three low-yield nuclear devices at its Mururoa test site in the Pacific June 5, June 27 and July 2, 1967. The tests, all conducted in the atmosphere, were aimed at developing an atomic triggering device for the detonation of thermonuclear weapons. The detonations, France's first nuclear testing since Oct. 4, 1966, raised to 12 the number of atmospheric tests conducted by France.

Red Chinese H-Bomb. China announced June 17 that it had successfully tested its first hydrogen bomb. A communique broadcast by Hsinhua, the Chinese Communist news agency, said: "Today, on June 17, 1967, after the five nuclear tests in two years and eight months, China successfully exploded its first hydrogen bomb, over the western region of the country." The French high commissioner for atomic energy, Francis Perrin, said June 17 that the Chinese test was a "very remarkable performance" but that it had "greater impact from the propaganda viewpoint than from the military viewpoint at least in the near future."

U.S. and USSR Back Non-Proliferation Draft; French Reaction. The United States and the Soviet Union submitted a draft treaty to prevent the further spread of nuclear weapons to the ENDC in Geneva August 24. Agence France-Presse August 25 quoted "responsible circles" in Paris as saying that France had not participated in the Geneva talks and thus had "no intention of signing this treaty."

CHAPTER X
FRANCE AND WESTERN EUROPE
EUROPEAN INTEGRATION; BRITAIN AND THE COMMON MARKET; RELATIONS WITH WEST GERMANY

De Gaulle Vs. British EEC Entry. Great Britain's 17-month attempt to join the six-nation European Economic Community (EEC, or Common Market) — France, Italy, West Germany, Belgium, Luxembourg and the Netherlands — was rejected by President de Gaulle Jan. 14, 1963 at his seventh presidential news conference.

De Gaulle said that Britain was not a European nation and could not become one unless it submitted to profound changes in its "nature" and "traditions." He warned that Britain's membership could weaken or destroy the EEC and other existing or planned European institutions. "England," said de Gaulle, "is... insular, maritime, linked through its trade, markets and food supply to very diverse and often very distant countries. Its activities are essentially industrial and commercial, and only slightly agricultural. The nature, structure and economic context of England differ profoundly from those of the other states of the continent."

De Gaulle was aiming at the United States as well as Britain. His declaration rejected policies that, he warned, could result in dissolution of the European community within an Atlantic community under U.S. tutelage. This stand was linked closely with de Gaulle's simultaneous rejection of U.S. proposals for a NATO nuclear force.

French Stand Assailed. De Gaulle's repudiation of British membership in the EEC was assailed January 14-15 by representatives of Britain and of the five other EEC nations.

The attack on the French position was disclosed in Brussels, where Britain and the EEC countries formally resumed their negotiations January 14 for the first time since Dec. 20, 1962. Edward Heath, Britain's chief representative in the negotiations, declared January 14 that he already had told de Gaulle that Britain would not accept "association" as a substitute for full membership in the Common Market.

De Gaulle's views were disavowed January 15 by the Belgian, West German, Italian and Netherlands representatives to the Brussels talks.

Franco-German Treaty. A treaty pledging cooperation and consultation between France and West Germany in foreign policy, defense and cultural affairs was signed in Paris January 22 by President de Gaulle and West German Chancellor Adenauer. The pact was viewed as a major

step in de Gaulle's plan for French leadership of a European community
freed from dependence on the United States.

The Franco-German treaty was concluded at the end of a two-day
Paris meeting held by de Gaulle and Adenauer. It was accompanied by a
joint declaration in which de Gaulle and Adenauer proclaimed their belief
that the treaty sealed "the reconciliation of the German people and the
French people, ending a centuries-old rivalry." The "reinforcement of
cooperation between the two countries," they declared, "constitutes an
indispensable stage on the way to a united Europe which is the aim of the
two peoples."

The pact, entitled a "Reconciliation Treaty," contained these provisions for Franco-West German consultation and cooperation:

Organization— The French and West German heads of state or
government were to meet at least twice yearly to determine general policy.

Foreign Affairs— "The two governments will consult before any
decision on all important questions of foreign policy..." These consultations would bear primarily on "problems relating to the European Communities and to European political cooperation, ... East-West relations,
both on the political and economic plans," and on NATO, the Council of
Europe, WEU, OECD, and the United Nations. The two countries would
seek to coordinate their programs of aid to less-developed countries.

Culture— The two countries would: (a) stimulate the teaching of each
others' language; (b) coordinate university degrees; (c) develop contacts and
information exchanges between scientific institutes; (d) organize collective
exchanges of youth, student, artisan and workers' groups.

Macmillan Rebuke to France. The British reply to de Gaulle's rejection of the United Kingdom's bid to enter EEC was delivered by Prime
Minister Harold Macmillan January 21. He rejected de Gaulle's stated
objections to British participation in the EEC and suggested that France
had not negotiated in good faith and that de Gaulle had not been wholly
honest when they discussed the talks at their last meeting, in December
1962. He asserted that de Gaulle's January 14 declaration had been a set-
back to the talks but not a fatal setback in view of the worldwide demand
for successful conclusion of the negotiations.

French Reaffirm Stand. De Gaulle's European policy declaration of
January 14 was reaffirmed by the French government January 24.
Addressing the National Assembly, Foreign Minister Couve de Murville
warned that Britain was not prepared for the vast changes necessary to
make its industrial, financial and agricultural sectors mesh with those of
the other European countries. He asserted that Britain had shown in the
Brussels negotiations that it was not prepared to accept the ECC treaty in
its entirety and that its demands for special concessions in fact amounted
to violations of the European community's rules and procedures. He
warned that if Britain and the six other European Free Trade Association
nations were permitted easy entry into the EEC, each with the special concession it would require, the current European community would become
"extra-continental" and would inalterably change its basic aims and
functions.

U.S. Opposes de Gaulle. American opposition to de Gaulle's European policies — particularly his rejection of British membership in EEC —
was made clear by President Kennedy at his news conference January 24.

Kennedy's statement rejected de Gaulle's thesis that the United States sought Britain's entry into the Common Market so that it could serve as the U.S. agent in Europe and assure the European Community's continued dependence on America. Kennedy reiterated the United States' past service to European unification and stressed that U.S. proposals for an "Atlantic partnership" of America and Europe called for relationship of equals.

France Keeps UK Out of EEC. Britain's one and a half-year effort to join the European Economic Community was ended January 29 when the six EEC nations informed Britain that they were unable to continue their Brussels negotiations on the British application for admission to the Common Market. The European nations' decision was reached at the end of a two-day Brussels meeting that had been called in the hope that settlement could be reached despite de Gaulle's opposition to Britain's entry to the EEC.

The formal breaking-off of negotiations took place when Edward Heath, Britain's chief European negotiator, was summoned by the representatives of the six EEC powers and told that, in view of France's opposition to continuing the talks, they had been unable to agree on a procedure for further meetings. The representatives of the five other EEC states told Heath that their governments had wanted to press for a successful conclusion of the negotiations and were certain that an agreement was possible but had been prevented from doing so by France.

Bonn Supports Renewed Talks with UK. The West German government's first formal expression of support for renewed United Kingdom-EEC negotiations was given January 30, after Chancellor Adenauer had met with his cabinet to discuss the results of the Brussels break. A government statement said: "The Federal government is convinced that the present situation must be constructively overcome. With this aim it will work for the restoration of unity ... among the Common Market partners and to facilitate the entry of Britain into the community." Fixing the blame for the break on France, the statement declared that the EEC nations "were unable to agree on ... continuing the negotiations with Great Britain despite the intensive efforts of five of the six."

Macmillan Criticizes de Gaulle. British Prime Minister Macmillan declared January 30 that the French veto of British admission to the Common Market had been dictated by President de Gaulle's apparent scheme for French domination of Western Europe. Addressing a TV audience that covered not only Britain, but the six Common Market countries, Macmillan blamed de Gaulle for "brutally" causing the collapse of the British-European negotiations and for jeopardizing the West's postwar steps toward unity.

Macmillan distinguished pointedly between France under de Gaulle and the other nations of Europe. In an obvious allusion to de Gaulle's allegedly autocratic methods of rule, he said: "I fear that France, or at least the present [de Gaulle] government ... are looking backwards; ... they seem to think one nation can dominate Europe or — equally wrong — that Europe can rule alone without friends and without allies."

ECSC, Euratom Talks Halted. Britain's negotiations for admission to the European Coal and Steel Community (ECSC) and European Atomic Energy Community (Euratom) were suspended January 30, following the collapse of the negotiations between Britain and the EEC.

Pompidou, de Gaulle on UK. Premier Georges Pompidou, in an address to Paris newsmen Feb. 5, 1963, confirmed that the British-U.S. Nassau agreement on creation of a NATO nuclear force had been a key element in de Gaulle's decision to veto Britain's EEC application. By the Nassau pact, he said, "Britain has shown that she is tied first of all to the United States, which is not in Europe."

Meeting with French deputies at a presidential reception in Paris February 5, de Gaulle declared that Britain had acted as a U.S. pawn in its application to join the EEC.

USSR Protests French-German Pact. The USSR protested against the Franco-German treaty in a note delivered to the French government February 5. The Soviet note had warned that if the Bonn-Paris alliance was used to provide West Germany with access to French nuclear weapons, the USSR would consider this action a direct threat and would "take immediately the...measures dictated to it by such a situation." France replied in a note delivered March 30 that the treaty was intended to build a French-German reconciliation that would be a safeguard for European peace. It declared that since the USSR had proclaimed repeatedly that it had "all the equipment needed for defense or attack," it could not possibly claim to be threatened by the treaty.

Adenauer Statement on EEC, French Treaty. West German Chancellor Konrad Adenauer, in replying to domestic criticism of his rapprochement with France and of de Gaulle's rejection of Britain's bid to join the Common Market, declared February 6 before the West German Bundestag that the break in British-EEC negotiations was temporary. Common Market nations, "especially we Germans," would work to revive the talks as quickly as possible. West Germany, said Adenauer, associated itself fully with Britain in its hopes for EEC membership and with the United States in its plans for strengthening NATO and making it a cornerstone of an Atlantic partnership. Defending the French-German alliance, Adenauer described it as a "historic necessity."

French-German Clash on Tariffs. Two meetings of the EEC Council held in Brussels April 22-23 and May 8-9, 1963 were marked by a clash between France and West Germany over a West German plan to generate further progress toward EEC goals by setting a timetable for action on tariff-reduction problems. The Bonn plan was designed to renew limited contacts with Britain and to prepare a coordinated EEC policy for worldwide tariff-cutting negotiations scheduled for 1964. France opposed the timetable on the ground it would postpone action on a common market in agriculture until after the world tariff talks opened; France wanted the farm problem settled to its advantage before agreeing to world tariff talks, at which the EEC might be forced to grant the United States concessions on farm imports.

French-German Treaty Ratified. The French-West German Treaty of Cooperation entered into force July 2. The French National Assembly June 14 ratified the pact by a 325-107 vote; the Senate ratified it June 21 by a 163-69 vote.

West Germany's ratification of the treaty had been approved by the Bundestag May 16 by a standing vote of approximately 400 deputies (only three of those present remained seated) and by the Bundesrat (Upper House) May 31 by unanimous vote. (The Bonn ratification law contained a preamble stating that the treaty did not supersede West Germany's commitments to NATO, its association with the United States, or its pledges that a united Europe would be open to Britain and European states not members of the European Economic Community.)

De Gaulle-Adenauer Meeting. De Gaulle and Adenauer conferred in Bonn July 4-5, 1963. The two were reported to have bypassed military matters to concentrate on European political and economic questions, particularly proposals for a renewal of British contacts with the European Economic Community.

UK, EEC Contacts Renewed. The foreign ministers of the six Common Market countries, meeting July 10-11 in Brussels, announced their agreement on resuming periodic contacts with Britain within the framework of the seven-nation Western European Union (WEU), comprising Britain and the six Common Market nations — France, Italy, West Germany, Belgium, Luxembourg and the Netherlands.* The agreement, made public July 11, provided for quarterly meetings among the seven countries in each of their capitals in rotation. Despite previous French objections, it was agreed that the talks, to take place as meetings of the WEU Council of Ministers, were to extend to economic as well as political and defense questions.

Brussels informants attributed the sudden reversal of France's position to a warning that the other five EEC countries would block an agreement on Common Market agricultural policy unless France agreed to accept at least limited contacts with Britain. The French were said to have agreed reluctantly, rather than face total isolation within the trade group and risk a farm settlement that did not give France's surplus-ridden farmers new European markets. Another factor in France's agreement to the proposal was the announcement July 11 that the EEC ministers had agreed to the signing July 20 of the Common Market's convention of association with 18 African countries, most of them former French colonies.

De Gaulle Threatens to Quit EEC on Farm Issue. A French demand for an EEC farm agreement by December 31 was made by de Gaulle at a Paris press conference July 29. Citing the repeated failure of the six EEC nations to come to agreement on the matter, de Gaulle said: "What would the very words 'European Economic Community' mean if Europe did not for the most part assure its food supplies from its own agricultural products...?" Acknowledging that the EEC's founding (1957) Treaty of Rome had dealt primarily with the question of industry, treating agriculture as a secondary issue, de Gaulle declared that the farm problem would have to be settled by December 31. By that date, he warned, "it will be necessary...that the Common Market be standing on its feet, complete and assured, or that it disappear." De Gaulle's statement was interpreted as a threat to quit the EEC if a farm agreement was not reached.

*The WEU, established by the 1955 Brussels Treaty to foster coordination and cooperation in defense, political, social, legal and cultural affairs, had gained in stature in recent years because it was the only European forum linking Britain to the six Common Market nations.

De Gaulle-Adenauer Meeting. De Gaulle and Adenauer, whose retirement as chancellor was imminent, met for their final conference Sept. 20-22, 1963 at Rambouillet, the French presidential estate near Paris. Their meeting ended with renewed pledges to strengthen the French-West German Treaty. (Adenauer, who termed the treaty the "most important work of my life," disclosed September 22 that he planned to continue to meet regularly with de Gaulle after his retirement.)

Britain-EEC Talks Begin in WEU. Foreign ministers of the seven WEU countries met in The Hague October 25-26, marking the first formal contact between Britain and the six EEC countries since the collapse of the Brussels conference in January. The major subject before the meeting — renewal of British-EEC discussions on trade and other related matter — was emphasized in the final communique issued October 26.

Erhard Disputes de Gaulle Thesis on United States. West German Chancellor Ludwig Erhard, who had succeeded Adenauer, visited Paris Nov. 21-22, 1963 for his first regular consultation with President de Gaulle under the Bonn-Paris treaty. In a brief statement made on his arrival in Paris, Erhard said it was his "credo" that "cooperation between our two peoples is essential if we wish to make of Europe something other than a vague geographic notion. Only then will we be able to throw all our weight into the balance, in view of a close Atlantic partnership." His remark was taken to mean that Bonn felt its new alliance with France could become an essential part of the Atlantic partnership advanced by the Kennedy administration in the United States and rejected by de Gaulle.

Erhard said in a talk to Paris diplomatic correspondents November 22, after his meetings with de Gaulle: "We Germans are convinced that we can and must rely on the Atlantic alliance. We feel sure that the United States would reply with all its force if Europe or any part of Europe was attacked." The French-German alliance was "a new force to lead Europe toward its common destiny." But this destiny was linked intimately with that of the United States, which had "encouraged European union with all its force a long time ago." West Germany had "the greatest respect for the French effort for atomic power," but it still relied on the United States nuclear deterrent to protect Western Europe.

French Victory in EEC Farm Accord. The six European Common Market nations reached a series of agreements Dec. 9-23, 1963 on the creation of a European-wide market in basic foodstuffs and the fixing of a unified policy on world tariff reductions.

The farm accords provided for the extension of Common Market practices, already applied to industrial and manufactured goods, to three of Europe's most basic agricultural categories: rice and cereals, milk and dairy products, beef and veal. The agreements were negotiated under a December 31 deadline imposed by President de Gaulle on July 29.

The accords generally represented a victory for France, the largest agricultural producer and exporter of the six; they represented a major concession on the part of West Germany, which had sought to retain some measure of protection for its relatively high-cost agriculture.

The Brussels talks were raised to the foreign ministers' level December 18. The farm question was set aside temporarily for a decision on the policy to be followed by the Common Market in the 1964 world-wide tariff negotiations. The foreign ministers reached agreement December 19 on a liberal policy, favored by West Germany, toward tariffs on manufactured and semi-finished goods.

The foreign ministers again took up the European farm problem December 21. They announced December 23 that they had reached a compromise agreement satisfying French demands for a common market in farm products that would pave the way for uniform pricing and free movement of basic foodstuffs among the six countries. The agreement: (1) ordered steps toward the gradual establishment of a common market in milk and dairy products; (2) provided for gradual creation of a common market in rice and cereals, with a common price pattern for cereals to be set by April 15, 1964.

The path to the December agreement apparently was opened by de Gaulle and Erhard at their Paris meeting held November 21-22. Although no detailed farm accord was produced at the meeting, it was clear that the two leaders had agreed on the basic pattern that led to the December accords: French acceptance of the West German demand for a liberal EEC tariff policy in the 1964 world trade talks; West German acceptance of a European-wide farm price system that would assure France continental outlets for its agricultural surpluses.

De Gaulle Repeats Stand on UK. President de Gaulle, in a New Year's statement broadcast to the French people December 31, reaffirmed his opposition to British membership in the Common Market. Citing what he said was France's major effort "to help build the Common Market and, in so doing, clear the path leading to a United Europe," de Gaulle asserted that these goals now were possible because France had refused to allow the EEC "either to disintegrate as a result of the admission of a new member which could not conform to the rules" or to be "annexed to a system existing on the other side of the Atlantic." France's European policies, he said, had been based on the reconciliation with Germany and on the determination "to see that the European Economic Community was truly a community and truly European." De Gaulle said that one of France's major tasks was "the union of Europe, including as soon as possible the regular and organized cooperation of Germany, Italy, the Netherlands, Belgium, Luxembourg and France in the political, defense and cultural domains, as will be the case of economics."

Erhard Seeks European "Summit." West German Chancellor Erhard proposed Jan. 9, 1964 that the leaders of the six Common Market nations — France, Italy, West Germany, Belgium, Luxembourg and the Netherlands — meet to deal with the "political malaise" arising from their differences over the admission of Britain and the political organization of Western Europe. Erhard, addressing the Bundestag, said that President de Gaulle had given his assent to the idea of a European summit conference during their meeting in Paris in November 1963. De Gaulle, said Erhard, had made it clear that he would support such a meeting to restore solidarity among the Common Market nations, but he would not agree to efforts to establish a closely knit European political union.

De Gaulle Bars European Government. President de Gaulle January 31 set forth his position on France's European policies at his ninth press conference. Asked for his views on the political future of the European Common Market, de Gaulle said that the six nations thus far had accomplished the objectives fixed by the Rome Treaty establishing the EEC but that in the attainment of these objectives they had "seen clearly that the executive power...belongs to the [member] governments alone." He conceded that the EEC Executive Commission, the Common Market's highest administrative body, had formulated the settlements ultimately adopted by the member governments, but he insisted that in each case "the [six] governments nonetheless found themselves obliged to take decisive steps and assume their responsibilities."

De Gaulle said that political union of the six EEC members was impossible because proponents of political union had formulated three "unattainable" conditions: "No European union, they say, unless through integration under supranational leadership. No European union, if England does not belong to it. No European union, without its being incorporated in an Atlantic community. Yet it is clear that not one of the peoples of Europe would allow their destiny to be handed over to an assembly composed mainly of foreigners. In any case this is true for France. It is also clear that England...would accept it less than anyone else. Finally, it is clear that to merge the policy of Europe in a multilateral Atlantic policy would be tantamount to Europe's having no policy itself and, in that case, we do not see why it would want to federate."

De Gaulle-Erhard Meeting. West German Chancellor Erhard met with President de Gaulle in Paris February 14-15 for a consultative meeting required by the French-West German Treaty.

The two leaders made no progress in resolving their differing views on the political organization of the EEC. They did, however, reach agreement concerning coordinated French-West German aid and investment programs for Africa and Latin America.

French, Italians Differ on European Unity. Italian President Antonio Segni visited Paris February 19-22 to discuss the European political question. A joint communique issued by Segni and de Gaulle February 21 said that they had agreed on the necessity for progress toward European political unity but had encountered "differences of concept" in their discussion. Foreign Minister Giuseppe Saragat, who accompanied Segni to Paris, in an address to the French Diplomatic Press Association February 20, stressed that Italy sought a European community whose members would "progressively transfer some of their sovereignty to joint institutions whose actions would be submitted to the control of an elected assembly."

French and Italian spokesmen February 21 confirmed that de Gaulle and the Italian leaders had failed to find any common ground in their discussions.

Bonn Opposes Paris-Backed EEC Grain Price Accord. West German Chancellor Erhard March 19, 1964 declared in the Bundestag that the "federal government will not accept a reduction in cereal prices in 1964-1965" and would not commit itself to any further reduction. Erhard's statement reflected Bonn's concern that the establishment of a single grain price for all EEC members would reduce the grain price received by West Germany's highly subsidized farmers. Erhard's government, facing general elections in 1965, was concerned with the political reaction if it deprived the German farmers of grain subsidies and forced them under a Common Market grain price agreement to compete against large French exports of surplus wheat.

Erhard's position was opposed by the French government which viewed early establishment of a Common Market-wide grain price as advantageous to French farmers. (The compromise farm program adopted by the EEC in December 1963 included the requirement that Common Market-wide grain prices be set in 1964.) French grain prices were substantially lower than those in West Germany's highly protected farm market. Implementation of a common market in grains and establishment of a single EEC price for grains would enable French exports of wheat to enter the German market.

De Gaulle-Erhard Meeting. President de Gaulle visited Bonn July 3-4, 1964 for talks with Chancellor Erhard. The meeting produced an agreed statement July 4 that "discussions on the political cooperation of Europe will be further intensified...with the objective of bringing into being a united Europe and a common European policy.... To this purpose, proposals will be made from the German side."

The statement was taken as proof that de Gaulle had abandoned a plan to create a French-West German committee to prepare proposals on European unity for submission to the four other EEC states. Although the July 4 statement made no mention of the French proposal, de Gaulle was known to have communicated it to the Bonn government before the meeting and to have taken it up with Erhard on his arrival in Bonn July 3. Bonn dispatches reported that Erhard had rejected the de Gaulle plan because he felt that the EEC states — particularly Belgium, the Netherlands, and Luxembourg — would regard it as an attempt to establish a legal French-West Germany hegemony over the six-nation community. In addition, it was apparent that the French plan was based on de Gaulle's concept of a confederation of sovereign continental European states, rather than on European political union open to Great Britain, as favored by West Germany and the smaller EEC nations.

De Gaulle Reiterates Opposition to European Union. President de Gaulle reiterated his opposition to political union of the six at his July 23 press conference. He asserted that France's opponents had invoked contradictory arguments in their rejection of the French plan for confederal cooperation among sovereign European states. He said that the plan had been rejected because it did not conform to its opponents' conception of a Europe that included Britain and was subordinated to "a commission of experts" (i.e., the EEC Executive Commission) and "a parliament [the advisory legislative body of the six with its seat in Strassbourg] cut off from national realities." De Gaulle added that "we have seen many people...advocate for Europe not an independent policy, which in reality they do not visualize, but an organization unsuited to have one, linked with...an Atlantic system,...and consequently subordinate to what the United States calls its leadership."

De Gaulle conceded that France's differences with its neighbors had stalemated the discussions on European political unity. He said that even France and West Germany, bound by a treaty of cooperation, had not been able to elaborate a common European policy because "Bonn has not believed...that this [European political] policy should be European and independent." He said that in the absence of any other acceptable proposal, France would wait patiently for the West German initiative foreseen in the statement issued in Bonn July 4 after his meeting with Erhard.

France Again Threatens to Quit EEC on Farm Issue. A French warning that France would withdraw from the Common Market unless West Germany permitted completion of a common European grain-price agreement was delivered in Paris Oct. 21, 1964. A statement issued after a cabinet meeting presided over by President de Gaulle declared that the government had "stressed once again that France will cease to participate in the European Economic Community if the agricultural market is not organized."

France's unyielding position had followed West Germany's refusal to negotiate at a Brussels meeting October 20 of Common Market agriculture ministers. French Agriculture Minister Edgard Pisani had reported to the cabinet that the Brussels deadlock, unless broken, would pose "very grave difficulties" in settling the grain-price question and carrying out the EEC plan for a uniform European farm system.

British-French Air Jet Project. The British government announced October 26 that it had informed France of its desire to restudy a joint Anglo-French project for construction of a supersonic airliner, the *Concorde*. The *Concorde* project to produce a prototype 1,450-mph. airliner by 1967 was being carried out by the British Aircraft Corporation and France's Sud Aviation Company.

British Aviation Minister Roy Jenkins conferred in Paris October 29 with Marc Jaquet, French transport minister, but reportedly failed to still French warnings that a British withdrawal from the project would endanger Anglo-French relations. (Britain contended that the project, initially budgeted at $240 million for each country, already had doubled and might cost even more to complete.) Jenkins, rejecting charges that Britain had made a deal with the United States to quit the project, told Parliament November 5 that no final decision had been reached on postponing or cancelling work on the *Concorde*.

Bonn Issues Unity Plan. The West German government Nov. 6, 1964 published a plan for the resumption of negotiations on the political unification of Western Europe. The Bonn program, submitted formally November 4 to the five other EEC member states, called for accelerated implementation of the Common Market at the same time that a committee of experts would draft a treaty for eventual political union.

The West German proposal was intended primarily to achieve a renewal of the European unity discussions halted by de Gaulle's opposition to any supranational political institutions that would diminish the sovereignty of the individual West European governments. It came at a time when France and West Germany were at loggerheads over terms for creating a Europe-wide agricultural market within the EEC.

French officials said in Paris November 6 that the West German plan could not be discussed before a settlement had been reached on a common farm market.

Bonn Agrees to Grain Price Reduction. The West German government announced November 10 its agreement to begin substantive negotiations on a reduction of its grain prices. The announcement followed France's October 21 threat to quit the EEC unless a grain settlement was reached by the end of the year. Meeting with the Common Market Council of Ministers in Brussels, West German Foreign Minister Gerhard Schroeder declared that Bonn was "prepared to reach an agreement now on common grain prices."

France Accepts EEC Tariff Position. The six Common Market states reached agreement in Brussels November 15 on a unified negotiating position for the world-wide Kennedy Round tariff-cutting talks due to be convened in Geneva the following day.

The agreement was made possible by France's announcement November 11 that it had dropped demands for final settlement of the European grain-price question as a precondition for Common Market participation in the Kennedy Round negotiations. The French reversal was announced in Brussels November 11 by Foreign Minister Couve de Murville at a meeting of the EEC Council of Ministers. Couve de Murville reportedly stressed that France did not believe the Kennedy Round negotiations could be successful unless the Common Market states first had settled their differences on agricultural matters. But, he reportedly said, France would not therefore delay negotiations on industrial tariffs, the primary concern of the Kennedy Round negotiations. It was apparent that French agreement to EEC participation in the Kennedy Round tariff negotiations followed West Germany's agreement November 10 to begin negotiations on the reduction of its grain prices.

EEC Present in "Kennedy Round" Talks. A new round of world tariff-cutting negotiations—the "Kennedy Round"—was opened in Geneva Nov. 16, 1964 by delegations representing 17 of the world's major industrial nations. The negotiations, convened under the auspices of the General Agreement on Tariffs & Trade (GATT), were considered the most important of GATT's six tariff-cutting conferences since its inception in 1948. Although the negotiations were in the hands primarily of the 17 largest industrial powers (including the six EEC members negotiating as a single bloc) affiliated with GATT, 73 states participated.

(The negotiations were known as the "Kennedy Round" in tribute to the late President John F. Kennedy, whose proposals for trade liberalization, embodied in the U.S. Trade Expansion Act of 1962, were the inspiration for the negotiations. The Kennedy Round negotiations were aimed at producing reciprocal tariffs cuts of 50% on the greatest possible number of industrial products involved in world trade.)

The Kennedy Round's substantive negotiations began in Geneva November 16 when the 17 principal industrial powers submitted lists of products they wished exempted from the negotiations. The joint list submitted by the six EEC nations was reported to apply to products constituting 19% of the EEC's total dutiable imports; according to the *New York Times,* the largest category of products on the Common Market list was machinery, ranging from tools to heavy industrial equipment.

EEC Grain Price Agreement. The EEC's Ministerial Council agreed in Brussels December 15 on uniform "target" prices for wholesale grain purchases throughout the Common Market. The agreement ended a year-long deadlock that had brought a French threat to withdraw from the Community.

The grain agreement was worked out at a Council meeting begun in Brussels December 12. Although West Germany initially expressed reservations at the price levels proposed, Bonn's representatives December 12 reaffirmed their government's commitment to negotiation of uniform grain prices.

De Gaulle Hails Accord. President de Gaulle, in a statement issued in Paris Dec. 16, 1964 following a cabinet meeting, declared that the Brussels grain-price agreement was a "capital" step that created "all sorts of possibilities in the way of European construction." In his statement, de Gaulle expressed gratitude to the EEC Executive Commission for its key role in arranging the grain-price accord, but he repeated his contention that the basic responsibility for such decisions remained with the six sovereign EEC nations.

France informed the other EEC nations December 17 that it expected the six-nation Common Market in agriculture to be completed in 1965. The French representative in Brussels submitted a timetable for completion of the required farm regulations which called for final establishment of EEC agricultural financial regulations and the conclusion of price agreements for meat, fruits and vegetables, rice, milk and dairy products.

Britain Warns EEC. The British representative to the EEC, Sir Con O'Neill, warned December 17 that the basis for the Western political and military alliance would be undermined unless the Common Market states worked toward political unity with Britain and the rest of Western Europe.

During most of 1964, Britain and the EEC nations had continued talks within the seven-nation Western European Union on proposals for economic and political cooperation. The WEU contacts had been set up by the seven countries following the collapse in 1963 of Britain's negotiations for membership in the Common Market. As in the past, the French delegation rejected every major British proposal submitted to the WEU for cooperation among the seven or for British participation in the EEC states' discussions of proposals for their eventual political association.

EEC, EFTA Cut Tariffs. The two rival Western European trade groups each reduced tariffs on industrial goods traded among its members by an additional 10% at the start of 1965.

The six-nation Common Market (European Economic Community or EEC) — France, Italy, West Germany, Belgium, Luxembourg and the Netherlands — put its new 10% tariff reduction into effect January 1. The cut brought EEC internal tariffs on industrial products down to 30% of the average tariffs in effect among the six states when the trade group began operations Jan. 1, 1958.

The British-led European Free Trade Association (EFTA) put its 10% tariff reduction into effect Dec. 31, 1964. This brought the level of EFTA internal tariffs on industrial goods down to 30% of the level existing among EFTA states when the association was formed in 1960. The EFTA planned to abolish its internal industrial tariffs entirely by late 1966, the same timetable contemplated by the rival Common Market. (EFTA member states: Britain, Austria, Sweden, Norway, Denmark, Switzerland, and Portugal. Finland was an associate member of the trade bloc.)

The EEC Executive Commission January 13 approved a plan to eliminate industrial tariffs among the six member nations by mid-1967. The tariffs which had been reduced to 30% of their original 1957 level, would be reduced an additional 10% Jan. 1, 1966 and the final 20% July 1, 1967. The original timetable had called for the complete elimination of industrial tariffs by 1970. The EEC apparently decided to accelerate the program to keep pace with its competitor, the EFTA, which had decided to aim for free internal industrial trade by 1967.

France Bars Unity Talks. Italian Foreign Minister Amintore Fanfani was reported March 18 to have suggested that the foreign ministers of the EEC countries hold a political unity meeting in Venice in May. French Foreign Minister Couve de Murville conferred with Fanfani in Rome March 27-29 and reportedly agreed in principle that a unity meeting would be desirable but rejected a spring date on the ground that there was insufficient evidence of agreement among the six EEC nations on goals and means for achieving European political unity.

De Gaulle Demands EEC Farm Agreement. De Gaulle insisted March 31 that talks on political "cooperation" among the EEC nations could take place only if there were a favorable outcome to EEC negotiations on a financial arrangement to cover the costs of EEC's farm program. De Gaulle also demanded completion of EEC negotiations on common prices for farm products. A government statement said a conference of the chiefs of state of the six nations would be "opportune" as soon as the Brussels discussions currently being conducted, "especially on the subject of agriculture," had been favorably decided.

Wilson- de Gaulle Meeting. British Prime Minister Harold Wilson and President de Gaulle conferred in Paris April 2-3, 1965. Wilson announced at a Paris press conference April 3 that the two leaders had agreed on Anglo-French cooperation in aircraft production and other technological areas. The British and French defense and aviation ministers were to continue the talks by considering the possible replacement of Britain's recently abandoned experimental TSR-2 jet bomber by a French-built Mirage-IV-C powered by British Rolls-Royce jet engines.

Merger Treaty Signed. Cabinet ministers of West Germany, France, Italy, Belgium, the Netherlands and Luxembourg signed a treaty in Brussels April 8 merging the EEC's three executive bodies into one executive and the three ministerial councils into one council, effective Jan. 1, 1966. Ratification by the national parliaments of the six member nations still was required. The three bodies to be merged were the European Economic Community (Common Market, or EEC), the European Coal & Steel Community (ECSC) and the European Atomic Energy Community (EURATOM).

EEC Fails to Reach Farm Agreement. EEC ministers met in Brussels May 13-14 but failed to establish an agricultural financing policy as demanded by France. The unresolved issues hinged on money needed to subsidize EEC farm surplus exports (mainly French), to transfer farm workers to factories, to modernize farm production and to support farm prices.

French-British Air Jet Accord. British Defense Minister Denis Healy told the House of Commons May 17 that Britain and France had signed a "memorandum of understanding" binding both nations to the joint development of two new military supersonic aircraft, a reconnaissance-strike plane and a fixed-wing trainer-combat plane. He said the pact "puts the seal on the recent understanding between President de Gaulle and Prime Minister Wilson."

De Gaulle, Erhard Clash on EEC Farm Plan. De Gaulle visited Bonn June 11-12, 1965 for discussions with West German Chancellor Ludwig Erhard. Their talks ended in disagreement over de Gaulle's insistence on a June 30 deadline for concluding an accord on establishing a Common Market agricultural finance plan. De Gaulle made the agricultural agreement a condition for a six-nation heads-of-state meeting desired by Erhard, to discuss European political integration.

EEC Deadlocked on Farm Finance Proposals. The EEC Council of Ministers met in Brussels June 15 in an attempt to establish a Common Market farm finance system before the June 30 deadline demanded by de Gaulle. At the meeting Foreign Minister Couve de Murville proposed a farm finance plan favorable to France's large agricultural industry (the largest of the EEC). The Council also had before it a farm finance plan proposed by EEC Executive Commission President Walter Hallstein. Hallstein's proposal was also advantageous to French farmers, but it contained provisions — unacceptable to the de Gaulle government — which would have given the EEC certain supranational budgetary powers. The Council meeting June 15 was unable to reach agreement on either the French or the EEC Executive Commission proposals.

Couve de Murville Rejects EEC Commission Plan. French Foreign Minister Couve de Murville June 16 declared that the EEC Commission's plan contained supranational aspects unacceptable to France. He explained the French position before the French National Assembly: "In our view,... [the] Assembly [the Parliamentary Assembly] should... remain within the limits of the role which is given to it by the Treaty of Rome, that is to say, a consultative role which... can also be important and useful."

Concerning a Commission proposal that members' customs collections be paid to an EEC Treasury after July 1, 1967, Couve de Murville said that the plan, "which would now allocate to the community receipts which would far exceed its annual expenditures... is an entirely abnormal decision, whose favor no serious reason has been brought forth." (The Commission had estimated community expenditures for 1967 at $1.237 billion and receipts from levies and customs duties at $2.3 billion. According to the Commission's proposal, the EEC Council would decide, on the basis of commission proposals, to what purposes this surplus would be put.)

EEC Farm Deadlock Brings French Boycott. The Council of Ministers of the Common Market convened in Brussels June 28-30, 1965 in an attempt to set up measures for financing EEC's agricultural program after July 1. (Measures adopted in January 1962 expired at midnight June 30.) At 2 A.M. July 1 Foreign Minister Couve de Murville adjourned the meeting unilaterally and announced that no agreement had been reached. The meeting's failure left EEC without an agricultural finance program. The French government, which had demanded settlement of the agricultural finance problem by the June 30 deadline, began an immediate boycott of Common Market institutions, bringing to a halt action on all EEC political and economic matters currently under discussion.

The commission's proposals to strengthen the supranational character of the EEC were backed at the June 28-30 meeting by foreign ministers Amintore Fanfani of Italy, Gerhard Schroeder of West Germany and Joseph Luns of the Netherlands. These three, together with EEC Commission President Hallstein, opposed Couve de Murville's demand for an agreement on agricultural financing arrangements by midnight June 30. They contended that an agreement could be reached but more time was needed. Luxembourg Prime Minister Pierre Werner attempted to compromise the opposing sides. Only Belgian Foreign Minister Paul-Henri Spaak supported the French view that an agricultural finance program was required by June 30; the supranational issues, he said, could be discussed later. Couve de Murville adjourned the meeting early July 1 after it became clear that the two groups had not been able to resolve their differences within the time limit demanded by France.

The French cabinet met in Paris July 1, with President de Gaulle presiding, to discuss the failure of the Brussels meeting. After the session, Information Minister Alain Peyrefitte read a cabinet statement saying the government had "decided for its part to draw the political, economic, and judicial consequences of the situation now created."

Paris announced July 6 that its permanent representative at EEC headquarters in Brussels, Jean-Marc Boegner, had been "invited" to return to Paris and that "for the moment" France no longer would take part in EEC Council meetings. Since all Council decisions required unanimous approval of the six, the French boycott of the EEC Council meetings in effect froze further economic or political integration of the EEC nations. (Under EEC's 1957 founding Treaty of Rome, after Jan. 1, 1966 the EEC Council of Ministers would be empowered to take decisions by qualified majority vote; that is, Germany, France, and Italy would be given four votes each, Belgium and the Netherlands two votes each, and Luxembourg one vote. Twelve votes would be sufficient for the Council of Ministers to make a decision.)

French officials boycotted an EEC meeting held July 6 on preparation of the EEC position in the Kennedy Round GATT tariff reduction talks scheduled to resume in Geneva September 16.

France Rebuffs EEC Concessions. The EEC's Council of Ministers met July 26-27 in Brussels to discuss revised proposals on agricultural finance submitted by the EEC Executive Commission. The new proposals, designed primarily to satisfy France, which boycotted this meeting, were presented by EEC Executive Commission President Hallstein. Two major concessions to France were included: (1) The Commission dropped its earlier plans under which EEC would have had an independent revenue from industrial duties and agricultural levies beginning July 1, 1967 and control over EEC's budget would be vested in the EEC Parliamentary Assembly. (2) The Commission accepted the French proposal, made at the June 15 and June 30 meetings of the Council, for adoption of an agricultural finance plan to run from July 1, 1965 through December 31, 1969.

French Premier Pompidou July 27 made no mention of the new proposals in a French TV interview in which he sharply criticized the Commission. Pompidou reiterated France's position that the six governments had agreed in 1962 to adopt, by June 30, 1965, an agricultural finance plan covering the period July 1, 1965-Dec. 31, 1969. The Common Market, he said, had "placed...French (industry)...in direct competition...with the powerful German industry. This could be tolerated only if it was compensated for by an agricultural common market, providing our agriculture with large outlets at remunerative prices, and thus enabling the state, largely released from the need for supporting our agriculture, to lighten the burdens borne by industry." In a direct criticism of the role of the EEC Commission, he declared that France "cannot leave to a commission which has no political calling the task of determining the living standard of the French people and ... the destiny of our agriculture and our industry."

De Gaulle Sets Terms, Opposes EEC Majority Voting. President de Gaulle Sept. 9, 1965 at his twelfth presidential press conference announced that France would end its boycott of ministerial meetings of the EEC only if France's EEC partners agreed to include an agricultural finance plan within the framework of EEC. De Gaulle simultaneously expressed his strong objection to EEC decision-making by majority voting of the EEC Council of Ministers.

Reviewing the EEC's failure to adopt an agricultural finance plan, de Gaulle declared: "... In Brussels on June 30, our delegation came up against a refusal with regard to final drafting of a financial regulation in accordance with the commitments made.... The Commission [the EEC Executive Commission] ... had formulated on the subject of this regulation conditions intended to give itself its own budget, ... as much as $4 billion, ... that would have made it literally a major independent financial power.... [The] combination ... of the supranational demands of the ... Commission [and] ... the support that several delegations declared themselves ready to give ... forced us to bring the negotiations to a close.

"... in the light of this event, we ... measured the situation in which our country would risk finding itself if one provision ... [of] the Rome Treaty were actually applied. Thus, in ... the text, the decisions of the Council of Ministers of the six would, beginning Jan. 1, 1966, be taken by majority vote; in other words, France would ... see her hand forced on any economic matter...

"... [France] is ready to participate in all exchanges of views.... If necessary, she envisages resuming the Brussels negotiations, once the inclusion of agriculture into the Common Market is truly adopted...."

French Boycott Blocks Kennedy Round. Kennedy Round negotiations for cutting world tariffs in farm commodities opened in Geneva Sept. 16, 1965 within the framework of the 79-nation General Agreement on Tariffs & Trade (GATT). The EEC, which previously had participated in GATT tariff cutting sessions, was absent from the session as a result of France's boycott of EEC. (GATT Executive Secretary Eric Wyndham White told reporters September 17 that the countries that had presented tariff reduction offers September 16 had restricted their offers to items that "in general excluded agricultural products of interest to the countries of EEC." He added that these countries would add to their lists when the EEC reentered the Kennedy Round negotiations.) An EEC spokesman in Geneva said September 16 that "for reasons beyond its control" the EEC could not submit its offers, but hoped it would be able to do so later.

EEC Urges French Return. Ministers of five nations of the EEC October 26 urged France to attend a special meeting of the EEC Council of Ministers to work out a solution to the EEC impasse resulting from France's boycott of its meetings. This special meeting would not include the EEC Executive Commission, which President de Gaulle had sharply criticized at his September 9 press conference.

France Eases EEC Stand. The French government announced Dec. 22, 1965 that it would accept a proposal for a meeting with the other five member states of the EEC in January 1966 to discuss all aspects of the current deadlock over EEC's financing and common farm market programs.

The announcement was made after a meeting of the French cabinet at which de Gaulle presided.

De Gaulle Announces French Return. President de Gaulle December 31, in his annual year-end TV address, declared that France was "able to resume the organization of the Common Market ... but under conditions which are equitable and reasonable and with the hope that on such a basis, other neighbors will join."

France Cuts EEC Tariff. France kept in step with its five European Economic Community partners (Italy, West Germany, Belgium, Luxembourg and the Netherlands) by reducing its tariffs to the other EEC members by 10 per cent, effective Jan. 1, 1966. The scheduled 10 per cent tariff reduction among the six Common Market nations brought duties down to 20 per cent of the levels that had prevailed Jan. 1, 1958, the date they began their first round of reductions.

France Meets With EEC, Sets Conditions. Foreign ministers of the six EEC nations met January 17-18 in Luxembourg. This was the first joint meeting they had had since July 1, 1965, when France began its boycott of EEC. As a concession to France, the meeting was held in Luxembourg, not at EEC Headquarters in Brussels. In addition, the meeting took place without the presence of the EEC Executive Commission, which had come under fire from President de Gaulle for its alleged supranational ambitions.

The major development of the two-day meeting was the presentation by Foreign Minister Couve de Murville January 17 of France's conditions for resuming normal relations between Paris and the EEC. Couve de Murville detailed a 10-point program reducing the power of the EEC Executive Commission. Among the major points were:

(1) A provision requiring the Commission to consult with the EEC states before adopting proposals of special importance to EEC member states,

(2) Closer control over the EEC budget by member governments and

(3) Creation of a joint public information office for the EEC Executive Commission and the EEC Council of Ministers with the Council, EEC's supreme policy making organ, retaining real control.

Couve de Murville insisted that the six nations subscribe to a "political agreement" not to invoke the majority voting provisions of EEC's 1957 (founding) Rome Treaty. Couve de Murville suggested that if any EEC member believed an issue before the Council involved vital national interests, the member could so declare and thereby remove that issue from the provisions of "qualified majority" voting.

Couve de Murville also pressed for quick ratification by the Netherlands, Italy, Belgium and Luxembourg of a treaty signed in 1965 by the six to merge the executive commissions of the EEC, the High Authority of the European Coal and Steel Community and the European Atomic Energy Community. It was reported that France backed the quick merger of the three commissions as a first step toward ousting EEC Executive Commission President **Walter Hallstein.**

Couve de Murville established the following timetable for implementing his proposals: Before the end of January, France wanted agreement on the question of majority voting, agreement on the 10-point program reducing the powers of the EEC Executive Commission and agreement on a date for depositing ratifications of the treaty merging the three commissions. In addition, Couve de Murville stipulated that the 1966 budgets of EEC and European Atomic Energy Community (EURATOM) be approved by February 7, that the agricultural financial program be adopted by March 31 and that the problem of adjusting members' tariffs to non-EEC nations, left pending since Dec. 31, 1965, be settled by April 30.

The ministers took no action on Couve de Murville's proposals; they agreed to meet again in Luxembourg Jan. 28, 1966.

EEC Deadlock Ends. Following a special meeting in Luxembourg January 28-30 of ministers of the six EEC nations, it was announced that France had ended its seven-month boycott of EEC and would return to EEC headquarters in Brussels for regular meetings of the Council of Ministers.

The dispute between France and the other five EEC members was resolved by a compromise agreement proposed January 29 by foreign ministers Spaak of Belgium and Luns of the Netherlands. The plan, embodied in a January 30 communique of the six, provided for a "gentleman's agreement" to disagree on the key issue of majority voting within the council; the communique stated simply that the six noted "a divergence of views on what should be done in the event of failure to reach complete [unanimous] agreement." In addition, it made concessions to France on the question of the powers of EEC's Executive Commission: (1) it gave the Council of Ministers increased supervisory powers over the Commission's preparation of EEC's budget; (2) it required the Commission to inform the member governments prior to making important proposals; and (3), the Commission was obliged to inform the Council of its proposals before releasing them to the press.

Erhard-de Gaulle Meeting. West German Chancellor Erhard met with French President de Gaulle and other top French officials in Paris Feb. 7-8, 1966. The meeting was the sixth of the semiannual heads-of-government consultations called for under the 1963 French-West German Treaty.

Both delegations expressed satisfaction with the talks during the two days, but no communique was released. Following a February 9 meeting of the French cabinet, at which de Gaulle presided, State Information Secretary Yvon Bourges read a cabinet statement on the Erhard-de Gaulle meeting. It said: "The construction of Europe was a desire shared by both delegations" although "the methods of political construction [of Europe] have not been detailed."

De Gaulle Hails EEC Agreement. President de Gaulle February 21, at his thirteenth presidential press conference, hailed the agreement reached at the January 28-30 Luxembourg meeting of the EEC Council of Ministers. The Luxembourg "agreement," said de Gaulle "...is of great and auspicious significance. Indeed, for the first time since the Common Market affair got under way, one openly departed from that sort of fiction in which the economic organization of Europe had to emanate from an authority other than that of the [six] states. If one of the [six] states...take[s] the initiative to propose a political meeting of the six governments, France would reply to it positively and wholeheartedly."

EEC Kennedy Round Agreement. The EEC Council of Ministers April 5 authorized the EEC Executive Commission to prepare joint EEC tariff reduction offers to be presented at the Kennedy Round of world tariff negotiations within GATT already under way in Geneva. EEC action on the Kennedy Round had been blocked since July 1965 as a result of France's boycott.

The authorization represented a compromise between France and the other five EEC members: France agreed to further EEC tariff negotiations within GATT in return for a firm commitment by the other five to agree by early May to the agricultural finance plan desired by France.

EEC Adopts Farm Finance Plan. The EEC Council of Ministers May 11, 1966 adopted financial regulations for the Common Market's agricultural program and simultaneously set a firm date (July 1, 1968) for the completion of a customs union covering virtually all EEC industrial and farm products.

The agreement on agricultural finance marked a major breakthrough for the EEC, which had been deadlocked on the issue since June 30, 1965, when the previous farm finance regulations (adopted in 1962) expired. The new agreement, which would operate retroactively from July 1, 1965 and continue through Dec. 31, 1969, covered the remaining four and a half years of the farm program's transitional period during which the program would still be partially financed by direct national assessments from the six EEC members. After Dec. 31, 1969, it had been stipulated in EEC's founding 1957 Rome Treaty, the farm program would be completely self-supporting.

The new agreement, which provided for gradually increasing coverage of the program's costs through the levies assessed on agricultural imports from non-EEC states during the four-and-a-half year period (July 1, 1965 to Dec. 31, 1969), conformed essentially to the demands made by the French government in June 1965; it was similar to compromise proposals presented in July 1965 by the EEC's Executive Commission.

EEC Sets Kennedy Round Proposals. The EEC Council of Ministers agreed in Brussels June 14 on tariff reduction proposals to be presented at the Kennedy Round of world tariff negotiations. The proposals set a common EEC tariff reduction position on grain, aluminium, paper and newsprint.

Pompidou-Wilson Talks. French Premier Pompidou, accompanied by Foreign Minister Couve de Murville, visited London July 6-8, 1966 for talks with British Prime Minister Wilson and Foreign Minister Michael Stewart on Britain's possible entry into the Common Market.

A communique on the Wilson-Pompidou talks, released in London July 8, said: "Mr. Wilson reaffirmed the readiness of Britain to join the EEC, provided her essential interests could be met. M. Pompidou recalled that nothing prevented the entry of Britain into the Common Market, provided that she accepted the Treaty of Rome (EEC's founding treaty) and the arrangement subsequently agreed."

EEC Farm-Price Agreement. The EEC Council of Ministers reached final agreement July 24 in Brussels on common prices for most farm commodities produced within the six-nation economic bloc. The agreement was to take effect on or before July 1, 1968.

The farm-price agreement was the necessary complement to EEC's May 11 finance agreement on the community's agricultural program of price supports, export subsidies and farm modernization. The July 24 agreement enabled the Council of Ministers to agree July 27, at another Brussels meeting, on their remaining agricultural offers for presentation in the Kennedy Round tariff negotiations under way in Geneva.

The July 24 agreement, together with the 1964 decision on grain prices, brought an estimated 86 percent of EEC's farm production within EEC's system of uniform prices.

De Gaulle Denounces Bonn's U.S. Ties. President de Gaulle, at his fourteenth presidential press conference Oct. 28, 1966, denounced West Germany's close relations with the United States. De Gaulle said that it was not France's fault if the 1963 French-German Friendship Treaty had been stripped of its "inspiration and substance" by Bonn's preferential ties" with Washington. "It is quite possible that as a result," West Germany may "have lost several opportunities" for joint French-German action.

Britain Renews Entry Bid. British Prime Minister Wilson informed the House of Commons November 10 of his government's "clear intention and determination" to bring Britain into the Common Market. Wilson said that, after having reviewed all aspects of Britain's relations with the EEC, "the government has decided a new high-level approach must now be made to see whether the conditions exist — or do not exist — for fruitful negotiations, and the basis on which such negotiations could take place."

Kiesinger Seeks Improved Bonn-Paris Relations. West German Chancellor Kurt-Georg Kiesinger, who had been elected Dec. 1, 1966 replacing Ludwig Erhard, made a major policy speech before the Bundestag December 13. He stressed that "the decisive role for Europe's future" depended on "a close and trusting relationship between Germany and France." Toward this end he pledged to honor the terms of the 1963 French-West German friendship treaty that had been largely abrogated under the administration of Erhard.

First de Gaulle-Kiesinger Meeting. President de Gaulle and West German Chancellor Kiesinger conferred in Paris Jan. 13-14, 1967. The talks, the first between Kiesinger and de Gaulle since Kiesinger became chancellor Dec. 1, 1966, were intended to revitalize the 1963 French-West German Friendship Treaty.

De Gaulle declared at the conclusion of the talks January 14 that the treaty, which had been "under a cloud," was "now reappearing in the light." He emphasized that "in today's Europe, even if occasionally the approach of French and Germans is not identical, there is above all the need, the benefit and the satisfaction of cooperating together." Kiesinger stated that there had been "an absolute reanimation of the friendship treaty in spirit and in content." He affirmed that a new period had begun in Franco-German relations.

The major agreements reached between de Gaulle and Kiesinger:

(1) West Germany would seek to establish normal diplomatic relations with the East European Communist countries as soon as possible. Kiesinger had called for the normalization of relations in his Dec. 13, 1966 policy speech.

(2) German reunification must be achieved through the general process of detente between Western and Eastern Europe. In the past, West Germany had insisted that a solution of the German question must precede any efforts to achieve detente.

(3) Discussion of Britain's bid to enter the EEC must be postponed until British Prime Minister Harold Wilson had concluded a tour of the six EEC capitals.

Kiesinger told newsmen in Bonn January 15 that, "if there is one constant factor in a changing world, it is the need for cooperation between Bonn and Paris." Although he admitted that there were areas of disagreement between the two countries — most notably with respect to British entry into the EEC, the North Atlantic Alliance and the nature of the Soviet threat to West European security — these, "differences of view between us were [not] so deep as to hamper cooperation," he declared. "We agreed together to make the fullest possible use of the Franco-German Treaty."

Anglo-French Plane Accord. French Defense Minister Pierre Messmer and British Defense Minister Denis Healey agreed in Paris January 16 on joint development of a swing-wing supersonic military jet plane. The agreement on the $600 million project put the French in charge of engine development and the British in charge of fuselage development. The two-engine plane was scheduled for operation by 1975. Its speed was to be two and a half times the speed of sound.

De Gaulle at Adenauer Rites. Former West German Chancellor Konrad Adenauer, 91, died at his home in Rhoendorf, West Germany, April 19, 1967. President de Gaulle in tribute to Adenauer said April 19: "His death causes me profound sorrow.... I bow with respect before one of the great statesmen of these times." De Gaulle attended a state funeral held in Bonn for Adenauer April 25.

Britain Renews EEC Bid. Britain May 11 formally reapplied in Brussels for full membership in the European Economic Community. (Denmark and Ireland also applied May 11 for EEC membership.) Britain's decision to once again seek Common Market membership had been announced by Prime Minister Wilson in the House of Commons May 2. After three days of debate May 8-10, Parliament May 10 approved by 488-62 vote a motion supporting the government's decision.

In his statement May 2, Wilson said the government was prepared to accept the Treaty of Rome, which established the Common Market in 1957, "subject to the necessary adjustments consequent upon the accession of a new member and provided that we receive satisfaction on the points about which we see difficulty..."

In an apparent effort to strengthen Britain's bargaining position vis-a-vis the Common Market members, particularly France, Wilson suggested in a TV interview May 8 that Britain might not purchase U.S. Poseidon missiles to replace the Polaris missiles currently being installed in several British submarines. "We are not going to throw into these [EEC] negotiations another Nassau, a new era of dependence on the Americans for nuclear weapons," Wilson declared. (The reference was to the December 1962 Nassau meeting between the late President Kennedy and Prime Minister Harold Macmillan, at which the United States agreed to supply Britain with Polaris missiles. It was generally believed that the Nassau agreement had been a factor in President de Gaulle's January 1963 veto of Britain's application to the EEC.)

De Gaulle Rebuffs Application. President de Gaulle's rejection of the British bid was delivered at his fifteenth presidential press conference in Paris May 16, 1967. His arguments were essentially the same as those he had raised in his January 1963 rejection of Britain's original bid for EEC.

De Gaulle cited these problems standing in the way of British entry into the Common Market:

> Britain . . . remains, because of the Commonwealth and because she is an island, committed far beyond the seas . . . . she is asking exceptional and prolonged delays and . . . that basic changes be made in the [Rome] Treaty's implementation. At the same time, she acknowledges that . . . it will be necessary to surmount obstacles that . . . [are] formidable.

> This is true . . . of the agricultural regulations . . . . Britain nourishes herself, to a great extent, on foodstuffs bought inexpensively throughout the world and, particularly, in the Commonwealth. If she submits to the rules of the six then her balance of payments will be crushed by [agricultural import] 'levies'. . . .

> Also, how can it not be seen that the very situation of the pound sterling prevents the Common Market from incorporating Britain. . . . Monetary parity and solidarity . . . could not be extended to our neighbors across the Channel, unless the pound appears, one day, in a new situation and such that its future value appears assured. . . .

> What is true, at this very moment, from the economic standpoint, would also be true . . . from the political standpoint. . . . Considering the special relations that tie the British to America . . . considering the existence of the Commonwealth . . . considering the special commitment that they still have in various parts of the world . . ., we cannot see how both [British and EEC] policies could merge, unless the British assumed again, particularly as regards defense, complete command of themselves, or else if the continentals renounced forever a European Europe. . . .

Wilson Rejects French "No." Prime Minister Wilson told the Confederation of British Industry May 17 that Britain would not take "no" for an answer to its application. He said that Britain was "determined not only to make these negotiations a success, but to carry them forward as quickly as lies in our power."

'Kennedy Round' Accord Reached. Fifty-three nations participating in the Kennedy Round tariff-cutting negotiations reached agreement May 15 on tariff reductions affecting about 60,000 items and more than $40 billion annually in world trade. The accord marked the conclusion of talks held since 1964 under the auspices of GATT. France participated in the negotiations and agreement through the six-nation EEC which negotiated as a unit.

Rome Summit Meeting. The heads of government of the six Common Market states met in Rome May 29-30, 1967 to commemorate the 10th anniversary of the signing of the Treaty of Rome. It was the first time in six years that the EEC heads of government had met together.

Among those attending the ceremonies: French President de Gaulle, West German Chancellor Kiesinger, Belgian Premier Paul Vanden Boeynants, Netherlands Premier Petrus de Jong, Luxembourg Premier Pierre Werner, and Italian Premier Aldo Moro.

A summit meeting of the six leaders and their foreign ministers was held May 30 in the Italian Foreign Ministry. According to news reports, the main topic of discussion was Britain's bid for membership in the EEC; all delegations except the French reportedly favored Britain's admission. A communique issued at the end of the meeting noted:

●At its meeting June 5-6, the Council of Ministers would examine the membership applications that had been submitted by Britain, Ireland and Denmark May 11.

●Another meeting of the EEC heads of state would be held, "probably" by the end of the year.

●The planned merger of the three communities — the EEC, the European Coal and Steel Community and the European Atomic Energy Community — would take place July 1.

Wilson Presses EEC Bid in Meeting with De Gaulle. British Prime Minister Wilson conferred in Paris with de Gaulle for five-and-a-half hours June 19; the two leaders met again briefly June 20 before Wilson returned to London. It had been agreed that no communique would be issued, and there was little information on the nature of the talks. Wilson told the House of Commons June 20 that the talks had been devoted in large measure to the Mid-East crisis and the Vietnamese War. With respect to Britain's EEC bid, Wilson said that he did not want to give the impression that de Gaulle was "more enthusiastic about British entry than he has been at any other time." But Wilson added that he had told the French president that "we do not intend to take no for an answer." Wilson reportedly had reaffirmed the British position that associate membership in the EEC was unacceptable, since it would entail adhering to the Common Market rules and policy without having a voice in influencing them.

France Blocks British Bid. At a regularly scheduled meeting of the EEC Council of Ministers in Brussels June 26, Foreign Minister Couve de Murville strongly opposed a proposal by the other five foreign ministers that Britain be allowed to present its case for membership at the Council's July meeting. He reportedly argued during the four-and-a-half hour session that Britain could not be granted a hearing until the Council had studied all the problems that would arise if Britain were to join the Common Market.

Couve de Murville again rejected the idea of British membership at a meeting of the EEC Council of Ministers in Brussels July 10. He argued that Britain's membership in the Common Market would open the door to all the other countries in Europe and that this would alter the basic character of the community. One of the consequences, he asserted, would be the transformation of the community into an Atlantic trading block; another would be an inevitable rise in Cold War tensions. West German Foreign Minister Willy Brandt rejected the French arguments asserting that Britain's membership in the Common Market would not change the Community and that there was nothing inherently wrong in the Community assuming a greater Atlantic orientation. Other speakers who challenged Couve de Murville were Belgian Foreign Minister Pierre Harmel and Netherlands Foreign Minister Joseph Luns.

Hallstein Out in Executive Merger. The long-awaited merger of the executive bodies of the three European communities took place July 1967 with the formation of a single 14-member European Commission. The organs merged: the Executive Commission of the European Economic Community (EEC), the High Authority of the European Coal and Steel Community (ECSC) and the Executive Commission of the European Atomic Energy Community (**Euratom**) The new commission was headed by Jean Rey, who had succeeded Walter Hallstein as president of the EEC Executive Commission June 5.

The merger of the three executive bodies, approved by the EEC Council of Ministers in March 1965, was to have gone into effect Jan. 1, 1966, but it was delayed by a controversy between France and West Germany over the status of Walter Hallstein, then president of the EEC Commission. Germany had wanted Hallstein to become president of the merged executives but France had opposed the nomination on the ground that Hallstein's supranational policies made him unsuitable for the post. As a compromise, President de Gaulle and West German Chancellor Kiesinger agreed during their meeting in Paris January 13-14 (reported February 21) to make Hallstein president of the new commission for an interim period of six months. However, it was reported May 6 that Hallstein had informed Bonn that he would not accept a temporary post on the new commission. The impasse was resolved after France nominated as Hallstein's successor Jean Rey, the EEC's chief negotiator at the Kennedy Round tariff-cutting negotiations and a vice president of the EEC Executive Commission. The EEC Council of Ministers approved the nomination June 5. Rey's term of office was two years, beginning July 1.

De Gaulle-Kiesinger Meeting. Kiesinger and de Gaulle conferred in Bonn July 12-13 for a semiannual consultation under the Franco-German friendship treaty of 1963.

In a statement made after the talks, de Gaulle July 13 listed these conditions as essential for the preservation of French and German "national personalities": (1) maintenance of the close Franco-German tie "to avoid the preponderance of America"; (2) maintenance of the Common Market as an assurance against U.S. domination; (3) understanding and cooperation between Eastern and Western Europe "so that there shall exist something other than the system of the two blocs."

Agreements reached by Kiesinger and de Gaulle called for: (a) the establishment of a joint commission to deal with the "political security" needs of the two countries; (b) the formation of a commission for economic, technical and industrial cooperation; (c) meetings in "special situation" at the highest level of the two governments; (d) a jointly sponsored study of the political and strategic circumstances in Europe in the 1970's.

French, British, German Air Projects. After protracted negotiations, a trilateral agreement to develop a short-to-medium-distance airliner was signed by Britain, France and West Germany in Bonn Sept. 26, 1967. The undertaking, the European Airbus Project, was expected to cost the three governments a total of $532 million when completed by 1973. The two-jet plane would have a maximum seating capacity of 300.

A joint British-French venture to develop a swing-wing (or variable-geometry) military aircraft was abandoned when France withdrew from the project. The disclosure was made in the British House of Commons by British Defense Minister Denis Healey July 5. France's cancellation of the $800 million project was made on "purely financial grounds," said Healey. (France's Dessault aircraft company announced November 27 that it had successfully tested its own swing-wing aircraft. The plane, called the Mirage G, was financed by the French government and was not expected to be serially produced before 1975.)

Not affected by the cancellation was the Franco-British project to build the Concorde supersonic airliner.

France Opposes UK Bid Despite Devaluation. Following British devaluation of the pound November 18, the EEC Council of Ministers met November 20 to deliberate on the British devaluation and to discuss its implications on Britain's bid for Common Market membership. All the ministers except the French viewed the devaluation as improving Britain's chance for Common Market membership. French Foreign Minister Couve de Murville argued that devaluation was not the fundamental point and bore no relation to the membership bid. He asserted that the problems associated with improving the British economy were still immense and that no immediate solution was possible. He declared that Britain would have to take all the necessary measures before negotiations on membership could begin.

President de Gaulle November 27 at his sixteenth presidential press conference again opposed Britain's bid to enter the Common Market. He declared: "... The present Common Market is incompatible with the economy, as it now stands, of Britain whose chronic balance-of-payments deficit is proof of permanent disequilibrium.... [The]... Common Market [is] incompatible [with]... the state of the pound sterling...."

De Gaulle added that a strong Common Market was necessary to "counterbalance the immense power of the United States...."

France Blocks British Bid. France Dec. 19, 1967 successfully blocked the efforts of the five other EEC members to open negotiations with Britain concerning its bid for Common Market membership. The action came at the close of a two-day meeting in Brussels of the EEC Council of Ministers.

The five advocates of opening negotiations with Britain — Belgium, Italy, Luxembourg, the Netherlands and West Germany — did not bring the issue to a vote for fear of forcing France to a veto and thus damaging the unity of the EEC. Rather, after it became apparent that France would not alter its stand the Council adopted a communique that said the application "remain[ed] on the agenda of the Council."

A statement issued by the British Foreign Office December 19 said: "It is a matter of grave concern that the government of France has been unable to accept the unanimous view of its partners that negotiations for Britain's accession to the European Communities should start at once. This can only delay the inevitable progress toward a united Europe, including Britain, which is in the interest of Europe as a whole. There is no question of withdrawing Britain's application...."

CHAPTER XI
INTERNATIONAL MONETARY POLICY

The de Gaulle government in 1963 and 1964 continued its policy of converting its holdings of U.S. dollars into gold thereby increasing the volume of its gold stock.

France Buys U.S. Gold. The U.S. Treasury reported March 5, 1964 that France was the largest purchaser of U.S. gold in 1963. France bought $517.7 million worth of gold. The next highest purchaser, Spain, bought $130 million worth.

France for New Monetary Unit. French Finance Minister Valery Giscard d'Estaing complained in an address Sept. 9, 1964 to the annual conference of the International Monetary Fund (IMF) that the balance-of-payments deficits of the two reserve currency nations — the United States and Britain — were at the root of the inflationary trends in other industrial nations. He suggested the creation of a new international monetary unit to replace or supplement the two reserve currencies (the U.S. dollar and the pound sterling) and thereby end a system under which, in his opinion, other countries faced inflation because they had to accept pounds and dollars in settlement of international obligations regardless of the deficit payments situations of the United States and Britain.

Paris Backs British Pound. France and 10 other nations pledged $3 billion in credits November 25 to the British government to bolster the pound sterling and maintain its official foreign exchange value.

De Gaulle Opposes Monetary "Hegemony." President de Gaulle, in his year-end nationwide broadcast December 31 expressed opposition to any economic or monetary system that "under the cover of supranationality, or integration or of Atlantism would keep us in fact under the hegemony that we know."

France Steps Up Gold Purchases. The Bank of France (France's central bank) Jan. 7, 1965 announced a decision to reduce its dollar reserves by increased gold purchases from the U.S. Treasury, which already was low in reserves of gold authorized to meet the demands of foreign dollar holders. The announcement said the "operation" of converting some of its dollars into U.S. gold was "identical" with its operations of July 1962 and July 1963 and would "involve $150 million."

($1.35 billion of France's total reserves of more than $5 billion was in dollars, the rest in gold; and the government had set a goal of reducing its dollar holdings to about $1 billion. Of the dollar reserves, about $650 million was required to meet France's long-term debt to the United States and Canada, and about $350 million was needed for France's current operations.)

De Gaulle for Gold Standard. President de Gaulle February 4, at his eleventh presidential press conference, called for a return to the gold standard. He attacked existing international monetary arrangements (the Gold Exchange Standard) whereby foreign exchange reserves included gold and the major currencies convertible into gold—U.S. dollars and British pounds. He described this system as especially advantageous to the United States and Britain because it permitted them to "issue" their own currencies to pay their foreign debts whereas other nations were required to obtain gold, dollars, or pounds to pay their foreign obligations. Demanding an end to the Gold Exchange Standard, de Gaulle declared: "... we consider that international exchanges must be established ... on an unquestionable monetary basis which does not bear the mark of any individual country. What basis? Actually, it is difficult to envision in this regard any other criterion, any other standard than gold. ..."

U.S. Opposes Gold Plan. The U.S. Treasury Department February 4 rejected de Gaulle's proposal of a return to the gold standard. A Treasury statement said that the gold standard had "collapsed in 1931 and proved incapable of financing the huge increase of world trade."

Giscard D'Estaing Details Gold Plan. Finance Minister Giscard d'Estaing announced February 11 France's intention to pay its balance-of-payments debts solely in gold. This would mean in effect a return to the gold standard by France. He called upon other nations "having international financial responsibilities" to consider similar measures. He recommended that an international collective reserve unit be established if it were found that international payments could not be financed under the French plan. Under the plan, France would be the first nation to pay its balance-of-payments debts in gold since the Bretton Woods monetary agreement of 1945, which permitted such debts to be paid in dollars rather than in gold.

U.S. Discloses Gold Purchases. The U.S. Treasury announced March 5 that French purchases of U.S. gold totalled $405 million in 1964. Total U.S. gold stocks at the end of 1964 were $15.471 billion.

Aid for British Pound. Finance ministers of the six EEC nations agreed in Cannes, France May 4, 1965 to a program for bolstering the British pound. Under the program, Britain would borrow in May about $900 million from the International Monetary Fund (IMF) and about $500 million from the General Agreement to Borrow, a monetary pool operated by the Group of Ten. The Group of Ten (sometimes called the "Paris Club") was made up of the 10 IMF nations that had pledged an additional $6 billion in September 1961 to assist IMF currency stabilization policies. They were the United States, Britain, France, West Germany, Italy, Belgium, Sweden, the Netherlands, Canada and Japan. They held approximately $52 billion of the free world's $69 billion reserves.

U.S. Gold Outflow. The N.Y. Federal Reserve Bank reported May 27 that the U.S. gold reserve had dropped $60 million in the week ending May 26 bringing the gold-stock level down to $14.293 billion, the lowest figure since 1938.

According to a separate Treasury Department report May 27, the U.S. gold loss totaled $833 million during January-March. France, the largest purchaser, bought $482-1/2 million worth, compared with $405 million worth purchased during all of 1964.

France to Repay Debts to United States. Finance Minister Giscard d'Estaing said June 16 that France would pay back $180 million on its postwar debt to the United States ahead of time.

U.S. Calls for Monetary Reform. In a major policy statement on world monetary problems, U.S. Treasury Secretary Henry H. Fowler proposed July 10, 1965 that a world conference similar to the 1945 Bretton Woods meeting be called to institute international monetary reform.

The world's major monetary problem, Fowler declared, was to assure sufficient international liquidity as the volume of world trade continued to increase. He said that U.S. "dollars — some $27 billion — account for the major share of international national liquidity." These dollars, held by foreigners, had been acquired, said Fowler, mainly as a result of 14 years of U.S. balance-of-payments deficits. The difficulty, he declared, was that continued U.S. deficits could not continue to supply the world's demand for international reserves. Fowler expressed fear that foreigners, alarmed by the U.S. payments deficits and losing confidence in the U.S. dollar, would return the dollars "to our shores as claims on our gold, thus depleting, instead of supplementing, world financial resources." "To prevent such a contraction in world liquidity," he declared, the United States "must reach and maintain equilibrium in our payments as a matter of highest national priority." "The paradox," he said, "is...that the very increase in...foreign dollar holdings that has fueled so much of the growth of the...world liquidity in the past...can no longer be allowed to continue if current international liquidity is to be protected. Yet without additions to the reserve dollars that our deficits have so long supplied, the world will need a new and assured source of growing liquidity to support increasing world trade and investment."

New sources of liquidity, said Fowler, had been under study by the Group of Ten; a report of a Group of Ten study committee, "submitted to the...Group of Ten on June 1,...examines...the possible paths to the creation of [new] reserve assets." The purpose of the proposed international monetary conference, said Fowler, would be to decide on new forms of international liquidity to supplement gold and dollars.

France Sets Conditions for Monetary Reform. French Finance Minister Giscard d'Estaing, in a statement released in Paris July 19, called Fowler's proposal of a world monetary conference "inopportune." He said two conditions had to be fulfilled before such a conference could take place: (1) France needed assurance that recent improvements in the balance-of-payments accounts of some deficit countries (the United States and Britain) will continue. (2) A "minimum of agreement" on the nature and objectives of reform had to be achieved, but the recent study by the Group of Ten study committee disclosed that profound differences still existed.

De Gaulle Reaffirms Stand on Gold. At his twelfth presidential press conference Sept. 9, 1965 President de Gaulle reiterated his stand that "gold...remains and...must remain...the only real standard."

France Refuses to Support British Pound. The Bank of England (Britain's central bank) September 10 announced a 10-nation agreement to support the British pound. Details of the accord were not disclosed. France, which had joined a similar agreement in November 1964 and in May 1965 did not take part in this accord. The agreement had been negotiated September 3-4 at the Bank of International Settlements (BIS) in Basel, Switzerland, at a meeting of central bank presidents.

U.S. Gold Outflow Continues. The U.S. Treasury Department September 8 disclosed that in the second quarter of 1965 the United States had lost $590 million from its stock of monetary gold. France led all foreign purchasers of gold in the quarter with $147.5 purchased.

Fowler on Monetary Reforms. U.S. Treasury Secretary Fowler reported to President Lyndon B. Johnson September 13 on the results of an August 28-September 11 trip to seven European countries to discuss the U.S. proposal for an international conference to reform the free world's monetary system. According to the report, released by the White House September 13, there was general agreement among the countries visited that "ways will have to be developed to expand international liquidity after the balance-of-payments deficits of the United States no longer exist."

Fowler reported a general agreement among the seven nations that the first stage of monetary reform should be negotiated by nations of the Group of Ten, with Switzerland as an observer. He expressed hope that the IMF, at its September meeting, would give the Group of Ten a mandate to resume its deliberations on monetary reform. He said he had "found support in many quarters" for including a wider grouping of nations in the second phase of negotiations.

During his trip Fowler conferred in Paris August 30-31 with French Finance Minister Giscard d'Estaing.

Group of Ten Agrees on Reform Procedure. At the annual meeting of the IMF and the International Bank for Reconstruction & Development (the World Bank), held in Washington September 27-October 1, the Group of Ten agreed September 28 to "resume on an intensified basis" their discussions on international monetary reform. They also agreed to renew through October 1970 their 1961 agreement to provide the IMF with "stand-by" funds totalling $6 billion to aid nations suffering balance-of-payments deficits.

The September 28 communique of the Group of Ten welcomed efforts by the United States to control its balance-of-payments deficits. At the same time it recognized that U.S. deficits had been "the major source of additional reserves for the rest of the world..." It was therefore understood, said the communique, that contingency planning was necessary to assure sufficient sources of world liquidity when U.S. deficits could no longer be counted as a major source of liquidity.

The first stage of contingency planning would take place within the Group of Ten; the Group of Ten's study committee was instructed to report by the spring of 1966 on its discussions concerning ways of improving the international monetary system and to establish "what basis of agreement can be reached,... including arrangements for the future creation of reserve assets. ..."

The communique recognized that at a later stage it would be necessary to "proceed...to a broader consideration of the questions that affect the world economy as a whole. This stage would necessarily involve discussions among all members of the International Monetary Fund."

France Presses for End of U. S. & British Deficits. French Finance Minister Giscard d'Estaing September 29, addressing the annual IMF-World Bank conference, argued that the solution of balance-of-payments deficits in the United States and Britain was a more pressing problem than planning for the expansion of world liquidity. "The problem," he declared, "in the immediate future is one of too much liquidity rather than too little." The present system was unfair, he argued, because nations "whose currencies are used as reserve currencies [the United States and Britain] are in a position to obtain implicit credit facilities . . . through the holding of their own currencies by partner countries." The major "contribution reserve countries can make to an international monetary reform is the restoration of a durable balance in their external accounts. This is the precondition for the study of any other device."

Giscard d'Estaing reiterated the French view that gold must be the sole standard in any reformed international monetary system. Referring to various plans to create additional kinds of reserve units, he insisted that any new reserve unit would have to be "linked to gold, which remains the necessary and unchanging reference basis." He emphasized that primary responsibility for monetary reform rested with the world's leading financial nations (i.e., the Group of Ten).

France Prepays U.S. Debt. The Commerce Department had reported Nov. 17, 1965 that France had repaid in advance $130 million of postwar debts.

U.S. Deficit, Gold Outflow Figures. Final figures on the United States balance-of-payments deficit for 1965 were disclosed Feb. 14, 1966 at a Washington news conference held by Secretary of the Treasury Fowler and Federal Reserve Board Chairman William McChesney Martin. The deficit for the year was $1.299 billion, down from $2.798 billion in 1964. The year 1965 was the United States' best payments year since 1957, when it had a payments surplus of $520 million. Fowler said the improvement was due in very large part to the program of voluntary business cooperation initiated by President Johnson in 1965.

The Treasury Department reported March 8 that more than half of the U.S. $1.655 billion gold loss in 1965 had been accounted for by French conversions of dollars. France purchased $884.2 million worth of U.S. gold (up from $405 million in 1964).

French Payments Surplus. The Paris newspaper *Le Monde* reported March 8 that in 1965 France had a balance-of-payments surplus of $1.1 billion, up from previous surpluses of $786 million in 1964 and $924 million in 1963. France disposed of the $1.1 billion surplus by: (1) repaying a $178 million debt to the U.S. Export-Import Bank (Eximbank) and thereby reducing its total foreign debt to $454 million from a 1958 total of $3.093 billion; (2) increasing by $360 million its reserves held by the Bank of France; (3) lending the IMF $560 million in francs to aid nations with payments problems.

France Dissents in Group of Ten Reform Accord. Finance ministers and central bank governors of the ten leading financial nations, the Group of Ten, met July 25-26, 1966 at The Hague to discuss international monetary reform.

A communique issued July 26 stated that nine of the 10 nations (all but France) had agreed to proceed to a second stage of monetary reform negotiations in which other members of the 103-nation IMF would be represented by the IMF's Board of Executive Directors.

In the communique, the 10 nations (including France) agreed on a number of general principles and objectives: "There is at present no general shortage of reserves." But they thought it "unlikely that the existing sources of reserves would provide an adequate basis for world trade and payments in the longer run." Continued U.S. balance-of-payments deficits "are not a satisfactory source of future reserve increases...nor are they acceptable to the United States."

"Consequently it was agreed that, at some point in the future, existing types of reserves may have to be supplemented by the deliberate creation of additional reserve assets." The 10 nations noted, however, that they "have not reached agreement on all points or presented a fully developed plan [to create additional reserves]." They stated certain premises on which a reserve-creation contingency plan would have to be based: Reserve creation should not be "directed to the financing of balance-of-payments deficits of individual countries" but would have to consider the "reserve needs of the world as a whole." Reserve creation would be the "particular responsibility" of those countries offering "financial backing for any newly created reserve assets [i.e., the Group of Ten]. Consequently, there is agreement that deliberately created reserve assets, as and when needed, should be distributed to all [IMF] members...on the basis of Fund [IMF] quotas or of similar objective criteria."

The points of the communique that France did not accept concerned (1) contingency planning for future reserve creation and (2) the decision to widen the monetary reform talks to include the IMF's Board of Executive Directors.

French Finance Minister Michel Debre (Debre replaced Giscard d'Estaing as Minister of Economics and Finance Jan. 8, 1966) told reporters July 26 that the French government objected to contingency planning because it believed that the existence of a contingency plan would operate as a temptation to implement the plan prematurely to solve the payments problems of deficit countries. Debre said the agreement on contingency planning implied that reserve-creating machinery would be set up before the U.S. balance-of-payments deficits were corrected. Debre said that although France opposed the decision to proceed with monetary reform negotiations, the French government would not boycott future talks.

France Ranks Second in World Reserves. The *Wall Street Journal* reported August 5 that France's reserves at the end of July stood at $5.967 billion, second highest in the world after the United States. All but an estimated $800 million of the reserves were in gold. France, according to the *Washington Post* August 9, had converted approximately $1-1/2 billion in U.S. dollars into gold during the previous 18 months.

EEC Adopts French Monetary Stand. The six European Economic Community (EEC, or Common Market) finance ministers met in Luxembourg Sept. 12, 1966 to discuss a common EEC position on international monetary reform. They said in a communique after the meeting:

(1) Serious and persistent balance-of-payments deficits must be eliminated if the international monetary system was to function effectively.

(2) A better equilibrium in the balance of payments of the United States and Britain and a collective agreement that a general insufficiency of reserves existed must *precede* any creation of additional international liquidity. Currently, such an insufficiency of reserves was not evident. The Group of Ten had a special responsibility in monetary reform decisions.

The positions taken in the communique had been pressed strongly in previous discussions by French Finance Minister Debre, who said he was pleased with the outcome of the meeting.

France Prepays U. S. Debt. U. S. Secretary of the Treasury Fowler announced September 16 that France had made a prepayment of $70.8 million on its remaining indebtedness to the United States, reducing to about $300 million the amount it still owed the United States on post-World War II reconstruction loans. Of the $1.85 billion France had repaid the United States since 1947, the Treasury said $810 million had been in the form of prepayments.

French View at IMF Meeting. The annual IMF-World Bank conference was held in Washington September 26-30. French Finance Minister Debre told the conference September 27 that France opposed the creation of a new international currency to replace gold, dollars and pounds. Debre asserted that gold and IMF reserves were the only feasible basis for the world's monetary system. Debre said that "the persistent deficit in the United States balance of payments" had brought "sickness" to the world's monetary system. He asserted that the "incessant issue" of dollars "provokes an excessive creation of money all over the world while also permitting an unlimited outflow of capital." "This state of things," he said, "is the cause of a worldwide inflationary trend which casts a growing shadow on the future."

At a news conference September 29, Debre indicated that France might support plans for the creation of new international reserves provided that no nation be released from the obligation to correct its own payments deficits.

French Purchases Drain U. S. Gold. The U. S. Federal Reserve Board reported September 30 that the U. S. stock of monetary gold had dropped by $94 million in August. The loss brought the total U. S. gold stock, as of August 30, to $13.319 billion, down $487 million from January 1.

The Federal Reserve Board reported December 15 that French purchases of U.S. gold in the period January through September 1966 totalled $601 million.

France Ceases Purchases of U.S. Gold. The Federal Reserve Board's gold transaction figures for the months October, November, and

December 1966 indicated that France had ended its policy of converting its holdings of U.S. dollars into gold.

France had begun regular monthly purchases in December 1964. At the end of 1964 French reserves included $3.7 billion in gold and $1.4 billion in dollars. At the end of September 1966, gold holdings were above $5.2 billion and dollar holdings were down to $685 million. During the same period, U.S. gold holdings had dropped $2.2 billion, of which French purchases accounted for two-thirds.

The *New York Times* reported October 27 from Paris that the decision to cease gold purchases had been made by Finance Minister Debre. According to the *Times*, the French government considered that its dollar holdings of $685 million were at the minimum level for current cash needs. In addition, the *Times* noted that estimates of French balance-of-payments indicated that the large $1 billion surplus for 1965 was not expected to be matched in 1966 and 1967. French prosperity and domestic expansion had increased imports and reduced exports, thereby reducing the volume of dollars available for conversion into gold.

In September 1967, the IMF agreed to reform the international monetary system by adopting a plan providing for creation of a new kind of international monetary reserves — "Special Drawing Rights" (SDR's). Monetary negotiations in 1967 centered for the most part on a deadlock between the United States and France over the form the new reserves would take.

The United States sought to make the proposed new reserve asset "as good as money," i.e., a monetary asset that could be transferred from one country to another without repayment obligations, whereas France had wanted to create the reserves in the form of repayable credit and to establish tight controls over its use.

The compromise finally reached provided that the assets (SDR's) would supplement gold, dollars and pounds, and thus be comparable to money, but that a certain percentage of them would be repayable; in addition, it was agreed that machinery would be created to limit the amount and frequency of the new asset's use.

France Makes Concessions on Reform. In an effort to achieve EEC unity on monetary reform, France made major concessions during a meeting of the EEC finance ministers in Munich April 17-18, 1967. Under pressure from Italy and the Netherlands, France (1) dropped its opposition to contingency planning, i.e., to the elaboration of a monetary reform plan that could be instituted when the need for new reserve assets became evident, and (2) agreed that, if the need arose for additional international liquidity, new assets could be created in the form of automatic drawing rights on the IMF. France insisted, however, that the drawing rights should be in the form of credit rather than in the form of a monetary unit that could be freely transferred between countries without repayment obligations.

The EEC finance ministers met again in Brussels July 4 and agreed, at France's insistence, that any new reserve assets to be drawn on the IMF should be repayable within a certain fixed period of time.

IMF Adopts Reform Plan. The 107-member IMF Sept. 29, 1967 unanimously adopted a plan to create a new form of international monetary reserves to supplement gold, dollars and pounds "as and when...[the need] arises."

This action was the highlight of the annual joint meeting of the IMF and the World Bank held September 25-29 in Rio de Janeiro. The plan had been worked out at an August 26 meeting of the Group of Ten and at previous joint meetings by the Group of Ten and the IMF's Executive Board. France took part in these negotiations.

The agreement on monetary reform ended negotiations that had been under way since early 1964. The accord was generally hailed as the most significant effort to regulate the international financial system since the creation of the IMF in 1945.

The monetary reform plan provided for the creation of Special Drawing Rights (SDR's) in the IMF, for which a special fund would be established. SDR's would be allocated to each IMF member nation as a percentage, uniform for all nations, of the member's IMF quota. The SDR's would then be used to supplement a nation's reserves in order to settle its international balance-of-payments accounts. Whereas existing IMF drawing rights had to be repaid in full, only 30% of the SDR's would be earmarked for eventual repayment to the IMF; the remaining 70% would be used like gold, dollars and pounds, to adjust accounts among IMF members. The SDR's therefore constituted a new, permanent reserve asset that would increase the world's money supply.

The actual issuance of SDR's would occur only after the IMF managing director had decided that there existed a need for more reserves and his proposal was then approved by nations having 85% of the weighted votes (based on each nation's IMF quota). If the proposal were adopted, SDR's would be automatically credited to each member's account in an amount equal to a percentage of its IMF quota. SDR's would normally be created at five-year intervals, except for the first five-year period, when it was generally assumed that the new reserves would be created on an annual basis. The plan did not specify how many SDR's would be created. IMF Managing Director Pierre-Paul Schweitzer said September 29 that the amount of SDR's created at first "would likely be on the conservative side."

The provision stipulating that SDR's could only be issued with the approval of IMF nations having 85% of weighted IMF quotas was strongly supported by France. The effect of the provision was to give the six-nation EEC (of which France was a member) veto power over issuance over SDR's since the six nations controlled 16-1/2% of the votes.

Although France agreed to adoption of the reform plan, Finance Minister Debre September 26 expressed reservations concerning the agreement. He referred to the current system of reserve currencies (dollars and pounds) as "an instrument of instability." "The more quickly we return to the gold standard, supplemented by a good organization of international credit," he declared, "the more quickly we shall provide the world economy with the conditions for recover." Referring to the monetary reform plan, Debre asserted that it was "impossible to imagine" the SDR's working properly until "the disappearance" of the U.S. and British balance-of-payments deficits. Maintaining that the SDR's would be more like credit than money, Debre said France had agreed to "nothing more" than to a "possible mechanism for new credits, accompanied by a reform" of IMF voting rules.

France Refuses Loan in Pound Crisis. Britain Nov. 18, 1967 devalued the pound sterling by 14.3%, from a par value of £1 per $2.80 to £1 per $2.40. In an effort to restore confidence in the pound and prevent renewed speculation, Britain applied for a $1.4 billion stand-by loan (which was granted November 29) from the IMF and sought $1.6 billion in loans from central banks of leading industrialized nations. The United States agreed November 19 to provide $500 million in loans; Germany and Italy agreed to provide $250 million each. French officials disclosed November 20 that France would not contribute.

France Out of Gold Stabilization Pool. Following the devaluation of the pound November 18, the dollar came under speculative attack with extremely heavy buying of gold in the London, Paris, Frankfurt and Zurich gold markets November 21-24. Buying eased November 27, however, after the world's major banking nations — members of the London Gold Pool — had affirmed their intention of maintaining the value of gold at the current rate of $35 an ounce.

A major factor contributing to the sudden speculation in gold was the confirmation by France November 20 that it had withdrawn in June from the London Gold Pool. (The pool was established in 1961 following a period of heavy monetary speculation to prevent disturbing fluctuations in the price of gold in the free market. The eight-nation pool had been built up by contributions of agreed quotas by the central banks of Belgium, Italy, the Netherlands, Switzerland, West Germany, France, Britain, and the United States.)

De Gaulle on Pound Devaluation. At his sixteenth semiannual press conference November 27, President de Gaulle expressed hope that Britain's devaluation of the pound would facilitate the end of the existing world monetary system (based on the U.S. dollar) and lead to establishment of a gold standard: "It is possible that the squalls [devaluation and related world monetary problems] currently being unleashed—without having anything to do with it — and which have swept away the rate of the pound and which threaten that of the dollar, [will] in the final analysis lead to reestablishing the international monetary system on the basis of immutability, impartiality and universality, which are the privileges of the gold."

De Gaulle attributed U.S. business control of many French industries to U.S. payments deficits. "It is true," he declared, "that we find ourselves faced with an American hold on certain of our businesses, but [it] . . . is due, to a great extent not so much to the organic superiority of the United States as to the dollar inflation that it is exporting to others under the cover of the gold exchange standard. It is rather remarkable that the total of annual deficits in the American balance of payments over the past years is exactly the total of American investment in the countries of Western Europe."

French Reserves Up. Figures issued by the French Finance Ministry Dec. 2, 1967 indicated that total French gold and foreign exchange reserves at the end of November stood at $6.18 billion, up $437.3 million from the first of the year. Sources in Paris said that most of the November gain had been in the form of dollars and had boosted French holdings of U.S. currency to about $1 billion.

CHAPTER XII

THE PROBLEM OF UNITED NATIONS FINANCE

France opposed efforts by the UN General Assembly to assess members for the costs of the UN's peace-keeping operations in the Congo and the Middle East. Refusing to pay these assessments, the de Gaulle regime contended that peace-keeping operations could only be ordered by the Security Council. A compromise arrangement reached in 1965 essentially upheld the French position.

France Refuses Congo Bond Payments. French Ambassador-to-the-UN Roger Seydoux told UN Secretary General U Thant Jan. 27, 1963 that France would not pay its share of principal and interest on UN bonds. Seydoux said France would deduct its share of servicing the bonds from its payments on the UN's regular budget. The bonds had been authorized by the General Assembly in December 1969 to meet the deficits incurred by operations of the UN's military forces in the Congo.

France Opposes Peace-Keeping Operations. The problem of financing the UN peace-keeping forces in the Middle East and Congo was the subject of a special session of the UN General Assembly held May 14-June 27, 1963. The special session adopted resolutions providing $42-1/2 million for expenses of the Middle East and Congo forces during the remainder of 1963.

France voted against the resolution providing $33 million for the UN Congo force and abstained on the resolution providing $9-1/2 million for the UN Emergency Force (UNEF) in the Middle East.

French Ambassador Seydoux warned the special session June 14 that France would not support any UN peace-keeping operation with which it did not agree. Seydoux took the position, also advanced by the USSR, that such matters were the exclusive responsibility of the Security Council. He accused the General Assembly of attempting to arrogate to itself the powers of a world government by running the Congo and UNEF operations.

U.S. Calls for Suspension of USSR Voting Rights. U.S. Ambassador-to-the-UN Adlai E. Stevenson Dec. 18, 1963 said that the United States would press for suspension of the USSR's General Assembly voting rights in 1964, when Soviet arrears for the UN's Middle East and Congo operations would exceed twice its share of the UN's normal operating budget, the point at which Article 19 of the UN Charter specified that a debtor nation forfeited its voting rights.

(The U.S. action ultimately posed a threat to France's voting rights in the General Assembly as a result of France's refusal to pay a share of the UN's Congo operations.)

De Gaulle Meets U Thant. President de Gaulle July 21, 1964 met with UN Secretary General U Thant in Paris. (The UN had ended its four-year operation in the Congo June 30.) De Gaulle told Thant that the UN had exceeded its powers by supporting an international force in the Congo instead of allowing the nations concerned to perform the necessary peace-keeping duties. (France's unpaid share of the UN's peace-keeping costs for the Congo totaled over $16 million by July 1964.)

Interim Agreement Averts Voting Impasse. The nineteenth regular session of the UN General Assembly opened Dec. 1, 1964 just an hour after a compromise agreement had been reached on the crisis threatened over the Soviet Union's unpaid peace-keeping assessments.

U Thant, representatives of the United States, France and the Soviet Union and other delegates agreed that items approved by the Assembly during December would have to be accepted by acclamation and that no votes would be taken until the conclusion of general debate (the opening statements of delegation leaders). This meant the postponement until early 1965 of a confrontation between the United States, the Soviet Union and France over the question of depriving the USSR and France of their vote because of their unpaid assessments.

Assembly Recesses. The nineteenth regular session of the UN General Assembly recessed December 30 without having taken any action on the unpaid peace-keeping assessments of the Soviet Union, six Soviet bloc countries and France, all of which were threatened with the loss of their Assembly vote if they remained more than two years in arrears.

De Gaulle for Five-Power UN Reform Conference. President de Gaulle Feb. 4, 1965 called for a five-power Geneva conference (including Communist China) to reform the UN. De Gaulle made the proposal at his eleventh presidential press conference:

> We all know what happened. Under the pressure of events in Korea, Suez and Hungary, and of the Soviets' excessive use of the veto, the so-called "united" nations, which were so no more, permitted themselves to exceed their nature and their possibilities. Failing to recognize the competence of the Security Council, they deviated from their Charter. In 1950 the General Assembly arrogated to itself the right to decide on the use of force, which made it the scene of quarrels between the two rivals. Through the disorder thus created, the then Secretary General was led to set himself up as a superior and excessive authority. Continuing these abuses, the Organization involved itself directly in the internal affairs of the Congo, sent there at great cost military troops furnished by States that were too often interested—which State is not?—and political, administrative and economic missions which, in fact, corresponded to the intentions of one great power. To be sure, this intervention has ceased thanks to the wisdom of the present Secretary General, and because of the expenditures—which France, let it be said in passing, could not for her part assume, since she has never ceased to disapprove of an unjustified undertaking and a procedure contrary to the San Francisco Treaty. But the profound transformation which the United Nations has undergone because of such distortions in legality clearly compromises its unity, its prestige and its functioning. Hence the present crisis into which it is plunged.

I will say frankly that, in my opinion, it is by returning to prudence and to the Charter that the United Nations can regain its equilibrium. In the present circumstances, it is clearly necessary for Washington, Moscow, London, Peking and Paris to agree to return to the point of departure, as they agreed to once in order to establish the United Nations. France, for her part, is ready to contribute to such an agreement by the five, and she feels that Geneva would be the obvious place for such negotiations . . . .

The official text of de Gaulle's remarks given above, issued by the French government February 5, quoted him as having praised "the wisdom of the present [UN] Secretary General [U Thant]" but having called the UN's Congo peace-keeping operation "an unjustified undertaking" and having stressed France's refusal to pay UN peace-keeping assessments. He had not made these remarks at the news conference.

U.S. Rejects De Gaulle Plan. In an implied rejection of de Gaulle's proposal for a five-power conference to reform the UN, President Johnson said at his press conference February 4: The United States took the position "that the problems of the United Nations are traceable not to the United Nations Charter but to those countries which have violated either the spirit or the letter of the Charter, because we believe that the framework for world progress and peace is in the Charter."

The U.S. State Department February 4 called de Gaulle's UN proposal "impossible" and "ridiculous," especially in view of the fact that Peking had just renounced all interest in the UN.

Communist Chinese Statement on De Gaulle Plan. Peking February 15 indicated approval of de Gaulle's February 4 call for UN reform. The Chinese view was given in the official *Jenmin Jih Pao* in an article that said: "even within the NATO bloc" there are demands for an end to "the state of affairs in which the United Nations is run by the United States"; "in general, what de Gaulle said . . . reflects an important trend in the present international situation; gone is the epoch of United States hegemony in the capitalist world".

France in Peace-Keeping Costs Committee. UN Assembly President Alex Quaison-Sackey and UN Secretary General U Thant February 27 announced the membership of a special 33-nation committee, authorized by the General Assembly to seek a solution of the peace-keeping and assessments controversies. The United States, Britain, France and the Soviet Union were named to the committee as major powers and permanent members of the Security Council.

The basic question the Special Committee on Peace-Keeping Operations was to delve into was the contention by the Soviet Union and France that only the Security Council and not the Assembly had the right to authorize peace-keeping operations.

France vs. Peace-Keeping Assessments. French Ambassador-to-the-UN Seydoux told the 33-member Special Committee April 23, 1965 that, in the French view, only the Security Council had the right to take peace-keeping actions and to make financial assessments for such purposes. He said the General Assembly could only make recommendations to the Council on matters such as economic sanctions and diplomatic relations.

U.S. Drops Funds-Voting Stand. U.S. Ambassador-to-the-UN Arthur J. Goldberg announced August 16 that the United States would no longer demand that voting rights in the UN General Assembly be denied to UN members who were more than two years in arrears in paying their assessments for UN peace-keeping expenses.

Goldberg told the 33-nation UN Special Committee on Peace-Keeping that the United States had to accept the "simple and inescapable" fact that a majority of the members of the General Assembly were unwilling to apply Article 19. "We will not," said Goldberg, "seek to frustrate that consensus, since it is not in the world interest to have the work of the General Assembly immobilized in these troubled days." Goldberg's speech meant that the United States would permit a resumption of regular voting at the twentieth session of the General Assembly, scheduled to convene in September.

The final meeting of the nineteenth UN General Assembly session was held September 1, and the Assembly approved a formula (adopted August 31 by its 33-member Special Committee on Peace-Keeping) to end the dispute on funds and voting rights.

In addition, the Assembly August 31 adopted a formula on voluntary contributions by UN members to cover the costs of peace-keeping operations. The formula, worked out by a group of Afro-Asian negotiators, had been submitted to the United States, France and the USSR for approval prior to formal adoption August 31.

French Representative Seydoux said August 31 that France considered the question of voluntary contributions as one to be studied in the "broader context" of the UN's "financial policy in general, including that of the specialized agencies."

De Gaulle Repeats Stand. President de Gaulle, at his twelfth presidential press conference Sept. 9, 1965, reiterated his opposition to UN assessments by the General Assembly for peace-keeping operations. He described these operations as "armed interventions which contradict the [UN] Charter." In his view, only the Security Council could order the use of armed force.

Couve de Murville Addresses UN. French Foreign Minister Couve de Murville addressed the UN General Assembly September 29. His speech marked France's first participation in the General Assembly's general debate since 1959. (French Information Minister Alain Peyrefitte said September 22, after a meeting of the French Council of Ministers with President de Gaulle presiding, that the participation of France's foreign minister in the general debate signified "that the UN had renounced an interventionist policy" with the August 31 agreement ending the dispute on assessments for peace-keeping operations voted by the General Assembly.)

Among points Couve de Murville made in his address:

UN budgetary crisis—"The French delegation does not conceal the satisfaction it feels at seeing a definitive close... to the crisis that last year prevented the normal meeting of this General Assembly.... This financial crisis should be taken as the opportunity to take a fresh look at the "financial" situation of the United Nations as a whole—including that of the specialized agencies...[and] to put an end to the continuous and systematic increase of our expenses of all kinds."

General Assembly's role—"The General Assembly is the expression of international public opinion, and it should consequently be the highest world political forum.... But the [Security] Council [represents]... the confluence of the world's major military, economic and political forces. It is normal that if action is required, the decision emanate from the Council...."

French View on Voluntary Contributions. The French representative on the General Assembly's Special Committee, Jacques Tine, said November 23 that France might consider making voluntary contributions to the UN if the Assembly approved a French proposal (currently under discussion in the Assembly's budgetary committee) calling for a study of the UN budget.

French Finance Study Adopted. The General Assembly's Administrative & Budgetary Committee Dec. 1, 1965 approved by 92-0 vote a French proposal to set up a 12-member committee to study ways to reform the UN's financial structure. French Ambassador-to-the-UN Seydoux had proposed the plan November 2. He held that since UN expenditures had been increasing, "it is appropriate... to draw up a complete and candid balance sheet... to introduce everywhere a spirit of order and economy."

Voluntary Contributions Voted. The Assembly December 15 adopted by 87-1 (five abstentions) a resolution calling on all UN members "to make voluntary contributions" to ease the financial crisis arising from nonpayment of UN peace-keeping assessments. France voted for the resolution.

France, USSR Hail End to UN Impasse. At the conclusion of President de Gaulle's trip to the Soviet Union, the June 30, 1966 French-Soviet declaration expressed approval of the solution of the UN's voting rights crisis over peace-keeping assessments by the General Assembly in 1965. The declaration said both sides took "note... with satisfaction of the progress made in the sense of realizing more exactly the role which belongs to the organization in accordance with its charter, and also of the efforts which are being undertaken for the introduction of greater financial and administrative strictness in its functioning."

CHAPTER XIII
ASIAN POLICY
SOUTHEAST ASIA AND COMMUNIST CHINA

During the period 1963-67 the de Gaulle government strongly opposed U.S. military intervention in Vietnam. De Gaulle repeatedly called for the neutralization of Vietnam through the reconvening of the nine nations which met in Geneva in 1954 to bring to an end the seven-and-one-half-year colonial war between France and the Communist Viet Minh rebels by dividing Vietnam into two states along the 17th parallel. De Gaulle also proposed that the 14-nation Geneva conference of 1962, which brought an end to the Laotian civil war and guaranteed the neutrality of Laos, be reconvened to assure the neutrality of Southeast Asia.

In a major policy initiative, the French government in 1964 became the first major Western power since 1950 to recognize Communist China.

De Gaulle Offers Aid for Neutral, United Vietnam. In his first major policy declaration on the developing Vietnamese War, President de Gaulle Aug. 29, 1963 proposed that Vietnam (North and South) be transformed with France's help from a divided, warring country into a unified, neutral state. De Gaulle offered French aid and cooperation if Vietnam was prepared to accept such a policy and throw off the foreign "influence" currently wielded by the United States and Communist nations. The de Gaulle proposal was made in a statement read to the French cabinet and released to the press.

Referring to "the work which France accomplished in the past in...[French Indochina which included North and South Vietnam], the ties which she retains in the whole country and the interest she has in its development," de Gaulle said that France appreciates "the role this people would be capable of playing in the present situation of Asia...once it is able to carry on its activity in independence from exterior influence, in internal peace and unity." He said France would be ready "to set up a cordial cooperation with this country" under such a policy.

The French proposal was rebuffed by U.S. President Kennedy September 2 as "irrelevant." In an interview granted CBS-TV, Kennedy emphasized his rejection of any policy that would lead to the withdrawal of U.S. troops from Vietnam before the Vietcong guerrilla menace had been crushed.

Paris Recognizes New Saigon Regime. France recognized South Vietnam's new provisional government Nov. 18, 1963. The South Vietnamese armed forces had ousted Ngo Dinh Diem as president in a violent coup d'etat November 1-2 and had established a provisional government.

Cambodia Asks French Aid. Prince Norodom Sihanouk, Cambodian Chief of State, was reported November 21 to have asked France to replace the U.S. assistance program, which the Cambodian government had canceled November 20. Agence France-Presse, the semi-official French news agency, said in Paris that Sihanouk had asked for French teachers to train engineers and technicians. Asserting that President de Gaulle was concerned with the maintenance of Cambodia's as well as Vietnam's neutrality, Sihanouk said "no one can accuse him of practicing imperialism or neo-colonialism here."

Sihanouk announced December 20 that after U.S. assistance terminated, "France will continue to have a much more privileged position in Cambodia than anyone else."

Peking on Ties with Paris. The "normalization" of relations between France and Communist China was suggested by Premier Chou Enlai in an interview filmed in Rabat Dec. 30, 1963 for France's state-run RTF radio and television network. Chou, asked about the possibility of closer Franco-Chinese ties, replied: "I am convinced that with...the normalization of relations between France and China, economic and cultural exchanges will develop."

France Recognizes Communist China. The French government announced Jan. 27, 1964 that it had agreed to establish diplomatic relations with Communist China and to designate an ambassador to Peking within three months. France became the second major Western power to recognize Communist China—Britain had done so Jan. 6, 1950—and the first NATO nation to establish relations with Peking since before the Korean war.

U.S. Deplores French Action. A U.S. State Department statement issued January 27, immediately after the Paris announcement, said that the French action was "an unfortunate step, particularly at a time when the Chinese Communists are actively promoting aggression and subversion in Southeast Asia and elsewhere." The statement said the United States would "stand firmly by its commitments" to Nationalist China, South Vietnam and other countries that might be affected by the French move.

The USSR and Soviet bloc countries welcomed the French announcement.

Nationalist China's Foreign Minister Shen Chang-huan declared January 28 that the French announcement was "a most unfriendly act" toward the Nationalist regime.

De Gaulle for Neutral Southeast Asia. President de Gaulle January 31, at his ninth presidential press conference, called for neutralization of Southeast Asia and discussed the implications of France's recognition of Communist China.

De Gaulle declared that France's recognition of the Peking regime had been dictated by the need to acknowledge "the world as it is." He asserted that it no longer was possible to ignore "the fact that for 15 years almost the whole of China is gathered under a government which imposes its laws, and that externally China has shown herself to be a sovereign and independent power."

De Gaulle made clear that his recognition of Peking was part of a wider French plan for a settlement of the continuing crisis in Southeast Asia—particularly in Vietnam, Laos and Cambodia. He said: "There is in

Asia no political reality...that does not concern or affect China. There is...neither a war nor a peace imaginable on this continent without China's being implicated in it. Thus it would be...impossible to envisage, without China, a possible neutrality agreement relating to the Southeast Asian states, in which...we French feel a very particular...interest — a neutrality which, by definition, must be accepted by all, guaranteed on the international level, and which would exclude both armed agitations...and...various forms of external intervention...."

LBJ Rejects De Gaulle Plan. The French plan calling for Southeast Asian neutrality was rejected by U.S. President Johnson Feb. 1, 1964 during his first formal presidential news conference. Johnson said that he would be prepared to consider "sympathetically" any plan that would insure the "neutralization of both North Vietnam and South Vietnam." "But I see no indication of that at the moment," he said. As long as the current Communist-inspired unrest in South Vietnam persisted, Johnson declared, "I think that the present course we are conducting is the only answer...."

Formosa Breaks with France. The Nationalist Chinese government announced February 10 that it had broken diplomatic relations with France because of the French recognition of Communist China. The Formosa announcement came only hours after the French Foreign Ministry had issued a statement in which it made clear that the de Gaulle government would no longer consider the Nationalist embassy in Paris to be the diplomatic representative of China.

French-Laotian Contacts. The *New York Times* reported from Vientiane, Laos February 10 that French representatives were in contact with Laotian leaders on President de Gaulle's proposal for neutralizing Southeast Asia. The French were reported to have offered to replace U.S. aid and influence in Laos and to assure the protection of a neutral Laos by means of an agreement under which Communist China would respect Laos' neutrality.

Paris-Peking Ties Established. A six-member Communist Chinese diplomatic delegation led by Charge d'Affaires Sung Chih-kuang arrived in Paris February 23 to establish formal relations with the French government. In a coordinated exchange, French Charge d'Affaires Claude Chayet arrived in Peking the same day with a French diplomatic mission sent to reestablish the French embassy in the Chinese capital.

De Gaulle Offers Cambodia Guarantees. De Gaulle offered France's help to Cambodia March 24 in arranging international guarantees of Cambodia's borders and its neutrality.

In a letter (published March 25) to Prince Sihanouk, Cambodian Chief of State, de Gaulle said he would urge the United States and Britain to agree to a new Geneva conference with Russia and Communist China participating. He advised Sihanouk, however, to first seek a settlement of Cambodia's border problems through direct talks with South Vietnam, Thailand and Laos. De Gaulle's letter was in reply to a message in which Sihanouk had sought French support for a 14-nation Geneva conference on Cambodia's political future.

France vs. SEATO Vietnam Stand. The Ministerial Council of the Southeast Asia Treaty Organization (SEATO) held its annual meeting in Manila April 13-15, 1964. The conference was marked by opposition within SEATO to France's proposals for neutralization of Southeast Asia. France abstained from voting on a section of a final communique issued April 15 that pledged SEATO support for South Vietnam against the Viet Cong guerrillas. The section was approved by Australia, Britain, New Zealand, Pakistan, the Philippines and the United States. Foreign Minister Maurice Couve de Murville, head of the French delegation, voted for the rest of the communique, which expressed SEATO determination to oppose overt Communist aggression in the area covered by SEATO.

De Gaulle Proposal on Laos Crisis. President de Gaulle proposed May 20 that the 14-nation (1962) Geneva conference on Laos reconvene to consider the latest military and political crisis in that country. (Troops of the pro-Communist Pathet Lao movement had broken a truce April 27 and launched heavy attacks on rightist and neutralist forces in northern Laos. The attack was attributed in part to the April 19 Laotian coup carried out by rightist military leaders against the coalition government of neutralist Prince Souvanna Phouma.)

De Gaulle's proposal was expanded to include South and North Vietnam and Cambodia in a statement made by Foreign Minister Couve de Murville May 21 at a cabinet meeting presided over by de Gaulle. Information Minister Peyrefitte quoted Couve de Murville as having told the cabinet: "There is no other solution to the problem of Laos than neutralization guaranteed by the signatory powers. A true...solution of neutralization must extend to all of Southeast Asia. It is the sole guarantee of the peace and independence of the states."

U.S. Rejects French Proposal. U.S. Ambassador-to-the-UN Adlai E. Stevenson, in an address to the UN Security Council May 21, expressed opposition to the French plan to reconvene the 14-power Geneva conference to consider the deteriorating situation in the former Southeast Asian states.

(The Council had been meeting in special session since May 19 to discuss Cambodian charges of "repeated acts of aggression by United States-South Vietnamese forces against...Cambodia." French Ambassador-to-the-UN Francois Seydoux May 25 called for adoption of a Security Council resolution "deploring" violations of Cambodian territory. Mentioning South Vietnam by name, Seydoux proposed that "those who bear responsibility" for the border attacks should compensate Cambodia.)

Soviet Union Backs French Plan. The French proposal for a Geneva meeting was supported by the Soviet Union in a May 23 Moscow announcement urging Britain, co-chairman with the USSR of the 14-nation 1962 Geneva conference on Laos, to join with the USSR in issuing an appeal that the conference be reconvened in June.

France Shuns Vientiane Meeting. Representatives of six of the 14 nations that had signed the 1962 Geneva neutrality agreement on Laos met in Vientiane, Laos June 2, 1964 to discuss the crisis in Laos. The United States and Britain had rejected the French proposal to reconvene the 14-nation Geneva conference for the purpose of assuring neutrality throughout Southeast Asia. They supported a proposal by Laotian Premier Souvanna Phouma that the 14 Geneva convention nations meet in Vientiane and confine their efforts to restoring the Laotian coalition government of rightists, neutralists and the Communist Pathet Lao.

France refused to attend the Vientiane meeting. Other signatories of
the 1962 agreement who boycotted the Vientiane meeting were the Soviet
Union, Communist China, Cambodia, North Vietnam and Poland.

Sihanouk Meets De Gaulle. Prince Sihanouk discussed the Southeast
Asian situation with President de Gaulle in Paris June 24-26. At a dinner
given in Sihanouk's honor, de Gaulle pledged "without reservation"
France's support of the Cambodian leader's appeal for reconvening of the
Geneva conference nations to guarantee Cambodia's neutrality. De Gaulle
assailed the "cruel divisions" of Southeast Asia, which, he said, were
heightened by "incessant foreign intervention." De Gaulle appealed to
other Southeast Asian states to pursue a policy of neutrality.

Paris-Saigon Tension. Relations between France and South Vietnam deteriorated after Vietnamese students damaged a French war
memorial in Saigon July 20 and had invaded the French embassy July 21.

France July 21 vigorously protested the incidents, demanded that the
South Vietnamese government pay for the damage, and asked for a public
apology. The South Vietnam Foreign Ministry responded July 25 with an
offer to pay for the damages but explained: "These incidents came about
under special circumstances, at a time when the French chief of state had
shown sympathy for the neutralization of Vietnam — a policy that Vietnamese public opinion has not ceased to judge incompatible with the higher
interests of the nation."

De Gaulle for Neutral Southeast Asia. President de Gaulle July 23,
at his tenth presidential press conference, reiterated his position calling for
neutralization of Southeast Asia. This implied, he declared, that the four
powers "which directly or indirectly bear a responsibility in what was or is
the fate of Indochina and which are France, [Communist] China, the Soviet
Union and America, [must] be effectively resolved to be involved there no
longer." To assure and provide "impartial control" for a neutralized Southeast Asia, de Gaulle suggested convening a Geneva conference which
would include "in principle, the same participants" as attended the 1954
Geneva conference. (The 1954 Conference included France, Britain, Communist China, the USSR, the United States, Laos, Cambodia, Vietnam,
and the Viet Minh Communist rebels.)

French Reaction to U.S. Bombing of North Vietnam. U.S. planes
Feb. 7, 1965 bombed and strafed the southern North Vietnamese military
base of Donghoi. South Vietnamese planes, escorted by U.S. jets, carried
out a follow-up attack February 8 against the North Vietnamese military
communications center in the Vinh Linh area. These were the first U.S.
bombings of North Vietnam in the war.

French officials in Paris indicated February 8 that the increased pace of the war in Vietnam demonstrated the imperative
need for negotiations with Peking and North Vietnam to settle
the conflict before it escalated into a wider war.

French-Soviet Peace Efforts. Soviet Ambassador-to-France Sergei
A. Vinogradov February 23 handed President de Gaulle a Moscow memo
that supported the French leader's proposal for settling the Vietnamese
war through the reconvening of the 1962 Geneva conference. (French
sources in Paris said that de Gaulle's government also was in constant contact with Communist China and North Vietnam.)

French Information Minister Peyrefitte said after a cabinet meeting February 24 that as a result of the de Gaulle-Vinogradov talks, France and the USSR had decided to press for an international meeting on South Vietnam.

After five days of talks in Washington with French Foreign Minister Couve de Murville, U.S. officials February 20 rejected French proposals for negotiations on Vietnam. At a meeting with President Johnson, Secretary of State Rusk and other administration leaders, Couve de Murville was said to have expressed fear of a possible Sino-U.S. war, which, he held, the United States would have to fight without allies. Couve de Murville said he believed China and North Vietnam would be willing to negotiate a "neutral" zone in Southeast Asia that would be free of Chinese as well as American influence. The U.S. officials reiterated the argument that North Vietnam was in direct control of the Viet Cong guerrillas in South Vietnam.

Paris-Hanoi Trade Pact. France March 16 agreed to renew a trade agreement with North Vietnam for one year and, for the first time, to extend medium-term credits to the Hanoi government. The announcement was made in Paris by Nguyen Tu, general director of Vietnamese Enterprises for Industrial Imports, before leaving for Hanoi. Tu said French-North Vietnamese trade had totalled $4 million in 1964.

French-Soviet Appeal. France and the Soviet Union April 29 urged reaffirmation of the 1954 and 1962 Geneva agreements guaranteeing the independence of Vietnam, Cambodia and Laos. Their call was issued in a communique based on talks Soviet Foreign Minister Andrei Gromyko held in Paris April 26-29 with French Foreign Minister Couve de Murville.

France Boycotts SEATO Meeting on Vietnam. The annual meeting of the Ministerial Council of the Southeast Asia Treaty Organization was held in London May 3-5, 1965. In a communique issued at the closing session, the conferees assailed the Communists for their role in the Vietnamese war. The communique was signed by the United States, Australia, Britain, New Zealand, the Philippines and Thailand. France did not sign. France had decided to boycott the meeting because of its opposition to United States Vietnam policy. France's regular delegate attended the meeting only as an observer.

In further expression of its opposition to the United States Vietnam policy, France announced April 23 that its war vessels would not participate in SEATO's May 1-24 naval maneuvers in the China Sea. Paris explained that French participation would create the impression that France supported the United States in Asia.

Paris Blocks NATO Statement on Vietnam. The NATO Ministerial Council met in London May 11-12. At the meeting U.S. Secretary of State Rusk sought support for U.S. continuation of the war in Vietnam. Opposition by French Foreign Minister Couve de Murville made it impossible to include in the Council's final communique a paragraph proposed by the United States condemning Communist aggression.

De Gaulle Scores U.S. Policy. President de Gaulle charged June 10 at an Elysee Palace reception that American forces were "involved in a dirty affair in Vietnam with their tanks, their trucks and their planes."

Saigon Ends French Ties. South Vietnam severed diplomatic relations with France June 24 but retained consular ties. In announcing the diplomatic break, Foreign Minister Tan Van Do charged that France "pretends to be a friend but isn't. The de Gaulle government has always directly or indirectly helped our enemies."

De Gaulle Repeats Stand. President de Gaulle, at his twelfth presidential press conference Sept. 9, 1965, again called for an "effective end of all foreign intervention [of Vietnam], and therefore complete and controlled neutralization of the zone in which there is fighting."

France Backs Red China for UN Seat. French Foreign Minister Couve de Murville September 29 declared before the UN General Assembly: "... The time will inevitably come when the People's Republic of China will represent [China]... in the General Assembly and in the Security Council.... [The problems of Asia] cannot be settled without the direct participation of the largest Asian power. By wishing to persist in excluding it, one simply risks seeing it continue to take its own initiatives on its own behalf."

The General Assembly November 17 defeated by 47-47 vote (20 abstentions) a resolution to seat Communist China in the UN and expel Nationalist China. (A two-thirds majority was required for adoption of the resolution.)

France voted in favor of seating Communist China. It was the first time since the issue came before the UN in 1950 that France supported seating the Peking government.

France Opposes UN Action. The UN Security Council met Feb. 1, 1966 to consider a U.S. draft resolution calling for Council action to arrange an international conference to bring peace to Vietnam and Southeast Asia. The Council agreed February 2 by 9-2 vote (the USSR and Bulgaria opposed; France abstained) to put the matter on its agenda.

The Council meeting had been requested January 31 by U.S. Ambassador-to-the-UN Arthur J. Goldberg. French Ambassador-to-the-UN Francois Seydoux argued February 1 that the UN was "not the proper forum for achieving a peaceful settlement" because North Vietnam and Communist China "are not represented in our organization."

De Gaulle Disapproves U.S. Bombing Resumption. The United States suspended air strikes against North Vietnam Dec. 24, 1965 and resumed air attacks Jan. 31, 1966. A French cabinet statement edited by President de Gaulle said February 2 that Paris "can only regret and disapprove of the resumption of bombing" of North Vietnam. The statement also criticized the U.S. action in taking the Vietnam case to the UN. It said that since North and South Vietnam and Communist China were not UN members, the UN was "not qualified to intervene." France suggested instead that the matter be taken up again by a reconvened Geneva conference.

De Gaulle was reported February 17 to have let President Johnson know of France's opposition to U.S. resumption of air strikes against North Vietnam. The French leader was said to have called military intervention self-defeating. De Gaulle's remarks had been made in a message sent to President Johnson February 9 in response to a letter de Gaulle had received from Johnson on U.S. peace efforts in Vietnam.

French Peace Offer. President de Gaulle informed North Vietnamese President Ho Chi Minh in a letter made public February 15 that France was ready to actively take part in exerting her influence to end the Vietnamese war as soon as possible. The message was in response to a note de Gaulle had received from Ho January 24.

De Gaulle Statement. At his thirteenth presidential press conference, President de Gaulle February 21 again called for a Geneva peace agreement "among all the parties concerned. The parties... are those who reached agreement in Geneva in 1954. The conditions for that peace are known.... They are an *entente*, and, as a start, contact between the five world powers.... Locally, they are an end to all foreign intervention. [and]... neutrality of the country. France... by withdrawing her troops [in 1954]... is all the better for it today."

France Shuns SEATO Meeting. The Ministerial Council of SEATO held its annual meeting in Canberra, Australia June 27-29, 1966. French delegate Achille Clarac, ambassador to Thailand, attended the Council conference only as an observer to exress disapproval of the organization's support of the United States in the Vietnamese war.

France-Soviet Statement. A French-Soviet declaration, issued June 30 at the conclusion of President de Gaulle's eleven-day trip to the Soviet Union, declared that both governments "continue to hold that the only possible way out of this situation, which is a threat to the cause of peace, is a settlement on the basis of the Geneva agreements of 1954 precluding any foreign interference in Vietnam."

French Statement on Haiphong Bombing. French government disapproval of the U.S. raids on the Hanoi-Haiphong oil depots (beginning June 29) was expressed in a statement released after a cabinet meeting July 2. Recalling that Paris had "made known its disapproval of what is called the escalation into which the United States had been drawn in Vietnam," the statement said France "even more strongly... condemns the recent bombing of Hanoi and Haiphong, which can only make any solution of this problem more difficult."

Mission to Hanoi. A former cabinet minister, Jean Sainteny, reported to President de Gaulle July 20 on a personal mission to Hanoi carried out at de Gaulle's request. Sainteny handed de Gaulle a message in which President Ho Chi Minh said "we are glad that France, signer of the 1954 Geneva accords on Vietnam, is trying to make an active contribution towards the reestablishment of peace in this region on the basis of the correct execution of these accords."

De Gaulle in Cambodia Urges U.S. Withdrawal. President de Gaulle called on the United States Sept. 1, 1966 to withdraw from South Vietnam as a step toward restoring peace in that country. De Gaulle, addressing an audience of 100,000 in Pnompenh, Cambodia, declared that a U.S. military withdrawal could be a prelude to genuine international negotiations on peace in Vietnam. (De Gaulle, on a scheduled 18-day 30,000-mile world tour, had arrived in Pnompenh for a state visit August 30 after a flight from Djibouti, French Somaliland. He left Pnompenh September 2 for Noumea, French New Caledonia.)

In his speech, de Gaulle strongly condemned U.S. policy in Southeast Asia. He praised Cambodia for its policy of neutrality and its effort to remain outside the conflict. France would "continue to lend it her help and support toward this goal," he said. De Gaulle argued that a policy of neutrality "alone could have spared" the other Southeast Asian states "from becoming a field of confrontation for rival dominations and ideologies and an attraction for American intervention."

To end the war, de Gaulle proposed an "agreement, just like the [Geneva] one of 1954...[with] the goal of establishing and guaranteeing the neutrality of the peoples of Indochina.... The contracting parties would therefore be the real powers being exercised there and among the other powers, at least the five world powers." (The United States, Britain, USSR, Communist China and France had participated in the 1954 Geneva agreements.)

De Gaulle said: Negotiations toward such an agreement "would depend, obviously," on a prior "commitment" by the United States "to repatriate its forces within a suitable and determined period of time." The United States, by "renouncing...a distant expedition once it appears unprofitable and...[by] substituting for it an international arrangement organizing the peace and development of an important region of the world, will not...involve anything that could injure its pride, interfere with its ideals and jeopardize its interests. On the contrary...what an audience would the United States recapture from one end of the world to the other, and what an opportunity would peace find on the scene and everywhere else. In any event, lacking this outcome, no mediation will offer a prospect of success, and that is why France, for her part, has never thought and does not think of proposing one."

De Gaulle, during his August 30 to September 2 stay in Cambodia, was accorded honors never before extended to a foreign head of state. He stayed at the royal palace in Pnompenh and attended in Siemreap September 1 a ceremony that included a specially staged recreation of the ancient rite of the coronation of the Khmer kings.

In a declaration signed September 2 at the royal palace, Prince Sihanouk and de Gaulle declared: "despite the disputes that have divided and still divide Vietnamese, it is essentially foreign intervention that, by turning a civil war into an international war, has given the hostilities their present dimensions. In order to end them, it is above all necessary for the powers whose interests and ideologies are confronting one another in Indochina...in conjunction with all the countries concerned...to observe strictly the clauses of the 1954 Geneva agreements, namely respect for the independence and sovereignty of Vietnam and non-interference in its internal affairs." Subject to the "agreement by all the Vietnamese, a status of guaranteed controlled neutrality should be conferred on Vietnam by international agreement." The agreement "should be applied to the entire Indochinese peninsula...."

LBJ Rejects De Gaulle Stand. President Johnson, at a news conference in Washington September 8, rejected President de Gaulle's suggestion, made in his September 1 speech in Pnompenh, that the United States could pave the way to Vietnam peace negotiations if it announced a timetable for withdrawal of its troops. "We don't have any information to that effect," Mr. Johnson declared. "No one has communicated any evidence to that effect to us."

Couve de Murville for U.S. Initiative. French Foreign Minister Couve de Murville called on the United States September 28 to make a "new move" toward a political solution of the Vietnamese war. Addressing the UN General Assembly, Couve de Murville declared that responsibility for a genuine peace overture rested with the United States. United States intervention, he said, had been one of the basic elements in the escalation, and the United States alone was in a position to "render everything possible, and first of all, peace...."

De Gaulle Repeats Call for U.S. Exit. President de Gaulle, at his fourteenth presidential press conference Oct. 28, 1966, said France had "no mediation of any kind to propose [in Vietnam]... for the good reason that peace is impossible at this time." For there to be a negotiated settlement of the war, he declared, the United States must: (1) withdraw its forces and adopt a policy of "controlled neutrality" for Southeast Asia, (2) provide economic assistance to allow Vietnam to "repair its ruins and resume its development" and (3) recognize that no treaty would be valid without the participation of Communist China. With respect to the latter point, the United States should draw the necessary conclusions concerning its relationship with China and China's "rightful place in the United Nations."

France Votes for Peking UN Membership. France joined 45 other UN General Assembly members in voting November 29 to seat Communist China and expel Nationalist China from the UN. The resolution was defeated with 57 negative votes.

De Gaulle-Kosygin Statement. A French-Soviet declaration issued Dec. 8, 1966 at the conclusion of Soviet Premier Aleksei Kosygin's visit to France and discussions with President de Gaulle "deplore[d] a situation the gravity of which results from external intervention; this situation also places the neighboring states in danger and constitutes at this time the main obstacle to international *detente* as well as to the establishment of lasting peaceful relations among numerous countries."

Anti-French Demonstration in Peking. Demonstrations were conducted at the French Embassy in Peking Jan. 31-Feb. 3, 1967 in protest against a clash in Paris January 27 between French policemen and a group of Chinese students who had attempted to march on the Soviet embassy. The French government lodged a strong protest February 1 after Chinese demonstrators had forced a French embassy official and his wife to stand seven hours in the cold following an alleged traffic accident.

General De Gaulle: Vietnam War "Detestable." President de Gaulle February 21 condemned the war in Vietnam as a "detestable conflict" and repeated his plan for neutralization of Southeast Asia. De Gaulle made the remark in greeting visiting Cambodian Chief of State Prince Sihanouk. The war would end, de Gaulle said, "only by the termination of the outside intervention that is its cause."

France Continues SEATO Boycott. France boycotted the annual ministerial meeting of SEATO held in Washington April 18-20. The meeting, devoted entirely to the Vietnam war, issued a communique condemning North Vietnam's "aggression" on South Vietnam.

De Gaulle Blocks "War Crimes Tribunal." President de Gaulle rejected efforts by a so-called "International Tribunal on War Crimes," created by opponents of U.S. policy, to hold its "trial" in France. (The trial had been organized by the British philosopher Bertrand Russell.) In a letter to Jean-Paul Sartre, executive president of the "court," de Gaulle April 19 forbade the holding of the "trial" on French soil. De Gaulle pointed out that the tribunal had no legal standing. He agreed that France opposed American policies in Vietnam. But he said that France was obligated to make certain that the United States, as a traditional friend of France, "shall not be the object of proceedings that are beyond the bounds of justice and international practices."

French-Polish Statements. On his arrival in Warsaw Sept. 6, 1967 for a six-day tour of Poland, President de Gaulle referred to Vietnam at a reception in his honor. He suggested that Poland and France "associate their efforts in favor of peace [in Vietnam] if the opportunity appears one day." He urged that the two countries "help in the implementation of the external and internal political status as established by [the Geneva] treaty 14 years ago."

The joint declaration issued September 12 at the conclusion of de Gaulle's visit said the Vietnamese War posed the major obstacle to the relaxation of international tensions. It did not accuse the United States by name and made no reference to de Gaulle's September 6 suggestion that Poland and France work together in bringing the war to an end.

France: U.S. Should End Bombings. French Foreign Minister Couve de Murville September 28 told the UN General Assembly that U.S. actions in Vietnam endangered world peace. He said the United States would have to take a "decisive initiative" to end the Vietnamese War. He held that the most fruitful step the United States could take to lead to peace discussions would be "the unconditional suspension, unlimited in time, of the bombing that is ravaging North Vietnam." He insisted that North and South Vietnam should be left to work out their differences "regardless of the regime that they might think fit to adopt." He said that it would be "quite illusory" for the UN to become involved in the Vietnamese struggle.

France Backs Peking UN Entry. France voted November 28 for a UN General Assembly resolution to seat Communist China and expel Nationalist China from the UN. The resolution was rejected with 58 nations voting against and 45 in favor.

CHAPTER XIV

THE MIDDLE EAST WAR (1967)

The war begun June 5, 1967 between Israel and the Arab states ended in an Israeli military victory within six days. France supported UN Security Council resolutions of June 6, 7, 9, and 12 calling for a cease-fire between Israel and the Arab states. French policy in the aftermath of the six-day war took a decidedly pro-Arab orientation.

French Efforts to Head Off the Crisis. The UN Security Council convened in emergency session May 24-30 to discuss the Middle East crisis caused by the withdrawal of the UN Emergency Force from the Middle East and the massing of Arab armies along Israel's borders earlier in May and by UAR threats to blockade Israeli shipping in the Gulf of Aqaba. President de Gaulle was reported to have proposed May 24 the convening of a conference of the U.S., Britain, France and the Soviet Union to resolve the crisis. Information Minister Georges Gorse said France regarded the 1950 tripartite Anglo-French-U.S. declaration on the Middle East as unrealistic since no cooperative international action could be taken in the region without Soviet participation. Under the tripartite pact, the three nations had pledged joint action to prevent violation of the truce that had ended the 1948-49 war between Israel and the Arab states.

Abba Eban Meets with French, British and U.S. Officials. Israeli Foreign Minister Abba Eban took up the question of the Egyptian blockade of the Gulf of Aqaba with French, British and U.S. officials in Paris, London and Washington May 24-26. Eban met with President de Gaulle May 24 and with U. S. Secretary of State Rusk and President Johnson May 25-26.

Reporting on his diplomatic endeavors at a news conference in Jerusalem May 30, Eban declared that Israel would continue the policy of attempting to open the Strait of Tiran, at the entrance to the gulf, "alone if we must, with others if we can." "Now it is clear from the contacts we have made with the major powers that there are others in the world who are prepared to make common cause for the restoration of the legal question in the Gulf of Aqaba." Eban had declared in a TV interview in London May 24 that the hasty withdrawal of the UN Emergency Force from the Gaza Strip and Sharm el Sheik "is why the world is in a state of tension now."

French Arms Embargo. The French government announced June 5 a suspension of shipments of military equipment and spare parts to the Middle East. The announcement followed the outbreak of hostilities and came after a meeting of President de Gaulle, Premier Pompidou, and

230

Foreign Minister Couve de Murville. Although the ban applied equally to both sides, Israel was most affected since it was the only country in the area largely dependent on French arms. Israel's air force was equipped mostly with French jets.

De Gaulle, Kosygin Confer. Soviet Premier Aleksei Kosygin met June 16 in Paris with President de Gaulle. Kosygin was en route to New York for an emergency session of the UN General Assembly convened to consider problems created by the Arab-Israeli conflict. De Gaulle was reported to have stressed France's policy of "deliberate objectivity" in the crisis in his talk with Kosygin.

De Gaulle Scores Israel, Links Conflict to Vietnam. President de Gaulle accused Israel June 21 of having started the war in the Middle East.

In a major statement on the crisis delivered to his cabinet and made public in Paris, de Gaulle said that France "condemns the opening of hostilities by Israel" even though France "disapproved the threat to destroy Israel brandished by her neighbors." "France," he declared, "accepts none of the changes effected on the terrain through military action as final."

De Gaulle held that the Middle East conflict stemmed from "the war [that] was started in Vietnam through American intervention." The violence of the Southeast Asian conflict, de Gaulle said, "cannot but spread disorder not only on the spot but far away." France believed that the Middle East crisis could not be settled peacefully "in the present world situation unless a new international element should come into sight. This element could and should be the end of the war in Vietnam through termination of foreign intervention."

The U.S. response to de Gaulle's remarks was delivered June 21 by White House Press Secretary George Christian. Christian said: "No one close to the situation sees any connection between the Middle East war and the situation in Southeast Asia."

The Egyptian government June 21 expressed satisfaction with de Gaulle's statement.

French Statement at UN. At the special session of the UN General Assembly, French Foreign Minister Couve de Murville June 22 questioned Israel's demand for direct negotiations with the Arab states. Couve de Murville said that serious obstacles to direct Arab-Israeli peace talks existed. The most important of these obstacles, he said, were Israel's conquest and retention of large Arab territories, its refusal to consider mediation by the UN or other third parties and its failure to define its terms for settlement. Under these conditions, he asked, "how can it be expected that these Arab countries, which for 20 years have refused to negotiate with Israel — however great a shock they may have suffered and possibly even because of this shock — will be any more ready to negotiate today than they were yesterday?"

Couve de Murville warned that Israel's retention of the Arab lands its forces had overrun could result in the "bringing about of incessant and dangerous incidents" of the type that had prevailed in the region before. In regard to Israeli occupation of Arab areas, "no *fait accompli* on the spot regarding the territorial boundaries and the situation of the citizens of the states concerned should be considered as permanent," he said. "Only a freely negotiated settlement accepted by all parties concerned and recognized by the international community could one day solve these problems as a whole."

France, he said, had a special role to play as a peacemaker in the Middle East because it was "entirely disinterested," because its only motive was peace and because it had a record of friendship and respect for both Jews and Arabs.

French Action on UN Resolutions. The UN General Assembly's emergency special session on the Middle East failed July 4 to adopt any of the four draft resolutions submitted to it dealing with the problems raised by the Arab-Israeli war. The Assembly did, however, approve a resolution declaring invalid Israel's June 28 reunification of the city of Jerusalem.

The Assembly's inability to reach agreement on UN action to assure peace in the Middle East was viewed as a defeat for the Soviet Union. The USSR had requested the emergency session in a bid to obtain Assembly condemnation of Israel and to force the withdrawal of Israeli troops from the occupied areas of Egypt, Jordan and Syria.

French votes on the four defeated resolutions were as follows:

(1) Abstained on Soviet draft resolution accusing Israel of "premeditated... aggression," demanding withdrawal of Israeli forces to 1949 armistice line, calling for Israeli reparations to Arab states, and calling for Security Council action to undertake measures "to eliminate all consequences of the aggression committed by Israel."

(2) Abstained on Albanian draft resolution condemning the United States and Britain for "participation" in the Israeli "aggression."

(3) Voted for a Yugoslav draft resolution calling for immediate withdrawal of Israeli forces to positions held before outbreak of fighting June 5, enforcement of the withdrawal through the offices of the UN Secretary General, and further Security Council action to resolve other issues related to the crisis.

(4) Abstained on Latin American draft resolution calling on Israel to withdraw its forces, requested all parties to conflict to end the state of belligerency, and reaffirmed earlier UN resolutions on the desirability of internationalizing the city of Jerusalem.

France voted for a Pakistani resolution, adopted by the General Assembly, declared invalid Israel's reunification of Jerusalem under a single administration.

French-Soviet Contacts. Soviet Premier Kosygin conferred with President de Gaulle and other French officials in Paris July 1. No communique was issued, but French officials indicated that the Middle East crisis had been discussed.

Commenting on his talks with de Gaulle, Kosygin declared at a Kremlin dinner honoring visiting French Premier Pompidou July 3 that the positions of the two countries were "close to each other on the main thing, namely to restore conditions of peace in the Middle East, liquidate the consequences of Israel's attack on the Arab states... [and] the hotbeds of aggression in other parts of the world."

Premier Pompidou discussed the Middle East crisis in Moscow July 4 and July 6-9 with Kosygin and other Soviet leaders. A joint communique issued at the conclusion of the talks July 9 said France and the Soviet

Union had agreed to work for peace in the Middle East and to safeguard the "rights for an independent existence of all peoples of the area." The statement recognized Israel's right to exist, but it said France and the Soviet Union would not recognize Israel's military conquest of Arab territories.

France Approves UN Peace Plan. The UN Security Council November 22 approved a resolution aimed at bringing peace to the Middle East. The resolution called for withdrawal of Israeli forces from Arab territories captured in June, for an end to the state of belligerency, for respect for the sovereignty and territorial integrity of all Middle East states, and affirmed the necessity for guaranteeing freedom of navigation through international waterways in the area. It empowered UN Secretary General U Thant to send a representative to the Middle East to maintain contact with Israel and the Arab states and assist efforts to achieve a peaceful settlement in accordance with the Security Council resolution.

The adoption of the resolution climaxed six weeks of Security Council public debate and private consultations. The Council's non-permanent members November 3 had turned over the task of drafting a resolution to the body's five permanent members — France, the United States, Britain, the USSR, and Nationalist China.

France Repeats Call for Israeli Withdrawal. French Foreign Minister Couve de Murville September 28, participating in the annual general debate of the UN General Assembly, said that each country in the Middle East had "the right to live and see its security guaranteed." He added that Israeli withdrawal from conquered Arab territories would be "the obvious preliminary" to a peaceful settlement, but he conceded that "no human eye can perceive the way" to establish peace there. He called for the UN to play a peacemaking role in the area.

De Gaulle Attacks Israeli Policy. President de Gaulle November 27, at his sixteenth presidential press conference, delivered a harsh attack on Israeli policy. He declared:

"The establishment of a state of Israel raised at the time a certain number of apprehensions.... Some even feared that the Jews — up to then scattered, but who had remained what they had been down through the ages, that is, an elite people, sure of itself and dominating — once they gathered on the site of their former grandeur, might come to change into a fervent and conquering ambition the very touching hopes that they had for 19 centuries.... Despite the tide ... of ill-will that they provoked, that they caused more exactly in certain countries and at certain times, a considerable capital ... or sympathy had formed in their favor ... in Christendom.... It must be said that ... since 1956 ... we saw in fact appear a State of Israel, warrior and determined to enlarge itself. Then, the campaign it conducted to double its population ... led one to think that the territory it had acquired would not be sufficient for long and that, to enlarge it, it would be led to use any occasion that would present itself. That is why ... the Fifth Republic freed itself ... of the special and very close ties that the preceding regime [Fourth Republic] had established with [Israel]...."

De Gaulle said that he had told Israeli Foreign Minister Abba Eban May 24 that if Israel were attacked, "... we will not allow it to be destroyed. But if you attack, we will condemn your initiative...."

"After attacking," declared de Gaulle, "... Israel took possession of the objectives it wanted to acquire.... For a settlement to be implemented, it would be necessary that there be the agreement of the great powers.... But one cannot see how any agreement could come into being ... so long as one of the greatest of the four [the United States] will not have disengaged itself from the hateful war it is conducting elsewhere.... Without the Vietnam drama, the conflict between Israel and the Arabs would not have become what it is...."

Reactions to de Gaulle's Statement. An Israeli government communique November 28 charged de Gaulle with "historical distortion" and called his remarks "a grave affront to the Jewish people and the state of Israel." Israeli Foreign Minister Abba Eban informed the French ambassador November 30 that de Gaulle's remarks had caused "grave injury" to French-Israeli relations.

The United Arab Republic chief government spokesman, Dr. Mohammed H. el-Zayyat, hailed de Gaulle's remarks November 29 as "heart-lifting, encouraging [and] courageous."

Jacob Kaplan, the grand rabbi of France, in a statement issued November 29, accused de Gaulle of "giving the highest possible sanction to a campaign of discrimination." Editor Hubert Beuve-Mery of the influential Paris newspaper *Le Monde* charged in a front-page editorial that de Gaulle's remarks had an "unpleasant smell of anti-Semitism."

CHAPTER XV
OTHER FOREIGN POLICY INITIATIVES
FRANCE AND LATIN AMERICA

In 1964 President de Gaulle made two official trips to Latin America for the purpose of increasing French political and economic involvement in the area.

De Gaulle in Mexico, French Caribbean Possessions. President de Gaulle flew from Paris March 15 to Pointe-a-Pitre, Guadaloupe beginning a ten-day tour of Mexico and the French Caribbean departments— Guadaloupe, Martinique and French Guinea. He flew to Mexico City March 16 where he was greeted by President Adolfo Lopez Mateos and hailed by enthusiastic crowds of Mexicans. Addressing an estimated 225,000 persons from a balcony of the National Palace, de Gaulle emotionally called for a new era of French-Mexican cooperation.

De Gaulle and Lopez Mateos, following three days of talks, issued a communique March 18 which pledged the two countries to new efforts to strengthen not only Mexico's ties with France but also ties between members of the Latin American Free Trade Association (LAFTA) and the European Common Market. The communique said that France and Mexico would study measures to increase their trade and cultural exchanges. It indicated that the two leaders had examined the possibility of a greater volume of French investment in Mexico in cooperation with Mexican capital.

De Gaulle returned March 19 to Pointe-a-Pitre, Guadaloupe to begin his tour of the French Antilles. Speaking at a rally in Pointe-a-Pitre March 20, de Gaulle declared that his Caribbean tour was only one manifestation of France's new initiative and independence and that friendly and allied nations would have to adapt themselves to the change. These words were taken as an allusion to growing French friction with the United States. But de Gaulle made it clear that France did not intend that its new initiatives, particularly in Latin America, should interfere with the traditional role and responsibility exercised by other powers in the hemisphere.

De Gaulle flew to Cayenne, French Guiana March 21 and to Fort-de-France, Martinique March 22. In both places, he delivered addresses stressing the economic and cultural ties that bound the French overseas departments with France. He was faced twice with demands for local autonomy, and he rejected each. In the first case, youths appeared March 20 during his Pointe-a-Pitre address carrying banners demanding autonomy; they were told that they were "a ridiculous little group" that could change nothing. In the second incident, Fort-de-France Mayor Aime Cesaire welcomed de

Gaulle to the city March 22 with a speech in which he demanded self-rule for the island; he was told publicly by de Gaulle that Martinique was thoroughly French and could be ruled only by France. De Gaulle March 23 flew from Fort-de-France to Paris.

De Gaulle South American Tour. President de Gaulle, accompanied by a party of about 100 persons, visited ten Latin American republics Sept. 21-Oct. 16, 1964. De Gaulle began his journey with a flight from Paris September 20 to Pointe-a-Pitre, Guadaloupe. His 12,500-mile itinerary thereafter: Venezuela September 21-22, Colombia September 22-24, Ecuador September 24-25, Peru September 25-28, Bolivia September 28-29, a cruise off Chile September 29-October 1, Chile October 1-3, Argentina October 3-6, Paraguay October 6-8, Uruguay October 8-10, a cruise off Brazil October 11-13, Brazil October 13-16. He flew back to Paris from Rio de Janeiro October 16.

During his trip de Gaulle stressed the unity of interest he claimed to find between his country and the nations of Latin America. In Venezuela, de Gaulle declared in a speech to Congress: "We cannot admit the right of any state, externally, to establish the direction of the economic or political affairs around them. I believe we agree that all oppression and all hegemony be excluded from our universe.... Between nations that everything invites to a closer relationship, the Atlantic Ocean cannot be an obstacle. How much truer this is for the Latin peoples that we both are."

De Gaulle met with Venezuelan President Raul Leoni. A communique issued said that France and Venezuela would negotiate a cultural and a commercial agreement.

De Gaulle visited schools in Colombia and proclaimed France's eagerness to contribute to Colombia's development.

De Gaulle stressed in Ecuador that France and South America had strong links based on their common Latin and Christian culture.

In Peru he conferred with President Fernando Belaunde Terry. Belaunde asserted September 27: "Peru has a very cordial friendship with both the United States and France. But it is a different kind of friendship." He called the bond with France mainly "spiritual." The two leaders said in a joint communique September 27 that France had agreed to send Peru more experts in electricity, mechanics and agriculture.

De Gaulle assured the Chilean Congress October 2 that an essential objective of French policy was to give developing nations more of a chance to export products and that France would support Latin America's drive for better trade relations with the European Economic Community.

De Gaulle conferred with President Arturo U. Illia in Argentina and agreed October 5 to expand trade and educational and scientific exchanges between France and Argentina. The two leaders also agreed on more strenuous efforts to obtain European economic assistance for Latin America.

De Gaulle warned Uruguayan government officials October 10 of the dangers of being trapped in a struggle between Washington and Moscow. He stressed the importance of world equilibrium and national independence.

De Gaulle conferred with Brazilian President Humberto Castelo Branco. In a joint communique, de Gaulle pledged France's support of Brazil's efforts to gain wider markets in Europe and more investment capital.

Pompidou on Latin Policy. Premier Pompidou told the National Assembly Oct. 30, 1964 that France expected to play a lesser role than the United States in Latin America. Commenting on President de Gaulle's September 21-October 16 tour of 10 Latin American republics, Pompidou said: "France cannot substitute herself for the economic effort being made by the United States. She does not want to, either, knowing perfectly well the solidarity created between the two American neighbors and the weight that the power of the United States represents. But all that does not mean that there is not, for us, something to do." He suggested possible cultural exchange programs and French industrial aid to Latin American development.

De Gaulle Reaction to 1965 Dominican Crisis. Following the outbreak of a civil war in the Dominican Republic April 24, 1965, U.S. President Lyndon B. Johnson decided to send in U.S. troops for the announced purpose of protecting and evacuating American nationals. Initially, only 400 marines were sent to Santo Domingo. However, Washington rapidly expanded the force to more than 19,000 by May 5, after charging that Communists had infiltrated and attempted to take over the rebel movement led by followers of ex-Pres. Juan Bosch, under the command of Col. Francisco Caamano Deno. Following a meeting of the French cabinet May 6, a government spokesman said that at the meeting President de Gaulle had criticized "the intervention of foreign troops in the Dominican Republic" and had expressed hope "they would be withdrawn." The official also disclosed that Paris was considering recognizing the Dominican rebel government headed by Col. Francisco Caamano Deno.

French government sources reported May 7 that Caamano's group had appealed to France for "moral and material support" against U.S. military intervention.

DE GAULLE'S 1966 WORLD TOUR

President de Gaulle Aug. 25, 1966 began a 19-day 30,000-mile world tour. The trip included visits to Cambodia August 30-September 2 and the French nuclear-testing center in the Pacific September 9-11. Among other stops on the trip: French Somaliland (August 25-26), Ethiopia (August 27-29), New Caledonia (September 3-5), the New Hebrides (September 6), Tahiti (September 7-9) and the West Indies (September 12). De Gaulle was accompanied by his wife and by French Foreign Minister Couve de Murville, Armed Forces Minister Pierre Messmer, Scientific, Atomic and Space Research Minister Alain Peyrefitte and Overseas Territories Minister Pierre Billotte.

Riots Greet De Gaulle in Somaliland. De Gaulle's visit August 25-26 to Djibouti, the capital of French Somaliland, was marked by rioting as Somali nationalists demanding independence clashed with French security forces. Four persons were killed and about 70 injured in the rioting. The rioting forced de Gaulle August 26 to cancel a scheduled open-air speech in the main square of Djibouti and to speak instead in the Territorial Assembly hall. He asserted in his address that "the placards that we have read [many demanding 'total independence'] and the agitation of those who carry them certainly do not suffice to demonstrate the democratic will of the French territory here." De Gaulle recalled that in 1958 the Somaliland Territorial Assembly had rejected (by a 27-4 vote) de Gaulle's offer of independence for the territory. De Gaulle said: "If one day...by regular and democratic methods, the territory were to express a new opinion about its destiny, France would take account of it."

De Gaulle in Ethiopia. De Gaulle conferred with Emperor Haile Selassie in Addis Ababa, Ethiopia August 27-29. A joint communique issued August 28 stated that the two countries "consider that relations between states should be based on the principles of strict respect for the independence of each and of non-intervention in the internal affairs of others." It continued: The heads of state "noted that...there existed between them a broad community of views on international problems. This holds particularly for the problems posed in Africa." The statement added that agreements on French-Ethiopian cultural, scientific and technical cooperation had been signed.

De Gaulle in New Caledonia. During his visit September 5 to Noumea, the capital of New Caledonia, de Gaulle told the Territorial Assembly: "History, geography and the will of the people of this territory combine to make this an important center of French influence." In Tahiti, de Gaulle promised September 13 to provide funds to build a highway through the interior of the island.

Somaliland Referendum Announced. After his return to France de Gaulle said Sept. 15, 1966 that "if they [the Somalis] want to separate themselves," France will not "present an obstacle." Overseas Territories Minister Billotte announced September 21 that a referendum on the country's future status would be held before July 1, 1967. The French cabinet approved the referendum bill October 27.

Somaliland Votes to Remain French. In the March 19, 1967, French-sponsored referendum 22,569 residents of French Somaliland voted for "increased autonomy" under French rule; 14,723 voters favored independence from France.

About 2,000 Somali nationalists rioted in the port city of Djibouti March 20 in the protest against the results of the referendum. French troops suppressed the disturbances, killing 12 Somalis and arresting 4,500.

The Djibouti violence was precipitated by nationalist charges that France had rigged the elections. (Neighboring Somalia, which claimed French Somaliland, charged in a broadcast after the balloting that "the people of French Somaliland have perhaps lost a battle by trickery, but not the war." Somalia had massed troops on the French Somaliland border during the election. Ethiopia, which opposed Somalia's annexation of French Somaliland, also had deployed soldiers on the French colony's frontier.)

President de Gaulle said March 22 that France would continue to rule French Somaliland despite the anti-French riots in Djibouti. Asserting that the March 19 referendum had "served its purpose," de Gaulle said the results showed that an "important and obvious majority" advocated continued protection by France.

FRANCE AND FRENCH CANADA

President de Gaulle in 1967 initiated a policy of closer ties between France and the French-speaking Canadian Province of Quebec. During a trip to Canada he ultimately called for a "free Quebec," the slogan of the Quebec separatist movement, and thereby seriously strained relations between the Canadian government and France.

French-Quebec Agreement. Quebec Premier Daniel Johnson announced May 22, 1967 in Paris that his province and the French government had agreed to cooperate on several cultural and financial projects. Ending a five-day visit to Paris, Johnson said that Quebec would contribute to a communications satellite system that would enable French radio and TV programs to be received in Quebec. Johnson also announced that a study group had been formed to spur the flow of investments between Quebec and France. Other programs would include the sending of young Quebec nuclear engineers and civil servants to France for advanced training and work.

President de Gaulle, meeting with Johnson twice during his visit, had applauded Quebec-French cooperation. At a banquet in Johnson's honor, de Gaulle had said that "all Frenchmen ... are profoundly convinced now of the great destiny which is common to them."

Canadian Manpower and Immigration Minister Jean Marchand applauded the Paris-Quebec agreements May 31 but expressed reservations about the satellite project because telecommunications were under Canadian federal jurisdiction.

De Gaulle for "Free Quebec." The separatist movement in Canada's French-speaking Province of Quebec received the blessing of the French government July 24, 1967 when President de Gaulle, on a state visit in honor of Canada's centennial, called for a "free Quebec."

This call, issued in a speech in Montreal, was viewed as an unprecedented interference in the domestic affairs of another country, and it prompted a sharp rebuke from the Canadian government July 25. Because of the Canadian rebuke, de Gaulle left Canada July 26, a day ahead of his scheduled visit to Ottawa, the Canadian capital, and his conference with government officials.

(De Gaulle began his trip July 15 aboard the cruiser *Colbert*, flagship of France's Mediterranean fleet. He arrived at the French territorial island of St. Pierre, south of the Newfoundland coast, July 20 and told a cheering crowd that St. Pierre and the neighboring French island of Miquelon represented "a token of our independence from everybody.")

In a reversal of the usual order of state visits, de Gaulle arrived in the city of Quebec rather than Ottawa July 23. (De Gaulle's itinerary had been worked out after months of negotiation between Ottawa, the city of Quebec and Paris. It represented a compromise between Quebec's desire to be the sole sponsor of the trip and Ottawa's insistence that the federal government have some hand in the visit because of de Gaulle's status as a head of state.) On his arrival in Quebec, de Gaulle told a welcoming crowd that he felt "at home" there. "What we are doing in France, you are doing here," he said, and added: "We will do it a little more together. Whatever is French has its role to play, as always." At a state dinner that evening, de Gaulle urged the people of Quebec to end their "second-fiddle" role, become "their own masters" and prevent "outsiders" from exploiting the province's natural resources. He urged them to join forces with other Canadians in order to "organize ways and means for safeguarding their essence and independence next to the colossal state [the United States] which is their neighbor."

De Gaulle traveled from Quebec city to Montreal by motorcade July 24 and in several speaking stops along the way referred to Quebec as "New France." At Donncona he told a crowd of 1,000 that "Quebec, alive, is on its way of becoming master of itself." At another point he asserted that Quebec "must depend on no one but itself."

On his arrival in Montreal later July 24, de Gaulle told a cheering throng of 10,000 French Canadians that he sensed "the same atmosphere" in Quebec that he had felt "during the liberation of France" in 1944. He concluded his speech by exclaiming: " *Vive le Quebec! Vive le Quebec libre! Vive le Canada Francais! Vive la France!"*

Canadian Prime Minister Lester B. Pearson and other Canadian officials July 25 denounced de Gaulle's use of the separatist " *Quebec Libre*" ("Free Quebec") slogan. Following a day-long cabinet meeting, Pearson issued a statement declaring that, while Canada had been pleased to welcome de Gaulle, certain of his statements "tend to encourage the small minority of our population whose aim is to destroy Canada, and, as such, they are unacceptable to the Canadian people and its government." Pearson continued: "The people of Canada are free. Every province of Canada is free. Canadians do not need to be liberated. Indeed, many thousands of Canadians gave their lives in two World Wars in the liberation of France and other European countries."

In obvious response to Pearson's critical statement, de Gaulle cancelled the remainder of his trip July 26 and flew back to Paris. Before leaving Montreal de Gaulle said: "On leaving, we want you to keep in your memory the few days that General de Gaulle spent in your midst. French Canada has become even more dear to France. We become closer in every way."

Pearson said July 26 that de Gaulle's cancellation of his visit to Ottawa was "understandable in the circumstances." He added that "those circumstances, which are not of the [Canadian] government's making, are greatly to be regretted." But Quebec Prime Minister Johnson declared July 28: "We must bitterly deplore that, caught up by the passion of extremist elements, the government of Canada felt obliged to make a statement that forced our guest to return to France without going to Ottawa."

Reaction in the French press to de Gaulle's remarks was largely unfavorable. Among press comments:

> *Le Monde* July 25—In de Gaulle's statements "the exaltation of nationalism, the anti-American phobia, the glorification of 'Francehood' reach a sort of paroxysm." As for the general's "rough interference in the internal affairs of a country": "Is the whole Gaullist doctrine of nonintervention, so often and so solemnly invoked, again very recently in the Middle East crisis and for years over Vietnam, merely a matter of circumstance?"

The French Communist daily *L'Humanite* July 27—While the French Communist Party favored self-determination for the people of Quebec, it also stood for the "noninterference in the internal affairs of foreign states."

Le Figaro July 27—"Thus ends, very badly, a trip which started out under the most agreeable auspices. This misadventure is without parallel in the presidential career of de Gaulle. . . . A scandal of this sort would have been conceivable with a Castro, or some little pinchbeck potentate, or even with Nikita Khrushchev, a past master of international bad manners—but de Gaulle! but France! It is absolutely unbelievable."

De Gaulle presented a report on the trip to the French cabinet July 31. After a four-and-a-half-hour meeting — reportedly the longest on record since de Gaulle came to power in 1958 — the cabinet adopted de Gaulle's report "unanimously." A communique summarizing the report, issued after the cabinet meeting by Information Minister Georges Gorse, stated in part:

. . . General de Gaulle took note of the immense French fervor everywhere he went. He noted that French Canadians were unanimously convinced that after a century of oppression following the English conquest, the second century under the system defined by the British North America Act of 1867 had not assured them of liberty, equality and fraternity in their own country.

He received from all sides fervent appeals addressed to France to organize and extend more and more her links with the French people of Canada, after 200 years of physical and moral separation. . . . Noting this indescribable wave of emotion and determination, General de Gaulle told the French Canadians and their government clearly that France intended to help them to reach the objectives of liberation that they themselves have set.

It goes without saying that France has no pretensions to leadership or, *a fortiori*, to sovereignty over all or part of the Canada of today. But, since France founded Canada and she alone for two and a half centuries administered it, peopled it and developed it, since she sees the existence and strong personality there of a French community of six and one-half million inhabitants, of whom four and one-half are in Quebec, she most certainly cannot either disinterest herself in the present and future fate of a people descended from her own people and admirably faithful to their country of origin, or consider Canada as a foreign country in the same sense as others.

Canadian Prime Minister Pearson Aug. 1 issued a short two-sentence reply that "noted" the Gaullist statement and declared that the Canadian government "has already made its position clear on the unacceptability of any outside interference in Canadian affairs and has nothing to add in present circumstances." There were reports that Pearson resisted cabinet pressure for a longer reply so that he could avoid expanding the incident into a diplomatic break.

French Aid to Quebec. France August 23 pledged a "considerable increase" in its aid to the Province of Quebec in order "to help the French of Canada to maintain and develop their personality." The promise was made after a two-and-a-half-hour meeting of the French cabinet presided over by President de Gaulle.

Announcing the cabinet decision, French Information Minister Gorse said that the aid would be in the "cultural, economic and technical fields" and that details would be worked out at future cabinet meetings. He said the increased aid would fall within the scope of the two cultural, scientific and technical cooperation agreements signed by France and Canada in 1965.

Canadian Prime Minister Lester B. Pearson said August 23 that he saw "nothing to be disturbed about in plans or programs for cooperation of this kind between France and Quebec or any other [Canadian] province." He noted that the French announcement referred only to maintaining and developing the "personality" of the Quebecois and did not mention "liberation."

As a follow-up to the announcement, French Education Minister Alain Peyrefitte conferred with Quebec Premier Daniel Johnson, Education Minister Jean-Jacques Bertrand and other officials in Quebec September 11-15. A communique issued at the conclusion of the talks September 15 said both sides had agreed to a ten-fold increase in cultural, scientific and technical cooperation over the next three years.

De Gaulle for "Sovereign Quebec." De Gaulle, at his sixteenth presidential press conference Nov. 27, 1967, called on Canada to grant Quebec the status of a sovereign state. He declared:

> By what one can only call a miracle of vitality, energy and loyalty,... a French nation, a piece of our people, is appearing today in Canada and wishing to be recognized and treated as such.... That Quebec be free, is indeed what is at issue.... Two conditions are necessary: the first entails a complete change regarding the Canadian structure such as it currently stands.... In my opinion, this will necessarily result in the advent of Quebec to the rank of a sovereign state and master of its national existence.

Canadian Reaction. In a statement read to the Canadian House of Commons November 28 Canadian Prime Minister Pearson said: "This [De Gaulle's] statement was not merely a commentary on Canadian domestic or foreign policies, which could have been ignored; it was an intervention in those policies by the head of a foreign state. As such, it remains unacceptable. Indeed, in this case it is intolerable that a head of a foreign state or government should recommend a course of political... action which would destroy... the unity of the Canadian state. The future of Canada will be decided in Canada, by Canadians."

Premier Johnson of Quebec Province declared November 27, at a conference of provincial premiers in Toronto, that he supported national unity for Canada. He said "the responsibility for establishing this [juridical and practical] equality does not rest with the Quebec government alone" but "is shared... by the other provinces and the federal government."

PART III

CRISIS AND CONCLUSION

(1968-1969)

CHAPTER XVI

POLITICS, GOVERNMENT AND THE ECONOMY (1968)

THE MAY-JUNE CRISIS

The May-June crisis was the most serious challenge to the de Gaulle regime since the Algerian war. Although President de Gaulle was able to stem the tide of economic disorder and social anarchy that erupted in the spring of 1968 and the Gaullists emerged with a decisive victory in parliamentary elections held in June, the convulsion left profound economic and social problems in its wake. These problems severely tarnished the image of political and economic stability that the de Gaulle regime had maintained during its first ten years in power.

The crisis was precipitated by student disorders in Paris and other university centers. Initially, the student demonstrators rebelled against what they considered an archaic university system. They demanded an end to overcrowded classrooms, abolition of year-end "all or nothing" examinations, increased contact with professors, improved curricula with more interdisciplinary courses, and — above all — a greater role for students in university administration. As the disturbances continued, the students rapidly broadened their demands to include a radical transformation of French society. Student-police confrontations and violence in Paris and other large cities sparked a wave of wildcat strikes and factory seizures by workers, which ultimately brought the entire economy to an almost complete standstill.

Student Demonstrations Lead to Violence. The disturbances began May 2, 1968 when six members of the "March 22 Movement," a coalition of leftist militants at the University of Paris' suburban Nanterre campus, occupied a lecture hall during a protest against "imperialism." (The "March 22 Movement" was named after a group of Nanterre students who had demonstrated March 22, provoking a closing of classes until April 1.) The militants' action, led by Daniel Cohn-Bendit (known as Danny-the-Red), resulted in the suspension of classes at the Nanterre campus later May 2.

Fighting between students and police erupted in the Latin Quarter of Paris May 3 after several hundred students had been forcibly removed from the university's Sorbonne campus, where they had organized a mass demonstration to protest against disciplinary action pending against Cohn-Bendit and other Nanterre students. More than 1,000 students were involved in the clashes, which raged through most of the Latin Quarter. Police used tear gas, and the students fought back with homemade grenades and cobblestones. Five hundred and ninety-six persons were arrested and students and police were injured in the rioting. Following the eviction of the students from the Sorbonne courtyard, the rector of the university closed the university gate to forestall further violence.

Violent rioting broke out early May 6 in the Latin Quarter between thousands of students and riot police. Students fought police with paving stones and gasoline bombs from behind barricades of overturned cars. By late night, an estimated 10,000 students had joined the rebels, who repelled several charges of police reinforced with armored trucks and water cannons. The May 6 fighting grew out of an illegal but peaceful demonstration for the release of arrested student leaders. By midnight, 422 students were under arrest and more than 700 students and police had been injured.

Violence Hits Provinces. Demonstrations occurred at major provincial universities May 7 in sympathy with the Paris students. Among the cities where demonstrations took place: Grenoble, Lyons, Nancy, Aix-en-Provence, Clermont-Ferrand, Marseille and Nice.

De Gaulle Warning. President de Gaulle May 8 issued a statement warning students against further violence. Following his warning, thousands of policemen cordoned off the Latin Quarter. Education Minister Alain Peyrefitte announced May 8 that classes would resume at the Sorbonne and Nanterre May 9, provided that students halted further violence. The move was interpreted as an effort to placate the students, who demanded the resignation of Peyrefitte and Interior Minister Christian Fouchet, the withdrawal of police from the Latin Quarter, and amnesty for all arrested demonstrators.

Renewed Student Violence; Police Withdrawn. Violence flared again late May 10, when an estimated 30,000 students gathered outside the Sorbonne to demand the removal of police from the buildings. By 10:00 p.m. student leaders issued orders to build barricades on major thoroughfares in the Latin Quarter. By early morning May 11, more than 60 barricades existed, made of cobblestones, overturned cars, buses, felled trees and construction materials.

The street warfare that ensued was more violent than the previous clashes. Three hundred and sixty-seven persons were injured and 468 arrested, and 188 cars were damaged or burned. The battle was regarded a victory for the students; when it ended, they occupied most of the Latin Quarter and the police had been withdrawn from the area.

The decision to remove the police was made at the direct request of Premier Pompidou, shortly after his return May 11 from a state visit to Afghanistan. After consulting with de Gaulle later that day, Pompidou announced that out of "profound sympathy" for the students and with "confidence in their common sense" all arrested students would be released and the university would be reopened May 12.

Communist, Catholic Labor Vs. Police Action. The Communist- and Catholic-led labor federations staged a nationwide 24-hour general strike May 13 in protest against "police brutality" in suppressing student demonstrations. Concurrently with the strike, organized labor in Paris participated in a massive demonstration of solidarity with the students.

The crowd, estimated variously at 200,000-500,000, marched for four hours from the city, chanting slogans backing the student revolt and denouncing de Gaulle.

Students Occupy Sorbonne. Students occupied the Sorbonne May 14. Lecture halls at the university were used for debates over educational reform. The action of the Sorbonne students was followed by students at most of France's other universities and high schools, who staged sit-ins, which were largely supported by faculty members.

Pompidou Statements. Speaking at a hastily convened session of the National Assembly May 14, Premier Pompidou referred to the student disturbances and declared: "Our civilization is being questioned, not the government, not the institutions, not even France, but the materialistic and soulless modern society."

Pompidou spoke again in a nationwide broadcast May 16. (President de Gaulle had conferred presidential powers on Pompidou two days earlier, before leaving Paris for a state visit to Rumania.) In his radio-TV address, Pompidou asserted that the government would take all measures needed to defend the Republic.

Factory Seizure Begins Strike Wave. A sit-in strike began late May 14 in Nantes, where 2,000 workers seized the Sud-Aviation aircraft factory and held the plant manager prisoner. Although the Nantes workers already had been on strike for higher pay, their seizure of the factory was without the authorization of the labor unions involved. After welding shut the main gate, the strikers camped on the site.

Wildcat strikes, accompanied by factory seizures, quickly spread to other industries, including the state-run Renault automobile plants, which were occupied by workers May 16. An estimated 20,000 workers took over the Renault plants at Boulogne-Billancourt (Paris), Le Mans, Flins, Orleans and Sandouville, near Le Havre.

The Renault workers demanded a reduction of the work week to 40 hours without loss of pay and a minimum monthly salary of 1,000 francs ($200). Currently they worked an average of 44-45 hours a week, and a pending reduction to 40 hours was to have been with pay loss. Among other plants struck May 16: an electrical equipment plant near Orleans, potassium mines in Alsace and glass works in Lorraine.

The strike movement spread to other sectors of the economy May 16. Directors and producers of RTF, the state radio and TV network, walked off their jobs in Paris in protest against what they termed government censorship. A partial strike of newspaper distributors prevented newspapers from reaching the newsstands.

Communist Party Vs. Student Demands. The French Communist Party and both the Communist-led and the Catholic-oriented labor federations, who initially had been hesitant to claim leadership of the widespread wildcat strike movement, moved May 16 to restore their authority and dissociate the workers' demands from those of the more revolutionary students. Labor leaders at the occupied Renault factory in Paris May 16 rebuffed university students when they marched to the plant to join the strikers. The students were told that their presence in the factory would give the government an excuse to intervene.

The Communist Party Political Bureau issued an appeal for leftist unity May 16. It declared that conditions were "rapidly ripening to end Gaullist power and set up a modern and authentic democracy." But the statement also warned workers and students against "taking instructions from adventurers [i.e., the radical student movement] who are likely to impede the movement." The warning was a reference to student leader Cohn-Bendit, who had denounced Communist Party leaders as "Stalinist creeps."

The uneasy alliance between student radicals and workers on wildcat strikes was strained further May 17, when Georges Seguy, general secretary of the Communist General Confederation of Labor, France's largest labor union, condemned a march on national radio and TV headquarters that students had planned for later that day. The students subsequently yielded and cancelled the march. After crediting students with sparking the current crisis, Seguy declared that "the working class has a majority and doesn't need meddling from outside influences." He said the union had not ordered a general strike but had merely called on its followers to participate in local strikes wherever they occurred.

Economic Paralysis Spreads. By May 17 the industries struck included: Several plants of the Rhone-Poulenc chemical company in Lyons and the lower Seine Valley; France's largest truck builder, Berliet, and a large synthetic-textile company, Rhodiaceta, both in Lyons; a government armaments factory in Bayonne, near the Pyrenees in the southwest; at least one-half dozen more Renault plants.

Air traffic came to a halt May 17 at Orly and Le Bourget international airports. By late evening the strike had spread to the national railroads and the post and telegraph services.

Communist Party Calls for Leftist Regime. Communist Party Secretary General Waldeck Rochet May 18 issued a call for an end to the Gaullist regime and the establishment of a popular front government of all leftist forces. The Communist Party, Rochet declared, was "ready to assume all its responsibilities." The party's decision, made at a Politburo meeting May 17, reversed its earlier hesitance to capitalize on the growing wave of economic disorder and violence.

The non-Communist Federation of the Left, led by Francois Mitterrand, had called May 16 for the resignation of the Gaullist government and for a general election.

De Gaulle Returns to Paris. President de Gaulle cut short by 12 hours his five-day state visit to Rumania and returned to France May 18. After conferring with key officials, de Gaulle promised reforms but warned citizens against continuing disorders.

Among activities affected by the strike May 18: Local and long-distance trains; the Paris subway and bus systems; taxi service was greatly reduced; the shipyards of St.-Nazaire on the Atlantic coast were occupied by workers; the employees of the state telephone and telegraph administration announced that they would transmit only telegrams and cablegrams that were a question of "life or death." The police occupied the international telephone and telegraph exchange in Paris May 18.

Ex-Premier Pierre Mendes-France, a member of Parliament, called May 19 for the resignation of the Pompidou government "so that economic, social and political transformation can begin in a climate of confidence."

Communist Party Renews Call for Leftist Regime. The Communist Party Politburo May 20 issued a statement describing the workers' strike movement as "tending toward the elimination of the Gaullist regime and government and the accession, with all the forces of the Left, of a veritable republican regime opening the way to socialism." The statement carefully distinguished the workers' demands from those of the radical student movement. The workers' demands were described as non-revolutionary and limited to improvement of their standard of living and working conditions.

In an effort to prevent violence, the Communist Confederation of Labor May 20 barred parades and demonstrations outside plants and succeeded in most cases in obtaining the release of plant managers who had been held prisoners by the workers. The police generally remained in the background and did not interfere with the protest movement.

Economic Paralysis Widespread. By the evening of May 20 most normal activity in France was crippled or halted. Trains were not running. Few planes operated. About 80% of public transportation in the cities was stopped. There were no mail deliveries in Paris and very few in the rest of the country. Automatic phone service was maintained, but manual calls could not be made. The government-owned power network continued to supply electricity, although the plants had been occupied by employees. Most newspapers continued to publish, and the unions urged truckers to continue bringing food supplies into the cities. Huge traffic jams developed in Paris and other cities. Food stores were swamped by housewives seeking to stockpile provisions, and depositors staged a run on banks.

Students continued to control most of the country's universities and many of the secondary schools. Teachers in the primary and secondary schools in Paris met with their students when they could but did not teach. The national teachers' federation issued a call for a full-scale strike beginning May 22.

The strike movement spread May 21 to include the Bank of France, the nation's nuclear facilities and Les Halles, the produce market in Paris. Strikes at the Simca auto factories in Poissy and La Rochelle and the Citroen auto plant in Rennes completed the shutdown of the French auto industry. Other industries or professions struck May 21: Pharmaceutical manufacturers, food processing plants, flour mills, oil refineries, actors, architects and meteorologists. Labor union leaders estimated that seven million workers, or a little more than one-third of the French labor force, were participating in the strike movement and that several million others were unable to go to work because of the breakdown of public transportation.

Pompidou Government Survives Censure Motion. The government of Premier Pompidou May 22 narrowly survived a parliamentary effort to overthrow it. A censure motion pressed in the National Assembly by the combined opposition of the Communist Party and the non-Communist left received only 233 of the 244 votes it needed. (Under the constitution, deputies seeking the downfall of the government needed a majority of the 487-member parliament.)

The censure motion, introduced by Francois Mitterrand, leader of the non-Communist Federation of the Left, charged that the government had failed to deal effectively with the demands of the students, teachers, workers and farmers, whose massive strikes and demonstrations had paralyzed the economy and caused widespread disorder.

The censure motion received the vote of 121 members of the Federation of the Left, 73 CP members, 34 centrists (out of 42), four independents and Edgar Pisani, a former Gaullist minister.

Prior to the vote, Pompidou promised wide-ranging economic concessions to the workers and educational reforms to the students. Admitting that "a critical point" had been reached since the wave of strikes hit the country beginning May 14, Pompidou declared himself ready "to start a dialogue with all the trade union organizations and... to call them in for talks." He asserted that the majority of Frenchmen opposed the disorder and that most workers were prisoners of their union leaders. "The government depends for its authority on the people and on those to whom the people have given constitutional powers," he declared. "It cannot give way to pressure from the streets."

Communist Party General Secretary Waldeck Rochet told the Assembly May 22 that the French people "have had enough of this regime of personal power." Referring to Pompidou's claim of popular support, Mitterrand asked the premier: "Where is the popular support that you claim? Go outside the Assembly Hall and you can see for yourself."

Journalists on Strike. The labor revolt spread to the press May 24 when *Le Parisien Libere*, the morning daily with the largest circulation, failed to appear on the stands because of the refusal of the printers to set a headline that they considered unfair and harmful to the strike movement. *France-Soir*, the largest evening paper, issued a statement May 24 that said: "*France-Soir*, like the other dailies, is appearing normally so that the public may continue to be informed. The journalists of *France-Soir* affirm, however, their solidarity with the general trend of demands sought by all the unions and all over the country." At Agence France-Presse, the semi-official French news agency, the staff unions May 24 established a "vigilance committee" to "continue to guarantee the objectivity" of the agency's news reports. Television newsmen went on strike May 25 with the charge that the government had prevented "impartial and objective" coverage of the crisis.

Renewed Student Violence. Violent street fighting between students and police erupted again in Paris. In the Latin Quarter of Paris May 23, an estimated 1,000 students and other youths battled riot policemen using tear gas and concussion grenades. Several hundred students and policemen were injured during the clashes, in which groups of youths hurled paving blocks and tear-gas grenades. Demonstrators erected new barricades and set fire to cars and to piles of garbage that had not been collected since the strikes started May 14. The fighting around the Latin Quarter grew out of a peaceful demonstration May 23 against a government decision to bar the readmission to France of Cohn-Bendit, the principal leader of the student revolt, who had gone on a speaking trip to West Germany.

De Gaulle Offers Referendum on "Participation." In an effort to end the student violence and the widespread work stoppages which had brought the French economy to a standstill, President de Gaulle May 24 called on the French nation, in a radio-television speech, to give him a personal vote of confidence in a referendum (to be held in June) or face the threat of "civil war." The referendum, he declared, would ask the nation to grant him a "mandate" to reform the universities and the economy in order to provide greater opportunities for student and worker participation in activities affecting them. He warned, at the conclusion of the seven-minute address, that if the referendum were defeated, he would resign.

Excerpts from de Gaulle's May 24 address:

Everyone realizes, of course, the far-reaching consequences of the current events—in our universities, then in the social field. One sees in them all the signs that demonstrate the necessity for a change in our society, and everything indicates that this change should include a broader participation by everyone in the conduct and results of the activity in which each is directly concerned. . . . the university crises . . . has, through contagion, unleased in many other groups a tide of disorders, abandonments or work stoppages. The result is that our country finds itself on the brink of paralysis. For ourselves and for the world, we French must settle a vital problem that our times create for us so that we may not slip, through civil war, into adventures and usurpations of the most odious and ruinous kind.

In view of the quite exceptional situation in which we find ourselves, I have therefore, on the government's proposal, decided to submit a bill to the vote of the nation, by which I ask it to give the state and, firstly, its head, a mandate for renovation.

To reconstruct the universities with regard not to their age-old customs, but to the country's real needs for evolution and to the actual opportunities in modern society for the student youth.

To adapt our economy, not to this or that category of special interests, but to the national and international needs of the present, by improving the living and working conditions of public service and company employees, by arranging for their participation in occupational responsibilities, by developing young people's training, by assuring them of jobs and by putting to work the industrial and agricultural activities within the framework of our regions. . . .

Police Battle Paris Students. Rioting erupted in Paris May 24-25, when an estimated 20,000 students, some workers and other youths clashed with police. The street fighting began shortly after President de Gaulle had finished his address to the nation. For the first time, the fighting involved the Right Bank, as one group of students attacked the Bourse (the Paris stock exchange) and set fires inside and in front of the building. By nightfall street fighting had spread over a two-square-mile area and had spilled into the Latin Quarter. About 30 running battles raged in scattered parts of the city by midnight. (At Paris' largest railroad station, the Gare de Lyon, one man pulled down the French tricolor and threw it into the gutter while thousands cheered. As the crowd sang the *Internationale*, the man hoisted a red flag over the station.) The Paris clashes, which lasted into the early hours of May 25, resulted in one death. More than 1,000 persons were injured.

Agence France Presse reported this tally of people injured and arrested during May 24 clashes: Paris — 456 serious, 500 minor injuries; 795 arrested. Violence in other cities May 24-25: Lyon—230 wounded, 27 policemen hospitalized, 200 arrested, Nantes — 80 wounded, including 57 policemen. Strasbourg — 50 wounded.

Responding to the renewal of clashes between students and police, Premier Pompidou May 25 issued a warning that new demonstrations would be "immediately dispersed with the utmost force." He charged that the disturbances in the Latin Quarter had been the action of "provocateurs" with an "obvious attempt to set off a civil war."

Gaullists Win By-Elections. In by-elections for municipal council seats in Dijon and Poissy May 26, the three seats contested were won by Gaullist candidates. The Gaullists defeated candidates backed by the Communists and the non-Communist Federation of the Left. In Dijon, Robert Poujade, secretary general of the Gaullist party, and Maurice Lombard, his associate, polled 24,504 votes. The candidate of the non-Communist Federation, backed by the Communists, polled 20,471. In Poissy, west of Paris, a Gaullist candidate, backed by the Democratic Centrists, defeated a Communist candidate supported by the non-Communist left.

Cohn-Bendit Back in Paris. Daniel Cohn-Bendit, the student leader whose agitation sparked the nationwide unrest, defied a government ban and returned to the Sorbonne in Paris May 28.

Following his departure for a speaking tour to Belgium and West Germany, Cohn-Bendit had been declared an undesirable alien by French police. This action barred him from re-entering France from Saarbrucken in West Germany May 24. (Cohn-Bendit, the son of German-Jewish parents who had fled from Germany to France during World War II, had been studying at the University of Paris in suburban Nanterre on a West German government grant.)

After dyeing his red hair black, Cohn-Bendit passed French border guards May 28 and showed up in Paris to give an after-midnight press conference May 29. He declared at the Sorbonne press conference that the aim of the student revolt that had swept France was to change governments and destroy capitalism.

Mendes-France Ready to Head Leftist Government. Ex-Premier Pierre Mendes-France May 29 declared his readiness to assume responsibility for a provisional government, which had been called for May 28 by Francois Mitterrand, leader of the Federation of the Democratic and Socialist Left. Mendes-France said that if he were called on to form a "popular government," the Communists would be part of it.

Meanwhile in Paris May 29, an estimated 200,000 persons massed in front of the Place de la Bastille to march through the city in a demonstration against the government called by the Communist-led General Confederation of Labor. The Paris demonstrators, like those in demonstrations held in other parts of France, demanded de Gaulle's resignation.

De Gaulle Confers with Army Command. Amid widespread speculation that de Gaulle might resign, it was announced May 29 at the Élysee Palace that he had left Paris by helicopter for his country home in Colombey-les-deux-Eglises, 135 miles east of Paris.

De Gaulle's arrival five and one-half hours later at Colombey (the flight normally took one hour) coincided with reports that he had in fact flown first to Baden-Baden, headquarters of the French armed forces in West Germany, to confer with army generals about the growing rebellion in France. (Although de Gaulle's visit to Baden-Baden was not confirmed by French government officials, a West German government spokesman, Gunther Diehl, disclosed May 31 that de Gaulle had been in Baden-Baden May 29.)

Reports also circulated in Paris that de Gaulle had conferred with local military commanders in Paris May 29 and had held a secret meeting with top military commanders in Mulhouse, near the Swiss border, later that day. Although government spokesmen denied that any of the French forces stationed in West Germany had been recalled, it was reported that some units had been seen in the outskirts of Paris May 30. The French Defense Ministry subsequently described the movements of troops around Paris, which included tank units, as "routine maneuvers." Observers, however, agreed that de Gaulle had held a secret meeting May 29 with General Jacques Massu, commander of the French forces in West Germany, and members of his staff in the Belfort-Strasbourg area in Alsace, near the West German border. These observers also concurred in the view that de Gaulle had sought the support of the French army before making a radio-television address to the nation May 30.

GAULLIST SWEEP IN ELECTION

De Gaulle Dissolves Assembly. In a move to end the nationwide disorder, President Charles de Gaulle May 30 announced the dissolution of the National Assembly and called for new elections to be held within the 40-day statutory period. The elections were scheduled for June 23 and 30.

Delivering an emotional radio-TV address, de Gaulle pledged to prevent a Communist "dictatorship" by all the means at his disposal. But he conceded that the disorder in the country made it necessary to postpone the referendum he had announced in his May 24 speech.

De Gaulle's May 30 address:

Frenchwomen, Frenchmen: Being the custodian of the national and republican legitimacy, I have examined, for the last 24 hours, all the eventualities that, without exception, would enable me to maintain it. I have made my resolutions. In the present circumstances, I shall not withdraw. I have a mandate from the people. I shall fulfill it. I shall not change the premier, whose worth, strength and ability deserve the tribute of all. He will propose to me the changes that will seem useful to him in the composition of the government.

I am dissolving the National Assembly today.

I have proposed to the country a referendum that gave the citizens the opportunity to prescribe a profound reform of our economy and our university system and at the same time to say whether or not they retained their confidence in me by the only path acceptable, that of democracy. I note that the present situation makes it materially impossible to proceed with this. That is why I shall postpone the date.

As for the legislative elections, they will take place within the time period provided by the constitution, unless some intend to muzzle the French people as a whole by preventing them from expressing themselves at the same time that they are being prevented from living, by the same means that the students are being prevented from studying, the teachers from teaching, the workers from working. These means are the intimidation, the intoxication and the tyranny exercised by groups organized long in advance for that purpose, and by a party that is a totalitarian enterprise, even if it already has rivals in this respect.

If this state of force continues, I shall have to take, in order to maintain the Republic and according to the constitution, other paths than the immediate polling of the country. In any case, everywhere and immediately civic action must be organized. This must be done to help the government first of all, then, locally, the prefects, who have become or become again commissioners of the Republic, in their task which consists of ensuring as much as possible the existence of the population and of preventing subversion at any time and in every place.

France is indeed threatened by dictatorship. Some want to force her to resign herself to a power that would impose itself in national despair, a power that would then obviously be mainly that of the conqueror, that is, of totalitarian communism. Naturally, to begin, it would be colored with a deceptive appearance, by using the ambition and the hatred of shelved politicians. After which, these people would carry no more than their own weight, which would not be great.

Well, no. The Republic will not abdicate. The people will collect themselves. Progress, independence and peace will prevail, along with liberty.

Long live the Republic!

Long live France!

Cabinet Revised. Premier Pompidou revised his cabinet May 31 amid signs of an emerging back-to-work trend among France's ten million striking workers and civil servants. The cabinet change appeared to most observers as a move by the Gaullist regime to remove men who had been compromised during the current disorders and to bring in new men who might enjoy the confidence of the striking workers and students during negotiations to end the country's paralysis.

Notable among the moves was the exchange of portfolios by Foreign Minister Couve de Murville and Finance Minister Michel Debre. Education Minister Alain Peyrefitte had resigned earlier after mounting student protests.

Composition of the third Pompidou government(former ministers in parentheses):

Premier—Georges Pompidou; *Foreign Affairs*—Michel Debre (Maurice Couve de Murville); *Finance*—Maurice Couve de Murville (Michel Debre); *Agriculture*—Edgar Faure; *Education*—Francois Ortoli (Alain Peyrefitte); *Justice*—Rene Capitant (Louis Joxe); *Social Affairs*—Maurice Schumann (Jean-Marcel Jeanneney); *Armed Forces*—Pierre Messmer; *Interior*—Raymond Marcellin (Christian Fouchet); *Cultural Affairs*—Andre Malraux; *Economic Planning*—Olivier Guichard (Raymond Marcellin); *Civil Service*—Robert Boulin (Edmond Michelet); *Housing*—Robert Galley (Francois Ortoli); *Industry*—Albin Chalandon (Olivier Guichard); *Transport*—Jean Chamant; *Posts & Telecommunications*—Andre Bettencourt (Yves Guena); *Information*—Yves Guena (Georges Gorse); *Youth & Sports*—Roland Nungesser (Francois Missoffe); *Exservicemen*—Henri Duvillard; *Overseas Territories*—Joel le Theule (Pierre Billotte); *Scientific Research*—Christian de la Malen (Maurice Schumann); *Ministers of State (without portfolio)*—Edmond Michelet, Henry Rey.

Return-to-Work Movement Gains. France's crippling labor strife appeared to be on the wane by May 31, when a general back-to-work movement picked up strength throughout the country. Observers agreed that the upheaval appeared to have reached its peak with President de Gaulle's radio address May 30 and the revision of the cabinet by Premier Georges Pompidou May 31.

Various union leaders and other political figures, who had earlier called for a provisional government, appeared to have accepted negotiations with both the management and the government as a means to end the prolonged general strike. But there were isolated areas where strikers held out pending favorable settlements.

By June 6, 1968, an appearance of normality returned to Paris for the first time in more than 20 days. Trains and Paris subways began running again. Although the schedule was sharply reduced, mail and phone services were resumed, and some banks reopened. The Paris stock exchange reopened June 7.

Work was resumed in most sectors of the economy, including the iron and steel industries of eastern France, the Lyons textile plants and the heavy industries around St.-Etienne, in central France, as well as those in and around Paris.

Services remaining under strike order were: most commercial air traffic; Parisian taxi drivers; merchant marine. About 60,000 high school teachers voted June 6 to remain on strike pending another round of negotiations with the government.

In the industrial sectors, resistance to ending the strike appeared to come from the major auto workers at all Peugeot, Citroen and Renault plants, the Michelin tire factory near Lyons and the Sud-Aviation aircraft factory in Nantes. Metal workers and laborers in the building trades remained on strike.

Election Campaign Begins. A three-week national election campaign was launched in France June 10. Opening the campaign for the government, Premier Pompidou June 12 appealed to the country to give the Gaullists a clear majority and thereby save France from Communist totalitarianism and subversion. He pleaded against the continuation of violence and warned that further disorders could destroy the country's political fabric.

Waldeck Rochet, secretary general of the Communist Party, June 12 rejected Pompidou's idea that the choice was between Gaullism and Communism. He charged the Gaullists with totalitarian tendencies and declared: "We love France, we stand for order, we represent political responsibility."

President de Gaulle had appealed to Frenchmen June 7 to "rally around their president so that the Republic may live and France may live." In a televised interview, de Gaulle promised France a new "society of participation" distinct from both capitalism and Communism. De Gaulle said that both were "bad solutions from the human point of view." De Gaulle said that he had been "tempted to resign" at the height of the current crisis, but he said he had remained in office to prevent a Communist takeover.

Workers Clash with Police. Violent clashes between workers and police took place June 7 in the nationalized Renault automobile assembly plant in Flins, 25 miles west of Paris. The fighting at the factory was the first violent confrontation between police and the striking workers since the nationwide factory sit-in movement had begun May 14.

The clashes in Flins began in the early morning of June 7, when about 4,000 workers, reinforced by some 200 militant students from Paris, assembled for a meeting in the town square a short distance away from the factory. The workers and the students then marched to the factory gates to demand the resumption of negotiations with the management and the removal of police from the plant. On June 6, the police had evicted the workers' pickets from the plant and had set up barricades at the factory gates.

The Communist-led General Confederation of Labor June 7 denounced the rioting and put the blame on "student agitators."

Student-Police Clashes. Scattered clashes flared between militant leftist students and police in the Latin Quarter of Paris June 10-11. The renewed street fighting grew out of a protest demonstration by students on the Left Bank of Paris June 10, following the death of a student demonstrator who had drowned in the Seine the same day. In the ensuing battle, students threw Molotov cocktails and debris on police from rooftops, erected new barricades and set cars on fire. As the police responded with massive salvos of tear-gas and concussion grenades, clouds of tear gas enveloped a 12-block area. Explosions rocked the Latin Quarter throughout the night and into the early morning of June 11, as the police, reinforced by gendarmes (military police), brought the fighting under control.

Violent street fighting broke out again in Paris June 11, following the fatal shooting of a young worker by police that day at the strikebound Peugeot automobile plant in Sochaux, near the Swiss border. In Paris, hundreds of barricades were erected and scattered rioting erupted and lasted until early June 12. Severe fighting between police and students occurred in the center of the city. Near the Notre Dame Cathedral, massive barricades made passage impossible. Two persons were wounded by rifle shots. Police made 1,500 arrests, and 93 persons were injured seriously enough to be hospitalized. Four police stations were attacked and 75 policemen were injured.

Workers throughout the country stopped work for an hour June 12 to protest the shooting at Sochaux. The work stoppages were called by the three major labor federations, which also demanded that police be removed from occupied factories.

Government Bans Student Groups. The Pompidou government June 12 banned all protest demonstrations in France during the election campaign and dissolved eleven extremist student organizations including the March 22 Movement led by Daniel Cohn-Bendit.

Police Retake Sorbonne. Paris police surrounded and cleared the Sorbonne of some 200 remaining students June 16. The students had held the buildings, the central campus of the University of Paris, since the beginning of the student strike movement.

De Gaulle Pardons Algerian Rightists. President de Gaulle June 15 pardoned former General Raoul Salan, serving a life sentence for his leadership of the "generals' revolt" in Algiers in April 1961 and of the underground Secret Army Organization (OAS). Thirteen other members of the OAS, who had fought against the granting of Algerian independence, were pardoned the same day. The pardoned men included six who had participated in attempts to assassinate de Gaulle in 1962 and 1964.

De Gaulle's move to free his former enemies was widely viewed as an attempt to win rightist support for the Gaullists in the parliamentary elections. On June 14, Colonel Charles Lacheroy, condemned to death for his role in the 1961 military uprising, had been allowed to return to France as a free man. He had fled to Spain and had been sentenced to death in absentia.

Ex-Premier Georges Bidault, at a Paris press conference June 9, had urged Frenchmen to vote against both the Communists and the supporters of President de Gaulle. Bidault's reappearance on the French political scene marked the end of his six years of self-imposed exile to Brazil and Belgium, where he had fled to avoid prosecution for alleged participation in the OAS.

Gaullist Sweep in Elections. Candidates supporting the de Gaulle regime won a landslide victory in a two-round general election for the National Assembly June 23 and 30. This was the first time in French republican history that any party had won an absolute majority of the Assembly seats. The opposition was reduced to little more than half the seats it had held in the outgoing Assembly.

Gaullists won 358 of 487 seats; the combined opposition won 128. (One seat remained to be filled after elections in July.)

The elections were held in two successive stages. In districts where no candidate won a majority of the total vote in the first round June 23, a second balloting was held June 30, and the candidate polling a simple plurality of the June 30 votes was declared the winner.

Responding to Gaullist campaign attacks on the recent nationwide disorders and the alleged threat of Communist totalitarianism, the voters dealt a massive blow to the opposition leftist parties. French Communist Party (PCF) representation was reduced from 73 to 34, a loss of 39, despite repeated PCF attempts during the campaign to repudiate responsibility for the crippling labor and student strife in May and despite the PCF position during the campaign of standing for order and discipline. The other big loser was the non-Communist Federation of the Democratic & Socialist Left, headed by Francois Mitterrand, which won 57 seats, a loss of 61. The Unified Socialist Party (PSU) lost all three seats it had held in the previous Assembly and was without representation. Its leader, ex-Premier Mendes-France, was defeated by a bare 132 votes in Grenoble by Gaullist ex-Welfare Minister Jean-Marcel Jeanneney. Democratic Moderate Center Party (PDM) representation was reduced from 39 seats to 29, one seat short of the minimum (30 seats) required to constitute a separate political group in the parliament.

The leftist parties suffered their losses despite an election strategy in which the weaker of the leftist candidates, where more than one remained in the race, withdrew in the second round in favor of the stronger. This strategy had been employed successfully in two previous elections, but in the current election, the single Federation-PCF slate sustained decisive defeats in both rounds.

The Gaullist candidates were grouped in two parties: The Union for the Defense of the Republic (UDR); and the Independent Republicans (IR), led by ex-Finance Minister Valery Giscard d'Estaing. The official Gaullist candidates (UDR) won 297 seats, a gain of 97; the IR won 61 seats, a gain of 18.

One hundred and sixty-six candidates, 152 of them Gaullists, were elected in the first-round balloting June 23. The Gaullist candidates, including the allied IR candidates, polled 10,581,144 (47.79%) of the 22,539,743 votes cast in the first round, a record plurality for any single political group. The PCF won 4,435,357 (20.03%), the Federation 3,654,003 (16.5%), the PDM 2,290,161 (10.34%).

The landslide trend to the Gaullist cause was continued during the second-round balloting June 30 in the 316 districts where no candidate had received a majority June 23.

Results of the second-round balloting in metropolitan France: Registered voters, 19,266,974. Valid ballots cast, 14,577,412. Abstentions, 22.7%. Party vote: UDR, 6,762,170 (46.39%). Communists, 2,935,775 (20.14%). Federation, 3,097,338 (21.25%). PDM (Centrists), 1,141,305 (7.83%). Splinter rightists, 496,463 (3.4%). Splinter leftists, 60,584 (.42%). PSU, 83,777 (.57%).

Representation of each party in the National Assembly as allotted by the Interior Ministry: UDR, 297 seats; IR, 61 (including three supported by the UDR); PCF, 34; Federation, 57; extreme left, 1; diverse left, 2; PDM (Centrists), 29; diverse right, 12.

De Gaulle went on the government's radio and TV network twice June 29 to plead with the voters "to give us an Assembly capable of backing the necessary policy with a strong, constant and coherent majority." He promised that in a "renewed France" the guiding principle would be "participation," which he defined as a system in which all workers in business or students at universities would be "associated directly with its [the business' or university's] functioning, with the results it achieves and with the contribution it makes to the nation."

Action to Curb Crisis Impact. The French government imposed a series of emergency trade and monetary controls to offset the threat of economic slowdown and to prevent the weakening of the franc in the wake of the strikes and social disorders. The impact of the strikes and the subsequent wage increases forced the government to dip into its gold and foreign exchange reserves.

Among the government's actions and related developments:

Monetary controls—The government May 31 imposed temporary but stiff control on the outflow of privately owned francs. The decree halted trading in francs in European currency exchanges but did not affect payments resulting from normal business transactions. The decree required government approval for most international transactions and payments involving gold, currency and securities. The Bank of France announced the same day that French tourists would be allowed to take only 1,000 francs ($200) per person out of the country for each journey. (Prior to the controls decree, the Bank of France had asked the Bank for International Settlements in Basel May 28 to buy, with French-owned dollars, French francs on the international currency markets to support the price of the franc.)

Bank rates up—The government announced July 3 that it had raised the basic interest rate from 3-1/2% to 5% in an effort to curb inflationary pressures on the franc and to help reverse the outflow of money. The announcement was made after the first cabinet meeting following the decisive Gaullist victory at the polls June 23 and 30. The government also: (a) increased the interest rates for loans on stocks from 5% to 6-1/2%,

(b) decided to raise $500 million in taxes and (c) approved a $1-1/2 billion supplementary budget for the current year. Reporting to the cabinet, Finance Minister Couve de Murville said that the $1-1/2 billion supplementary budget had been made necessary by the large-scale wage increases, benefits and strike indemnities resulting from the strike settlements and that the budget increase would raise the year's deficit from the envisaged $1-1/2 billion to $2 billion.

Reserves down— The Finance Ministry disclosed June 4 that France's gold and foreign exchange reserves had dropped by $306.6 million during May to a total of $5,720,500,000. A further decline of $203.6 million was reported July 5, which brought reserves down to a total of $5.52 billion. The latter figure included $885 million drawn from the International Monetary Fund by June 17 to supplement France's gold and foreign exchange reserves. The IMF drawings were the first by France in a decade and exhausted France's automatic drawing rights in the fund.

Financial sources in Washington, Paris and other capitals reported in late June and in July that France had sold $75-$100 million worth of gold to the United States and several hundred million dollars' worth to the central banks of other countries in June and early July in exchange for dollars and other foreign currencies.

Trade curbs— Foreign Minister Debre announced June 14 that France was asking its European Economic Community partners for special temporary exemption from earlier commitments to end all industrial trade barriers among member states July 1. Among the products included in the exemption were appliances and automobiles.

The government June 26: (a) limited imports of automobiles, trucks, textiles, appliances and steel to no more than 7%-15% above 1967's imports, (b) reduced interest rates on government loans to exporters from 3% to 2% and (c) promised to subsidize exports not covered by the existing "economic insurance risk" program. The subsidy, designed to offset unforeseeable rises in the cost of production, was based on wages; it would amount to 6% in the period July-October 1968 and 3% in November 1968-January 1969.

(The government also indicated that it would take "necessary measures" against price increases beyond 3% in domestic markets. But it apparently did not intend to inhibit export price changes. Renault, Peugeot and Citroen, France's three major auto manufacturers, announced July 25 that they would raise the prices of their products by 3%.)

Couve de Murville Premier. President de Gaulle July 10 appointed Maurice Couve de Murville to replace Georges Pompidou as premier of France. Two days later, Couve de Murville announced the formation of his cabinet, which consisted largely of members of Pompidou's cabinet.

The dropping of Pompidou so soon after the spectacular Gaullist victory at the polls, for which Pompidou had been popularly assumed to deserve a large share of the credit, caused widespread bitterness in Gaullist circles and sparked speculation as to its motive. Generally two theories were advanced to explain it: (1) Pompidou had been long regarded as an heir apparent to de Gaulle; some observers believed that Pompidou's removal from the premiership was a prelude to his eventual elevation to the presidency when de Gaulle's term expired in 1972. (2) According to other observers, Pompidou had been dismissed because of policy disagreements between him and de Gaulle; as the chief architect of the landslide Gaullist victory, Pompidou had become a powerful political figure in his own right with considerable following.

Pompidou submitted his resignation to de Gaulle July 10, as required by Article 8 of the constitution. In his letter of reply of the same day, de Gaulle praised Pompidou for his success in handling "the grave crisis which the country traversed last May and June." A phrase in which de Gaulle held out the prospect of future mission for Pompidou was regarded as significant. De Gaulle said in the letter: "Wherever you will be, be assured, my dear friend, that I will be anxious to keep particularly close relations with you. Finally, I wish that you keep yourself ready to accomplish any mission and assume any mandate that the nation may one day bestow upon you." After declining an offer to become president and whip of the Gaullist group in the National Assembly, Pompidou was unanimously elected July 10 to honorary presidency of the group. His only other post was that of Assembly deputy.

Among key cabinet members, Michel Debre was kept as foreign minister, Andre Malraux as cultural affairs minister, Pierre Messmer as armed forces minister and Raymond Marcellin as interior minister.

Among appointments causing the most surprise were the shifting of Francois-Xavier Ortoli, a friend of Pompidou's and education minister in the previous cabinet, to the finance ministry, and the naming of ex-Premier Edgar Faure to be the education minister. Both portfolios were regarded as crucial in the coming months as attempts were made to solve pressing problems emphasized by the May-June crisis.

Composition of the Couve de Murville government:

> *Premier*—Maurice Couve de Murville.
> *Ministers of State: Cultural Affairs*—Andre Malraux; *Social Affairs*—Maurice Schumann; *Relations with Parliament*—Roger Frey; *Minister of State*—Jean-Marcel Jeanneney.

> *Ministers: Justice*—Rene Capitant; *Foreign Affairs*—Michel Debre; *Interior*—Raymond Marcellin; *Armed Forces*—Pierre Messmer; *Finance*—Francois-Xavier Ortoli; *Education*—Edgar Faure; *Equipment*—Albin Chalandon; *Industry*—Andre Bettencourt; *Agriculture*—Robert Boulin; *Transport*—Jean Chamant; *Veterans Affairs*—Henri Duvillard; *Posts & Telecommunications*—Yves Guena; *Scientific & Atomic Affairs*—Robert Galley; *Town & Country Planning*—Olivier Guichard.

> *Secretaries of State responsible to the premier: Information*—Joel le Theule; *Civil Service*—Philippe Malaud; *Youth & Sports*—Joseph Comiti; *Overseas Territories*—Nicolas Inchauspe; *Social Affairs*—Marie Madeleine Dienesch and Pierre Dumas; *Foreign Affairs*—Yvon Bourges and Jean de Lipkowski; *Interior*—Andre Bord; *Economy & Finance*—Jacques Chirac; *Education*—Jacques Trorial; *Industrial Equipment & Housing*—Philippe Dechartre.

(Jacques Chaban-Delmas was re-elected National Assembly president July 11 on the opening of the new Assembly session.)

ATTEMPTS AT REFORM

Radio-TV System Revamped. The French cabinet July 31 announced the reorganization of the French radio and TV system, ORTF, a government monopoly. One hundred and two newsmen were dismissed or transferred, and the only unrestricted news program was canceled. ORTF newsmen had gone on strike in May in protest against censorship and biased coverage of the student riots. The newsmen had demanded a revision of the 1964 radio-and-TV law and greater autonomy and freedom of reporting.

1969 Budget Cuts Back A-Force. The French cabinet September 4 approved the 1969 budget, which scheduled expenditures at 150 billion francs ($30.6 billion) and foresaw a $2.3 billion deficit. The budget provided for cutbacks in military spending (including expenditures for the French nuclear strike force) and in overseas aid; an increase in luxury taxes; a 10% tax credit on the price of all equipment bought before Jan. 1, 1970; a more progressive income tax schedule (a 15% increase on higher incomes and a 15% decrease on lower incomes).

Exchange Control Ended. The French government ended currency exchange controls September 4. The controls, instituted May 31 to halt a run on French monetary reserves, did not prevent French reserves from dropping by 1/4 — to $4.5 billion August 30.

De Gaulle Calls for Senate Reform. President de Gaulle September 9, at his first press conference since Nov. 27, 1967, announced a referendum would be held on a proposal to strip the French Senate of its powers and transform it into an advisory council for social and economic problems. "The Senate," he declared, "no longer has to play, as in the past, the role of counterbalance to the Chamber of Deputies for, since 1958, the chief of state himself has had the responsibility and the means of preventing excesses and of maintaining the balance...."

Referring to the student-worker unrest in May and June, de Gaulle said that reform was necessary. He again called for reorganization of the universities and the economy to allow students and workers opportunities to "participate" in decisions affecting their interests.

De Gaulle warned that the government would suppress all internal "threats and violence" and would no longer tolerate the occupation of public installations by students or workers.

Referring to his dismissal in July of Premier Pompidou, he said that Pompidou might be called upon to serve France at a later date. This was interpreted as an indication that de Gaulle considered Pompidou as his eventual successor as President.

Poher Elected Senate President. The Senate October 3 elected Alain Poher, a Center Democrat and conservative anti-Gaullist, as the new Senate president. Poher, former leader of the European Parliament, replaced Gaston Monnerville, a Radical Socialist and anti-Gaullist liberal.

In Senate elections held September 22 little change occurred in the composition of the Senate.

Educational Reform Voted. The French National Assembly October 11 passed a controversial educational reform bill by a 441-0 vote, with 39 abstentions (33 Communist and 6 Gaullists). The bill, drafted by Educational Minister Edgar Faure and backed by President de Gaulle, had been adopted by the cabinet September 19.

The reform bill was designed to overhaul and decentralize the national educational system, unchanged since its creation by Napoleon in 1808. The measure was also considered the government's answer to the massive student disturbances that had paralyzed the country during May and June. Faure told the Assembly October 11 that "if we refuse this liberty we will have revolution. Your only chance to contain the students is to grant this liberty."

Under the bill, to become effective Feb. 15, 1969, power that had been invested in the Education Ministry would be transferred to individual universities. Each autonomous university would elect its own council from among faculty and students; the faculty would provide at least 50% of each council's members. Each council would have the power to (a) fill the newly created post of university president, (b) control the budget and seek endowments from other than government sources, (c) propose measures dealing with curriculum, examinations, administration, and teaching methods, and (d) maintain discipline. The role of the rector, who was appointed by the Education Minister, would be reduced to that of a chancellor, who would maintain liaison with the government. The bill would give students the right to hold political meetings in specially designated university halls.

Under the bill, French universities would offer for the first time, on an experimental basis, courses in night schools and thus permit full-time workers to obtain university degrees.

Before its approval in the Assembly, the bill had been opposed bitterly by a powerful conservative faction within the Gaullist party and the cabinet. Criticism of the bill centered especially on the provision permitting political activity on campuses.

After some hesitation, the French National Students' Union, the largest French student organization, declared October 18 that it opposed the reform. Jacques Sauvageot, vice president of the union, urged students at a rally of about 1,000 students in Paris October 16 to boycott elections to the new governing councils. By participating in the councils, he warned, students would back "the reactionary policies of the teaching body." "It is not our task to improve the universities," he said. "It is to make the students politically conscious." "We have to create within the universities a number of bastions and a number of breaking-down points. The universities must become the focal point of the struggle of students in cooperation with the workers," he declared.

Soustelle Returns. Jacques Soustelle returned to France from Switzerland October 24 after living in exile since August 1961. The French National Assembly July 23 had voted a general amnesty to all convicted persons or fugitives involved in the 1954-62 Algerian uprising. Soustelle, former governor-general of Algeria, had opposed de Gaulle's Algerian independence policy and was charged Sept. 23, 1962 with leadership of the outlawed National Resistance Council.

Bank Rate Raised. The Finance Ministry November 12 raised the Bank of France lending rate from 5% to 6% (the rate had been raised from 3-1/2% to 5% July 3). Reserve requirements were tightened from 4-1/2% to 5-1/2% on demand deposits and from 2% to 2-1/2% on other deposits.

Austerity Policy Spurs Dissent. The Gaullist government's decision to introduce a strict program of austerity to defend the franc, approved November 27 by the National Assembly, was greeted with immediate opposition from worker and student elements. The Communist-led Confederation Generale de Travail (CGT), France's most powerful labor organization, declared November 27 that the new policies (which called for increased taxes on many consumer goods) were a "heavy threat to the living conditions of wage-earners."

Workers at five Renault automobile factories staged a token one-half day strike December 5. The protest, the first major strike since the May-June French labor upheaval, was supported by all three of France's major union federations — the CGT, the Socialist Force Ouvriere (FO) and the Catholic Confederation Democratique et Francaise du Travail (CDFT). Students also joined the protest in some areas, though the workers prevented them from entering the Renault plants; union leaders were careful to keep the strike an orderly protest over economic issues and not a political demonstration. The strike was called to protest a reduction in Christmas bonuses and a statement by management that the 1969 wage increase would be small.

The strike took place the same day that the National Assembly passed a law giving legal recognition to labor unions in all enterprises of more than 50 employees. The law also included the right of union representation and collection of dues.

Georges Seguy, secretary general of the CGT, and Jacques Sauvageot, head of the French National Student Union, met in Paris December 4; it was the first time the two conflicting groups had met since the May social unrest started by the students and then joined by the workers. According to CGT leaders, the students were told that the unions would work with them only if they gave up their attempts to become a mass political movement.

Student Unrest. A new outbreak of protests and strikes by French university and high school students prompted the issuance December 14 of a government decree threatening the expulsion of student agitators.

The decree restored disciplinary jurisdiction to university rectors, empowering them to transfer or dismiss rebellious students at schools closed by strikes. The powers were to remain in force until the formation of faculty-student disciplinary councils provided for under the university reform act, to become effective Feb. 15, 1969.

Students clashed with police and staged school boycotts and demonstrations December 13 in Marseilles, Lyons, Bordeaux, Nantes and Clermont-Ferrand. The most serious trouble centered at the suburban Nanterre campus of the University of Paris, the focal point of the May student rebellion. The university was closed by a student-faculty strike to protest the arrest of one student and the detention for questioning of eight others suspected of participating in a series of bombings in Paris December 8.

Education Minister Edgar Faure December 18 ordered the withdrawal of police cordons surrounding the university. At the same time he announced that students involved in the Paris strikes would lose their scholarships and military deferments.

CHAPTER XVII

FRANCE AND WESTERN DEFENSE

FRENCH POLICY AND NATO

France to Pay Relocation Costs. It was reported March 7, 1968 that France had agreed to pay NATO $17-1/2 million for the building in Paris that had housed the North Atlantic Council. The Council had been moved to Evere, Belgium in October 1967 at a cost of $14 million.

France to Maintain NATO Ties. West German Chancellor Kurt Georg Kiesinger said in an interview published in the *New York Times* May 19 that President de Gaulle had assured him that France would not denounce the NATO treaty in 1969 unless something unforeseen were to develop. Kiesinger said de Gaulle had given him this assurance "quite explicitly and decisively" during talks they had held in Paris February 15-16.

A-Force Delayed. French Foreign Minister Debre announced June 14 that the development of the French nuclear armed force, the "force de frappe," would undergo a one-to-two-year delay as a consequence of economic problems resulting from the month-long national strike. Debre said "certain financial difficulties" would "naturally hamper the buildup of France's nuclear striking force," and "certain goals we were scheduled to reach in a year or two will be reached one or two years later."

Missiles Tested. The French Armed Forces Ministry announced July 4 the successful testing in France of two new long-range ballistic missiles. The first missile, a sea-to-ground, 2-stage, remote-controlled rocket with a 1,550-mile range, was launched July 2 in the Landes area. The 2d, fired July 3 from an underground silo, was a 2-stage, ground-to-ground weapon with a 1,864-mile range.

De Gaulle in Turkey. Making the first visit by a French chief of state to Turkey, President de Gaulle conferred with Turkish leaders in Ankara Oct. 25-29, 1968. Industrial, technical and cultural topics were discussed, but the only concrete result was an accord for technical cooperation signed October 29.

In his opening address October 25, de Gaulle warned Turkish leaders against the growing "hegemonies" (the United States and the Soviet Union) that were dividing Europe. In an oblique suggestion that Turkey reduce its military participation in NATO (which de Gaulle hinted was a dilution of Turkish sovereignty), de Gaulle urged Turks to "maintain their integrity and independence, to let no one dispose of their soil, their airspace, their coasts and their forces." Turkish President Cevdet Sunay disagreed with de Gaulle's view. Sunay held that the Soviet invasion of

Czechoslovakia in August and the Soviet fleet buildup in the Mediterranean had increased NATO's importance.

French Test Sub Missile. The French Armed Forces Ministry announced November 18 that a 2-stage strategic ballistic missile had been fired successfully from the submerged submarine Gymnote off the southwest coast of France November 16. The range of the missile was estimated at about 1,100 miles.

Anglo-French Missile Plan. British Defense Minister Denis Healey and French Defense Minister Pierre Messmer, meeting in Paris to review joint Anglo-French defense projects, agreed December 6 on the joint production of a new missile. The Martel air-to-ground missile, designed for long distances, was to be built by French and British firms.

A-Force Program Delayed. The Paris newspaper *Le Monde* reported Jan. 4, 1969 that influential French army officers had recommended that the United States be asked to help in developing France's atomic weapons. France's nuclear weapons system had been delayed; Mirage IV bombers armed with atomic bombs were to have been ready in 1966, but actual delivery of the planes and bombs was not made until May 1968. Informed sources also said that testing of intermediate-range nuclear missiles, scheduled for 1968, had just begun. Under France's recent austerity program, the 1969 nuclear testing program had been cancelled.

U.S. Bills France for Bases. According to U.S. sources in Paris, Washington had asked Paris to pay for the U.S. installations in France vacated after NATO troops and commands were expelled by the government of President de Gaulle. The *New York Times*, reporting January 7, said that the amount claimed was expected to amount to over $300 million.

To date, the French had paid for the former NATO Council headquarters in Paris ($17.5 million), and for some movable U.S. property ($51.5 million). The new claim involved two naval depots, nine airfields, warehouses, communications centers, offices, post exchanges, schools, railway sidings and commissaries.

Nixon Visit Improves U.S. Relations. U.S. President Richard Nixon made an eight-day trip to five European nations Feb. 23-March 2, 1969. He conferred with West European leaders in Brussels, London, Bonn, West Berlin, Rome, Paris and the Vatican, as well as with NATO officials and with the U.S. negotiating team at the Vietnam peace talks in Paris.

Arriving at Orly Airport February 28 for a three-day visit to Paris, Nixon hailed France as "America's oldest ally and America's oldest friend." General de Gaulle, welcoming Nixon at the airport, described his visit as a "joy" and an "honor."

De Gaulle and Nixon conferred over two hours February 28 at the Elysee Palace. They held a second round of talks March 1. Ronald Ziegler, Nixon's press secretary, said that "the President feels that the unprecedented amount of time devoted to the talks provided an opportunity for a full exchange of views and for significant progress toward developing a cooperative approach to some of the issues involved."

Following a final discussion at the Elysee Palace, de Gaulle broke traditional protocol and accompanied Nixon to the airport and to the steps of the plane. The general told Nixon: "We are enchanted with your visit. It is a success." Nixon announced that de Gaulle had accepted his invitation to visit Washington in 1970.

De Gaulle at Eisenhower Rites. President de Gaulle March 30-31, 1969 attended funeral ceremonies in Washington honoring former U.S. President and World War II hero Dwight D. Eisenhower, who died March 28. De Gaulle March 28 declared: "I see disappear with much sadness a dear companion in arms and a friend... for whom I had a deep affection."

France Reaffirms NATO Tie. In an address to the National Press Club in Washington April 9, French Foreign Minister Debre affirmed France's loyalty to NATO. (Debre was in Washington for ceremonies commemorating NATO's 20th anniversary.) He said: "We exclude integration, and this refusal is decisive... France intends to keep command of her defense, as she intends to keep control of her policy. This is a fundamental requirement." But he declared that his presence in Washington indicated France's belief that NATO had not lost its meaning. Debre also stressed that France's differences with the United States over the future of Western Europe did not exclude cooperation on other issues. "The new climate of trust that has been established in French-American relations comes from a more accurate evaluation of the European goals of French policy, which President Nixon has analyzed perfectly," he declared.

DISARMAMENT AND NUCLEAR TESTING

France vs. Non-Proliferation Pact. The United States and the Soviet Union Jan. 18, 1968 submitted a revised and complete draft treaty to prevent the further spread of nuclear weapons to the UN's Eighteen-Nation Disarmament Committee (ENDC) in Geneva (which France continued to boycott).

French Armed Forces Minister Pierre Messmer denounced the treaty January 22 as "dangerous and doomed to failure." He charged that, if adopted, it would "lead to tensions and create new, dangerous situations."

France Abstains in UN Vote on A-Pact. The UN General Assembly June 12, 1968 adopted a resolution recommending the draft nuclear nonproliferation treaty submitted to it March 15 by ENDC. The vote was 95-4. France was among the 21 nations which abstained.

Explaining France's abstention, French Ambassador-to-the-UN Armand Berard said June 12 that disarmament could not be made effective in the absence of a "true detente" between East and West. However, he said that France would abide by the treaty's major provision, which barred the nuclear-weapon states from providing such arms or the means of manufacturing them to the non-nuclear-weapon states.

France Resumes A-Tests. France resumed its nuclear testing program July 7 with the explosion in the atmosphere of a conventional atomic device of "moderate strength." The warhead was detonated from a balloon about 1/3 mile above the French Pacific testing ground at Mururoa Atoll, approximately 750 miles southeast of Tahiti. The nuclear test, France's first since July 2, 1967, raised to 13 the number of French atmospheric detonations.

The test began the third series of French atomic tests in the Pacific and was believed to be a prelude to France's first attempt at a hydrogen-bomb explosion. The second test in the series was conducted July 15 at Mururoa Atoll, and a third test was held August 3.

France Tests H-Bombs. France exploded its first thermonuclear hydrogen bomb August 24 and became the world's fifth thermonuclear nation. (The other four: the United States, USSR, Britain and Communist China.) The device was suspended from a balloon 1/3 mile over the Mururoa Atoll test site in the Pacific Ocean.

Research Minister Robert Galley said in a news conference in Paris August 27 that the thermonuclear blast had released energy equal to that produced by the explosion of two million tons of TNT (or about 100 bombs of the kind dropped on Hiroshima).

France conducted its 2d hydrogen-bomb test Sept. 8, 1968 at the Mururoa Atoll. There were no details about the strength of the detonation. France September 9 announced the end of the 2-month test series, which included three atomic and two thermonuclear explosions.

EAST-WEST RELATIONS

France, United States, Britain to End Occupation Rights in West Germany. France, Britain, and the United States informed West Germany of their readiness to relinquish their remaining World War II occupation rights and restore full sovereignty to Bonn. In a note delivered Dec. 13, 1967 and made public Jan. 18, 1968, the Western powers said that the restoration of full sovereignty would be made after the parliament had passed "emergency laws" that would provide, among other things, for the use of the army as police in an emergency. The Bonn parliament adopted the "emergency laws" May 30 (Bundestag) and June 14 (Bundesrat).

Hungarian Leaders Visit France. Prime Minister Jeno Fock and Foreign Minister Janos Peter conferred with French leaders March 25-30 in Paris. Fock, the first Hungarian prime minister to visit France since World War II, described the talks as a "turning point" in Franco-Hungarian relations. President de Gaulle announced March 30 that he would visit Hungary in "the foreseeable future."

The two countries agreed to establish a joint commission to promote scientific, industrial and technical cooperation. Fock further proposed French investment in the Hungarian aluminum and petroleum industries. French leaders agreed to talks on the manufacture of computers and to discuss ways of changing the pattern of mutual trade. (In 1964-67 Hungary's trade deficit with France had amounted to $80 million.)

West Warns Soviets on Berlin Access. Britain, France and the United States March 13 reminded the Soviet Union of its responsibility to ensure free access to West Berlin. The warning was in response to an East German government decree March 11 which had barred members of the extreme right-wing National Democratic Party from using West Berlin's access routes.

The three Western powers again protested April 19 following an East German announcement that top West German officials would be barred from traveling to West Berlin via land routes across East Germany.

East Germany April 26 barred West Berlin Mayor Schutz from traveling to Bonn in his capacity as Bundesrat president. Two days later, on April 28, the three Western powers filed a note with the Soviet Union protesting the April 26 incident.

De Gaulle in Rumania. President de Gaulle May 14-18, 1968 made a state visit to Rumania. During his stay he conferred with Rumanian Communist Party General Secretary Nicolae Ceausescu and toured a number of Rumanian cities where French-built industries were located.

Throughout his stay, de Gaulle emphasized the themes of national independence and noninterference in the affairs of other states and stressed the necessity to promote a European detente. Addressing the Rumanian Grand National Assembly May 15, de Gaulle declared: "Each nation should speak with its own voice, act only for its own account.... Rumania has chosen this path and so has France." Foreign Minister Couve de Murville, who accompanied de Gaulle, said May 18 in a Radio Bucharest interview: "We seek ... to establish the best possible relations ... with the other countries of what is called Eastern Europe ... what this involves, in brief, ... is to put an end to the cold war, to put an end to the division of the continent, and to put an end to what is generally called bloc policy."

A final communique of the de Gaulle-Ceausescu talks said that both sides would promote increased trade, scientific and cultural exchanges. A mixed Franco-Rumanian commission was established to promote economic cooperation. Regarding Europe, the two sides noted with satisfaction the progress achieved toward establishing a "normal situation" on the continent, "namely the road of detente and cooperation." The problem was to open the way for cooperation in all of Europe. This would create, little by little, conditions which would allow discussion of the great problems "upon whose settlement depends the establishment of a lasting peace based on independence and territorial integrity of the states in Europe."

France Joins Western Protest Vs. East German Travel Restrictions. East Germany June 11 announced a number of regulations governing travel by West German citizens between West Germany and West Berlin. The new regulations required every West German traveling to or from West Berlin to obtain a round-trip transit visa at a cost of $2.50. Previously, West German travelers had been required only to show their identity cards. In addition, the tax on travel and shipping between West Germany and West Berlin was increased.

The United States, Britain and France issued a joint statement June 12 denouncing the travel restrictions and declaring them invalid. The statement said that the three governments were in consultation with the West German government on how best to deal with the situation and would communicate with the Soviet government, which shared with them the responsibility for unhindered Berlin access.

France Supports NATO Action on Berlin. In the first substantive Western counteraction to East Germany's restrictions on access to West Berlin, the NATO Permanent Council in Brussels June 20 approved rules barring travel to NATO countries by East German political figures, journalists and parliamentary delegations. Other East Germans would be required to pay a $5 fee to visit the West. The fee would be waived in the case of elderly people who wished to visit friends or relatives in the West. The Permanent Council approved the restrictive rules on recommendation of the United States, Britain, France and West Germany.

France Vs. NATO Action on Soviet Naval Threat. The North Atlantic Council, holding its regularly-scheduled semiannual meeting at the ministerial level in Reykjavik, Iceland June 24-25, directed NATO's Permanent Council to seek ways of protecting the alliance's southern flank. The NATO action was in response to the USSR's deployment of some 40 naval vessels in the Mediterranean.

The move was not supported by France, which had dissociated itself in 1966 from the alliance's military aspects.

France joined with the other NATO members in an appeal, made in a communique issued June 25, to the USSR and its Eastern European allies for a "mutual and balanced" reduction of forces to promote East-West detente in Europe. The communique described East German restrictions on access to Berlin as "a deliberate attempt to jeopardize detente, from which West Berlin and its inhabitants must not be excluded."

De Gaulle Denounces Czechoslovak Invasion. De Gaulle Aug. 21, 1968 scored the Soviet-led Warsaw Pact invasion of Czechoslovakia as "an attack on the rights and destiny of a friendly nation." De Gaulle said the action was a continuation of the "policy of blocs, which was imposed on Europe by the effects" of the 1945 Yalta Conference, at which the United States, Britain and the Soviet Union had agreed on the division of responsibilities in post-war Europe.

France August 23 joined six other UN members in sponsoring a Security Council resolution condemning the Soviet Union and its four Warsaw Pact allies for invading Czechoslovakia. The resolution received a 10-2 vote (three abstentions) but was defeated by the USSR's veto.

The resolution called on the USSR and its allies to "withdraw their forces" and to "cease all other forms of intervention in Czechoslovakia's internal affairs."

French Foreign Minister Debre met with Soviet Ambassador-to-France Valerian A. Zorin September 2 to demand that the Soviet Union immediately withdraw its forces from Czechoslovakia. Following a meeting September 7 with West German Foreign Minister Willy Brandt, Debre said: "The chances of a return to normality in Europe are directly linked to a detente and it is up to the Soviet Union to show by her decisions that she has not renounced such a detente."

French Communists' Rift on Czechoslovakia. Following the Soviet-led invasion of Czechoslovakia the French Communist Party Politburo August 21 issued a statement voicing "surprise and reprobation" and disclosed that its leaders had cautioned Moscow against the use of military force. This condemnation was considered the PCF's first public disagreement with Moscow and it produced dissension within the party. It should be noted, however, that the French CP—unlike the other large Western Communist Party, the Italian CP—did not call for the withdrawal of Warsaw Pact troops from Czechoslovakia. The French CP Politburo September 3 approved the Soviet-Czechoslovak August 27 Moscow agreement providing for the "temporary" stationing of Soviet troops in Czechoslovakia. (At a Central Committee meeting in Paris October 20-21, Jeannette Thorez-Vermeersch, widow of ex-PCF leader Maurice Thorez, and leader of the PCF's pro-Moscow wing, resigned from the Politburo and Central Committee in protest over the August 21 condemnation.)

West Warns USSR on Use of Force. Soviet threats to use military force against West Germany evoked warnings by the United States, Britain and France September 17 that any such action would result in an "immediate allied response" under the North Atlantic Treaty.

The Western reaction, contained in separate statements, was designed to relieve West German fears arising from a Soviet note to Bonn July 5 warning of the USSR's right under the UN Charter to intervene unilaterally, if necessary with force, in West Germany "against renewal of aggressive policy by a former enemy state" of World War II.

De Gaulle to Continue to Seek Detente with USSR. President de Gaulle September 9, speaking at his presidential press conference, condemned the Soviet occupation of Czechoslovakia, but said that it would not deter his efforts to continue to seek a political detente with the USSR.

Among de Gaulle's remarks:

> The division into two blocs . . . is a misfortune for it [*Czechoslovakia*] which follows other misfortunes. Indeed, that division constitutes, for the people of our continent, a permanent encroachment on their right to independence. . . . Moreover, to distribute the nations of Europe into two camps, dominated by two rivals, is to prevent them from normally establishing between them the economic, cultural and human relations that are consistent with their nature and tendencies. . . . Finally, the political and military tension maintained between them constantly puts peace in question. . . . France has condemned that situation since its origin . . .

> Since 1958 we French have not stopped working to end the system of the 2 blocs. Thus, while maintaining close relations with the countries of Western Europe . . . . we have gradually detached ourselves from the military organization of NATO which subordinates the Europeans to the Americans. Thus, while participating in the Common Market, we have never agreed to the so-called "supranational" system for the 6 which would engulf France in a stateless entity. . . .

> At the same time, while we were making the advent of a Communist regime at home impossible, we have renewed with the countries of the East, and first with Russia, growing practical relations. . . .

> . . . the events of which Czechoslovakia has just been the scene and the victim within the Communist bloc are to be condemned, notably because they are absurd when viewed in the perspective of European detente. We had considered as a sign of an evolution favorable to the whole of Europe, the fact that [*Czechoslovakia*] . . . who, in 1948 . . . found itself incorporated in the Soviet bloc by a Communist *coup de force*—was showing its intention of recovering possession of itself to some degree and of opening itself a little toward the West. On the contrary, the return to submission demanded and obtained of the Prague leaders through armed intervention under cover of what those concerned call "socialist solidarity"—which is nothing but the expression of Soviet hegemony—reveals to us the persistence of the Eastern

bloc and consequently of the Western bloc in what is furthest
removed from what Europe deserves. . . .

It is, indeed, too late for foreign domination to win the support of nations anywhere, even when it has conquered their territory. As for converting them, it is too late for any ideology,
notably Communism, to prevail over national sentiment . . .
it is too late to succeed in dividing Europe forever into two
opposed blocs. . . . France, . . . come what may, will continue to
work everywhere, . . . for *detente, entente* and cooperation, in other
words for peace.

France in NATO Warning to USSR.

A three-day meeting of the
NATO Council of Ministers was concluded in Brussels Nov. 16, 1968 with
a sharply worded communique warning against further direct or indirect
Soviet interference in Europe and the Mediterranean area. The ministerial
meeting, usually held in mid-December, had been moved forward as a result of the Soviet occupation of Czechoslovakia. Although the wording of
the final communique reportedly was softened at the insistence of the
French, Danish and Canadian ministers, the text clearly reflected
heightened Western solidarity and was signed by France.

The communique's major points:

New Soviet move would bring crisis: Clearly any Soviet intervention directly or indirectly affecting the situation in Europe or in the
Mediterranean would create an international crisis with grave
consequences.

Like all other peoples, the people of Czechoslovakia must be
free to shape their future without outside interference. Agreements concluded under the pressure of occupying forces can
provide no justification for challenging this basic concept.

The contention of the Soviet leadership that there exists a
right of intervention in the affairs of other states deemed to be
within a so-called "socialist commonwealth" runs counter to the
basic principles of the United Nations Charter, is dangerous to
European security and has inevitably aroused grave anxieties.

East-West detente threatened: The Soviet intervention in
Czechoslovakia has seriously set back hopes of settling the outstanding problems which still divide the European continent and
Germany and of establishing peace and security in Europe, and
threatens certain of the results already achieved in the field of
detente.

The ministers reaffirm the determination of the alliance to
persevere in its efforts to contribute to a peaceful solution of the
German question based on the free decision of the German people
and on the interests of European security.

Berlin security pledged: . . . The ministers confirm the support
of their governments for the declared determination of the
(France, Britain, United States) powers to safeguard Berlin's
security and to maintain freedom of access to the city.

Defense improvement planned: The quality, effectiveness, and
deployment of NATO's forces will be improved in terms of both
manpower and equipment in order to provide a better capability
for defense as far forward as possible.

NATO Warning Rebuffed. Responding to the November 16 NATO ministerial communique, the Soviet Union, in a statement issued by Tass November 23, warned that the Warsaw Pact allies were prepared to take "appropriate measures to insure the security of the states of the Socialist community" against any NATO actions.

French CP on Independent Course. In a move towards more independence from Moscow leadership the French Communist Party (PCF) asserted Dec. 6, 1968 that in developing a Socialist program for France, it intended to take into account "French particularities." In a 45-page manifesto, the PCF declared that "it is possible and necessary to consider opening the way to socialism by other means than those used in Russia and other countries."

Following a two-day meeting of French and Russian CP leaders in Moscow November 4-5, the PCF November 7 issued a statement that indicated that the PCF had not been willing to retract its statements on the invasion of Czechoslovakia but that the two Communist parties had reached "broad agreement." The statement declared that "beyond the respective opinions of the two parties about events in Czechoslovakia, the Moscow encounter will make it possible to strengthen the friendship and joint action of the French and Communist parties."

USSR-French Trade Pact. After a week of negotiations in Paris, the Soviet Union and France agreed Jan. 7, 1969 to double their trade in 1970-74. The agreement, negotiated by Foreign Minister Debre and Soviet Deputy Premier Vladimir R. Kirillin, provided for the delivery of French equipment to construct a refinery in the USSR, the building of a French factory in the Soviet Union to produce 500,000 tons of cellulose annually, and collaboration in the metal-working, food and light industries.

At a news conference January 8, Debre said that French-Soviet trade under the existing trade pact had reached $700 million, a year ahead of the planned schedule. The new five-year trade agreement would become effective when the present agreement expired at the end of 1969.

West Protests Berlin Access Curbs. France joined the United States and Britain in protesting East German blockades on road traffic in and out of West Berlin in early March. The East German government had announced February 9 that the members of the West German Federal Assembly would be prohibited from entering West Berlin across East German territory for the West German presidential election scheduled for March 5 in West Berlin. Despite East German traffic harassment March 1, 2, 4, 6, 7, and 11-12, the election was held. The three Western powers protested these harassments through their military representatives in East Berlin.

CHAPTER XVIII
FRANCE AND WESTERN EUROPE
RELATIONS WITH WEST GERMANY; BRITAIN AND THE COMMON MARKET

De Gaulle-Kiesinger Discuss UK Common Market Bid. West German Chancellor Kurt George Kiesinger and President de Gaulle conferred in Paris Feb. 15-16, 1968, in a regular meeting provided for by the 1963 Franco-West German Friendship Treaty. In a joint statement issued February 16, the two leaders agreed in principle to enlarge the European Economic Community (EEC,or Common Market) with Britain and other West European countries. But the statement added that such an enlargement could come about only after "these countries are in the position to either enter effectively into these communities or, as the case may be, to link themselves in another form." The statement added, however, that for the immediate future, "all the efforts" of the two governments should be devoted toward strengthening the existing community.

French-Backed Dairy Price Policy Approved. The agricultural ministers of the six member states of the EEC agreed May 29 to a unified price policy on dairy products. Action on the policy was forced by France, which had warned that lack of a dairy agreement might prevent it from carrying out the EEC industrial tariff reductions scheduled for July 1.

France Announces Import Quotas. The French government June 26 unilaterally imposed quotas on steel, textiles, automobiles and household goods and provided subsidies to French exporters. The measure was designed to soften the impact of "sudden and unexpected paralysis" of the French economy following the May-June student and worker disturbances. Approximately 10% of France's total imports were affected by the quota system, of which 7% consisted of exports from the five other Common Market nations.

France Joins Kennedy Round Cuts, Completes EEC Tariff Reduction. Eighteen member-nations of the General Agreement on Tariffs and Trade (GATT) July 1, 1968, carried out tariff reductions stipulated under the Kennedy round tariff-cutting agreement. For most of the 18, the reduction represented 40% of the total envisaged under the year-old agreement. The pact was intended to cut the Western world's tariffs by 35% over a five-year period. The countries reducing tariffs under the agreement included the Common Market nations (France, West Germany, Italy, Belgium, the Netherlands and Luxembourg). The Common Market nations simultaneously abolished all tariffs remaining among themselves and aligned their common external tariff with the Kennedy round reductions.

A GATT meeting in Geneva, called July 1 in response to France's June 26 imposition of import quotas, set up a "working party" to study the measures. The group's first report, unanimously adopted by the organization July 19, criticized France for not consulting GATT before acting and declared that the good of the international economic community should take precedence over individual nations' interests. However, the report did not formally condemn the French action and did not examine the legality of the measures vis-a-vis GATT rules and regulations.

EEC Agrees to French Quotas. The EEC Executive Commission agreed July 23 to permit France to impose import quotas and export subsidies as announced by the French government June 26. The Commission did not extend the quota system beyond December 31, and it retained the right to annul the arrangement if France's industrial position improved. It was the first time in 10 years that an EEC country had been permitted to impose import restrictions.

France Bars UK from EEC. The third French veto of British entry into the European Economic Community was, in effect, cast Sept. 27, 1968, when France rejected a West German interim plan that could have led to UK membership. The West German proposal, advanced by West German Foreign Minister Willy Brandt, would have cut industrial tariffs between Britain and the EEC by 30% over a period of three years and would have increased technological cooperation and regular ministerial contacts.

At a closed-door meeting in Brussels, French Foreign Minister Debre told the EEC's Council of Ministers that France could not accept preferential arrangements with Britain and would consider only tariff cuts that could be offered to all European countries. He added that such trade arrangements could in no way be considered a prelude to EEC membership by nations involved. Debre pointed out that France opposed any enlargement of the EEC.

De Gaulle-Kiesinger Meeting. The French rebuff to British membership coincided with President de Gaulle's annual visit to Bonn September 27-28 for talks with West German Chancellor Kiesinger.

In Bonn September 28, de Gaulle pledged that France would support West Germany in case the conflict within the Soviet block spread into Western Europe. His pledge came in response to a series of Soviet warnings and threats to Germany following the invasion of Czechoslovakia. De Gaulle reiterated his opposition to British membership in the Common Market.

France Thwarts WEU Action on Britain. Belgian Foreign Minister Pierre Harmel October 3 announced a proposal to revitalize the Western European Union (WEU) in order to expand Britain's role in Europe without facing a French veto. The WEU includes Britain and the six EEC countries as members.*

At a WEU meeting in Rome October 21-22, a move toward British entry into the Common Market was thwarted by France. Harmel proposed the establishment of an intergovernmental organization to study possible collaboration between Britain and the EEC nations on political, defense, monetary, technological and youth problems. French State Secretary for

---

*Britain had been trying to turn the WEU into an organ for discussion of common European policies.

Foreign Affairs Jean de Lipkowski, while agreeing to the idea of a study group on collaboration, rejected proposals that would permit the study group to formulate policy by majority vote, and thereby bypass the French veto.

France Backs Wider European Trade. At a meeting of the EEC Council of Ministers in Brussels Nov. 5, 1968, French Foreign Minister Debre introduced a nine-point program for increased trade between the EEC and other European nations. The plan suggested new European-wide tariff reductions with industrial tariffs to be cut by 30% over a four-year period. The reductions would be in addition to the cuts previously implemented under Kennedy round tariff negotiations by GATT members. Another proposal advocated European-wide action to reduce restrictions on agricultural imports. Debre also proposed measures for increased EEC technical cooperation with Britain on "specific and practical projects."

Debre emphasized, however, that his proposals for expanded EEC-European trade were not intended to open the Common Market to membership by any other nation. West German Foreign Minister Willy Brandt said in Brussels November 5 that the Bonn government hoped the French proposal would lead to a widening of EEC membership, but as a reported concession to France he refrained from directly coupling tariff reductions to the Common Market's admission of Britain and other nations. Few objections were raised to Debre's proposals, and the Council of Ministers directed the EEC's Executive Commission and ambassadors to study the proposals.

Euratom Maintained. An eleventh-hour effort by the ministers of the six-nation European Atomic Energy Community (Euratom) December 21 saved that agency from extinction. France had sought to reduce Euratom's 1969 budget from $80 million to $20 million, but the other five nations rejected the cut. A compromise was reached when the five agreed to budgetary cuts—but not to the extent France had wanted.

EEC to Take France to Court. The Common Market Executive Commission announced Jan. 16, 1969, that legal proceedings before the EEC's Court of Justice would be instituted against France for its failure to adhere to a scheduled reduction of the special export subsidy, adopted in June 1968, in the form of a low interest rate on government loans granted to exporters.

Such credit subsidies had been declared illegal in the Common Market and were abolished July 1, 1968. France, however, had been given special dispensation to institute the subsidy because of its weakened economic situation following the May-June student-worker upheavals; under the agreement, the Bank of France was allowed to discount export loans at a rate three percentage points below the official French bank rate (5% at that time), but was to narrow the margin to 1.5 points by Oct. 31, 1968, and was to abolish the subsidy by Jan. 31, 1969.

In announcing the decision to take court action, the Executive Commission indicated that the French bank rate was 6%, but export credit was still being extended at 3%.

France Boycotts WEU on UK Issue. Accusing Britain of attempting to use the WEU as a back-door entrance to the EEC, France announced that it was ceasing all participation in WEU activities for an indefinite period. The French action came on the eve of a regular fortnightly meeting at the organization's headquarters in London February 18. The meeting was held as scheduled, though France did not attend.

Dispute over de Gaulle-Soames Talk. British-French tension over Britain's efforts to join the EEC developed into a sweeping diplomatic crisis Feb. 21, 1969, with the publication in London of far-reaching proposals for a future European organization, allegedly outlined by French President de Gaulle at a meeting February 4 with British Ambassador to France Christopher Soames. French government sources immediately disputed British accounts of the meeting, and a verbal diplomatic war ensued.

According to the British report, published by the *London Times* February 22, de Gaulle told Soames that British membership in the European communities would inevitably change the nature of the organization. De Gaulle reportedly suggested that the current Common Market be supplanted by a larger form of free-trade association governed by a four-power inner council composed of France, Britain, West Germany and Italy. He said that such an organization should be based on a totally independent Europe. De Gaulle explained that, once an independent Europe was achieved, there would no longer be a need for NATO, which he termed an American-dominated organization. The British reports stated that de Gaulle also told Soames, in the *London Times'* words, "that he would be quite prepared to discuss with Britain what should take the place of the Common Market, and would like, as a first stage, political discussions between Britain and France."

French official sources immediately denied the accuracy of the London reports. A statement issued in Paris February 21 through Agence France-Presse declared that the reports were sensationalized and that, in his meeting with Soames, de Gaulle had expressed no views different from those "which had been publicly and constantly defined by himself in the course of the past few years."

British officials February 21 affirmed the accuracy of their report of the meeting. They said the decision to make public the details of the meeting was made after inaccurate accounts had appeared in two French newspapers early February 21.

The controversy deepened February 22. The French repeated their accusations that Britain had dramatized and distorted de Gaulle's proposals, and the British strongly denied the charges. At the same time, officials at the French Foreign Ministry denied that they had ever endorsed Soames' record of the meeting, as the British had asserted. Foreign Minister Debré, in a television and radio interview February 22, accused Britain of leaking to other West European governments the contents of what France had viewed as a confidential meeting.

British Foreign Secretary Michael Stewart, speaking in Parliament February 24, admitted that Prime Minister Harold Wilson February 12 had told West German Chancellor Kiesinger of the Soames-de Gaulle meeting before France had been informed of Britain's intention to do so, but he added that "it would have been entirely improper to have allowed these conversations [during Wilson's trip to Germany]... to conclude without Dr. Kiesinger being made aware of what had happened." He added further: "It was, of course, understood between the French government and ourselves that these conversations were confidential from the public at large, but we never entered into, nor would we have thought it right to enter into, any undertaking to conceal [them] from our allies and partners in Europe..."

The French government February 24 delivered a formal protest to Soames; it complained that Britain had leaked false information to its allies and the press. The French Foreign Ministry issued a detailed statement of the incident February 24, which asserted that Debre had "denied" Soames' version of the de Gaulle discussion. (Soames and Debre had met alone February 8, and there was no official record of their conversation.) Soames March 1 delivered a note in Paris replying to the French Foreign Ministry's February 24 protest. According to the *London Times* March 3, the British note reaffirmed the British government stand outlined earlier by Soames and by Foreign Secretary Stewart. That position stressed that Debre had seen Soames' account of the meeting and had told the British ambassador February 8 that it was correct.

WEU Meets Without France. The Permanent Council of the Western European Union met at its London headquarters Feb. 26, 1969, with all members except France in attendance. West Germany earlier had recommended that the Council meet March 5, the regular date for the bimonthly meeting; Germany apparently hoped that the French could be persuaded to attend the later session. However, France stated February 24 that it would attend neither the February 26 nor the March 5 meeting, nor any other meeting until the Council agreed to its demand that decisions to call meetings be made unanimously.

France also boycotted a March 12 meeting of the WEU Council.

Concorde Debut. The controversial Anglo-French supersonic Concorde airliner made its first test flight March 2 in Toulouse, France, one year behind schedule and two months after the maiden flight of the Soviet Union's supersonic TU-144.

The droop-nosed plane, designed to carry up to 140 passengers at a cruising speed of over 1,450 m.p.h. (twice the speed of sound), had been constructed jointly by the British Aircraft Corporation and France's Sud Aviation. According to their estimates, the plane could be in regular service by late 1973, three to six years ahead of the supersonic airliner planned by the United States. The Concorde had cost more than $725 million, well above the $420 million originally budgeted in 1962. Official estimates indicated that total costs would probably be close to $1.37 billion.

British Concorde Test Flight. Concorde 002, the first of the British-French supersonic airliners to be assembled in Britain, completed a successful 22-minute maiden flight from Filton to Fairford, England, April 9. Concorde 001, assembled in France, had made its first flight March 2 and had made eight more test flights since then.

France Sues EEC. *Le Monde* of Paris reported March 7 that France had filed suit in the European Court of Justice against the EEC's Executive Commission. Challenging the Commission's earlier decision to take France to court for failing to reduce its special export subsidies. France asserted that its preferential subsidies were not an illegal aid to exports, and it demanded that the court annul the Commission's decision that they be reduced.

Summit Meeting. A semiannual French-German "summit" meeting, held in Paris March 13-14, was marked by an atmosphere of open disagreement between the two nations. Both French and West German spokesmen emphasized that President de Gaulle and Chancellor Kiesinger had reached no agreements on European issues and that the differences between the two nations over British entry into the Common Market had not been narrowed.

President de Gaulle was reported March 14 to have set out for Kiesinger two alternative routes for the future of European maintenance of the present European Economic Community with six members, or formation of a larger and more loosely organized group which could include Britain, Scandinavia and, in de Gaulle's words, "the Turks and the Swiss." (Such a proposal had been the subject of the British-French dispute over published reports of the meeting February 4 between de Gaulle and British Ambassador to France Christopher Soames.)

De Gaulle was said to have been unmoving in his stand on the crisis within the WEU. Contending that the quarrel did not interest France, he was reported to have repeated his claim that recent WEU Council meetings had been held in violation of the organization's constitution and that France would continue its boycott of the meetings.

At a press briefing in Paris March 13, West German spokesman Guenther Diehl had said that because of the two nations' "so very different views" on important European issues, the talks had "descended rapidly and inexorably" to more practical topics of bilateral cooperation. De Gaulle and Kiesinger agreed to establish a regional commission to aid development of the Saar and Lorraine, on their common border. In addition, West Germany committed itself to purchase at market prices large quantities of French-produced Algerian oil. The two leaders also agreed to proceed with a European "airbus" project, without the participation of Britain if necessary.

Airbus to Proceed Without UK. Cabinet ministers of France, Great Britain and West Germany announced April 10 that Britain was withdrawing from the European A-300B airbus project. They said that the project would be continued as a French-West German program.

CHAPTER XIX

INTERNATIONAL MONETARY POLICY

French Reserves. The French Finance Ministry reported Jan. 2, 1968, that total French gold and foreign exchange reserves had fallen by the equivalent of $74.3 million in December 1967 to a year-end total of $6.108 billion. The December decline was the first since April. Over-all, French reserves had increased by $363 million in 1967.

The Finance Ministry announced March 1 that France's reserves of gold and foreign exchange had declined by the equivalent of $93.6 million since the beginning of the year—$55.1 million in January and $38.5 million in February. Total French reserves as of the end of February: $6.014 billion.

Gold Crisis. A giant wave of speculative buying hit the world's gold markets March 1, and by March 14 the gold trading had swelled to record proportions. During the 10 days of market activity: (a) an estimated $1 billion worth of gold — about 900 tons — was believed to have changed hands in the London market alone, as compared with normal trading of three to five tons daily, and (b) the price of gold rose in the Paris market March 15 to a record $44.36 per ounce, compared with the official exchange rate of $35.

The United States and the other six active members of the London Gold Pool (Belgium, Britain, Italy, the Netherlands, Switzerland and West Germany) attempted to dampen the speculation by feeding large amounts of gold from their treasuries into the London market. France, which had withdrawn from the Gold Pool in June 1967, did not join in this action.

The U.S. Treasury disclosed March 8 that the U.S. gold supply had been decreased by a total of $771.2 million during the fourth quarter of 1967 because of the operations of the London Gold Pool. The bulk of the loss had occurred immediately following the devaluation of the British pound at the end of November.

"Two-Price" Gold System Established. Britain closed trading in gold on the London market March 15, 1968, when it became apparent that efforts by the Gold Pool to end speculation had failed. At the request of the United States, a high-level meeting of the seven active Gold Pool members was then held in Washington March 16-17, and a plan was adopted to resolve the crisis. (France did not participate in the Washington meeting.)

The seven nations agreed to stop buying and selling gold in the international markets in an effort to prevent any further loss of their monetary gold to private speculators. At the same time they affirmed that gold transactions between monetary authorities would continue to be based on the official exchange rate of $35 an ounce.

The effect of the agreement was to establish a "two-tier" pricing system for transactions in gold: (1) a private market price that would be allowed to fluctuate according to supply and demand and (2) an official monetary price of $35 an ounce that would pertain to gold transactions between governments. The agreement marked the end of a system, in effect since 1961, under which the Gold Pool members had sought to maintain a more-or-less uniform world gold price by intervening in the market whenever the market price of gold rose above or fell below the official rate of exchange.

International reaction to the Washington agreement was generally favorable. But most government and financial officials emphasized that the solution was only a temporary one and that long-term stability in the international monetary system could be achieved only if the U.S. and Britain took immediate measures to end their persistent balance-of-payments deficits

France Dissents on IMF Special Drawing Rights. Nine of the 10 leading financial nations known collectively as the Group of 10 (Belgium, Britain, Canada, France, Italy, Japan, the Netherlands, Sweden, the United States and West Germany), meeting in Stockholm March 29-30, 1968, issued a communique March 30 indorsing the plan of the International Monetary Fund (IMF) to create a new form of monetary reserves to supplement gold, dollars and pounds. The dissenting member, France, in the final paragraph of the communique, dissociated itself from the operative paragraphs of the document. France held that there were "differences" between the plan as presented at the March 29-30 meeting and the "outline adopted" at the annual IMF meeting in Rio de Janeiro Sept. 29, 1967. As a result, the French delegation "reserve[d] its position" pending "possession of the final texts..."

The IMF had agreed at its meeting in Rio de Janeiro to create the new reserves, known as "special drawing rights" or SDRs. The plan approved March 30 was to take effect when it was ratified by 60% of the IMF members having 80% of the weighted voting (i.e., those who contributed 80% of the Fund's gold and foreign exchange holdings). The actual creation of the SDRs would require the further approval of members having 85% of the weighted voting.

French Finance Minister Debre urged March 29 that the agenda of the meeting be broadened to include what he termed a "frank and open reflection on all the [financial] problems of the present day." Debre said that France had "no hostility against special drawing rights" *per se,* since "in the future monetary order, means of international credit could by this means be supplemented in a very useful way." But he attacked the role of the dollar and the pound as primary reserve currencies and asserted that the price of gold should be raised. At the insistence of West German Economics Minister Karl Schiller and others, however, the conference members voted against turning the meeting into a general debate on the nature of the world monetary system.

In an effort to win French acceptance of the plan, the United States agreed March 30 to several compromises that generally favored France and its five partners in the European Common Market.

The most important compromise was agreement on a plan to amend the IMF voting rules in such a way that the 85% majority vote required for activating the SDRs would also apply to such normal IMF operations as raising quotas in the Fund and effecting a uniform change in the par values of member-currencies, an operation equivalent to raising the official price of gold. The effect of the amendment would be to give the Common Market countries veto power over these operations, if they voted as a bloc, since the six member nations collectively controlled 16 1/2% of the weighted votes. The current rules required an 80% majority vote for increasing quotas (which meant that only the United States, with about 22% of the votes, could exercise veto power).

The United States did not accede to French demands that the SDRs be created only after equilibrium was restored in the United States' balance of international payments. Debre said in a statement issued March 30: The SDRs "are no longer that form of supplementary credit which we had judged useful: they are, I fear, an expedient, unless they are the blueprint for a so-called currency which will bring great disillusion to those who might trust in it..."

The IMF Board of Governors in Washington June 3 adopted a resolution embodying the SDR plan and the other amendments to the IMF's articles of agreement. An IMF spokesman said that the resolution had been adopted by a "substantial majority" of the governors (a simple majority of those members with at least two thirds of the Fund's voting power was required). Informed sources said that France and its allies in the so-called "franc zone" had abstained. Following the Board of Governors' indorsement, the amendments were submitted to each of the 107 IMF members for ratification.

France Refuses Credit to Britain. It was announced in London July 8, 1968, that Britain had received assurances of a $2 billion medium-term (10-year) sterling support package from 12 central banks and the Bank for International Settlements (BIS) in Basel, Switzerland.

Agreeing to provide the stand-by support, in addition to the BIS, were the central banks of Austria, Belgium, Canada, Denmark, Italy, Japan, the Netherlands, Norway, Sweden, Switzerland, the United States and West Germany. France also participated in the discussions but declined to participate in the credit arrangement. A Bank of England communique noted, however, that France had "expressed its sympathy with the steps being taken to deal with this problem."

French Crisis; Reserves Drop. The international monetary system was shaken in November 1968 by its third major crisis in a year. Initiated by massive speculation against the French franc in favor of the West German mark, the crisis led to the institution of French and West German measures to strengthen the international financial and trade situation without changing the parities of their currencies. Speculation also struck the British pound, forcing the Bank of England to intervene and the British government to order strict measures to control consumer demand and improve Britain's trade balance.

Stimulated by rumors of an impending West German revaluation (i.e., increase in the mark's exchange value), the crisis had built up due to a persistent and increasing flight from the franc to the mark. Approximately $1.7 billion in francs were sold during the first three weeks of November, and France was forced to use its already depleted gold reserves to support the franc's parity. (French reserves had been decreasing since the student-worker upheavals in May and June.) The Bank of France reported November 28 that total French reserves had decreased to $3.819 billion by November 21, a decrease of $3 billion since May.

In attempts to shore up the franc, the Paris government November 12 had raised the Bank of France discount rate from 5% to 6% and had announced a series of credit-tightening measures. The restrictive measures included the imposition of a 4% growth ceiling on short-term non-priority bank loans to the private sector for the remainder of the year. French Finance Minister Francois-Xavier Ortoli said November 12 that the restrictions had been made necessary by the depletion of reserves. President de Gaulle followed this action November 13 with an announcement to a cabinet meeting that devaluation of the franc "would be the most absurd thing there could be..."

Basel Meeting on Crisis. A regular meeting of 11 central bankers at the BIS in Basel, Switzerland, November 16-17 did nothing to resolve the crisis. Though the meeting was shrouded in secrecy, France was reportedly offered a $1 billion credit package to be financed mostly by West Germany. France, however, rejected the proposal, reportedly due to the "string" attached to it. No details were given.

France Cuts Budget. Premier Couve de Murville assured the French people November 18 that France's allies had offered "all the help she might need or will need in the future, without any reservation." In an attempt to hold down fears of a devaluation of the franc and to prepare the public for austerity measures, he added that the National Assembly would be called upon to make sharp cuts in the state budget and a "fundamental reform" of the French financial market.

The speculation in European foreign exchange markets continued and increased November 18-19. The French government November 19 ordered budget cuts of $400 million, and the action was approved by the National Assembly later that day.

France Receives Credits in Emergency Talks. In a new attempt to halt the intense speculation, foreign exchange markets in the major European capitals were closed November 20 and remained closed for the rest of that week. West German Economics Minister Karl Schiller, acting chairman of the IMF's Group of 10, called an emergency meeting of financial leaders, held in Bonn November 20-22.

The meeting in its November 22 communique pledged $2 billion in short-term credits to help France reinforce its financial position; $600 million was to be provided by West Germany, $500 million by the United States, $200 million by Italy and $100 million each by Belgium, Britain, Canada, the Netherlands, Switzerland and the Scandinavian countries as a unit, $50 million by Japan and $50 million by the BIS.

The communique indorsed West Germany's decision to maintain the value of the mark unchanged. It described Bonn's decision, announced November 19, to impose export taxes as "a significant contribution to the stability of the monetary system..."

The Bonn meeting was held in secret and no details were released to newsmen. However, reporters said that most of the discussion had consisted of an extensive debate on devaluation of the franc and that the

French delegation, though unwilling to change parity without a corresponding move by Germany, had finally decided on a small change in the franc's value. Almost everyone connected with the meeting was apparently convinced that the franc would be devalued despite the lack of a formal communique to that effect. The conferees apparently agreed to leave the details and the announcement of devaluation to France.

De Gaulle Rejects Devaluation. President de Gaulle stunned the financial world November 23 with an announcement that France would not devalue the franc. His brief statement, issued by the Presidential Palace at 7:45 p.m., said: "The President of the republic announces that after a meeting of the cabinet today, November 23, the following decision has been taken: The present parity of the French franc is maintained."

Addressing the French people on radio November 24, de Gaulle said that the crisis in France was "the consequence of the moral, economic and social upheaval...suffered last May and June..." He called for an enforced halt to "all agitation and demonstrations, all tumult and parading, which prevent work and offend sensible people..." He hypothesized that devaluation would have "run the strong risk of being not a remedy at all, but a ruinously easy and momentary device...[with] the reward paid to those who gambled on our decline." Insisting that the French economy was basically sound, de Gaulle called for stringent economic austerity, including a wage-price freeze and further budget cuts, in lieu of devaluation.

De Gaulle's decision was given the indorsement of U.S. President Lyndon B. Johnson in a telegram dispatched November 24. Johnson wished de Gaulle success in his austerity program and added that "we are ready to cooperate in any way we can to achieve your objective consistent with our national purpose."

When the European foreign exchange markets reopened November 25, the franc and the pound both gained, while the mark fell in light-to-medium trading. However, some dealers still expressed doubt as to the ability of the measures announced in Paris, Bonn and London to restore equilibrium and establish confidence in the franc and the pound for more than a limited time.

Exchange Controls Announced. In an effort to defend the value of the franc, the French government November 25 announced a series of exchange control measures which essentially confined currency transactions to authorized agencies; the free convertibility of the franc was halted. French nationals were required to deposit their foreign securities in authorized banks in France; exporters were required to repatriate earnings from foreign transactions; and restrictions were placed on commercial payments overseas. In addition, foreign travel allowances were limited to 700 francs ($40) for French tourists and 2,000 francs, with a maximum of 200 francs per day, for businessmen; the regulations were to stay in effect five weeks for businessmen and until January 1969 for tourists.

French Austerity Program Adopted. A strict austerity program was presented to the National Assembly November 26 by Prime Minister Couve de Murville. The measures included a further cut in the 1969 budget deficit, from the originally planned 11.7 billion francs ($2.34 billion) to 6.35 billion francs ($1.27 billion). The military budget was slashed by $80 million and the 1969 nuclear test program was cancelled. Couve de Murville also announced a cut of 60 million francs ($12 million) in the French contribution to the British-French Concorde supersonic jetliner project, but reports indicated that the 1969 program would not be greatly affected by the reduction.

To achieve the proposed cuts in the budget deficit, the government asked for an increase in the value-added tax—a charge placed on the value added to a product at each level of its production. This increase was expected to more than compensate for the revenue loss caused by the government's abolishing a 4.25% payroll tax paid by employers.

The value-added tax, borne largely by the consumer, was to be increased in four categories: from 6% to 7% for items such as foodstuffs, from 13% to 15% in the category including fuel and petroleum, from 16.66% to 19% on a large group of manufactured goods and from 20% to 25% on items such as automobiles and luxury goods.

The bulk of the budget cuts affected subsidies to nationalized industries. As a result, effective December 1, government-owned corporations raised rail freight rates by 6.2% and gas and electricity rates for industrial users by 4.8%.

The National Assembly approved the government's austerity program November 27 by a vote of 391 to 91; Senate approval followed on November 28 by a vote of 157 to 87.

Enforcement measures announced November 30 aimed at preventing prices from rising beyond the level reached after the cost of the added-value taxes had been calculated. All businesses were required to keep detailed records so that profit margins could be gauged. In addition, several hundred new agents were to be hired to join tax inspectors, customs officers and police personnel in detecting unjustified price increases.

Speculation Resumes. After almost two weeks of relative, though uneasy, calm in European foreign exchange markets, a new wave of speculation Dec. 5, 1968, sent the British pound to its effective floor and forced the Bank of England to take action to support it. At the same time, the franc and the dollar fell on German money markets, and the West German Bundesbank reportedly registered an intake of $300 million in foreign currencies. The main cause of the new round of speculation was thought to be the publication December 4 of the West German government's Economic Advisory Panel's report indicating that the mark eventually would have to be revalued and that the German export tax measures announced November 19 were not an adequate substitute for revaluation.

Reserve and Trade Figures. The French Finance Ministry announced December 5 that total reserves had fallen by $280 million in November. The decline, the largest since July, resulted mainly from the speculative flow of French francs into West German marks. The actual loss in reserves was believed to have been greater than that reported, since France had a $1.3 billion swap agreement on which it could draw to support the franc.

The Finance Ministry reported December 10 that the surplus of imports over exports for November totaled one billion francs ($200 million). The trade deficit was almost three times higher than the October deficit of 319 million francs ($63.8 million). November imports totaled 6.65 billion francs ($1.33 billion), while exports were only 5.65 billion francs ($1.13 billion). Financial sources attributed this situation in large part to inflationary wage increases and consumer spending following the May-June social unrest.

New Exchange Curbs. In a further effort to restore confidence in the franc, the Bank of France Jan. 20, 1969, ordered curbs on the outflow of foreign currencies. Under the new regulation, foreign currencies deposited in French banks by French residents or companies established in France could be lent only to other French residents; if such currency were lent to a foreign institution, the lending bank was required to deposit with the Bank of France an equal amount of that currency. The regulation, effective in two stages February 25 and March 25, affected all banks in France, including foreign banks and branches.

France in Monetary Talks. Central bankers of the major financial powers (including France), meeting in Basel at a regular BIS session, agreed February 9 on a program designed to prevent currency speculation from leading to devaluation. The plan was to be referred to the countries' political authorities for approval.

Although details of the plan remained secret, informed sources indicated that no formal or specific procedure was to be established and that the bankers had decided to rely on quick action on a crisis-by-crisis basis.

Reserves Fluctuate. France's holdings of gold and foreign currency reserves showed a slight increase in January but dropped significantly in February. The French treasury reported February 4 that reserves increased by $14.9 million in January to a total of $4.214 billion. February's figures, reported March 4, showed a decrease of $89.7 million, leaving total reserves at $4.13 billion.

Renewed Speculation Against Franc. Monetary tensions rose again in Europe in February and early March 1969 as French labor unrest and rumors of an imminent devaluation of the franc fed speculation on the gold and foreign currency markets. The free market price of gold hit record highs, and an increasingly weak French franc (still somewhat unstable as a result of the November 1968 monetary crisis) led to a faltering British pound as well. However, fears of a major international financial crisis subsided when it became clear that a one-day general strike staged in France March 11 had not led to a renewal of the May 1968 unrest and that the franc would not be devalued.

As gold prices reached record highs, the franc came under new pressure, and fears of its devaluation weakened the British pound. (French workers were demanding 1969 wage increases of up to 12% in addition to the 12% won in 1968; the French government felt that any increase of more than 6% would force devaluation of the franc.) Both the French and British central banks were forced into the market to support their currencies.

In an effort to curb the smuggling of francs out of France, the Bank of France March 7 ordered the BIS, acting as its agent, to reduce the price at which it would buy French banknotes from Swiss banks to about 9% below the official price in Swiss francs. The move penalized anyone attempting to convert French banknotes into Swiss francs or dollars in order to buy gold; Swiss banks would not exchange francs at a rate above that used by the BIS.

Central bankers of the major industrial nations expressed a belief that the franc would retain its current value. Holding a regular meeting at the BIS in Basel, Switzerland, the bankers March 9 decided that the current situation required no special action if the French labor problem remained under control.

Following the one-day French general strike, gold prices fell March 11 in Zurich, London and Paris. The French franc and the British pound strengthened. The trend continued March 12 as fears of devaluation of the franc diminished.

Reserves Drop. French gold and foreign exchange reserves had dropped by $139.1 million during March, the French Finance Ministry reported April 2. The decrease brought total French reserves to $3.93 billion at the end of March, down from $5.9 billion a year earlier. Reserve losses in the first quarter of 1969 totaled $213.9 million.

New Governor for Bank of France. Oliver Boris Wormser was named governor of the Bank of France April 9. Former head of the economic section of the French Foreign Ministry and ambassador to Moscow, Wormser succeeded Jacques Brunet, who retired after nine years in the post.

De Gaulle's Resignation Spurs New Speculation. De Gaulle's resignation April 28, 1969, led to renewed monetary speculation and a strong demand for gold that same day, but intervention by the French, British and West German central banks kept the situation under control. European money markets had moved erratically since April 22, due, at least in part, to uncertainty about the French referendum.

In a pattern reminiscent of the November 1968 crisis, the value of the French franc and the British pound fell April 28, while that of the West German mark rose. In addition, the free market price of gold in the Paris market rose to $49.06 an ounce, a record high. Commodity and metal markets also rose sharply.

Bankers in Frankfurt estimated that $200 million in foreign funds had come into Germany April 28. The mark rose to its ceiling rate against the U.S. dollar, while the franc fell to its lowest value since November 1968. The pound dropped sharply during the day, though it later recovered. (According to the *London Times,* the New York Federal Reserve Bank had intervened in the market to aid the pound.) In an attempt to slow the flow of funds into Germany, the Bundesbank, late April 28, reinstituted a 100% reserve requirement on foreign funds retroactive to April 15. Bundesbank President Karl Blessing said that central banks stood "firmly and united" behind the franc and indicated that any massive flood of speculative funds into Germany "would be swapped right back out."

CHAPTER XX

MIDDLE EAST POLICY

1967 Letter to Ben-Gurion Made Public. The French government Jan. 9, 1968, made public an exchange of letters between President de Gaulle and former Israeli Premier David Ben-Gurion dealing with de Gaulle's Nov. 27, 1967, press conference remarks describing Jews as an "elite people, sure of itself and domineering."

Denying that he had any intention of offending the Jewish people, de Gaulle said in his Dec. 30, 1967, reply to Ben-Gurion that his remarks could not be considered "disparaging" because it was due to the characteristics he had mentioned that "this strong people was able to survive and to remain itself after 19 centuries spent in unimaginable conditions." But de Gaulle reiterated his opinion that Israel should not have attacked the Arab states June 5, 1967.

Ben-Gurion's Dec. 6, 1967, letter to de Gaulle had rejected de Gaulle's press conference remarks as based on "incorrect and imprecise information" and had described them as "harsh and wounding expressions."

Iraq to Receive French Jets. The French government agreed April 6, 1968, to sell Iraq 54 French Mirage supersonic fighter-bombers at a cost of $70 million. The signing of the accord, in Baghdad, was reported April 12. Delivery was expected to start at the end of 1969. France had contracted its first arms deal with Iraq in 1967, when it agreed to supply 75 self-propelled tracked machinegun carriers.

Premier Pompidou was reported to have informed Israeli Ambassador-to-France Walter Eytan in March that the French government arms embargo against Israel, imposed during the June 1967 war, would remain in effect. This decision continued to block the shipment of 50 Mirage jets ordered by Israel in 1966. Israel April 16 paid the third and final installment on the $1 million plane contract, thus paving the way for possible Israeli legal action against France for breach of contract.

Official sources in Paris disclosed June 26 that France had authorized the delivery to Israel of 25 disassembled Fouga-Magister twin-jet planes. The sources emphasized that the jets were for training purposes and thus did not violate the French arms embargo to Israel. However, the *New York Times* reported June 27 that the 50 Fouga-Magisters owned by Israel before the 1967 war had been flown on bombing and close-support missions.

UN Condemns Israel. The UN Security Council August 16 unanimously adopted a resolution condemning Israel for a retaliatory air strike August 4 against Jordan. French delegate Claude Chayet had asserted during debate August 6 that the Israeli attacks "could not be justified by statements of legitimate defense, since they are reprisals and the very idea of military reprisals has never been acceptable to us."

The Israeli government March 30 formally rejected any Big Four proposals on the Middle East that were contrary to Israel's vital interests, rights and security. The statement, issued after a cabinet meeting, detailed Israel's own position on a peace settlement:

"Israel entirely opposes the plan to convene the representatives of states that lie outside the Middle East [the United States, France, Britain and the Soviet Union] in order to prepare recommendations concerning the region. Such a procedure undermines the responsibility devolving on the states of the region to attain peace among themselves."

Big Four Talks Begin. The Big Four representatives to the UN opened formal joint discussions in New York April 3 on a peaceful political solution of the Middle East conflict. A second conference was held April 8.

The first meeting was held at the residence of Armand Berard of France and was attended by Charles Yost of the United States, Lord Cara-don of Britain and Yakov Malik of the USSR. A communique issued after four hours of talks said: "The four powers are agreed that the situation in the Middle East is serious and urgent and must not be permitted to jeop-ardize international peace and security..." The communique promised that "active consultations will continue" and indicated that Israel and the Arab states would be apprised of progress.

Just before issuance of the Big Four statement, Yosef Tekoah, Israeli representative to the UN, had said that "nothing good can come of the talks" because anything approved by France and the Soviet Union would be "inimical to Israel's vital interests."

(The Big Four representatives to the UN suspended their talks on the Middle East July 1. A U.S. diplomat at the UN said that the talks were deferred, apparently for the remainder of the summer, in the hope that progress would be made in U.S.-Soviet discussions that had commenced at the end of May.)

CHAPTER XXI
OTHER FOREIGN POLICY DEVELOPMENTS

THE NIGERIAN CIVIL WAR

France Backs Biafra. The French government July 31, 1968, issued a statement of support for secessionist Biafra by calling for an end to the Nigerian civil war on the basis of self-determination. The statement came after a weekly cabinet meeting and prompted speculation that France would move unilaterally to recognize the secessionist state.

The policy statement said: The French government "notes that the bloodshed and suffering endured by the peoples of Biafra for more than a year show their will to affirm themselves as a people. Faithful to this principle, the French government believes that, as a result, the present conflict should be resolved on the basis of the right of peoples to self-determination and implies the undertaking of appropriate international procedures."

The Nigerian government said August 2 that the civil conflict was an internal matter and "therefore deplores this intrusion into her internal affairs by the government of France."

De Gaulle: France Aids Biafra. President de Gaulle Sept. 9, 1968, at his presidential press conference, said that France was giving aid to Biafra in its military struggle against Nigeria. Explaining his stand, he declared: ". . . why should the Ibos [the Biafrans], who are mainly Christian, who live in the south in a certain way and who have their own language, why should they be subject to another ethnic fraction of the [Nigerian] federation? . . ."

"In this affair, France has helped Biafra. . . . She has not taken the action which for her would be decisive, recognition of the Biafran Republic . . ., [but recognition] is not excluded in the future."

France Arms Biafra. The *Manchester Guardian* reported Oct. 1, 1968, that a French airlift, based in Libreville, had begun September 25 with an estimated 30 tons of arms and munitions flown to Biafra each night. *Newsweek* reported November 18 that an estimated 1,000 tons of arms had reached Biafra since the start of the French airlift and that, in addition, French mercenaries had entered Biafra to train soldiers.

French Policy Uncertain. There were reports during May 1969 that the U.S. had appealed to France, Biafra's main arms supplier, to cut down arms shipments in the interest of obtaining a negotiated peace in the area. However, a Paris report in April indicated that the French had discontinued all arms shipments to Biafra.

The *Washington Post* reported May 10 that "informed officials" in the U. S. government said that France had been asked to reduce or stop its arms supply to Biafra. But the State Department later May 10 officially denied the *Post* story, and said that the U. S. had merely "exchanged information and views from time to time with other interested governments including that of the French. We anticipate such exchanges will continue."

The Paris satirical weekly *Le Canard Enchaine* had reported in mid-April that a member of the French Secret Service had visited Biafra "not later than April 4" and had informed the government that French arms deliveries would be suspended. He reportedly suggested that Biafra negotiate a peace with Nigeria. The change in French policy, the magazine suggested, was due to a Nigerian pledge that French oil interests would be respected in Biafran territory captured by the Nigerian army. The *London Times*, reporting on the story, said April 20 that it was "generally accepted in Paris that French deliveries of arms to Biafra have stopped."

A two-man French parliamentary delegation had carried out a one-week fact-finding mission in Biafra for President de Gaulle beginning March 2. The two were Raymond Offroy, former French ambassador to Nigeria and president of the Action Committee for Biafra, and Jacques Marette, a member of the National Assembly.

The Nigerian radio reported May 8 that French Foreign Minister Michel Debre had given assurances that France would not recognize Biafra. Debre was said to have spoken with Dr. Okoi Arikpo, Nigerian External Affairs Commissioner, who had just returned from a visit to London and Paris.

The *Washington Post* reported May 16 that British officials blamed the French for deliberately scuttling chances for peace negotiations in September 1968 by beginning arms shipments to Biafra. The article said that Biafra had made overtures to Britain about the start of peace talks with Nigeria, and Lord Shepherd, Commonwealth Minister of State, had been dispatched to Lagos to work out arrangements. However, the start of arms deliveries by the French had encouraged the Biafrans to continue the war.

(The Nigerian radio reported March 1 that France had purchased ten million rounds of ammunition from Bulgaria for delivery to Biafra. Two million rounds were reported already in transit in Gabon, which had recognized Biafra, and the rest was awaiting shipment in France.)

FRENCH CANADA

De Gaulle Receives Acadians. A delegation of four French-speaking Acadians from New Brunswick, Canada, paid a two-week visit to France in mid-January 1968. Gilbert Finn, one of the delegates, said that they had been invited to France by President de Gaulle "to see how things are done in the university, newspaper and different fields." (The Acadians, descendants of early French settlers in the Maritime provinces, numbered about 250,000 in New Brunswick [total population: about 625,000], and there were smaller Acadian populations in Nova Scotia and Prince Edward

Island.) At a formal luncheon for the Acadian delegates in Paris January 20, de Gaulle said that "we have forgotten you and neglected you." He proposed to "reestablish" relations between France and the Acadians, who "remain more French than ever." (French officials had announced January 11 that the French government would help to finance *L'Evangeline*, the only French-language newspaper in New Brunswick.)

France-Quebec Satellite Project. Quebec Premier Daniel Johnson said June 8, 1968, that work was continuing on an eventual communications satellite linkup between France and Quebec. He said "several Quebec engineers" were currently working at the French national space research center, and "a close cooperation has been established" between Radio-Quebec and the French government broadcasting system.

Couve de Murville-Trudeau Talks. Canadian Prime Minister Pierre Trudeau conferred for 90 minutes with French Premier Maurice Couve de Murville in Quebec Sept. 30, 1968. The meeting, which had been arranged September 29 at the request of Canada, was held after the funeral of Quebec Premier Daniel Johnson, who died September 26. Trudeau, who had succeeded Lester Pearson as Prime Minister earlier in the year, was a French-Canadian and a strong opponent of Quebec separatism.

Speaking at a news conference after the meeting, Couve de Murville said that there would be no substantial change in France's relations with Quebec. He accused the press, however, of "exaggerating small differences" between France and Canada. While there had been "ups and downs" in recent relations between the two countries, they had been "nothing fundamental." Couve de Murville said: "There is nothing conflicting in the interest of France and the interests of Canada."

Quebec-French Ties Bolstered. Quebec and French delegates met in Paris November 15-16 and agreed on an expansion of cultural, educational and technical cooperation between France and Quebec. The representatives, meeting in the sixth session of the permanent Franco-Quebec Commission, agreed on a $1 million program of scientific and technical research in Quebec during 1969-70. They also agreed on an exchange of teachers, students and journalists.

Canadian Ambassador Presents Credentials. Newly appointed Canadian Ambassador-to-France Paul Beaulieu presented his credentials to French President de Gaulle Dec. 16, 1968. He asserted that Canada was "wholly open to French life and means to become for it...a particularly favorable environment." De Gaulle replied that Canada was still "in the very midst of evolution" and that the English and French living there would have to agree, "but on conditions that their national personalities be respected and remain distinct." De Gaulle expressed the hope that "one day Canada may find her equilibrium under new conditions in the shape of organized cooperation between two equal people."

Trudeau on de Gaulle Policy. Canadian Prime Minister Trudeau charged in a Jan. 2, 1969, interview that French President Charles de Gaulle had "retarded the cause of Canadian unity by some substantial degree—but amongst those classes that are not very large in numerical terms."

Quebec-French Ties Strengthened. Representatives of Quebec and France signed three letters of agreement January 24 on scientific and economic matters, thus raising the question of Quebec's infringement, with the backing of France, on foreign affairs matters under the jurisdiction of the Canadian government.

The letters were signed by a seven-man Quebec delegation, led by Education Minister Jean-Guy Cardinal and Industry and Commerce Minister Jean-Paul Beaudry, which visited Paris January 22-26 and was received with the ceremony usually reserved for representatives of a foreign country. Most commentators saw the five-day visit as another move in President Charles de Gaulle's campaign to increase French influence in Quebec at the expense of Canadian unity.

De Gaulle welcomed the Quebec delegation January 22 at a gala dinner in the Elysee Palace and said that the "links forged once more between Quebec and the mother country make us stronger to fight in all modern activities." De Gaulle declared that "the exchange of personal contact between our two governments has the character of a striking and capital event. I am speaking of course of the establishment of direct relations between New France and France, between Quebec and Paris." Paul Beaulieu, the Canadian ambassador in Paris, was not invited to the dinner. However, he did attend a luncheon given for the Quebec group January 23 by Foreign Minister Michel Debre. Cardinal met with de Gaulle January 22 and January 24.

Cardinal and Debre announced January 24 that they had signed agreements on new joint programs. The most significant pledged both parties to study a satellite communications system between France and Quebec. Although the project had been mentioned earlier, under the new accord Quebec technicians would work on the French-West German Symphonie satellite system to gain experience for their own project. The other two letters set up a special committee to stimulate private French investment in Quebec and established a program under which France would provide a number of teachers and researchers for the University of Quebec.

Canadian External Affairs Minister Mitchell Sharp said later January 24 in Ottawa that the three letters of agreement would not be considered valid by Canada if they did not come under the terms of the Franco-Canadian cultural and scientific exchange treaty of November 1965. Sharp declared that constitutional responsibility in the field of telecommunications was with the Canadian government. "It is therefore clear," he added, "that all international cooperation concerning satellite communications requires the concurrence and full cooperation of the Canadian government." Sharp told the Canadian House of Commons January 31 "that the participation of the federal government will be required in any satellite scheme, and therefore consultations will of necessity be involved." Sharp said that Quebec should have been "willing to take into its confidence the government of the country and to disclose its intentions before making them known and including them in letters of intent to the government of another country."

VIETNAM AND CHINA

Paris Picked as Vietnam Peace Talks Site. The United States and North Vietnam, climaxing 34 days of negotiations that had started with President Johnson's announcement March 31, 1968, of a limited bombing halt of North Vietnam, agreed May 3, 1968, on Paris as the site for their preliminary talks on Vietnam. The parley, Hanoi said, would start May 10 or shortly thereafter. North Vietnam's statement accepting Paris "welcome[d] the French government's willingness to offer Paris as a site for the talks." It cited the suggestion as having been advanced April 18 by French Foreign Minister Couve de Murville.

Thant, Debre for End to Bombing. UN Secretary General U Thant called Sept. 16, 1968, for "a complete and unconditional cessation of the bombing of North Vietnam." Speaking at a Paris news conference after meeting with French Foreign Minister Michel Debre, Thant said: "Without this I do not see how the problem can be moved from the battlefield to the conference table." Debre said that President de Gaulle supported Thant's view because "it conforms to reality if one wishes to assure a solution of the Vietnamese problem."

Debre vs. Foreign Intervention. Foreign Minister Debre Oct. 7, 1968, at the UN General Assembly said that the Vietnamese war illustrated "a people's difficulty in itself determining its own regime in the presence of foreign interference." He added that a permanent settlement could come about by implementation of the 1954 Geneva Agreements but that the initiative would have to be a halt in the U.S. bombing of North Vietnam.

(The United States halted all air, naval and artillery bombardment of North Vietnam on Nov. 1; the decision to stop the bombing was made by President Johnson and publicly announced by him in a TV-radio address the evening of Oct. 31.)

France Backs Communist China for UN Seat. The UN General Assembly November 19 rejected a resolution calling on the UN to seat Communist China and expel Nationalist China; 58 countries voted against the resolution, 44 voted in favor, and 23 abstained. France voted for the resolution.

CHAPTER XXII

POLITICS, GOVERNMENT, THE ECONOMY (1969)

Consumer Prices Up. The government increased prices on a wide variety of consumer products Jan. 2, 1969, in a move to reduce buying power in order to halt inflation. The cost of gasoline was boosted to the equivalent of 85.65¢ a gallon; the price of automobiles went up by 5.8%, pharmaceutical products 2%, some durable goods and foods 1% - 1 1/2% and certain services 2.6%.

Breton Nationalists Arrested. French police January 1-14 arrested 28 suspected members of a nationalist group accused of engaging in violence to enforce their demands for autonomy for Brittany. The nationalist group was called the Liberation Front of Brittany (LFB), and its followers were said to have been responsible for bomb attacks on public buildings in Brittany since the summer of 1967. The explosive raids against government buildings, tax offices and a police station had been stepped up in recent months.

The leader of the Liberation Front, Yann Goulet, in an interview published January 13 in the weekly *Nouvelle Observateur* in Paris, said that if de Gaulle "does not give the Breton people the freedom indispensable for their material and spiritual development, the tempo of military operations will only accelerate."

De Gaulle Vows Full Term. President de Gaulle pledged for the first time January 22 at his weekly cabinet meeting that he would serve out his presidential term, which was to expire December 1972. "In the fulfillment of the national task that devolves on me, I was reelected president of the Republic on Dec. 19, 1965, for seven years. I have the duty and the intention to fulfill my mandate."

De Gaulle's statement was said to be aimed at offsetting reports that he planned to retire before 1972 and at countering former Premier Georges Pompidou's announced availability for the presidency. During a visit to Rome January 17, Pompidou had said that if de Gaulle "should retire . . ., I would be a candidate to succeed him."

De Gaulle in Brittany, Announces Referendum. President de Gaulle visited Brittany January 31-February 2 in the midst of a nationalist campaign for greater autonomy in this northwestern province. Some Bretons greeted de Gaulle with coolness and some with open hostility.

The highlight of de Gaulle's tour took place at Quimper February 2 when he announced that a referendum would be held in the spring on constitutional reforms to expand regional authority and reduce the powers of the Senate. Under the proposal, some powers, currently held by the central government in Paris and still to be defined, would be granted to France's 21 regions. The authority would be given to assemblies composed of local councilmen, National Assembly deputies and representatives of labor, farmer and business groups and universities. The regional prefects would carry out the measures adopted by these groups.

De Gaulle said that the Senate reforms would transform the Senate, currently elected by councilmen of the country's 95 departments, into a body representing the regional assemblies. The Senate could affect legislation by delaying but not blocking bills by the National Assembly. Under the proposed rule, the Senate would be reduced to a consultative body that would study all economic measures before they were submitted to the National Assembly.

At the start of his tour of Brittany January 31, de Gaulle had been booed by about 100 young demonstrators in front of the Rennes city hall. They shouted "Free Brittany" and "De Gaulle to the museum."

Referendum Criticized. De Gaulle's referendum plan was assailed Feb. 3, 1969, by his political opponents. Rene Billeres, of the Radical Socialists, and Jean-Louis Tixier-Vigancour, of the ultrarightist Republican Alliance, urged a "no" vote. Guy Mollet, secretary general of the Socialist Party, called de Gaulle's proposal a "fake regionalization, a fake participation, proposed in a fake referendum," but he did not recommend that voters reject it. Jacques Duhamel, leader of the centrist opposition bloc in the National Assembly, criticized de Gaulle for including Senate and regional reforms in one package. Duhamel said he favored more powers for the regions, but he did not advocate changes in the Senate.

Student Unrest. French students demanding educational reforms clashed with police January 23 in Paris, Vincennes, Caen and Besancon.

The most violent disturbance took place in Paris, where militant high school and university students seized the offices of the rector of the Sorbonne and of the dean of the university's Faculty of Letters. The raiders sacked the rector's office but were evicted two hours later by the police.

(The high school students demanded the same autonomy granted university students in the government's educational reform bill of October 1968. They also insisted on the right to hold political meetings in the schools. The government thus far had rejected both demands. The high school students' other grievances were similar to those of university students: overcrowded classes, outdated educational concepts and unfair admission policies.)

Thirty-four of the Sorbonne students involved in the attack on the rector's office were expelled February 3. Eleven of them lost their military deferments and were called up immediately for army service. The Sorbonne was occupied February 12 by 200 militant teachers protesting the call-up of the students, but police moved into the building three hours later and evicted them.

The departure for the army of six of the drafted students February 13 precipitated widespread disorders by university students and teachers in Paris. A group of demonstrators stormed the railroad station (Gare de l'Est) in an unsuccessful attempt to block the train carrying the draftees, while flash demonstrations were staged in other parts of the city. Police arrested more than 600 persons in the day's disturbances.

General Strike. France was partially paralyzed by a nationwide 24-hour general strike of industrial workers March 10-11. The strike was called by the country's three major labor federations — the Communist-led General Confederation of Labor, the Catholic Democratic Confederation of Workers and the Socialist Workers Force — to support demands for wage increases of up to 12%, a 40-hour week, a wage-price escalator clause, lower taxes and a retirement age of 60.

The work stoppage started at 9:30 p.m. March 10 with a two-and-a-half hour power blackout in most sections of Paris. The full effect of the strike was not felt until the following day, when a major portion of the country's heavy industry was forced to close as workers quit their jobs and the power blackout was reimposed.

The day was marked by huge workers' demonstrations in Paris and in provincial cities. The largest turnout was in the capital, where an estimated 200,000 workers marched from the Place de la Republique to the Place de la Bastille.

De Gaulle vs. Strike. In a major radio-TV address March 11, originally intended as an appeal for a "yes" vote in the referendum set for April 27 on regional and Senate reform, President de Gaulle charged that the general strike had been organized "by the same assailants, backed by the same accomplices [involved in the May-June 1968 disorders], using the same means and threatening again to sink money, economy and republic. Need I declare that they will be firmly defended?"

Poher, Giscard d'Estaing Oppose Referendum. Alain Poher, the president of the Senate, warned April 1 that the upper house would not accept its abolition without a fight. Poher indicated that he would vote against the reform plan. Calling the referendum "useless," Poher noted that it was the fourth time in eight years that revision of the constitution had been sought. Parliament, he said, would have indorsed regional reforms if it had been asked to do so. Poher declared his opposition to the "disappearance" of the Senate and the inclusion of Senate and regional reforms in one package, calling for a "yes" or "no" vote.

De Gaulle's plan to reduce the Senate to a consultative body was assailed April 9 by Valery Giscard d'Estaing, leader of the Independent Republican Party. Citing the plan under which the Senate could only propose amendments to the National Assembly, Giscard said "for those who know the indifference of parliament to advice from outside, this procedure runs the risk of remaining a formality without any practical effect."

De Gaulle Threatens to Resign. De Gaulle declared April 10 that he would resign if his regional and Senate reform bill was defeated in the April 27 referendum. In a nationwide television interview he said: "Here I am, submitting a solemn proposal of reform to our country. If the French people, by chance — for that is the word — were to oppose this reform, what kind of a man would I be if I failed to draw the consequences of such a profound rupture at once and ridiculously maintain myself in my present functions."

Shopkeepers Strike. Operators of small private shops and enterprises staged their second one-day nationwide strike April 16 to protest against the government's tax and economic policies. Their first strike had occurred March 5.

De Gaulle Resigns Following Referendum Defeat. Charles de Gaulle, 78, resigned as president of France April 28, 1969, after his government's proposals for Senate and regional reforms were rejected by a national referendum held the previous day. The final results of the referendum announced April 29: "no votes — 12,004,970 (52.40%); "yes" votes — 10,905,453 (47.69%). Of the 29,394,456 registered voters, 5,832,452 had abstained.

In his statement of resignation, issued from the Elysee Palace, de Gaulle said: "I cease to exercise my functions as president of the Republic. This decision takes effect today at noon." De Gaulle had issued a final appeal to the voters April 25 for "a show of confidence" to permit him to serve out his third seven-year term, which was to end in 1972. "If I am solemnly disavowed by a majority of you, I will cease to exercise my functions immediately," he had said.

De Gaulle had not been legally required to submit his reform plan to a public vote. He could have sent the bill to the National Assembly, and the Gaullist majority there would have assured its passage. But de Gaulle had decided to make the issue one of public confidence in his rule despite the strong objections of several cabinet ministers and leading Gaullist politicians.

Less than three hours after the polls closed, Premier Couve de Murville had conceded defeat. He said: "A majority of the French people has pronounced itself against the reforms that were submitted to it, with all the political consequences that this rejection entails. Beginning tomorrow a new page will be turned in our history."

Waldeck Rochet, secretary general of the French Communist Party, called de Gaulle's resignation a "victory," which "bears witness, above all, to the profound will for democratic change among our people." "In rejecting personal power, the workers, the nation, have expressed their refusal of all reactionary power, any attempt to continue the same policies under different colors," Rochet said.

Poher Becomes Interim President. In accordance with French constitutional provisions on presidential succession, Alain Poher, 60, president of the Senate, was installed as interim president April 28. He was to serve pending the election of a permanent president no less than 20 days and no more than 35 days from the date of de Gaulle's resignation. Premier Couve de Murville and his cabinet were to remain in office as a caretaker government for this period. One cabinet member, Justice Minister Rene Capitant, a left-wing Gaullist, refused to serve and resigned.

Following his installation as interim president April 28, Poher, in a television address to the nation, lauded de Gaulle for his "outstanding services of the past." Conceding "the divergencies disclosed in yesterday's voting," Poher appealed to Frenchmen to "save the unity of the nation." He expressed confidence that "we will succeed through scrupulous respect for the law, which is the duty of the interim president, of the government, which remains in operation, of the elected assemblies and of all Frenchmen."

Poher had been a French resistance leader in World War II. First elected to the Senate in 1946, he became Senate president Oct. 2, 1968, succeeding Gaston Monnerville, who had held the post since 1947. Poher had joined the Popular Republican Movement (MRP), a Christian Democratic party, at the end of the war and remained a member until its dissolution in 1967. As chief of the personal staff of Robert Schuman, then (in 1946) finance minister, Poher was known as an early champion of European unity. In addition to his Senate duties, Poher had served as mayor of Ablon-Sur-Seine, a Paris suburb.

Poher was hostile to de Gaulle's reform program from the beginning and had expressed his opposition to it in a Senate speech April 1. He gained national prominence as the result of a television address April 17 in which he had urged the electorate to cast a negative vote in the referendum.

International Reaction. U.S. President Nixon April 28 expressed "deep regret" at de Gaulle's resignation. In a personal letter to the French leader, Mr. Nixon said: "I have greatly valued the frank and comprehensive exchanges of views it has been my privilege to have with you, both as a private citizen and as Vice President and President of the United States. Nor shall I forget the courtesy of your welcome and the wisdom of your counsel during my recent visit to Paris."

Although no West European country, with the exception of West Germany, immediately issued a formal statement, the initial reaction to de Gaulle's withdrawal from the political scene was one of hope that it would increase the chances of West European unity.

Britain, which de Gaulle had blocked from entering the Common Market, pledged to work for greater European unity in a joint declaration with Italy issued April 28. The statement was made during a state visit to London by Italian President Guiseppe Saragat. A "joint declaration of policy," signed by Italian Foreign Minister Pietro Nenni and British Foreign Secretary Michael Stewart, said that Italy and Britain "believe the common interests of the continent, its security and its prosperity, demand union." Alluding to France's objections, under de Gaulle, to enlargement of the Common Market, the declaration said that expansion of the current six-member grouping would "not alter its nature but insure its fulfillment." After meeting with Prime Minister Harold Wilson, Saragat told a joint meeting of Parliament that Italy hoped for "full participation by your country in the establishment of the new Europe."

A statement issued by the West German government April 28 said that Bonn was "in debt to Charles de Gaulle because he established West German-French friendship, independent of the change of majorities and governments, as an elemental ingredient of the common European policy of peace."

The Soviet government newspaper *Izvestia* contended April 28 that de Gaulle's withdrawal from politics was being used as a pretext by "rightist" forces to redirect French foreign policy toward "Atlantism," a closer relationship with the U.S.

Israelis, embittered by de Gaulle's shift from a pro-Israel policy to strong support of the Arab cause, expressed satisfaction with the general's resignation, although there was no official comment from the government. A leading newspaper, *Maariv,* said April 28: "The world, including Israel, has been saved from the obstinacy of a stubborn, vindictive and vengeful man."

Egypt expressed praise for the general in a statement issued April 28 by Mohammed H. el-Zayyat, the official government spokesman, who described de Gaulle as "a man who lived by his principles" and "should be a shining example for statesmen everywhere."

Presidential Nominees. Three French parties nominated candidates for the scheduled June 1, 1969, presidential elections, at which a permanent successor to de Gaulle was to be chosen.

Ex-Premier Georges Pompidou announced his candidacy April 29 and was indorsed later April 29 by the Union for the Defense of the Republic (Gaullist party). The two other candidates, selected May 5, were Marseilles Mayor Gaston Defferre, Socialist, and Jacques Duclos, 72, Communist.

Francois Mitterrand of the Convention of Republican Institutions had declared after his party's congress May 4 that he would not run. Mitterrand had polled 45% of the vote against President de Gaulle in the previous presidential election in 1965.

The June 1 presidential election date was selected May 2 at a cabinet meeting presided over by Interim President Poher. If no candidate obtained a majority, a runoff between the two leading contenders would be held two weeks later.

In announcing his candidacy April 29, Pompidou said that he felt duty-bound "to maintain continuity and stability and hope in preparing for the future."

Valery Giscard d'Estaing, leader of the Independent Republicans, announced April 30 that he would not be a candidate. He gave his support to Pompidou.

Defferre's candidacy was approved by 2,032 delegates (227 voted against it) at a Socialist congress May 5. The vote came after Defferre's only rival, Alain Savary, withdrew. That same day the party changed its name to Socialist Party. Heretofore, it had been known as Parti Socialiste SFIO (Section Francaise de L'Internationale Ouvriere).

Duclos was chosen by the Communist Party's Central Committee May 5 after failure to agree with the Socialists on a possible single candidate for the entire Left.

Poher Enters Race. Interim President Poher May 12 announced his candidacy in the June 1 presidential elections. Poher's entry into the race increased to seven the number of presidential candidates. In addition to Pompidou, Defferre and Duclos, the latest announced nominees were Michel Rocard, 36, head of the non-Communist Unified Socialist Party (he declared May 1), Alain Krivine, 27, of the Communist League (Trotskyist) and a leader of the 1968 student revolt, and Louis Ducatel, an independent, former Paris City Councillor and strong advocate of free enterprise.

Former Premier Pierre Mendes-France entered the election campaign May 15 as Defferre's Socialist running mate. Both men announced that if Defferre was elected, Mendes-France would become his premier. They said they advocated de-emphasizing the powers of the presidency and placing the major responsibility of government in the hands of the premier. Pompidou and Poher had come out for maintaining a strong presidency as it existed under Charles de Gaulle, relegating the premier to a subordinate position.

Pompidou Veers Away from Gaullism. In his first formal policy statement of the campaign, Pompidou had told the Central Committee of the Gaullist party May 9 that if elected he would change de Gaulle's policies on foreign and domestic affairs. Pompidou said that he would "favor the enlargement of Europe when the circumstances are fulfilled as far as our potential partners are concerned, in order to lead this Europe to a political consciousness permitting it to assume the position it deserves."

As for domestic affairs, Pompidou said that he was "determined to assure freedom of information" and to give Parliament a strong hand in "controlling government." Pompidou's remarks on freedom of information were in response to Poher's repeated charges of government control of the state radio and television network. In his latest statement on the issue May 15, Poher charged that for the past few days the network had "ceased to observe" his earlier order for "objectivity and impartiality." Poher said that the radio and television media should abandon the propaganda role it had played under the de Gaulle regime.

Pompidou said May 14 that "Britain must enter Europe" and asserted that "General de Gaulle well understood this." Pompidou, however, did not specifically refer to Britain's entry into the European Common Market, from which it had been blocked by de Gaulle.

Closing Days of the Campaign. Among the major statements made in the closing days of the election campaign:

Pompidou pledged May 16 that if elected he would not "imitate the style of General de Gaulle. I am a different man. I plan a policy of openness and dialogue.... The administration must become more flexible, more efficient, less meddlesome." Pompidou warned that if he lost the election France would face violent disorders, similar to the unrest in 1968.

Jacques Duclos declared May 16 that only the Communists offered a real change of policy. He called Pompidou and Poher "two candidates of the same clan" of high finance. Duclos deplored the failure of the Socialists to agree on a common program and a single candidate. He charged that the Socialist candidate, Defferre, would support Poher in a runoff.

In an interview published in *Paris-Match* May 20, Poher advocated a reversal of Charles de Gaulle's policies toward Europe, NATO and the Middle East. He indicated that he favored direct talks with Britain on its future membership in the European Common Market. Poher said that he supported stronger French ties to NATO because France "cannot assure alone the effective protection of her borders." As for the Middle East, Poher opposed de Gaulle's unilateral arms ban against Israel. Asserting that he could not support "a discriminatory embargo," Poher said that France "must always be fair to the belligerents" in the Middle East.

Poher May 27 reiterated support of a French role in NATO. France, he said, "must find the guarantee of her independence and security in a renovated Atlantic alliance in which a United Europe will be the equal partner of the United States." Poher again called France's arms embargo against Israel "unacceptable." He pledged that if elected he would restore French participation in the Geneva disarmament conference and other international parleys.

In a final television appearance of all seven candidates May 27, Poher charged that Pompidou, as premier under de Gaulle, had done the opposite of what he was now promising the voters in foreign and domestic affairs. Poher asked whether Pompidou had been "liberated" from his Gaullist views by the defeat of de Gaulle's referendum April 27. "If you were not in agreement with the policy that you carried out between 1962 and 1968, you should have let the country know before the referendum," Poher said.

(De Gaulle had left France for a vacation in Ireland May 10. Government officials said that he would not return until the election of a new president.)

Pompidou, Poher to Face Runoff. Pompidou won more than 44% of the vote and Interim President Poher received 23% in the French presidential elections held June 1. Communist Jacques Duclos ran a surprisingly close third with 21%. The remaining votes were shared by the four other candidates. Since no candidate obtained a majority, a runoff between the two leading contenders — Pompidou and Poher — was to be held June 15.

Final results of the first round of the elections, announced June 2: Pompidou 10,050,804 votes (44.46%); Poher 5,268,414 (23.31%); Duclos 4,811,037 (21.28%); Defferre 1,133,241 (5.01%); Rocard 816,410 (3.61%); Ducatel 268,481 (1.27%); Krivine 239,078 (1.06%). Of the 29,512,878 registered voters, 22,898,669 went to the polls. Invalid ballots totaled 293,200 and there were 6,614,209 abstentions.

The French Communist Party's Central Committee urged its followers June 2 to abstain from voting in the presidential runoff on the ground that Pompidou and Poher both were reactionaries and "stooges of capitalism" and that the working class, therefore, could not vote for either. The CP action was regarded as virtually assuring Pompidou's election because it would deprive Poher of needed leftist votes. Assuming Duclos' election boycott appeal was obeyed, the number of votes required for a majority would be reduced, further enhancing Pompidou's chances of victory.

Gaullist leaders had started a drive June 1 to persuade Poher to withdraw in the hope that Duclos would enter the runoff. The Gaullists believed that with Duclos in the race Pompidou could win as much as 80% of the vote. Despite Gaullist pressure, Poher insisted that he would be a candidate in the runoff.

Several political leaders who had backed Poher until the June 1 vote said that they would switch to Pompidou. Among them were rightist Jean-Louis Tixier-Vigancourt and Bertrand Motte, a conservative member of Parliament.

Pompidou Elected President. Georges Pompidou was elected to a seven-year term as president of France June 15, 1969, by defeating Interim President Alain Poher in a runoff election. Pompidou was to assume office June 20 after the election results were certified by the Constitutional Council.

Final results announced by the Interior Ministry June 16: Pompidou 11,060,181 votes (58.2%); Poher 7,942,915 (41.8%). Of the 29,488,640 registered voters, 20,307,013 went to the polls and 9,181,672 abstained. Invalid ballots totaled 1,303,914. The large number of abstentions was partially attributed to the Communist Party's June 2 call to its followers to abstain from voting in the runoff on the ground that Pompidou and Poher were both reactionaries. The CP's Politburo June 17 called the abstentions "the most important feature" of the election. It said that the more than nine million abstainers had denied Pompidou "the right to speak in their name."

In a statement conceding defeat June 15, Poher said that the millions who had voted for him constituted an opposition group whose unity must be maintained. Pompidou pledged in a victory statement that he would "be the president of all Frenchmen." In a message sent to Pompidou from his vacation retreat in Ireland June 15, de Gaulle said "for all national and personal reasons I address you my most cordial felicitations."

(Pompidou had said June 9 that if elected he would resign from the Gaullist party.)

Pompidou Forms Cabinet; Chaban-Delmas Premier. Pompidou took office as president of France June 20 and appointed Jacques Chaban-Delmas, president of the National Assembly, to succeed Maurice Couve de Murville as premier. The formation of a new cabinet, consisting of 18 ministers and 20 secretaries of state, was announced June 22. The cabinet members assumed their duties June 24.

Michel Debre was replaced as foreign minister by Maurice Schumann. Debre was shifted to the post of defense minister. Valery Giscard d'Estaing became finance minister. Pompidou had first offered that position to Antoine Pinay, but Pinay had refused it June 21. Pinay, a former premier, had served as de Gaulle's first finance minister in 1958.

Two key members of de Gaulle's cabinet were dropped by Pompidou. They were Cultural Affairs Minister Andre Malraux and Education Minister Edgar Faure. Chaban-Delmas said that Faure had been offered another cabinet position but had declined.

Chaban-Delmas had been active in the French resistance in World War II. He entered politics in 1946, winning a seat in the National Assembly. He was elected mayor of Bordeaux the following year and has held that post ever since. Chaban-Delmas served as minister of public works in the cabinet of Premier Mendes-France in 1954 and as minister of state and later as minister of defense in the cabinet of Premier Felix Gaillard from November 1957 to May 1958. He was first elected president of the National Assembly in 1958.

Schumann, a strong advocate of European unity, was said to have been chosen as foreign minister over the strong objections of conservative Gaullists. He had been a prominent member of the World War II resistance and after the war became a close associate of Premier Robert Schuman. The two men had been among the leaders of the Popular Republican Movement (MRP), the Roman Catholic party that led the fight for European unity.

The new cabinet:

Ministers of state and ministers: Premier—Chaban-Delmas; *Defense*—Debre; *Culture*—Edmond Michelet; *Relations with Parliament*—Roger Frey; *Justice*—Rene Pleven; *Finance and Economic Affairs*—Giscard d'Estaing; *Education*—Oliver Guichard; *Interior*—Raymond Marcellin; *Foreign Affairs*—Schumann; *Planning and Development*—Andre Bettencourt; *Overseas Departments and Territories*—Henry Rey; *Equipment and Housing*—Albin Chalandon; *Industrial Development and Scientific Research*—Francois-Xavier Ortoli; *Posts and Telecommunications*—Robert Galley; *Agriculture*—Duhamel; *Transport*—Raymond Mondon; *Labor, Employment and Population*—Joseph Fontanet; *Health and Social Security*—Robert Boulin; *Veterans*—Henri Duvillard.

Secretaries of state responsible to the premier: Attached to the premier—Leo Hamon, Joseph Comiti, Philippe Malaud, Jacques Baumel; *Defense*—Andre Fanton; *Parliamentary Relations*—Jean-Louis Tinaud, Jacques Limouzy; *Foreign Affairs*—Yvon Bourges, Jean de Lipkowski; *Interior*—Andre Bord; *Finance*—Jacques Chirac, Jean Bailly; *Education*—Pierre Billecocq; *Industrial Development*—Gabriel Kaspereit, Bernard Lafay; *Equipment and Housing*—Marcel Anthonioz, Robert-Andre Vivien; *Agriculture*—Bernard Pons; *Labor, Employment and Population*—Philippe Dechartre; *Public Health and Social Security*—Marie-Madeleine Dienesch.

Eleven ministers and 17 secretaries of state belonged to the Gaullist Democratic Republic for the Union (UDR). Pleven, Duhamel and Fontanet were members of the centrist Progress and Modern Democracy Group (PDM); and Giscard d'Estaing, Marcellin, Bettencourt, Mondon, Malaud, Tinaud and Anthonioz were independents.

H

I

J

K

FRANCE under DE GAULLE

Contents:

- Moslems in Algeria Rebel against French Rule
- Fifth French Republic Formed with De Gaulle as President
- De Gaulle Offers Algerians Right to Choose Independence
- Referendum Leads to Independence for Algeria
- De Gaulle Starts Equipping France with Atomic Weapons; France Explodes Atomic Devices in Atmosphere
- Downing of U. S. U-2 Spy Plane over USSR Wrecks East-West Summit Conference in Paris
- European Common Market Created; De Gaulle Vetoes British Membership
- French Gold Purchases Add to U. S. Gold Drain
- France Recognizes Communist China
- De Gaulle Causes Tension with Canada by Calling for a 'Free Quebec'
- Student Violence and Labor Strikes Shake Regime
- France Supports Secessionist Biafra in Nigerian Civil War
- De Gaulle Resigns after Defeat in Referendum on Senate and Regional Reforms

FACTS ON FILE, 119 W. 57th St., NEW YORK, N.Y. 10019

INTERIM HISTORY

The Bridge Between Today's News and Tomorrow's History